Foundation Mac OS X
Web Development

Phil Sherry

friendsof

DESIGNER TO DESIGNER™

an Apress® company

Foundation Mac OS X Web Development

Credits

Lead Editor
Gavin Wray

Technical Reviewers
Jake Smith, Max Hazelhurst

Editorial Board
Steve Anglin, Dan Appleman,
Ewan Buckingham, Gary Cornell,
Tony Davis, Jason Gilmore,
Chris Mills, Steve Rycroft,
Dominic Shakeshaft, Jim Sumser,
Karen Watterson, Gavin Wray,
John Zukowski

Project Manager
Beth Christmas

Copy Edit Manager
Nicole LeClerc

Copy Editor
Ami Knox

Production Manager
Kari Brooks

Production Editor
Kelly Winquist

Compositor
Dina Quan

Proofreader
Katie Stence

Indexer
John Collins

Artist
Kinetic Publishing Services, LLC

Cover Designer
Kurt Krames

Manufacturing Manager
Tom Debolski

Dedicated to the two Macs
that I wish I still had in my life:
Joe & Linda

CONTENTS AT A GLANCE

CONTENTS

Web page editors: Adobe GoLive vs. Macromedia Dreamweaver 23
Vector animation: Adobe LiveMotion vs. Macromedia Flash 25
And the overall winner is 26
Typography 27
Color 27
Web-safe colors 28
Some web rules for print designers 29
Page layout considerations 31
Transferring print layouts to the Web 32
Making fonts legible on the Web 32
Cross-platform testing 33
Copyright issues 34
Designing on a Mac in a PC environment 34
File suffixes 34
Designing with accessibility in mind 35
Chapter review 36

Chapter 3: Developing Static Websites 39
Overview 40
Site editing tools 41
Macromedia Contribute 41
Administering users in Contribute 42
BBEdit 45
World Wide Web Consortium (W3C) 46
Accessibility 47
XHTML 47
Enter XML 47
Skip to the end 48
DOCTYPE 48
Namespace 48
Tags 48
Div 49
Cascading Style Sheets 49
Linkage 49
link 49
import 49
embed 49
CSS basics 49
CSSEdit 50
My first style sheet 51
Positioning 53
Green color scheme 57
Purple color scheme 58
Large type scheme 60
Reversed color sheet 60
JavaScript 61
Status bar message 62

FOREWORD

From the very beginning of getting into this industry some people still call "new media," I've been using a Mac. In fact, it was a Mac that got me into graphic design and subsequently web design. I had a sort of epiphanic moment when I first used my Dad's 180c PowerBook. Think John Belushi handspringing down the church aisle in *The Blues Brothers* and you've got the idea of how big an impression using a Mac for the first time left on me. There's just something about the Mac that distinguishes it from their Wintel cousins. The interface doesn't get in the way. You just want to make stuff with Macs. You want to design, code, draw, play. And of course, you want to make websites.

So why has it taken so long for a book like this to come along? Well, let's face it, in the old days Macs were temperamental, to say the least. They would crash at least a few times a day, especially when you had a lot of applications open, as you do when designing websites. But then OS X came along. Built on a rock-solid UNIX core, Mac designers now have the stability of UNIX coupled with a graphical, easy-to-use interface.

For a web designer, the Mac is now a dream development box. Amazingly, the world-famous Apache web server is built right in. In typical Macintosh fashion, you just turn on Personal Web Sharing and the world's most ubiquitous web server fires up. Then just go ahead and turn on PHP, install MySQL, and you have one heck of a development platform. The Mac used to be the tool for just creating the graphics elements of web sites. Now though, you can design and develop full sites all on a Mac: server-side scripting, databases, the power of UNIX coupled with the famed Macintosh ease of use.

With all this power though comes a need to find out exactly what this "baby can do," and finally a book has arrived that will show you exactly that. Phil has written the ultimate guide to using a Mac for web development. Having known Phil for a number of years, his sense of humor shines through as he takes you through all you need to know in an easy-to-understand, conversational tone. Team Phil with my old buddy, Jake Smith, as the book's technical editor, and you have an expert dream team on Mac web development! Jake was, and still is, my first port of call when I have technical problems with my Mac. It's often said that Mac users are like members of a cult when it comes to their passion for the platform. With Phil and Jake, you have two high priests of that "cult." What they don't know about development on the Mac isn't worth knowing. This book gives you all their knowledge gleaned over several years at the coalface of web design. Read it. Consume it. Then do what every Mac user does: go and make stuff.

Brendan Dawes
Creative Director, magneticNorth
www.magneticn.co.uk
www.brendandawes.com

ABOUT THE AUTHOR

 **Phil Sherry** is a self-taught web developer during the day in Liverpool, and a freelance web anarchist for the remaining hours of the day. With lingering bad memories of having to use dial-up connection for years, he still does his best to design sites for the lowest common denominator. That means lower resolutions too, as well as people with slower machines (let's not mention those poor Windows users).

Together with this book's technical reviewer, Jake Smith, several rock gods have had their web presence greatly enhanced over the years, including Andy Rourke, the ex-bass player from The Smiths. Phil has previously worked on several friends of ED books, and also beta tested several key Adobe products.

A self-confessed geek, Phil can usually be found in a room full of computers, surrounded by screens of ASCII. When asked about how people should approach this book, he said, "I'm not going to teach them how to set the world on fire, but I'll show them how to strike the match. The rest is up to them."

ABOUT THE TECHNICAL REVIEWER

 **Jake Smith** is creative director with JP74, based in the Northwest of England. With a portfolio that includes work and awards for blue-chip and FMCG clients, he still takes the time to further his knowledge with projects like an online Speak & Spell emulator written in Flash, and to collaborate in web antics with the author. Jake has also written chapters for Flash-based books and monthly columns for *.net* magazine.

Having worked with multimedia since 1995 and been a Mac activist for even longer, Jake has an expansive knowledge of both the technical and creative sides of the web development process, proven by being a longtime beta tester for Adobe and Macromedia, and on the flip side, a former games tester for Sony PlayStation Europe.

He also has two cats, Sonic and Tails.

ACKNOWLEDGMENTS

This book couldn't have been written without the considerable help, patience, guidance, and gadgetry of the following:

My family for putting up with the mood swings; Paul "The Man" Baines, for taking great photographs; Simon Bondar, Gareth Heyes, Rob Ryan, and Jake Smith for contributions above and beyond the call of duty; Dave Hartley for the loaner iMac; Mark and Tracy Axelson, and Bradley and Annie Allen for long distance support; Gavin "The Gavinator" Wray, Beth Christmas, and all at friends of ED/Apress . . . Thanks for believing in me.

Big thanks to Underworld, Nine Inch Nails, Jane's Addiction, Rush, NoMeansNo, Led Zeppelin, Miriam Lamen, and Intentions Of An Asteroid for making music that inspired me to write every day.

I'd like to thank Bob Morris for asking so many questions, but I'm not going to.

Apple Computer, Inc., for making some of the coolest things known to mankind.

I should *probably* thank all my friends for keeping me out of the pub, so I could write and meet my deadlines. I will.

Later, I said . . .

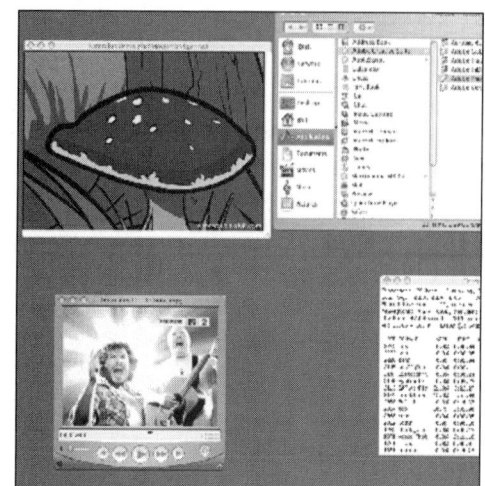

Chapter 1

INTRODUCTION TO MAC OS X PANTHER: THE NEW FEATURES

What we'll cover in this chapter:

- All change
- OS 9 vs. OS X
- Web development
- Internet connectivity
- Web development applications
- Useful shortcuts
- Accessibility

Let's go back . . .

Walk with me a moment. Anyone remember the Commodore PET? I saw one on the cover of a magazine in my father's newspaper shop. Wow. I instantly wanted one. No, wait . . . what's *that* inside? An Apple II? Sign me up for one of *those* things! I don't know why (and am still not really sure), but that Apple machine just sang to me. I never really forgot that song.

In 1981, my friend acquired a kit-form Sinclair ZX 81 (www.old-computers.com), and we both sat putting it together with *huge* grins on our faces—okay, his grin was bigger than mine because it was his computer. I seem to remember having to be asked to leave and go home so that my friend could do his homework in peace. The walk home seemed twice as long that day.

I managed to get a Commodore VIC-20 a few weeks later, and I was officially a nerd. I spent more time programming that thing than playing games. I dived straight in, learning all I could about BASIC (CBM BASIC V2, to give it its full title). Like everyone else, I started (of course) with the obligatory lines, as you can see in Figures 1-1 and 1-2.

```
10 PRINT "PHIL IS BOSS! ";
20 GOTO 10
RUN
```

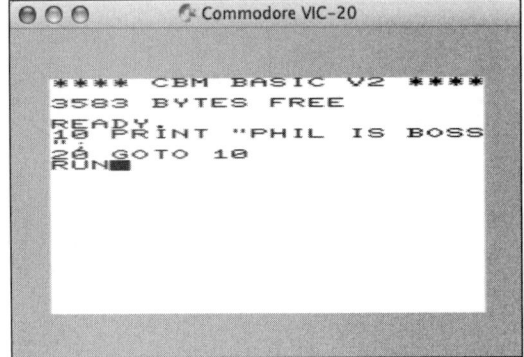

Figure 1-1. Ahh, VIC-20's BASIC. Those were the days.

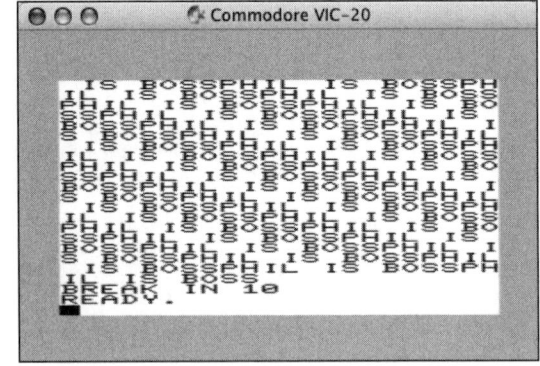

Figure 1-2. Look at those graphics! Dazzling!

It was around 1991 when I had my first encounter with Redmond (MS-DOS 5.0 to be precise) on an IBM 286, which led to Windows 3.1 (I still have the nightmares occasionally), Windows 95, and so on. Something was wrong though; I still wasn't happy. I started teaching myself some HTML and threw a few basic sites together. Eventually, I had a few clients, things were going okay in that department, but I still wasn't happy. The Windows environment was, simply put, driving me crazy.

All change

My life changed in 1998: My Nan bought me my first Mac—a 266MHz iMac (which I used for the screenshots in this book)—and I finally left the world of Windows behind me. Mac OS 8.5 was my first taste of the Macintosh operating system and I liked it . . . at first. For a start, it wasn't Windows. Everything just looked cool and things felt . . . different.

Then, as I began actually *using* my Mac for web development, I realized that the honeymoon period was over. Sure, I could use all of the same applications that I was using on Windows, but having to wait for one application to boot up before you could switch to another? Random freezes and crashes? Software that was seemingly unstable? Wait a moment, what was happening? Was this the same OS that I'd previously thought was going to save my sanity from years of Windows torture?

Back in those days, the Macintosh wasn't really built for serious multitasking. It was great for Photoshop, Illustrator, and QuarkXPress (but this was *only just* possible at the same time). Just using Word, browsing the Internet, and sending some e-mail, sir? Yeah, it could manage that. Using Dreamweaver, Fireworks, Flash, Freehand, Photoshop, Word, an FTP application, a browser, and e-mailing your client to see if that last update was satisfactory? The only chance of this happening was **no** chance.

Clearly, something had to change. And with talk of a completely new operating system on the way from Apple, things sounded good.

NeXT!

Back in December 1996, Apple Computer purchased NeXT Software (an English guy called Tim Berners-Lee *invented* the web on a NeXT computer at the Cern labs in Switzerland; for more info, see http://wwwpdp.web .cern.ch/wwwpdp/ns/ben/TCPHIST.html). Basing their brand new OS on NeXTSTEP and FreeBSD UNIX, Apple was touting OS X as "**the** most stable OS *ever*." People began to see NeXT's Rhapsody making an appearance on the Macintosh platform (later renamed Mac OS X Server), and things started to get exciting. Then, towards the latter half of 2000, Mac OS X Public Beta hit the streets and things were different. Three years on, and many revisions later, you now have **Mac OS X 10.3**, also known as **Panther**.

With the arrival of Mac OS X, not only do you as a Mac user have the most stable OS of any home computer, but you also have everything you need to be a real web developer:

- A solid UNIX-based OS (including Perl and Sendmail)
- The Apache web server application
- The PHP scripting language and MySQL database

OS 9 vs. OS X

Okay, enough history. What are the main differences between the Macintosh OS 9 and OS X?

Dock

I think the first thing you'll notice when you boot up OS X is the **Dock**. "What's that thing?" is the first thing I usually hear people say. The Dock, shown in Figure 1-3, is like OS 9's Application Switcher gone loco! You can also keep frequently used applications in here, a folder full of shortcuts, frequently used documents, and so on. Basically, in short technical jargon: You can keep your stuff in the Dock.

Figure 1-3. The Dock in all its default glory

Finder

At first glance, Finder just sits there looking identical to how it used to—until you create a new folder. Apple changed the shortcut key from ⌘+*N* to SHIFT+⌘+*N*.

> When mentioning the ⌘ key, I'm referring to the Command key, which is more commonly known as the Apple key, as it has the Apple logo on it.

So what happens when you open a Finder window? Oooh, columns! And buttons to take you places! As you can see in Figure 1-4, there's also a preview pane, which plays your QuickTime movies in it. With Panther, you have even easier access to your files, and the Search facility is right there at the top right of the Finder window (convenient, as well as lightning fast).

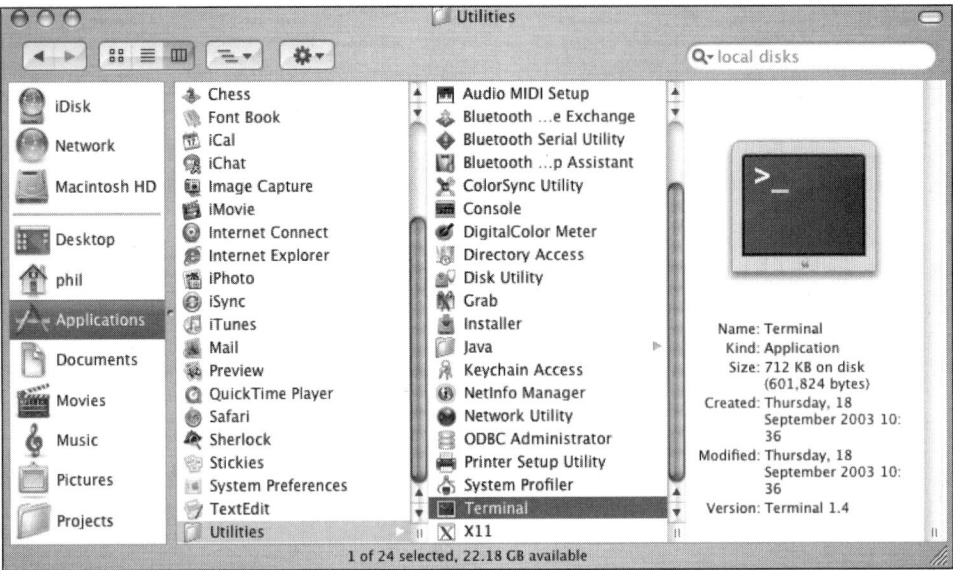

Figure 1-4. The Finder in OS X 10.3 with the new "brushed metal" look

One thing was missing from Finder from the first version of Mac OS X and irked a lot of people: Labels. Previously only available through a third-party plug-in (Unsanity's LabelsX: www.unsanity.com/haxies/labels), Labels are now back as a feature of the OS. In Panther, Finder can read all of your old OS 9 Labels just fine and works exactly the same.

Memory

Memory management was a nightmare in OS 9. Quite often, you would install an application and, when you tried to use it, would be greeted with an error message telling you that you didn't have enough memory to run the darn thing! You had to manually assign how much memory an application could use but, even then, you weren't guaranteed to be successful and had to shut other applications down to give full power to the main one (see Figure 1-5). This is no longer a worry, as OS X has an advanced memory protection and management system.

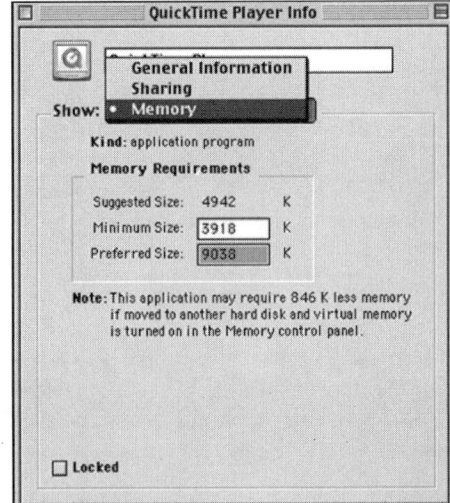

Figure 1-5. Via Get Info, you needed to manually configure the memory allocation. This is no longer necessary in OS X.

Networking

In OS 9, you could connect to other local Macs via **AppleTalk**. All you had to do was turn AppleTalk on, use Chooser or Network Browser to select the Mac you wanted to connect to, and then enter a user name and password. Easy, not exactly "h4ck1ng teh G1bson, d00d!" like in the movie *Hackers*. Connecting to a computer running a different OS was a bit involved though. You had to install a third-party application for a start, and even then it was no easy ride.

With OS X, connecting to other machines on a **L**ocal **A**rea **N**etwork (LAN) is so easy that even my Dad could do it. Look . . .

Open a Finder window, click the Network icon, and select your server from Local as shown in Figure 1-6. That's all there is to it. Finder scans the entire local network and locates all the Macs.

Need to connect to PCs? You should see your PC Workgroup/Domain in here too. Whether it's Windows or UNIX (permissions withstanding), you are only a few clicks away and you don't have to install any third-party software.

Font Book

For the average designer who switches between jobs all day, font management previously called for a third-party application (such as Extensis Suitcase). The reason for this was that a folder full of fonts slowed your system right down, and you didn't need them all active anyway. (Show me a designer who has less than 1000 fonts on their system!) Also, in OS 9 there was a limit to how many fonts could be read.

A brand new feature of Panther is set to change this. With **Font Book**, you can group your fonts, and activate or deactivate them as shown in Figure 1-7. Apple seems to be eradicating the need for third-party applications but, as you'll see in other sections of this book, it's a purely personal choice which applications you use. Weigh up the odds, and go for what you feel is best for your projects.

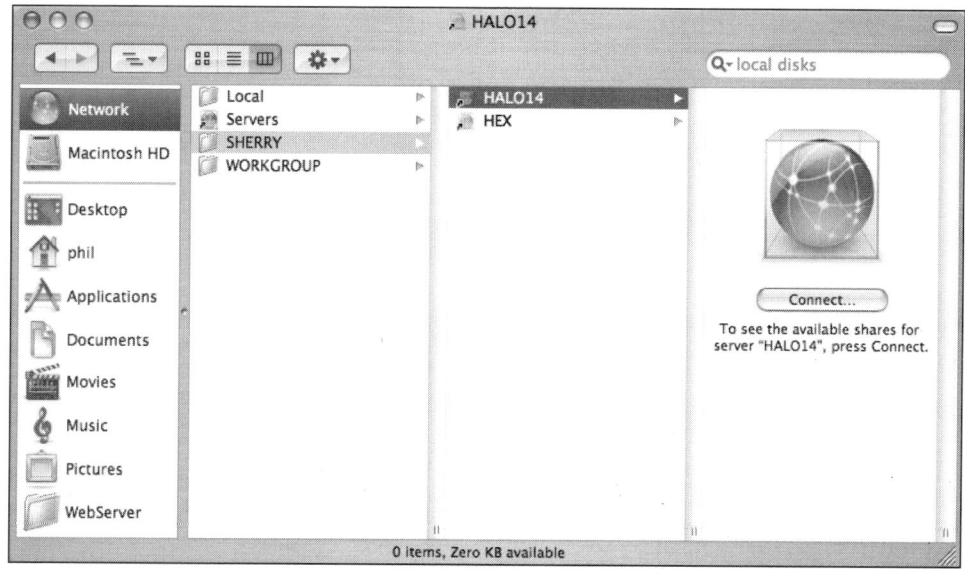

Figure 1-6. Connecting to a PC network is as easy as falling off a log.

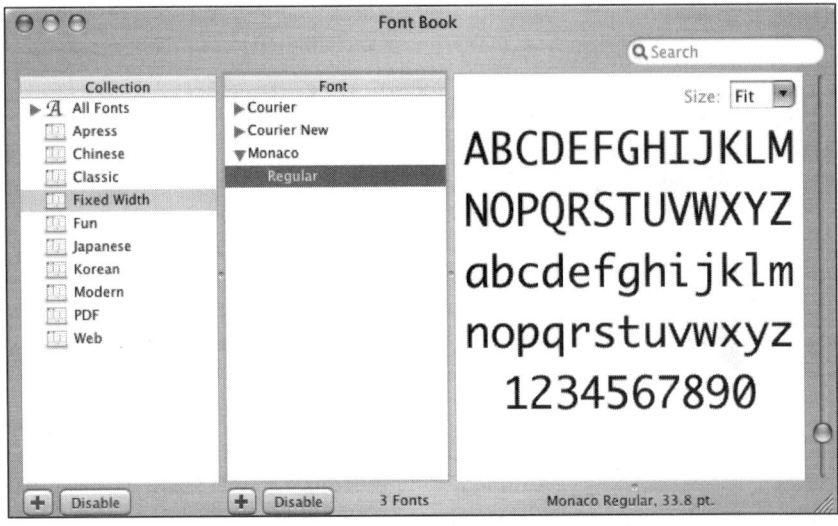

Figure 1-7. Turn fonts on and off easily with Font Book.

Graphics

"Macs are good for graphics, but not much else."

If I had a penny for every time I've heard this, I'd have at least $5.63 by now. My own opinion is that the origin of this statement dates back to the time when Adobe PageMaker was a Mac-only application, as were Photoshop, Illustrator, Freehand, and QuarkXPress. Therefore, if you wanted to do any serious pixel pushing, you did it on a Mac.

These days, however, the way Mac OS X approaches graphics surpasses anything seen before. Enter **Quartz Extreme**, which uses the graphics card in your Mac to relieve the main PowerPC chip of on-screen calculations. This dramatically improves system performance, making OS X much more responsive.

As this uses the **P**ortable **D**ocument **F**ormat (PDF) as its basis, you can create PDF files from pretty much any application, then view them in Preview, without the need to spend money on Adobe Acrobat (see Figure 1-8).

To create a PDF from an application such as Safari, choose Print ➤ Save As PDF.

Exposé

If you're trying to work with a screen resolution of 1024×768 or less, things can soon become pretty cluttered on the screen. With several applications open, it's easy to lose windows underneath each other, and it takes time to dig around and find them.

With **Exposé** in Panther, you just hit the *F9* key and all your open windows shrink and tile so that you can see what's open, as shown in Figure 1-9. Mouse around, select the window you want, and release the key. Awesome. Got a lot of Dreamweaver windows open? Hit *F10* and the open applications' windows tile. Groovy. Need to see the desktop? *F11* is your friend. All these keys are changeable, by the way, and you can also assign Screen Corners for each action. This is one fantastic time saver, if you're anything like me and tend to have a lot of applications open at the same time.

Figure 1-8. Preview opens images or PDF documents.

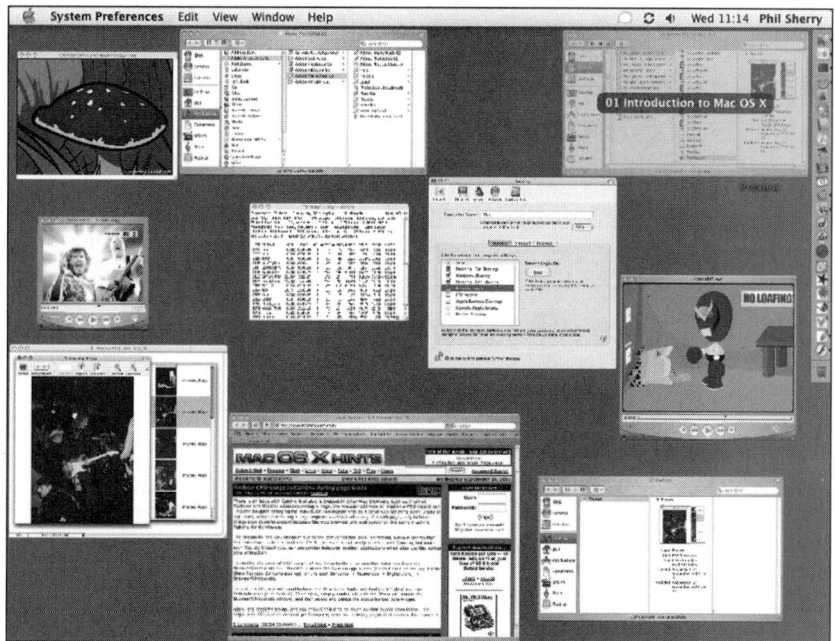

Figure 1-9. Once you use Exposé, you'll wonder how you managed without it.

Web server

If you're serving web pages, you should do it properly, which means one thing and one thing only: **Apache**. Apache 1.3.28 is bundled as the web server application with Panther. At the time of writing, Apache serves 64 percent of the websites online, according to their website (http://httpd.apache.org/). This makes it more widely used than all the other web server applications put together.

To serve up your pages, you just leave your HTML documents and images in your Home/Sites directory or in the root directory of the web server (/Library/WebServer/Documents). To view them in your browser, go to http://127.0.0.1/~username/, where username is, um, your user name (see Figure 1-10). You have to tweak the configuration file a little bit so you can do a few server-side things, but that's a bit too heavy for Chapter 1, so I'll cover all that when I get my geek hat on later in the book.

Fast User Switching

Multiple accounts on the same Mac have been possible for years, but having to close all running applications and documents before switching users was always a real pain. OS X users were envious of the Windows XP feature where you can switch between users without having to quit all your open applications. A quick trip into System Preferences ➤ Accounts ➤ Login Options, and you can activate this new feature (see Figure 1-11).

Figure 1-11. Fast User Switching is more than simple.

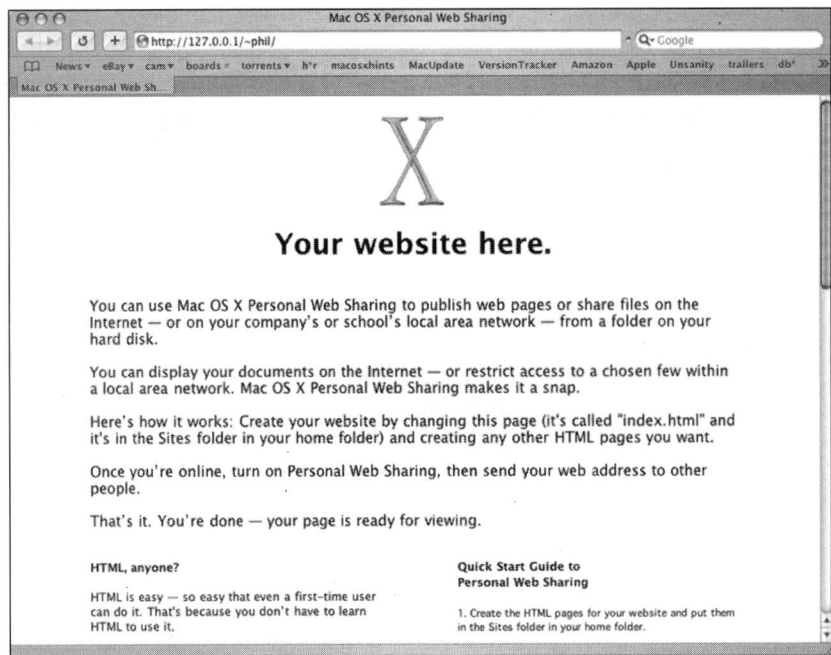

Figure 1-10. Web serving, the easy way

When you enter your password, the screen whizzes round on the side of a cube (very cool), then you're logged in. Easy.

> Note that the Fast User Switching animation is only availabe on Macs with Quartz Extreme enabled. To check whether you have this capability, take a look at www.apple.com/macosx/features/quartzextreme/ for more information.

FileVault

If you're of a paranoid persuasion, you'll like FileVault, shown in Figure 1-12. Your whole Home directory is encrypted with 128-bit keys. Deleted files are exactly that: deleted. Random data immediately overwrites them. Gone. You can access it through System Preferences ➤ Security.

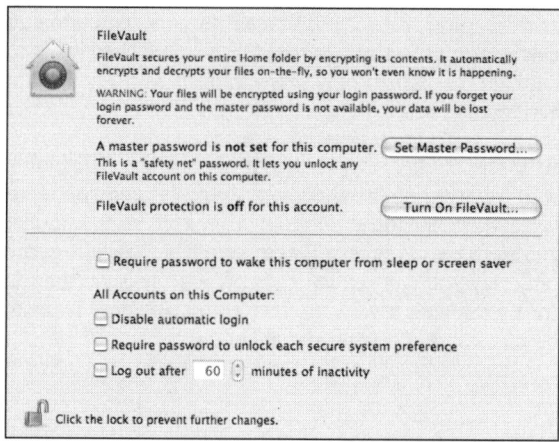

Figure 1-12. FileVault is like having Judge Dredd on board: Safe.

FileVault also allows your Mac to be logged out after a set period of inactivity, which is useful if you're away from your desk often. You can also use the screen saver as a lock, requiring a password to turn it off.

Web development

In the old days of OS 9, developing with PHP and/or MySQL usually meant using a remote UNIX server, but not any more. But what are they though?

PHP

PHP (www.php.net) is a widely used general-purpose scripting language that is especially suited for web development and can be embedded into HTML. Unlike JavaScript, which you may already be familiar with, PHP is a server-side language. Let's take a look at a quick example:

```
<html>
<head>
<title>friends of ED</title>
</head>
<body>
<?php
echo "This is some very basic PHP code!";
?>
</body>
</html>
```

As the code is executed on the server, before it is sent to the browser, all end users see is the result. If they viewed the source of that resulting web page, all they would see is this:

```
<html>
<head>
<title>friends of ED</title>
</head>
<body>
This is some very basic PHP code!
</body>
</html>
```

This means that they don't get to see the code you've spent hours developing, nor any passwords you might have in the code for connecting to a database. You can connect via Flash too (as well documented in other books from friends of ED and Apress). You can now download a Mac OS X package in the download section (www.php.net/downloads.php), which means that you don't even need to compile it yourself.

I just mentioned databases, so let's have a quick look at the one that works best with PHP: MySQL (www.mysql.com/). The MySQL database server is the world's most popular open source database, and PHP has a lot of functions built in to allow you to do some great stuff with minimal headaches. It too is available as an easy point-and-click package from their website.

Another scripting technology you might have heard of is Macromedia's ColdFusion. This works equally well with MySQL, and the same Flash connectivity is present as with PHP. Macromedia bought ColdFusion from Allaire several years ago, and it is now a part of the MX stable. In fact, at the time of writing, Macromedia's website is powered by ColdFusion.

As well as the standard point-and-click installers that most Mac users are familiar with, both PHP and MySQL are available as source files (if you want to tell your friends that you compiled it yourself). This is a far more UNIX-y way of installing an application, which involves running a configure script, and then actually making the application. I'll cover this in more detail in Chapters 6 and 7.

UNIX

UNIX is a rock-solid operating system. The Internet was built on it, and it has a reputation for hardly ever crashing, or, as we say in the trade, "falling over." It was built by geeks, for geeks, but the days of "The Geek shall inherit the earth" are coming to an end. With Mac OS X, the average home user can have this hugely powerful OS at their fingertips, along with all its benefits, and yet be up and running in minutes thanks to such easy installation.

With protected memory and preemptive multitasking, Mac OS X lets you keep working day in and day out. Yes, some applications will probably still crash from time to time, but your whole system won't go down with it. This **has** to be a bonus for the developer (unless you're one of those "Uhh, I can't work right now, I'm rebooting" slackers).

A lot of people are scared by one thing in Mac OS X: **Terminal** (/Applications/Utilities/Terminal.app). The very presence of a **C**ommand **L**ine **I**nterface (CLI) seems to make some people shudder. This is UNIX,

people. Having your Mac speak exactly the same language as the backbone of the Internet has significant advantages. You get the chance to develop on the same system that your work will be hosted on, for a start.

> Hold down ⌘+V on startup to see the geeky UNIX stuff under the hood.

For the web developer, Terminal is extremely useful and shouldn't be thought of as intimidating. If you plan on using a database, such as MySQL or PostgreSQL, then you'll most likely have to get to grips with Terminal.

You may be wondering, as a Mac user, just how much of this UNIX stuff you need to know. I'll run through some Terminal tips throughout the book, so be prepared! Although you can do some serious damage via Terminal, this will certainly not be covered in this book; just the good stuff. Some tips will seem essential to you eventually; others are just useful to know. They will also help you to just become more familiar with Terminal in general.

As the Mac OS X Finder is UNIX-based, files beginning with a period (.) are seen as system files and rendered invisible in a Finder window. This isn't very useful if you're using .htaccess files in your site. Therefore, the only way you can see your .htaccess file is via the CLI (or by opening it with the text editor, BBEdit). This will be discussed in further detail in Chapter 6.

Internet connectivity

During the last couple of years, the World Wide Web has altered our daily lives. In the old days, you'd arrive at work, read the paper, and check your mail by opening some envelopes. Today, the first thing most people do is open a news site in a browser and check their e-mail. In fact, if you spend too much time with that browser window open, you might get fired . . . by e-mail!

Browsers

Web browsers. There are thousands of them. Well, not exactly thousands, but certainly enough to keep today's web developers up all night trying to make sure their pages render properly in **all of them**, as well as in the handful of PC browsers. At the time of writing this, I can name ten OS X browsers: Camino, Firebird, iCab, Internet Explorer, Lynx (text-only), Mozilla, Netscape, OmniWeb, Opera, and Apple's very own Safari.

Interestingly enough, Microsoft has stopped further development of Internet Explorer for the Mac. Why? Safari. They figured it wasn't worthwhile, as Apple had "easier access" to the code that makes OS X tick. How do you choose the one for you? They all have their quirks, glitches, and oddities, but these will be covered in detail in Chapter 4.

E-mail

When I used OS 9, I used Eudora for e-mail. It worked and was good at its job. When I switched to OS X, I tried Eudora's new X-friendly beta. I didn't like it, no sir. But, wait. Bundled in with OS X is Mail.app, and it's full of useful features, such as the Junk Mail feature that seriously weeds out the ton of spam we're all plagued by. To be fair to Eudora, that was a long time ago, and they've gotten back up to scratch since (or, so I hear). Also, Mail.app will import all your mail from pretty much any application that you currently use these days.

If you're a PC-to-Mac switcher and you used to use Microsoft Outlook for your entire daily needs, fear not. Mac OS X even has Microsoft Office (which Microsoft claim to be their best version of Office), including the Mac equivalent of Outlook called **Entourage**.

Web development applications

> "But, you can't get most of the good applications for Mac, can you?"

Myth deleted. All the popular web development applications are now Mac OS X native and are some of the most valuable tools for today's web developer:

- **Adobe's** Acrobat, GoLive, Illustrator, InDesign, Photoshop, and ImageReady
- **Macromedia's** ColdFusion, Contribute, Director, Dreamweaver, Fireworks, Flash, and Freehand

InDesign outputs to GoLive. Illustrator and Freehand can output SWF files straight for use in your web pages. All these applications are all working together these days, for you, the web developer.

Useful shortcuts

If you're totally new to Mac OS X, having only used OS 9 before (or even Windows), you may not be aware of the startup shortcuts. You can boot from a CD (*C*), etc. You may also find the following shortcuts useful:

- If you have a multiboot system (maybe you have OS 9 or Linux on a partition), you can hold down the *OPTION* key to allow you to select which Startup Disk you want (only applies to Macs from iMac onwards).
- Hold down the *X* key during boot to force your Mac to boot into OS X.

One other shortcut you might be pleased to know has finally come of age is *ALT+TAB* (see Figure 1-13). Earlier versions of OS X had some basic functionality for switching between applications, but Panther's version now does the job properly.

Figure 1-13. Use *ALT+TAB* to scroll through your open applications.

Accessibility

There's a whole host of features for those who are hard of hearing, or have impaired vision or another disability (see Figure 1-14). With just a few clicks, you can have your Mac talking alerts to you, and you can reverse the on-screen colors or use grayscale. If you can't always hear the alerts, the screen can flash to alert you.

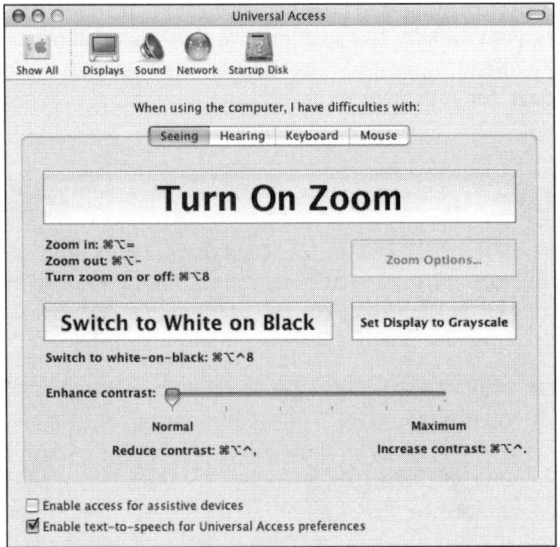

Figure 1-14. Universal Access allows disabled people to change the way they see and hear their Mac.

All of these features are already available in Mac OS X. They just need switching on in System Preferences ➤ Universal Access.

Chapter review

Hopefully, by now you've finished reading this chapter in the bookstore, you're standing at the checkout, and you're waiting to buy this book because you've realized it's aimed at you. May I suggest you swing by the record store and grab some Underworld and Nine Inch Nails albums too, just to help you get the right vibe.

This book doesn't aim to turn you into a PHP guru or an expert web developer. It's purely aimed at people who need to learn the fundamentals of web development using Mac OS X as a platform. Maybe you're from a print background or you've only just switched to using Mac OS X.

You'll be taken through some real-life examples, which you should be able to put into practice on your own sites. PHP and MySQL will be discussed, and how to get both of these up and running on your Mac in a matter of minutes, with only a brief excursion into Terminal. Terminal will also be tackled in more depth from Chapter 5 onwards.

For the purposes of this book, I'll be using Macromedia's Dreamweaver MX 2004, Fireworks MX 2004, and Flash MX 2004. You can download trial versions of these applications from www.macromedia.com. I'll also be referencing a text editor called BBEdit, which is available from www.barebones.com.

Okay.
Book . . . Check.
Mac OS X . . . Check.
Software . . . Check.
Underworld or Nine Inch Nails on **LOUD** . . . Check.
Let's get started!

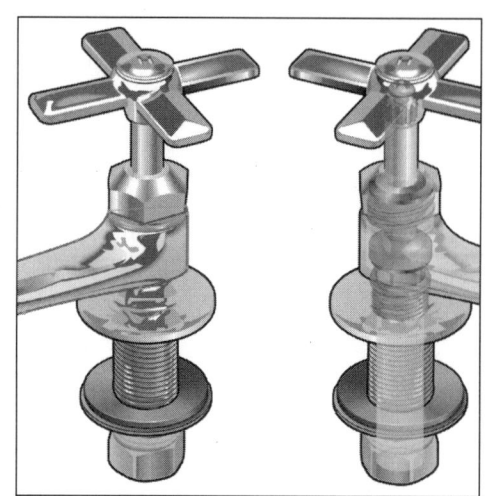

Chapter 2

MAC GRAPHICS AND DESIGN ISSUES

What we'll cover in this chapter:

- Design product overviews
- Typography
- Color
- Some web rules for print designers
- Designing on a Mac in a PC environment
- Designing with accessibility in mind

In this graphics-oriented chapter, I'm going to guide you around some of the new facets of designing for the web and cross-platform media. If you're coming to this book from a print background, then some of this information will be invaluable. If you're a programmer, you probably want to skip it and get down with the Terminal, but I urge you to have a quick read anyway, because you never know when you may need something from this chapter in the future. We'll be looking at

- Some background history of the primary design applications
- Basic web design knowledge, such as fonts, color, and layout
- Working with your PC teammates on a project
- The main "gotchas" when designing on a Mac for a primarily PC-based audience

With the Mac's proven track record in the design and print industry, it would be very stupid to switch platforms and tools just to design for a slightly different medium, and so it's a good thing you don't have to . . . the Mac has everything it needs to be both a cutting edge graphics tool and an industrial-strength web server and development environment, all in one box. So, bring on the tools . . .

Design product overviews

Ladies and gentlemen, step right up for the software slugging match of the century, Adobe vs. Macromedia. Both of these corporations are vying for graphic designers' attention and cash. Both companies and their products have their pros and cons, have similar strengths but capitalize on the other's weaknesses. They both also bundle their primary digital design applications in a set, which is heavily discounted, enticing the user to "buy one–buy all" of the company's applications:

- **Macromedia Studio MX 2004:** Dreamweaver MX 2004, Flash MX Professional 2004, Fireworks MX 2004, Freehand MX
- **Adobe Creative Suite:** Photoshop CS, Illustrator CS, InDesign CS, GoLive CS, Acrobat 6.0 Professional, Version Cue

Let's see how they stack up against each other . . .

Vector graphics and line art: Adobe Illustrator vs. Macromedia Freehand

Freehand (shown in Figure 2-1) and Illustrator are two applications that do the same job. You use them to create vector or line art for use as EPS files, the print designer's standard vector format of choice (it's Quark friendly), or JPEGs, TIFFs, and PNGs (bitmap images) to drop into Photoshop or to import into Flash. Anyone coming from the print world will be fluent with the use of vectors and EPS files but, for those who aren't, vector artwork is usually used for logo designs and flat artwork, whereas bitmap graphics are generally used for images that contain large gradations of color, like a photograph.

Vectors are different from bitmaps, as they are mathematically plotted on a work area (as opposed to being pixels, precise definitions for each visible square of the work area). The points and curves of a vector are all stored as numbers for x and y coordinates and degrees for angles. This means that vector art has two distinct advantages:

- You can scale the artwork indefinitely, as scaling the artwork by 400 percent just means multiplying the vector coordinates by 400 percent.
- Files created with these two applications will be much smaller than JPEG, PNG, or TIFF files typically created with Adobe Photoshop or Macromedia Fireworks.

So, all through college I was a Freehand activist. I understood how the application worked (or at least the bits I needed to use to do my job) and could work quickly without too much trouble. Illustrator at the time, on the other hand, was completely alien to me. Some of the concepts of the drawing tools and the way points didn't have to be joined to make a fill were at odds with everything I knew from Freehand. Consequently, Illustrator and I didn't get on . . .

Fast-forward five or six years, and Illustrator and I are now good buddies. I still use Freehand for the majority of my day-to-day vector work, but I also seem to use either application depending on which tool is more

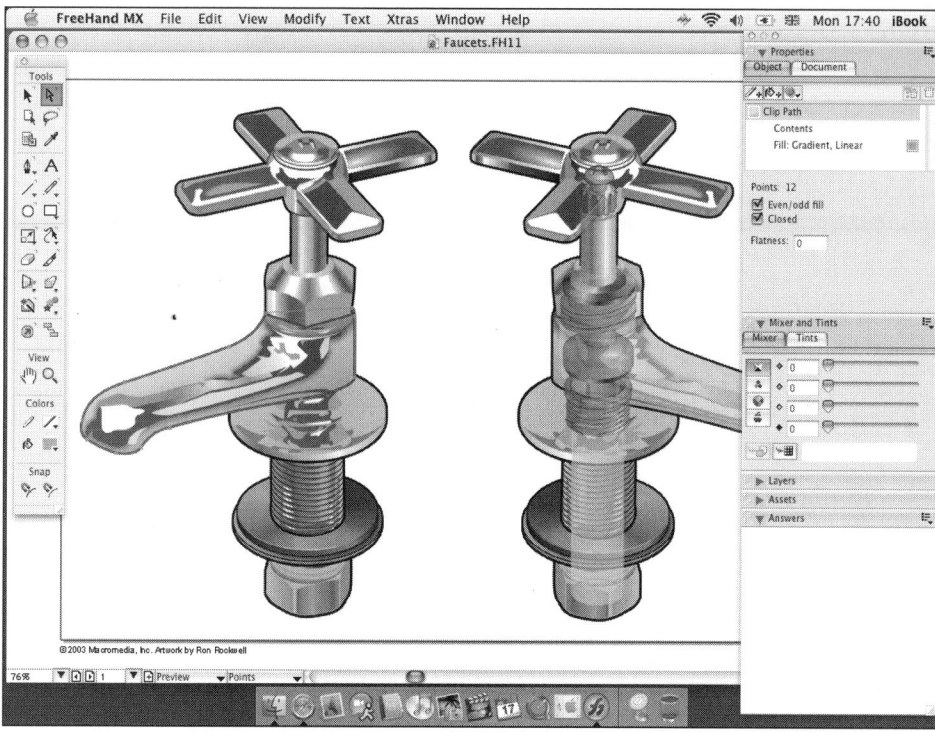

Figure 2-1. Macromedia Freehand MX

suitable for the task at hand. For example, if the artwork is destined for Flash, then, naturally, saving the work in Freehand and importing the Freehand document is the way to go, due to the tight integration through the Macromedia family of applications. But wait, I find the color matching from Freehand to Flash is very poor. The colors look totally different in my Flash movie from what they did in my Freehand document, so I use Illustrator to export the Flash SWF and import this into Flash. Both applications have grown closer over the years, and their functionality and feature set seem to get more similar each time I have a task to complete. Maybe I'm growing more tolerant in my old age . . .

Gripes? If I had to pick faults, then Freehand's use and implementation of layers is abysmal. The Layers palette hasn't had a brush up since about Freehand 5 (we're at version 11 now) and is put to shame by Illustrator's intuitive Photoshop-like handling of layers. Secondly, the Align tab in Freehand is a law unto itself. Though Macromedia's Studio MX 2004 family of applications do follow many of the same design principles, some tools behave differently in each application, leaving a feeling that the left hand is not quite talking to the right hand through the development process.

Illustrator is no angel though—you're still only allowed to use one page per document. Freehand capitalizes on multiple page document layouts by allowing them to act as an animation when exported as a Flash SWF or when importing the Freehand document into Flash. Because Freehand's drawing tools are light years ahead of Flash's in many respects, I can see traditional animators who are familiar with Freehand loving this capability.

Pixel pushers: Adobe Photoshop vs. Macromedia Fireworks

You might think that this is a bit of an unfair contest, especially as Photoshop has its trusty web imaging sidekick ImageReady in its corner too, but Fireworks squares up well, compensating handsomely in some specific areas, ducking and weaving like a true contender.

Photoshop, shown in Figure 2-2, is an image editing application. Its core trade is editing pixels. When you paint or fill an area, it directly colors each individual block, or pixel, to form the image. Photoshop has grown to encompass vectors, but primarily it's a bitmap image editor, and different from the previously mentioned Illustrator and Freehand.

Fireworks is a hybrid image editor and vector drawing tool. Neither pixels nor vectors seem to have precedence, but the application looks and acts like Photoshop in many ways. For us web developers, both Fireworks and Photoshop will commonly be used to output our standard web image format GIF and JPEG files, so Fireworks can stay in the realm of image editors for this comparison.

Photoshop really doesn't need an introduction. If you work with graphics, the odds are that you spend nearly all day with Photoshop open while you work. It's one of the most well-known, well-used, and essential tools in the industry because it's such a capable and reliable application. Traditionally a print-focused application, Adobe started to add web-specific features slowly—a little too slowly for the speed at which the Internet was developing—to give designers the tools they needed for the Internet and other digital media. This was when Macromedia saw the hole in the market and smartly filled it with Fireworks. Macromedia used to have a heavyweight print-oriented photo editing application

Figure 2-2. Adobe Photoshop CS

called Xres, which died a quiet death, and I have a feeling that Fireworks is the phoenix from the ashes. Fireworks's raison d'etre was to allow web designers access to all the web-oriented techniques like animated GIFs, image maps, and sliced rollovers. Fireworks not only chops up and exports your graphics, but it also writes all the HTML that holds the image together and writes all the JavaScript required to make the rollovers function in a web browser! Let's take a look at this in action:

You have a layered Fireworks document ready for slicing:

Now you have it sliced, with hotspots:

Adding status bar, rollover code, and links is easy:

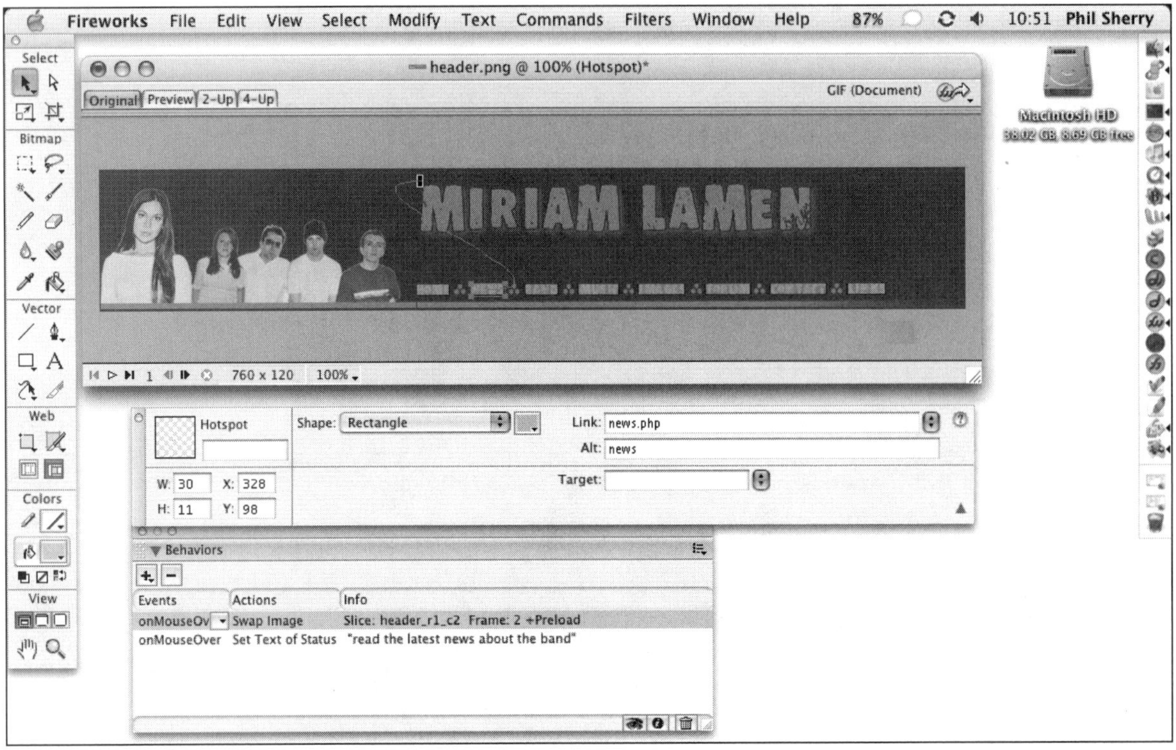

Now go into Dreamweaver, and punch the Fireworks
button to start importing . . .

...then find the .htm file exported from Fireworks:

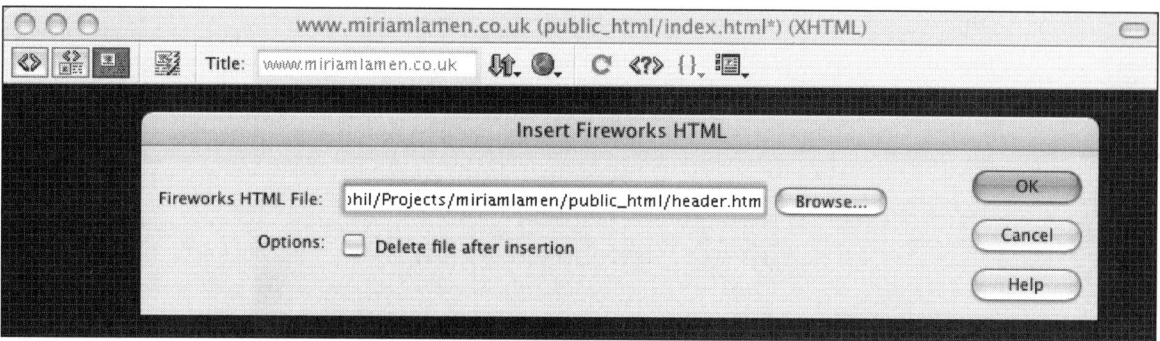

There you have it. All graphics and code imported in a
few clicks.

Ergh, but wait a minute. What's with all this bloated JavaScript on each page? I think not! We'll deal with that in the next chapter.

```
9   <script language="JavaScript" type="text/JavaScript">
10  <!--
11  function MM_preloadImages() { //v3.0
12    var d=document; if(d.images){ if(!d.MM_p) d.MM_p=new Array();
13      var i,j=d.MM_p.length,a=MM_preloadImages.arguments; for(i=0; i<a.length; i++)
14      if (a[i].indexOf("#")!=0){ d.MM_p[j]=new Image; d.MM_p[j++].src=a[i];}}
15  }
16
17  function MM_swapImgRestore() { //v3.0
18    var i,x,a=document.MM_sr; for(i=0;a&&i<a.length&&(x=a[i])&&x.oSrc;i++) x.src=x.oSrc;
19  }
20
21  function MM_findObj(n, d) { //v4.01
22    var p,i,x;  if(!d) d=document; if((p=n.indexOf("?"))>0&&parent.frames.length) {
23      d=parent.frames[n.substring(p+1)].document; n=n.substring(0,p);}
24    if(!(x=d[n])&&d.all) x=d.all[n]; for (i=0;!x&&i<d.forms.length;i++) x=d.forms[i][n];
25    for(i=0;!x&&d.layers&&i<d.layers.length;i++) x=MM_findObj(n,d.layers[i].document);
26    if(!x && d.getElementById) x=d.getElementById(n); return x;
27  }
28
29  function MM_swapImage() { //v3.0
30    var i,j=0,x,a=MM_swapImage.arguments; document.MM_sr=new Array; for(i=0;i<(a.length-2);i+=3)
31     if ((x=MM_findObj(a[i]))!=null){document.MM_sr[j++]=x; if(!x.oSrc) x.oSrc=x.src; x.src=a[i+2];}
32  }
33
34  function MM_displayStatusMsg(msgStr) { //v1.0
35    status=msgStr;
36    document.MM_returnValue = true;
37  }
38  //-->
39  </script>
40  </head>
```

To be honest, I was unimpressed with the first version of Fireworks, eschewing it in favor of my longtime friend Photoshop until Fireworks showed me some of its tricks, like the image slicing. Adobe paid attention too, and quickly produced an application called ImageReady, which is practically a direct competitor to Fireworks yet is still overshadowed by Photoshop. ImageReady handles all of your animated GIF requirements, and the fancy rollover menus and HTML/JavaScript output those familiar with Fireworks have grown to love, but keeps the Photoshop interface and tools, so users will feel at ease straight away. Indeed, Photoshop itself has many facets of the web design application in there, but Adobe had the good sense not to try and cram everything into one application. When you buy Photoshop, you get ImageReady thrown in. Very sensible.

A couple of notable points about each application. Fireworks and Freehand work very well together, as you'd hope (or expect). When you import a Freehand document into Fireworks, it keeps all the type and vectors just as you originally made them, and they remain in vector form so you can edit them further. It'll also output SWF files too, saving you a trip into Flash for some quick animations or for laying out screen designs with actual graphic elements that need to end up in Flash.

And Photoshop? Do I really need to point out all the good things about this application? It's amazing. ImageReady probably needs more of the praise, taking Photoshop's layered PSD files straight from Photoshop so you can perform your animations, timings, slicing, dicing, and optimizing. Then at the click of a button, you can send them back to Photoshop for editing without causing any file format inconsistencies or hiccups. They complement each other well as an integrated pair of applications should.

Both Photoshop and Fireworks have too many strengths to mention, and their weaknesses pale in comparison to what these remarkable applications enable you to achieve. Almost everyone will choose Photoshop straight away, but you should be aware of the Swiss Army Knife that is Fireworks.

Web page editors: Adobe GoLive vs. Macromedia Dreamweaver

Now this is where the competition steps up and competes head-on for the web designer's screen real estate, time, and cash.

These two applications compete unapologetically. They are both, for all intents and purposes, **W**hat **Y**ou **S**ee **I**s **W**hat **Y**ou **G**et (WYSIWYG) **H**ypertext **M**arkup

Language (HTML) page editors that have grown with each version to encompass all the new or prevalent web technologies such as CSS, XHTML, PHP, and JSP, as they've emerged and become more important.

In the simplest terms, both of these applications enable you to create a new HTML page, drop your text into the page, align it, color it, and specify the font. You can set background colors and pictures with a few clicks, and drop in all the images required for each page. You can then use the familiar layout metaphors to align items and set widths and heights.

Adobe inherited GoLive from what used to be GoLive CyberStudio at version 3, and is arguably the more mature of the two applications, but Dreamweaver isn't lacking. Both applications follow the interface guidelines of their related applications. For example, GoLive has similar palette layouts and tool colorings of Photoshop/Illustrator (see Figure 2-3), whereas Dreamweaver has the same palette design and layout as Flash/Fireworks. Whether you like it or not, this will

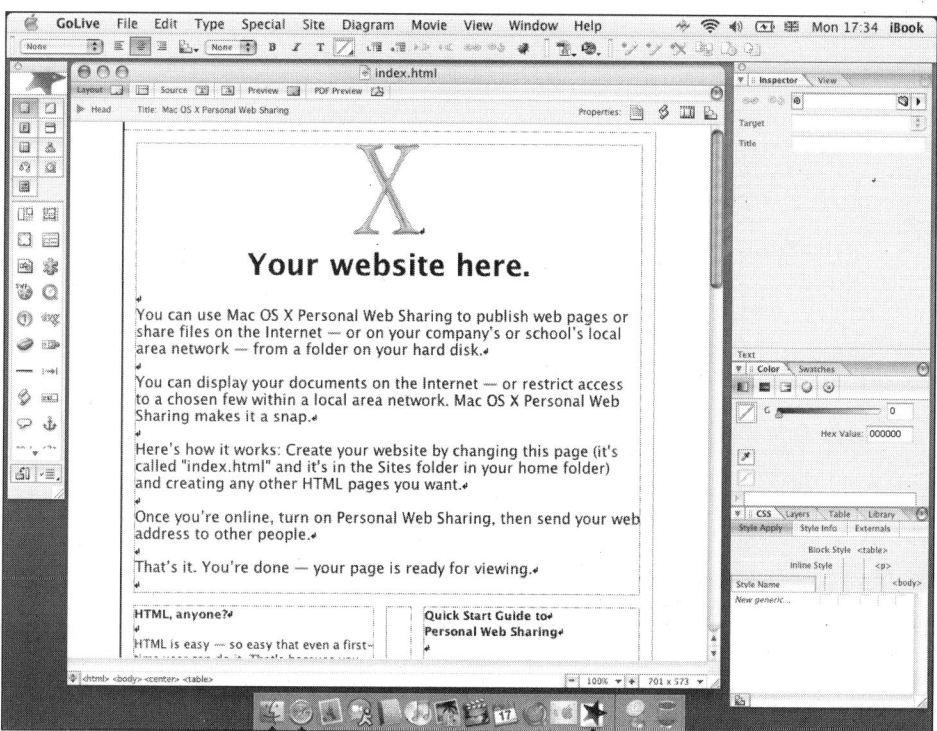

Figure 2-3. Adobe GoLive CS

probably influence your immediate decision about which application to start with.

If you're a newly arrived print-oriented designer, you'll get to grips with GoLive the quickest of the two applications. The process of laying out tables and dropping images in place isn't particularly difficult, but it's the positioning of palettes and the way tools work that'll help you get comfortable. GoLive is simply a more visual layout tool than Dreamweaver.

Dreamweaver appeals to coders and developers, to the more hardcore factions of web development. The interface can be confusing for first-timers, a fact that Macromedia has tried to address in the latest release by streamlining the toolbars and initial tools available. However, when people start diving under the hood, Dreamweaver catches the attention of coders in a way GoLive doesn't seem to have managed. Both applications have hundreds of add-ons and plug-ins to aid in repetitive or difficult tasks. They also feature heavy

integration with the other applications from their respective MX 2004 or CS stable.

Dreamweaver works very well with imported Fireworks and Flash files, retaining links to the original files, which makes updates very simple. Select the graphic you want to update, CMD-click and choose Edit with Fireworks MX 2004. Fireworks opens up, and you can edit your graphic in Fireworks. Once you've finished, one click takes you back to Dreamweaver with the newly changed graphic in place and the original source file updated and saved (known as **round trip editing**, as shown in Figure 2-4).

GoLive has the same functionality, only it's implemented in a slightly different way. GoLive uses Smart Objects to import and control assets from other applications. You can drop a Photoshop PSD file into a GoLive HTML page, and a module opens with resizing and optimization controls from Photoshop. This

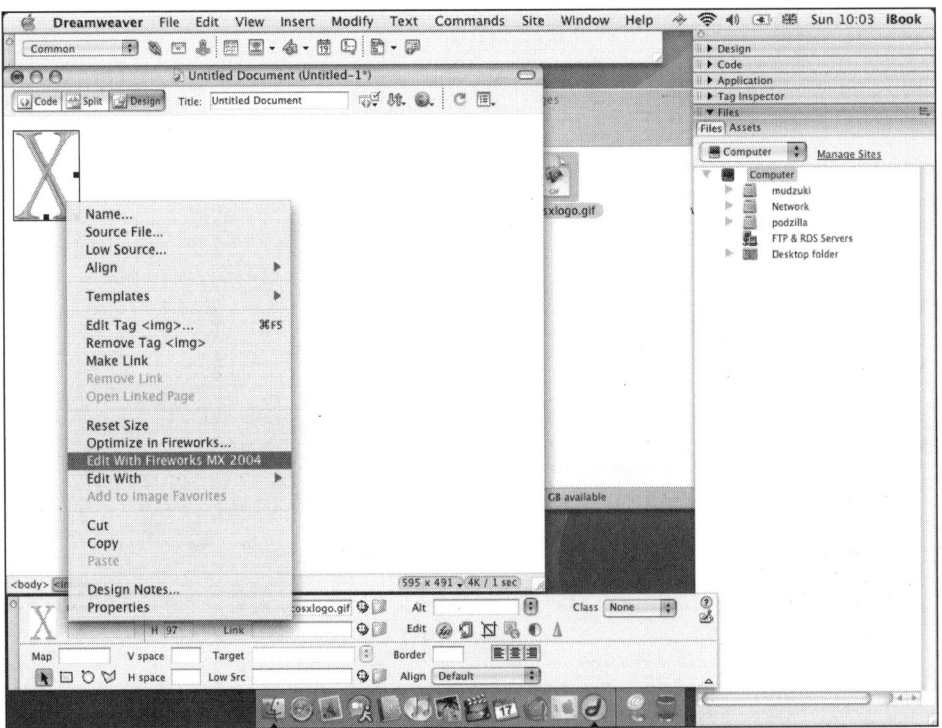

Figure 2-4. Round trip editing: the option to jump from Dreamweaver into Fireworks and back to edit your image files

provides the same functionality as you'd have if you were exporting a GIF or JPEG from Photoshop.

The choice between GoLive and Dreamweaver is a very personal one. Again, no right or wrong answer. Go and download the trials and see which one meets your needs and suits you best. But don't forget, at least look at both of them!

> *You can download the trial applications of Dreamweaver and other Macromedia applications from* www.macromedia.com/downloads/ *(beware, the file sizes are anywhere from 50 to 100MB in size). Similarly, you can download trials of the Adobe applications at* www.adobe.com/support/ downloads/main.html *(where the files will be a similarly fat size).*

Vector animation: Adobe LiveMotion vs. Macromedia Flash

The winner, in the first round, with a technical knock-out is Flash! OK, maybe this a bit severe but, despite outputting the same file format (SWF), these two applications are light years apart.

I think everyone reading this knows about Macromedia Flash (shown in Figure 2-5). You may have only heard the name, you may be familiar with it, or you may work with it for a living. Regardless, Flash is eponymous with Internet developments of the last three or four years, for better or worse. Flash is responsible for many brilliant websites laden with entertaining games, lush graphical and aural content with loads of slick animations, wipes, and action. Flash is also responsible for some of the true crimes and atrocities against web design perpetrated this decade. Although it's wrong to hold Macromedia to blame, overly eager teenagers who have downloaded every "kool" script to make text

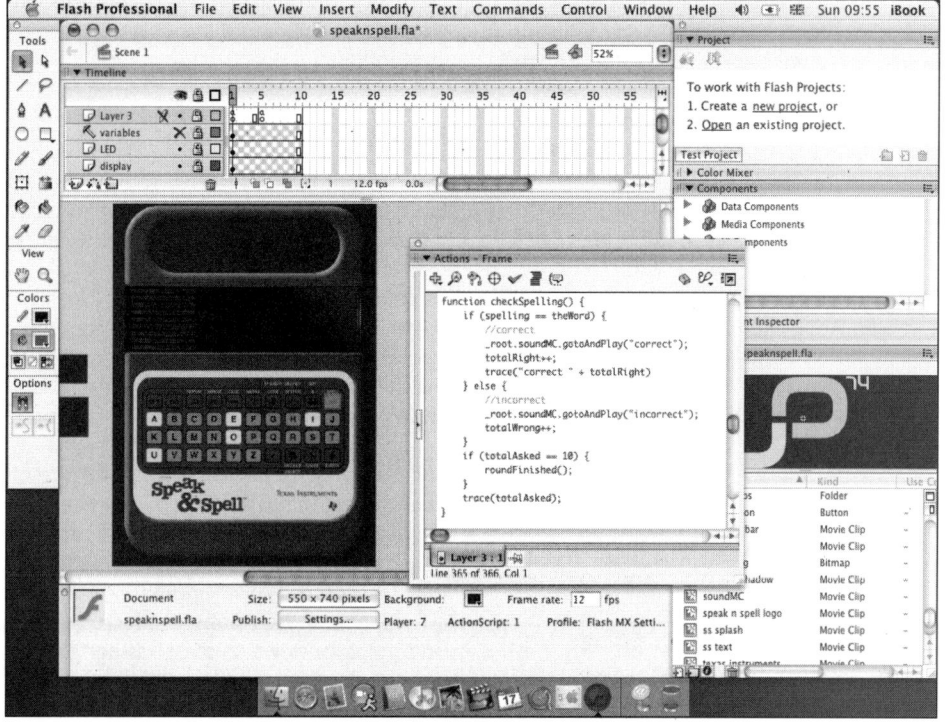

Figure 2-5. Macromedia Flash MX 2004

twirl and spin, with banging techno tunes and retarded navigation schemes, have done a lot to damage Flash's reputation.

There is always a usability debate on using Flash, where the purists try to ban Flash from the Internet, citing reasons of accessibility as the main bugbear (more on accessibility in Chapter 3). It won't happen, of course, it's just a case of choosing the wrong tool for the job. Why use Flash for an animated intro when the rest of the site has been built in pure HTML? Or why use Flash to create animated headers and menus when a simple set of JavaScript rollover buttons made with Fireworks will do the job just as well? Well, the simple answer in one word is "clients!" Quite often the client wants all these awesome animations and killer sound effects, but on a website selling garden furniture? It's the job of the web designer to educate clients and guide them in the direction of making informed decisions, but sometimes you just can't win this argument or they'll go elsewhere looking for that Flash intro.

Back to LiveMotion. What is LiveMotion's purpose? Who's it aimed at? It's obviously not aimed at the same crowd who use Flash daily, is it? LiveMotion is very akin to another Adobe product, After Effects (www.adobe.com/products/aftereffects/main.html), a tool that "delivers the speed, precision, and powerful tools you need to produce visually innovative motion graphics and effects for film, video, DVD, and the Web." It was an attempt to aid the transition into the online world for those people who work daily with video editing software and motion graphics. To this end, it's effective, providing a quick learning curve as the familiarity of the Adobe tool set is all there and it follows concepts the motion graphics designer will be used to. LiveMotion even allows for the programming of ActionScript, the language behind all the very clever Flash sites.

Flash, on the other hand, is the daddy of online interactivity. Since its inception in the summer of 1995, known then as FutureSplash, there have been literally hundreds of thousands of online games and interactive content sites created, all programmed in Flash. The Flash community is huge, with hundreds of sites dedicated to sharing knowledge, scripts, and workarounds for free to aid the learning of everyone in the group.

Some of the well-recognized Flash artists like Josh Davis, Yugo Nakamura, and Brendan Dawes have achieved rock star–like status in these communities, appearing at heavily attended conferences all over the world. Compare these guys with Jakob Nielson, the usability guru who insists that all sites should have the design impact of a phone book . . . guess who gets chosen as a role model?

Here are some recommended viewing Flash sites, for very cool scripts, ideas, discussions, and downloads:

- Flash Kit: www.flashkit.com
- www.actionscripts.org/
- www.actionscript.com
- Colin Moock: http://moock.org/webdesign/flash/

Flash has provided the biggest digital revolution since PageMaker opened up DTP to the masses, or the conception of the Internet. I can't seriously recommend anyone going with LiveMotion—this is a no-win situation, stick with Flash all the way. (Also, effective from November 2003, Adobe have ceased distributing LiveMotion.)

And the overall winner is . . .

Well, it's not really fair to match some of these applications head-on and compare them directly, as they're designed for different target audiences. I've also not scored each application separately, as I believe you can't force your opinions about the applications on someone else (with the obvious exception of Flash and LiveMotion), as each application is very competent in the field it operates in, and other users will nearly always work in a different way than you do. If you're happy with GoLive, then great, stick with it full time, but it's always good to be aware of the other options open to you. It's also good to have general knowledge about each of these other applications. If you're trying to get a job in the world of web design, the chances are that the company you apply to will have already purchased one of the Adobe or Macromedia bundles, and isn't going to buy a fresh set as part of your demands. Get on with the job in hand with the tools at hand.

Typography

For print designers, type can be the only thing that drives a design. The whole ethos of a brochure can be within the color and spacing of a font. A web designer can be at the mercy of end users, hoping they haven't set Comic Sans or the Star Trek typeface as their default viewing font.

The Internet was made by techies. Fact. But what do techies know about design? Very little, which explains why there is very little scope for control over design-related issues in standard HTML pages, such as fonts. You have no control over leading or letter spacing. If you want to achieve this, you have to do a lot of leg-work with "invisible spacers," which are 1X1 pixel transparent GIFs. But what point size is this? How about `<font size="1">`. What kind of measurement is 1? 1 what? 1 elephant? 1 apostrophe? What is worse, this indiscriminate measurement of 1 is actually different on a PC than a Mac! And then there's the range of fonts. Because you can't enforce every viewer to down-load a font before they look at your site, you're stuck with choosing a font from a list that (you hope) will be available on the user's machine. This list of fonts is usu-ally comprised of Times, Arial, Verdana, Georgia, and Comic Sans. Awesome! Now try explaining to a client why they can't use their corporate font throughout their site's body copy.

There have been several attempts over the years to develop things like "web fonts," where a font is stored on a server and, with a plug-in, the font is pulled into the page and used from the existing servers. This never took off, which was probably due to licensing and pay-ment issues.

So, if you need to have a fancy font for a header, do it as a graphic, simple as that!

Generally, every way of implementing type design on the web has been an afterthought, except for Cascading Style Sheets (CSS). CSS allows designers to specify leading and letter spacing, as well as use more meaningful font size measurements, such as points or ems. The world of CSS is a whole book unto itself, but it's very important to be aware of what it is and how it can benefit you, even at the simplest level of specifying a font across the whole site.

Imagine, for instance, you design a 300-page site for something tedious that needs 300 HTML pages of nearly solid text, and you use Arial throughout the site. Next, a manager decides that they actually don't want Arial to be used, they would prefer Times to be used all the way through the copy. You probably would have to do a search and replace through every page, changing every source code instance of `<font face="Arial">` to `<font face="Times">`. Although GoLive and Dream-weaver will do this with a "find and replace" command throughout a site folder and every subdirectory, you still run the risk of messing up and, believe me, it's easily done.

With CSS, you edit *one document* and the change is visible through every single page in the 300-page site. That's pretty powerful, isn't it? It also vastly reduces the amount of code in a standard HTML document because the code for the fonts isn't repeated every time there is a new paragraph of copy. Therefore, your pages are smaller, they load faster, and use less band-width. This is probably the first tentative step any designer makes into CSS. Don't be shy, dip your toe in. It's pretty nice in here (CSS will be covered in much more depth in Chapter 5).

Finally, a much welcomed new feature of Mac OS X is the ability to use TrueType fonts, the standard PC font format, without any conversions or messing about. Just drop the font into one of two places, ~/Library/Fonts (in your Home directory) for the font to be available to just you, or in /Library/Fonts to be available to every user on the computer. The major bonus in now being able to use TrueType is that free fonts on the Internet are invariably in TrueType format, so you instantly have access to all the fonts that are marked for PC, as well as your standard PostScript fonts, as favored by the majority of graphic designers.

Color

Once print designers have specified the Pantone colors (Pantone is the universal standard for specifying exact colors for accurate print) and paper stock, they know exactly how the print is going to look in the final prod-uct. Now welcome to the world of web design. A world where you don't know if the end user is going to be viewing your web page on a laptop, a desktop 21" TFT screen, a set-top box/TV, or a dirty, dingy, and dark 12" 640×480 monitor. Here lies one of the biggest problems in web design for a Mac user, but fortunately it's one that is simply resolved.

The default Mac gamma setting and, indeed, pretty much any Mac monitor setting that has been "color-sync'd" for print, is too light and too bright for web design. Without calibrating your monitor to mimic a PC or TV set, your graphics will look washed out and faded on an average PC monitor. The solution? Step through the **ColorSync** setup again and create a very dark profile for your monitor.

Go to System Preferences ➤ Displays, and click the Color tab. Click the Calibrate button and you can step through the process of calibrating your monitor, paying particular attention to the Television Gamma option (see Figure 2-6).

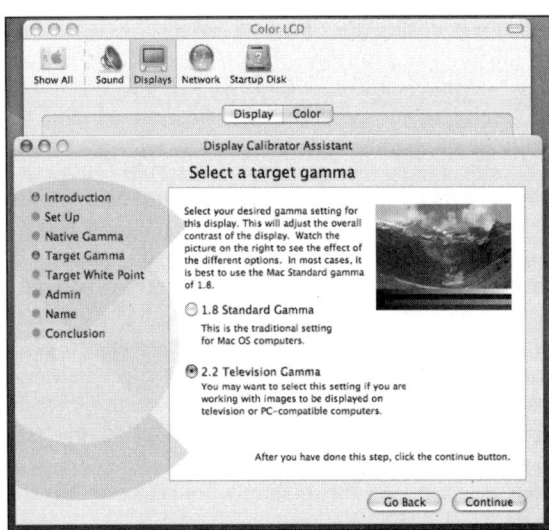

Figure 2-6. Calibrating the display in Mac OS X

Here's another very helpful color correction tip specifically for Adobe Photoshop: Choose View ➤ Proof Setup ➤ Windows RGB and your artwork should become noticeably darker. Remember, Photoshop doesn't use the same ColorSync profile as your monitor unless you set the Color Preferences up this way. With all this advice, you can get your artwork to a color state that closely matches that of a standard PC setting but, as always with web design, it's a good idea to test early and test often.

Web-safe colors

You may be asking yourself, "Hang on? What's a web-safe color and why do I need to use it?"

A long time ago, in a galaxy far, far away . . . most of the computers hooked up to the Internet had poor 8-bit video display cards, which were limited to displaying a maximum of 256 colors on screen. And what's more . . . the Mac and PC didn't even share the same 256-color palette. They shared 216 colors that looked exactly the same on each type of computer. So, a good web designer, back in the day, would choose colors from this set of 216 colors to use in all the text, table cells, and flat graphics, and dither all the GIF image files down to use only colors from this palette.

This is very, very rarely done in today's web design galaxy. Most users have a graphics card with over 8MB of video memory and every display is in millions of colors, but you can still see the roots of this 216-color chart when using the color chip picker in the Macromedia applications.

If you're a coder getting a little stuck with all this talk of design and color, and are asking yourself how this chapter can help you, fret not; I can help make your ASCII text, table cells, and general color choices look good. A simple application of color theory can work wonders for a site and really create a cohesive design. Help is at hand in the form of **Color Consultant Pro** (www.code-line.com/software/colorconsultantpro .html), shown in Figure 2-7. This is a very helpful tool that aids the design by applying color theory into an interactive color wheel, making the whimsical task of color picking a lot quicker and helping you feel more confident that your selection of colors does actually work together . . . scientifically! See, nerds, you knew I'd come good and help you out there. Actually, I'd recommend this application to anyone who has to pick colors to use together, no-matter what field they are working in. It removes a lot of indecision and time wasting when picking complementary colors.

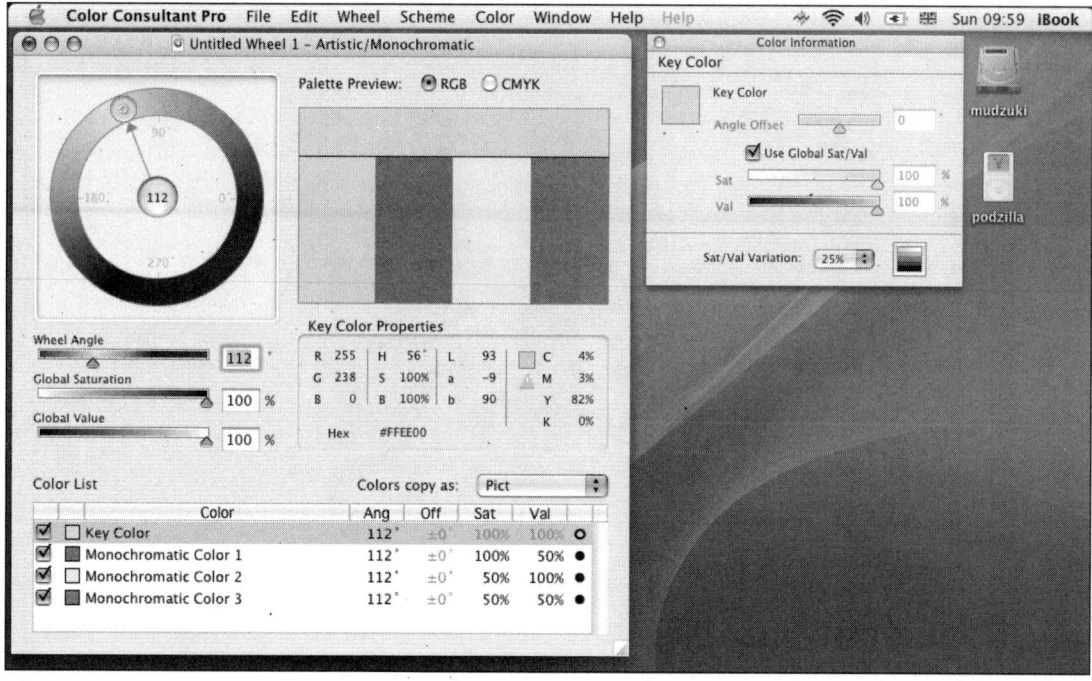

Figure 2-7. Color Consultant Pro: invaluable in helping you pick complementary colors

Some web rules for print designers

When saving graphic files for use on the Internet, there are three main file formats: JPEG, GIF, and the less-used PNG taking third place. Just to reiterate, very quickly, JPEGs are great for landscape scenes, pictures of people, and general photographic scenes that have large tonal graduations of colors, as they use the full range of millions of colors.

GIFs are good for stylized text headings or corporate logos, as these types of images usually only contain two or three colors and some site "furniture," such as buttons and arrows. Although JPEGs can't contain transparency, GIFs can, albeit a little blocky around the edges. GIFs can have a maximum of 256 colors in each file, but you would tend to aim for about 8 to 32 colors to keep the file size low.

JPEGs and PNGs are limited to a single frame (they are static), but GIFs can be made up of a series of frames shown in succession, which produces a simple animation effect.

PNGs can have an 8-bit alpha mask, using 256 shades of gray to give you superb alpha transparency, but not many browsers support PNG by default.

One thing to watch, print designers, is that you must *always* save your images in RGB format when creating graphics that are going online, because the work is going to be displayed on a monitor that uses Red, Green, and Blue elements to create a pixel on screen. There's no place for CMYK here.

You can change the format of an image in Photoshop by choosing Image ➤ Mode ➤ RGB Color. Also, using the File ➤ Save for Web option automatically handles the CMYK-to-RGB conversion (see Figure 2-8).

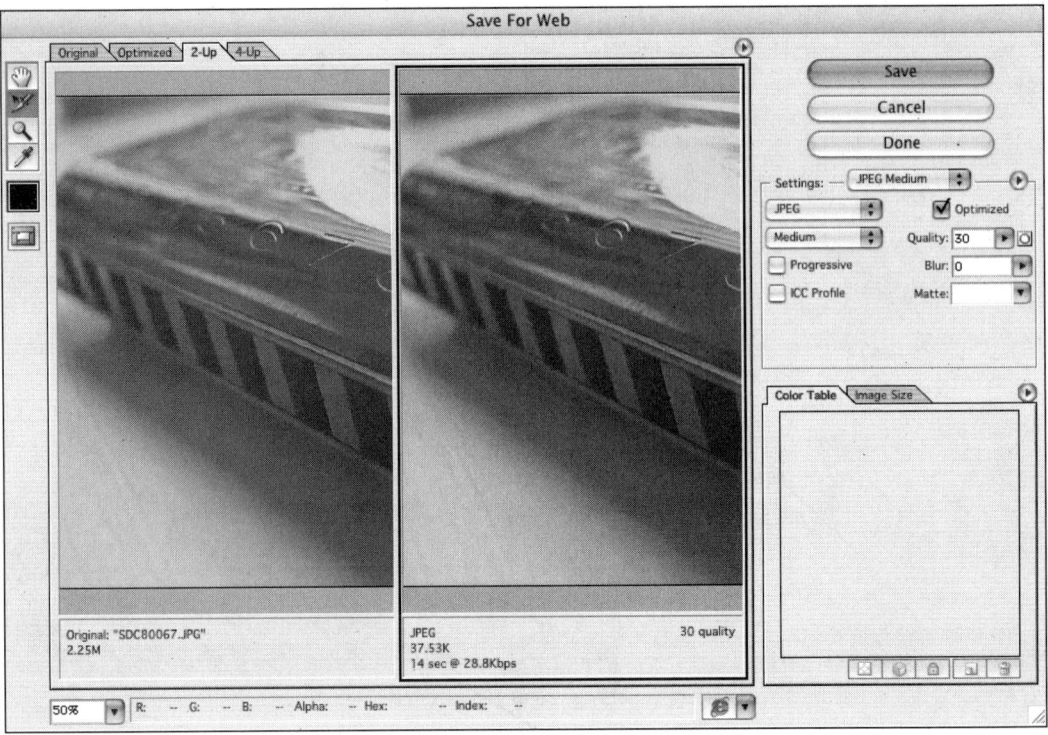

Figure 2-8. Photoshop's Save for Web option automatically converts the color mode to RGB.

In Fireworks, everything it exports—whether it's a JPEG, PNG, or GIF file—is in RGB mode, so you're okay here. If you save a JPEG in CMYK mode, you're wasting file size by including four color channels of information in the file instead of three. However, even more importantly, it won't display in most browsers, as they simply can't show a CMYK JPEG, expecting RGB instead. You can then waste a lot of time checking the page code, file location, and graphic over and over, saying things like "But it works on my machine, look, I can open in it Photoshop!"

Secondly, file sizes in the web design world are the complete opposite of the print world. Smaller is better! An average website clocks in at under 2MB in file size for the whole site! Compare a standard JPEG file of around 15 to 30K with your average 20 to 30MB CMYK TIFF images, and you can imagine how much faster Photoshop will run. The reason for this extreme difference, quite simply, is the resolution that you create the graphics at. Print designers aim for something like a 300 dpi (dpi stands for "dots per inch") image to retain

the highest quality when designing Photoshop work for a brochure or other printed matter. Web designers aim for the bare minimum data required to show an image at screen resolution, because all their work will be shown on a monitor. This means 72 dpi for web designers, or anyone whose output goes to TV or monitor.

So, working with images that are a roughly a quarter of the dpi, and with much smaller dimensions (you don't need to design A4/A3 paper–size screens!), you now have less time to sit on your bottom watching progress bars. It will affect a lot of things; you work faster, you don't need as much free hard drive space for Photoshop to use as a scratch disk, you're never constantly running out of disk space . . . oh wait, that'll never change.

And, finally, you know that Pantone color reference booklet next to your desk? At times, you might as well stick it under the short leg of your desk to stop it wobbling. When you start dealing with clients on a variety of PC monitors, all the Pantone reference charts in the world won't help you get a color right. With the best intentions in the world, you're still going to have to compromise and shift colors to get them close to the original but still appear in the same color field across a range of displays.

Page layout considerations

When initially designing a website layout, it's a common mistake for a print designer to jump in and design a layout with a portrait format, much like an A4 page and, I guess, around 90 percent of the things they produce. The typical computer screen, however, is landscape in layout. After you factor in toolbars and menus, the area left to display your page in is more like a widescreen movie space.

This doesn't help when the maximum screen real estate on the Mac is different than that on the PC! Using the same browser on each platform will give different default sizes due to the system bars and buttons being different sizes. The best thing to do is get a PC (or PC user) to take a snapshot of a screen with the browser open and the default set of page buttons and adornments in place, and then use this snapshot as the base layer in a Photoshop document. You can then snap a standard Macintosh desktop with open browser, and drop that picture into Layer 2 of your Photoshop document. Change this layer's opacity to 50 percent, and you can see which areas of the two browsers overlap and how much space remains for you to design in from the outset.

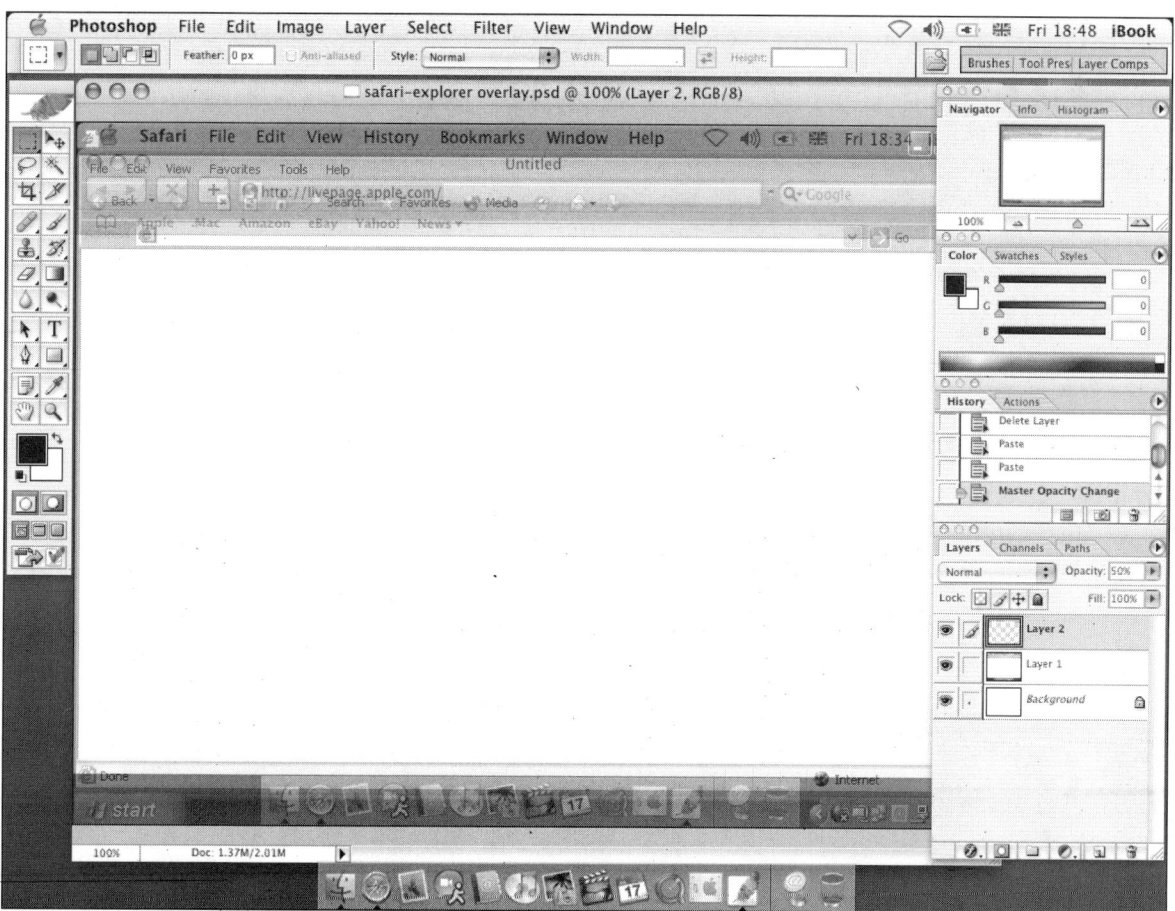

Transferring print layouts to the Web

Imagine that you're working on a print job using InDesign. As per the client's request, you have generated some raw Illustrator and Photoshop files. You lay them out using InDesign but notice that part of a graphic just isn't quite right. All you have to do is *CTRL*-click the offending PSD or AI file and choose Graphics ➤ Edit Original. This opens the graphic file in its original application so you can alter it. Once you've finished making the change, all you have to do is save it and, when you return to InDesign, you'll see the amended graphic immediately.

The next thing you know, the client is on the phone wanting it to go online. Easy:

1. In InDesign choose File ➤ Package for GoLive.

2. Now open GoLive and choose File ➤ Import ➤ From InDesign.

That's about as easy as it comes: from print layout to web in a few clicks.

Making fonts legible on the Web

The second biggest problem for a print designer making the transition into web development is understanding font sizes and legibility issues in web browsers and when designing at 72 dpi. You can't assume that the 7 pt Helvetica Neue Light text you've set in Quark is going to be at all legible in a website. Laying out type for headers and copy should really be done in Photoshop and at 72 dpi; otherwise, unless you're very familiar with sizing and results, you'll just be fooling yourself.

As a quick example, create a new Photoshop document of about 480×60 pixels at 72 dpi in size and try dropping your reams of copy in there. Test out reducing the point size as much as you can yet keeping the type legible. Shocking isn't it?

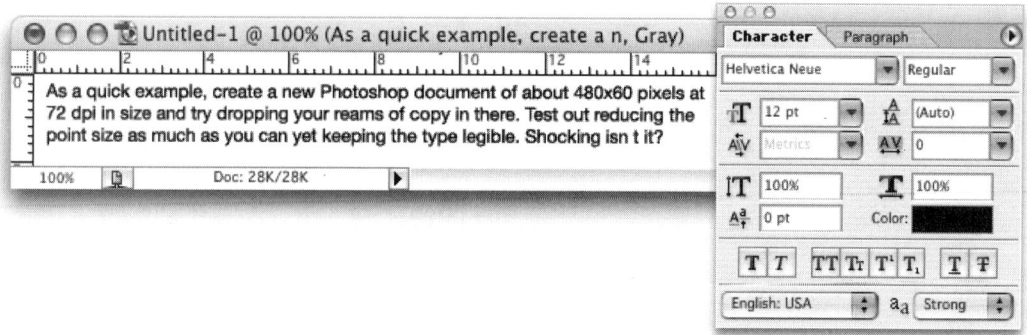

In my best Columbo voice, "One more thing." Mac and PC browsers don't render things in exactly the same way. There are a few nuances about borders and table alignments, but the main problem lies in font rendering. The PC uses a standard size of 96 dpi to render screen type, which of course makes it look bigger than the Mac's old standard of 72 dpi. What you find in the latest versions of the browsers is that the Mac is making 96 dpi the default setting, putting all browsers on an even footing.

Cross-platform testing

If you want a good test base for visually designing sites that will be cross-platform, test everything on Internet Explorer 5 (IE5) on the Mac. It has one of the strictest HTML rendering engines out there, which is good. If the site looks good on IE5 on the Mac, you can bet that it's only a few tweaks away from running well on all browsers. Safari is another great browser for following standards, but is a little more relaxed about certain bits of code when compared to IE. However, for CSS and JavaScript, Safari is better. Basically, you can't win; you have to test on both a PC and a Mac, and in different browsers!

Another advantage of the Macintosh is that, besides running the Mac OS and a UNIX base layer, you can run a full Windows system through emulation. Today's G5s, the G4s, and even G3s are powerful enough to run

Windows 98, 2000, and XP on Microsoft's Virtual PC (the application formerly known as Connectix Virtual PC). With this up and running, you can test your websites as you develop them on a "real" PC browser. You can set up Virtual PC to access your site folders as shared drives or, for the über nerds, if you've set your Mac up with Apache as a web server and are serving your sites as you develop them, you simply type in your Mac's IP address or full domain name in the PC browser and you can view and test the site "live" . . . all from one Macintosh box.

> For more details on Microsoft's Virtual PC, check out www.microsoft.com/mac/products/virtualpc/virtualpc.aspx?pid=virtualpc.

In fact, it's very good practice to design your web pages for client approval in Photoshop or Fireworks (I'd avoid Freehand, Illustrator, and especially Quark—it can be a real pain getting certain graphics out of Quark later on). It's easy to see if the supplied copy will fit in header or body copy areas, whether the copy needs a rewrite or needs addressing and moving onto two pages. Using a screenshot of a PC web browser with the blank content area punched out and your design placed within it will also rest a client's mind, helping prevent questions like "Will you be making one that works on a PC too?" Clients may be unused to the Mac interface. If they can get to grips with what's surrounding your design quickly, then they're less likely to throw up problems and questions, and you can get down to the task at hand. Give them something they know and are familiar with and get them on safe ground. You're supposed to be on the client's side, after all.

For HTML design, once a client has approved the look and feel, Photoshop and Fireworks now have very powerful slice commands. These aid you in chopping up a complete layout into all the relevant little pieces that are stitched back together in your HTML editor. Remember, don't work hard, work smart.

A plus point that print designers can bring to web design is simply their knowledge of page layout formats. Most web pages are single columns of text broken occasionally by a picture that's invariably centered in the page. Coming from a different background, you should be able to put a fresh slant on some of your clients' layouts and give web page design a kickstart.

Copyright issues

Designers are more aware of copyright issues than the average bear. What you might not be aware of is that the copyright laws for images from an image library will vary depending on whether you use your images in print or online. The quality doesn't have to be as high with images online, but they will potentially be viewed by more people. The rules on this differ from image library to image library, but are usually well documented. Remember, the Internet is a medium that deals in more than just visual entertainment. A lot of websites depend on music and audio content to drive their impact, but copyright extends to the use of music, samples, and loops too.

Okay, this may seem like common sense to a lot of people, but what you need to know is what to do about it. There are quite a few online stores where you can purchase royalty-free music, sound effects, and music loops to go on your website. I'd definitely recommend Sound Dogs (www.sounddogs.com). The prices start at little more than a couple of cents for some of the sound effects and, invariably, they have exactly what

you're looking for at a bit rate (the sound quality) that suits you. There's no point paying for a CD-quality music sample if it's just going to be mangled from stereo into mono and reduced to a low bit rate. All delivery of the sound files is done online, so you receive an e-mail with a login and password to a secure FTP site to download your files, usually within minutes of your order being accepted. You can also sleep well at night, knowing you've not ripped anyone off, the DMCA Police will be off your trail for a little longer, and you've helped a starving artist somewhere in the world.

Designing on a Mac in a PC environment

Despite what any system administrator says ("Sorry, we don't have any Mac 'ports' on the walls for you to use"), your Mac plays very well with other Windows machines on a network. As detailed in Chapter 1, you can see and access other PCs on the network, they won't distinguish you from any other PC, and they can see your Mac as a shared PC, thanks to Mac OS X's built-in **Samba sharing**. This means that files can be swapped very easily between teams of people working on the same project, sharing Photoshop documents, GIFs, JPEGs, and HTML files without a second thought. Actually, wait, there is just one thing you need to do.

File suffixes

Do you remember how for years Mac users laughed at PC users for having to add a suffix to each file, such as .doc for a Word document, in order for the system to recognize which application it came from? Well, chow down on humble pie, because you need to start adding these suffixes to any files you want to share with Windows and UNIX machines on your network.

Actually, Mac OS X adds these file suffixes automatically when saving files. If you can't see any, it's because they're hidden by default. Mac OS X uses a hybrid of both file name extensions (like UNIX and PC machines do) and the old Mac OS way of identifying a file by its creator types in the resource fork. Indeed, any files you intend to publish online require a file suffix, because it's probable that it's a UNIX or Windows machine running as the web server.

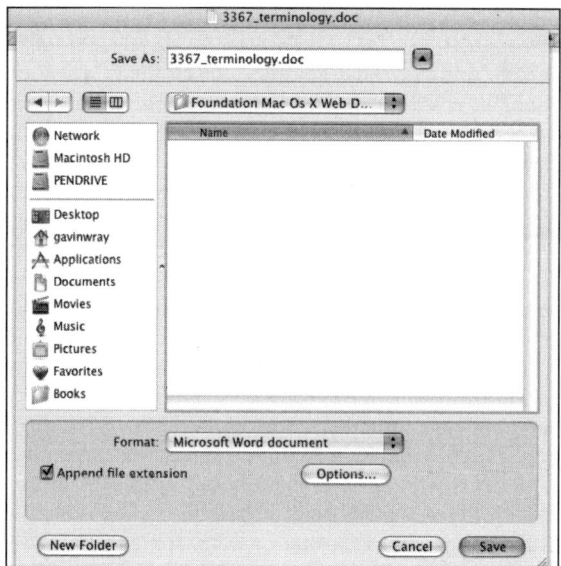

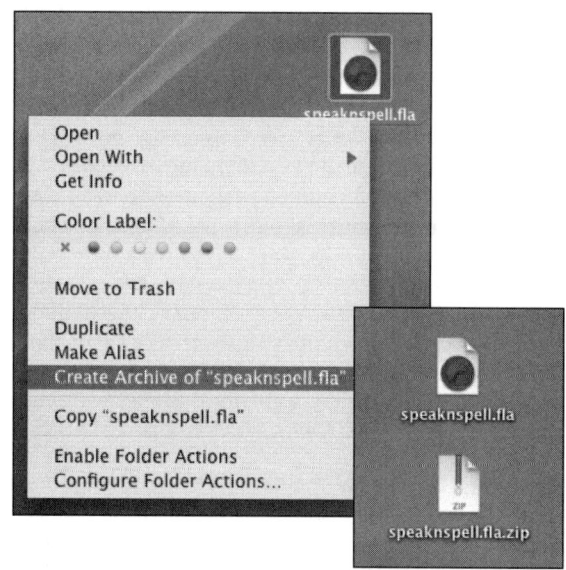

This naming convention can be difficult to stick to at first, as some of the print-based designers I know add periods and three-letter abbreviations all over a file name, including letters irrelevant to the type of file. It makes the file name look like some secret coded message, incomprehensible to all, but obvious for the person saving and naming the file. It doesn't matter if their work is generated on a Macintosh and sent to printers who all use Macintoshes, so the document never steps foot on another file system.

Working on a Mac within a PC workplace also requires you to play nice with the Windows users too. When you compress files, make sure you use a compression format other people can use too, as there's no point in archiving a project if no one else can then access it at a later date. The ZIP compression format, typically used on PCs, is a good choice because it's now built in at system level with Mac OS X 10.3. Just *CTRL*-click any file and select Create Archive of <your file>. Few PC users have StuffIt for PC installed, even though SIT files are the most eponymous compression format to Mac users.

Designing with accessibility in mind

This is where your design skills or programming knowledge will show through, not how well you know a program. But there's a slight snag . . .

Designing to web standards is difficult, as a lot of the CSS sites you see are hand coded so, if you're a designer, hook up with a good programmer if you need to create a well-designed and accessible site. Likewise, if you're a good coder, get yourself a competent designer. You'll find everything you do will benefit from a well-coded page or an attractively designed layout. There aren't many people out there who can both code and design to a high level.

When designing anything that's dominated by a focus on accessibility, the golden rule is "Keep It Simple," at least until you've created a few accessible sites and know how to handle the problems. You'll find out more about hand coding and designing sites that deal with these problems later in the book, but the technical details I've mentioned in this chapter will help both a coder and designer communicate in the same language to achieve a good site.

Chapter review

At first, it seems that there is a lot to learn and remember when designing graphics for use in the web environment. Measurements are in pixels instead of something more normal like millimeters or inches, and colors don't look the same on every monitor. You can't rely on Pantone standards, must use RGB color channels instead of the CMYK you're used to, and need to change the gamma settings of a monitor. The list seems to go on! After a few weeks though, these things become second nature, and you won't need to think about them. As a graphic designer in the print world, you already come to the web world armed with your most useful tool: your creativity.

Don't forget to look at the positive side of things. As a print designer, you already use applications like Photoshop and Freehand on a full-time basis, so there's nothing to relearn there. At the simplest level, Dreamweaver and GoLive do the same job for web design as Quark and InDesign do for page layout design: They help you arrange text and images on the screen.

In fact, don't give the graphics side of things a second thought; you'll have them boxed off and in the bag in no time. We'll move on to concentrate on developing new coding skills, such as learning CSS and XHTML from scratch to create a web page layout. Using Dreamweaver and GoLive makes designing a web page a breeze, but you really should have a bit of an understanding about how web pages hang together and exactly what it is that GoLive and Dreamweaver output once you've finished laying out a page. It may sound tough, but it's very important to understand the mechanics that drive everything, even if it's a rudimentary "I know enough to fill the back of a stamp" kind of knowledge. It will help you understand why certain layouts won't work, and it might help you to explain to a client why it's technically impossible to achieve the crazy design they've come up with. It'll also help you understand why the push for standards and accessibility is making strides and give you an idea where the future of web design is heading. So without further ado, let's code . . .

Chapter 3

DEVELOPING STATIC WEBSITES

What we'll cover in this chapter:

- Site editing tools
- World Wide Web Consortium (W3C)
- XHTML
- Cascading Style Sheets
- JavaScript
- Templates and Library Items
- XHTML time

Before you plunge into the waters of dynamic websites, you should learn the basics first. "Don't run before you can walk" is currently more applicable in the world of web development than it has ever been. Why? The way the web works is changing. Hacked up old HTML documents full of `<font>` tags are out; unforgiving XHTML and CSS documents are very much here to stay, and the Web is to be made accessible for everyone. In this chapter, you'll learn about why this is happening, what it means for you as a developer, and, more importantly, what on earth XHTML and CSS are actually all about. By the end of this chapter, you'll have made a basic web page that is totally XHTML/CSS valid and meets the new accessibility laws. It will have alternate style sheets, including large text and reverse colors for the visually impaired, making it easier for them to read.

Overview

For years, people have talked about making websites for a living or as a hobby. More often than not, it was very difficult to get these sites to work the same in the main two browsers (PC Internet Explorer and PC Netscape 4+). You would code some elements that would look fine in one browser, but in another it would look awful. Compromise was often the order of the day. The choices were

- Use a detection script to send the user to a browser-specific version of the site (a very popular technique that's still in use today).
- Design purely for PC Internet Explorer, which is currently the most popular browser in use (a bad technique, as it blocks some users, creating a bad impression).
- Get the site looking "near enough" as you want it to in the main two browsers, and ignore all the other users. (Far too common. I'm sure some designers never knew there was life outside IE and Netscape.)
- Code properly! (More about this later.)

In all of these scenarios, one set of users was guaranteed to come off worst of all: Mac users. I'd be willing to put all my Macs up as a stake and bet that nine out of ten designers who designed websites on a PC have *never* tested their work on a Mac. The sad fact is that the majority don't seem to care.

I, for one, always thought about both platforms, as I used both of them at work and home. I would often design a site at work using Windows as the test platform and the site would work just fine. Testing it at home on my Mac though was an entirely different story: There would be large gaps in the layout, misbehaving tables, and general funk occurring all over the place.

A designer could make far too many mistakes and simply get away with it. "Missed some closing tags off? Not a problem, I'll just render the page the way I think it should be!" said Internet Explorer, while Netscape would crank up the king of all tags (`<blink>`), and actually flash where the error was! Of course, a lot of this bad coding was done by hand and usually to impossible deadlines for evil tyrant dictators (a.k.a. The Client). No syntax coloring + no visual guides = No Fun, and a greater risk of mistakes being made. I regularly used to code 90K HTML pages in Notepad that were full of nested tables. Eating in a restaurant one night after work, a waiter said to me:

"I'm afraid there's a problem with your table, sir."

"Check both the `<tr>` and `<td>` tags are closed properly," I said, without even thinking.

The look of confusion on the guy's face was classic, until I realized and explained. That's when I knew things really *had* to be done a different way. I managed to convince my boss to let us use Dreamweaver, and deadlines were never as scary from that day forth.

I started in this business by hand coding, and I'm still glad I did. I know how things work, and why. I can fix bits of code if I need to and make tiny adjustments without having to start up Dreamweaver. Hand coding is very useful, but let's be realistic here. If a client is banging on the door, wondering where their overdue 200-page site is, it's time for action.

This action comes in the form of What You See Is What You Get (WYSIWYG) web page editing software such as Dreamweaver or GoLive (these applications are discussed in detail in Chapter 2). Used in conjunction with their graphics counterparts (Fireworks and ImageReady, respectively, in the case of the Dreamweaver and GoLive), today's developer can save a serious amount of time. In fact, you would have to be quite mad to shun tools like these. How about the ability to lay out your page, slice up the graphics, create image maps, add rollovers, add <alt> tags and status bar messages, then import all that into your HTML document with a single click? Does that do anything for you? It certainly makes things easier for me!

Site editing tools

In Chapter 2, you looked at the heavyweight editors, Dreamweaver and GoLive. With full-on site management, visual CSS support, and everything else they have to offer, you can quite easily get lost in options if all you need to do is maintain an existing site. You might only want to make a few text changes. Or, maybe you've left users in charge of their own updates, and a program like Dreamweaver would be far too much for them to handle. Time to look at site editing tools!

Macromedia Contribute

Contribute is an interesting application that can be set up in a number of ways, depending on your requirements and users' needs. First, imagine that you are the administrator of a site with total control and you're giving your client only very basic rights, such as allowing the client to just edit text, change certain images, and so on. In a nutshell, you can allow your client to edit only certain regions of the site.

1. Click the Create Connection button, shown in Figure 3-1, to invoke the Connection Assistant. Note the option to connect to your iDisk (which you can use, if you have a full .Mac account).

2. Fill in the User Info.

3. Type in the web address (see Figure 3-2). Let's stay local and use http://127.0.0.1/ (I've left the example from the previous chapter in the root of my web server, to replace the default Apache index page).

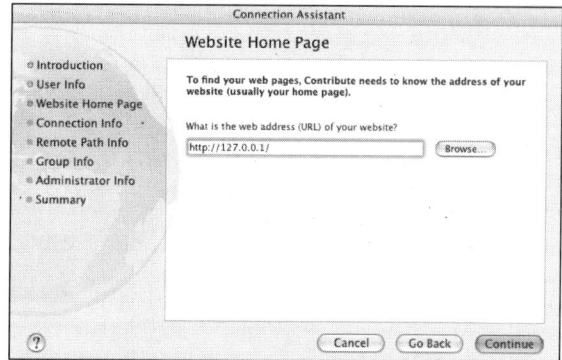

Figure 3-2. Type in the local IP address for your web server.

4. Select Local/Network on the Connection Info page, as shown in Figure 3-3.

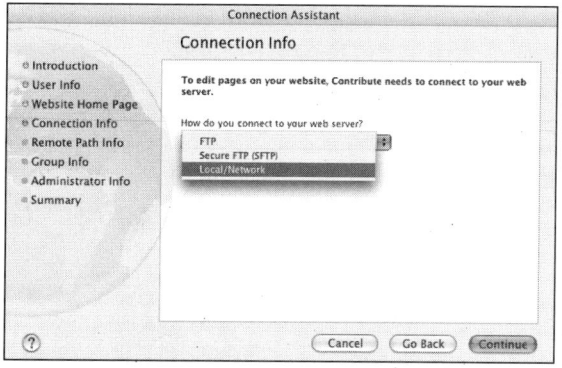

Figure 3-3. Choose the Local/Network option from the menu.

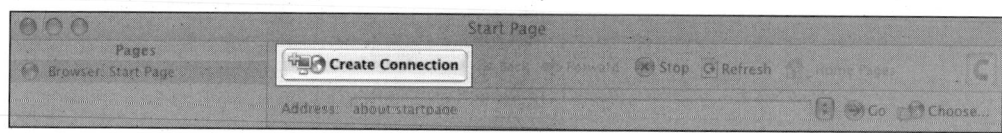

Figure 3-1. Click the button to start.

5. Still on the Connection Info page, browse to the network path of your web server: MacintoshHD/Library/WebServer/Documents (see Figure 3-4).

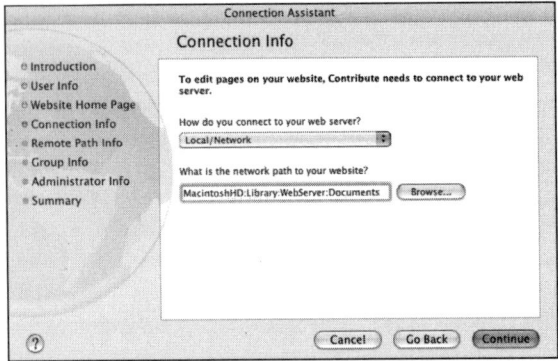

Figure 3-4. Use the Browse button to select the path to the web server's documents folder.

6. You want to administer the site, so click the Yes, I want to be the administrator button and then enter the password you want to use (see Figure 3-5).

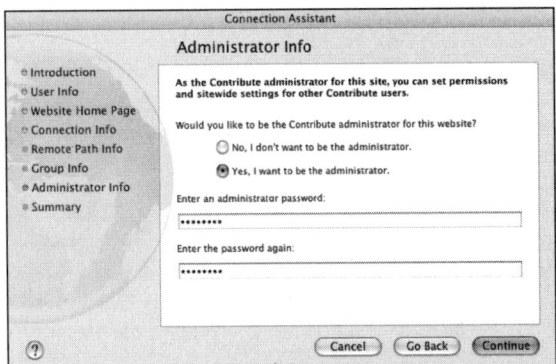

Figure 3-5. Insert a password—make sure it's one you'll remember.

7. The Summary page should tell you that you've been successful, so click Finish.

8. You'll be asked if you want to change the settings for the website, so click Yes, because you want to administer the users (see Figure 3-6).

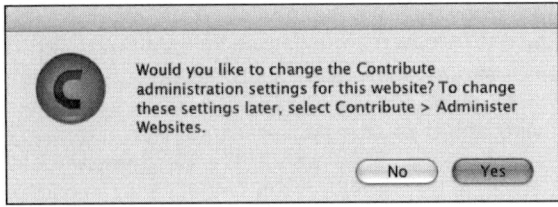

Figure 3-6. Click Yes, although you can do this part later too.

Administering users in Contribute

I'm going to set up Jake, my Technical Reviewer, as a user, and then have Contribute create a key to e-mail to him.

1. Click the Send Connection Key button, shown in Figure 3-7.

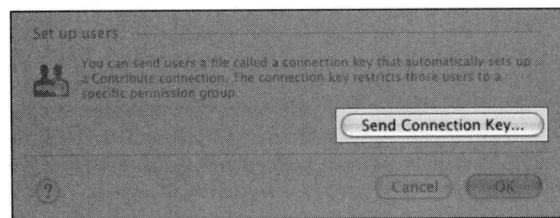

Figure 3-7. Hit the Send Connection Key button to start the export process.

2. Select the No radio button to customize the connection settings for others as shown in Figure 3-8 and click Continue.

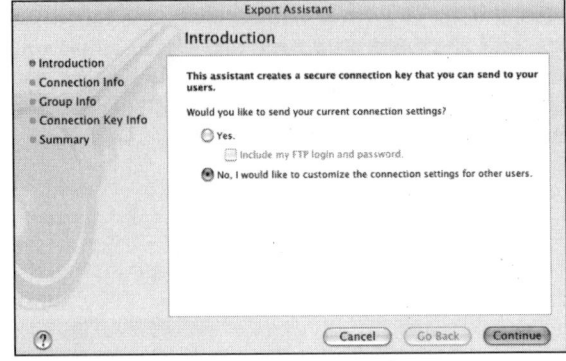

Figure 3-8. Select Customize.

3. On the Connection Info page, select and then fill in your SFTP settings (see Figure 3-9). The Export Assistant will now check the settings.

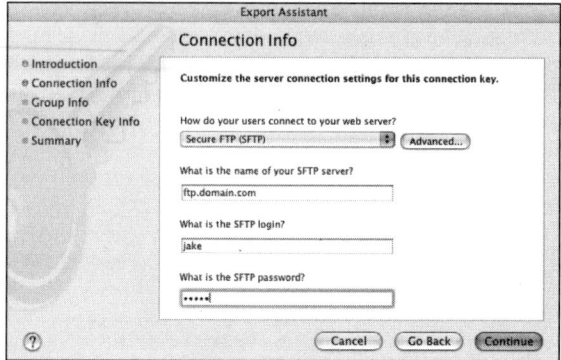

Figure 3-9. Insert your SFTP details.

4. Select Users on the Group Info page.

5. I'm going to mail Jake his key, so I leave the Send in e-mail option selected as shown in Figure 3-10 and provide him with a password, which I will have to tell him.

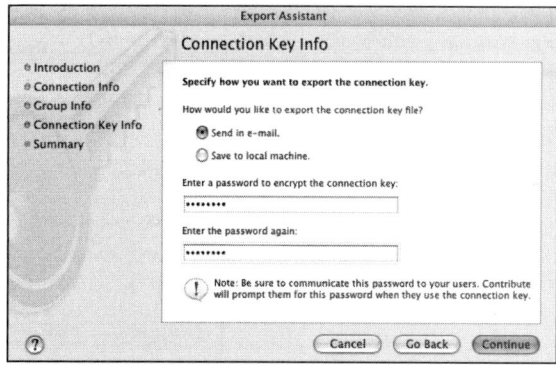

Figure 3-10. Enter the password for the key.

6. When I click the Continue button, my e-mail application opens, attaches the encrypted key, and waits for an e-mail address. As you can see in Figure 3-11, the body of the e-mail is already filled in nicely, ready to go.

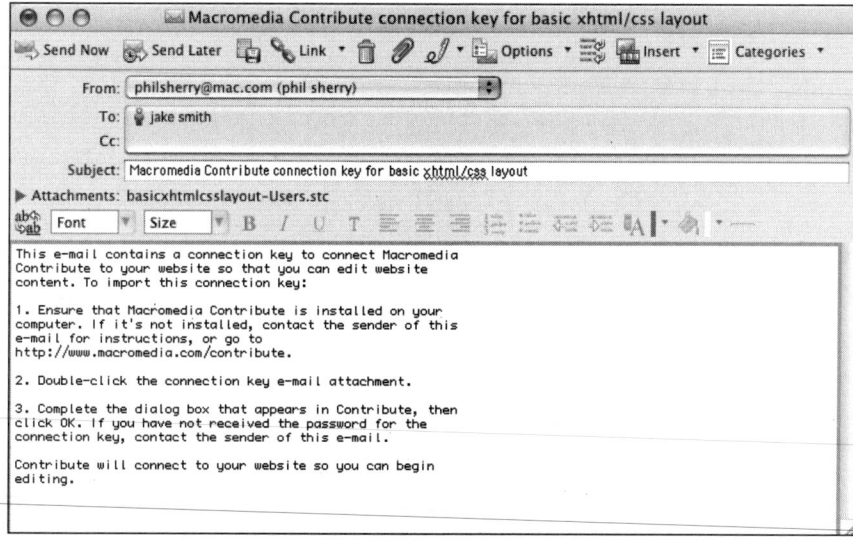

Figure 3-11. Contribute words the e-mail and attaches the file.

Users can be allowed to alter a certain image or specific text sections, for example, all of which are definable by you. This ensures that they can't completely destroy the layout (and all your hard work!) but don't have to trouble you every few days when they want to update the site. There's even a one-click command to specify that they can only edit blocks of text (see Figure 3-12).

All of this works alongside Dreamweaver too. If you use **templates** (discussed later in this chapter), you can specify which regions you want the user to be able to edit via Contribute. The Check In/Out feature (see Figure 3-13) is in full effect too, which protects against accidental overwrites (by either party!). This feature tells you whether someone else is actually working on a file currently and, if true, prevents anyone else from making changes to that file.

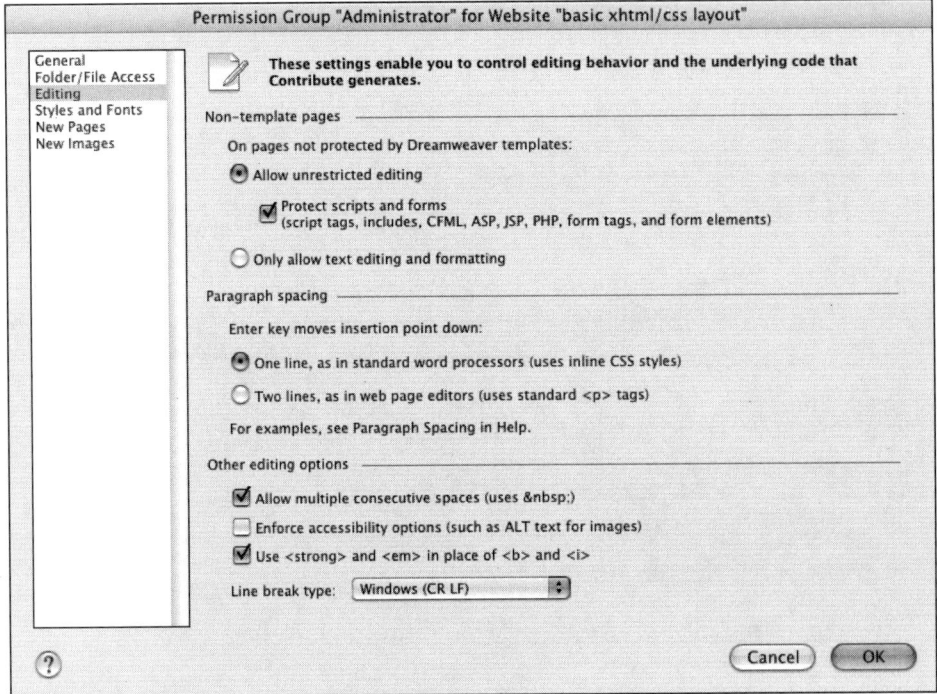

Figure 3-12. Define what the user is able to alter.

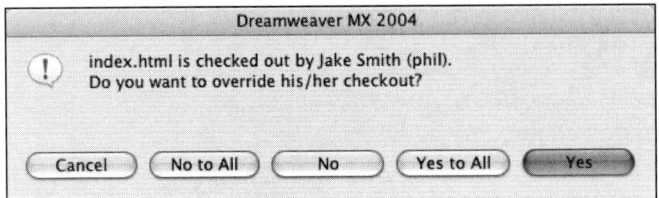

Figure 3-13. The Check In/Check Out feature tells you if a file is in use.

No longer will you have to trust your clients with FTP login details and worry about them deleting the whole site at 7 p.m. on a Friday night, just as you're about to go and party for the weekend. I'm sure you've all had that emergency phone call, something like "I think I've done something wrong and the CEO needs to see the site in 5 minutes. Can you help!?" Ugh, party postponed. Not any more though!

BBEdit

As text editors go, BBEdit is the king. I find this application quite invaluable. It has syntax coloring for HTML, XHTML, XML, CSS, PHP4, JavaScript, Java, Perl, C/C++, Ruby, Python, Pascal, and much more, with plug-ins for other languages (such as SQL) available on its website (www.barebones.com/products/bbedit). It even has a glossary menu full of code snippets (from Apache through to XSLT), which you can just drag or click to insert into your document.

The built-in FTP browser is also useful. Feed in your FTP settings, and you can edit documents live on the server, eliminating the need for extra FTP software. This is one speedy FTP application too!

The tie-in with Dreamweaver is really cool. I often have the same page open in both Dreamweaver and BBEdit at the same time. Edit the code in one application, and it's updated in the other one automatically. Dreamweaver hiccups a little bit and asks if you want to reload the page, but BBEdit handles itself like a champ.

Opening "hidden" documents, (system files such as the Apache configuration document `httpd.conf`, `.htaccess` files, and so on) is extremely easy. In BBEdit, go to File ➤ Open Hidden and locate your file, or you can use the command line. When you first run the application, you're asked whether you want to install the command line tool as shown in Figure 3-14. Do so, as this is a *very* useful feature.

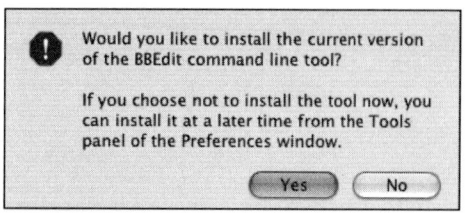

Figure 3-14. Install the command line BBEdit tool.

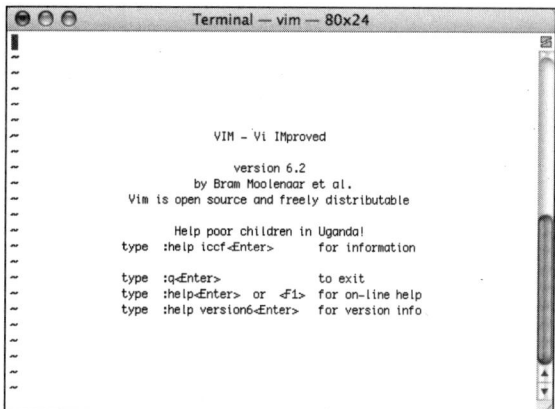

Figure 3-15. Vim command line text editor

If you're scared by the command line text editor Vim, shown in Figure 3-15 (and I don't know anyone who isn't, at first), and don't really want to learn about Pico or Emacs (see Figures 3-16 and 3-17) just yet, then all you have to do is open Terminal and type in

```
bbedit /etc/httpd/httpd.conf
```

BBEdit will open the file. If there are Root User permissions attached to the file, you can just authorize with your Admin password, amend the file, and then reenter the password to save the document. Easy.

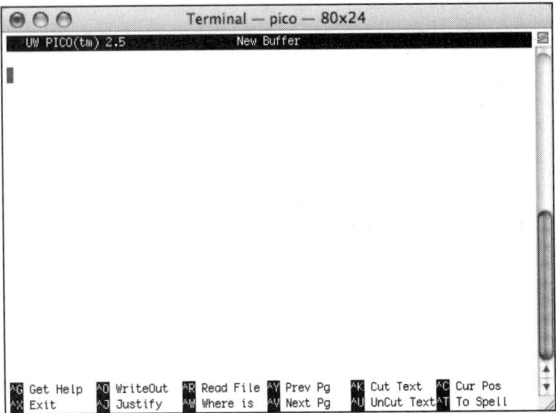

Figure 3-16. Pico

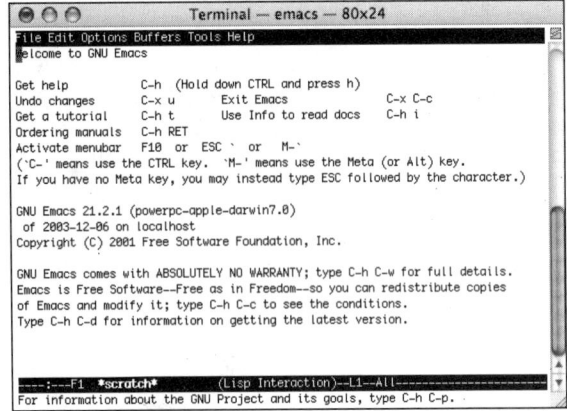

Figure 3-17. Emacs

World Wide Web Consortium (W3C)

> "The World Wide Web Consortium (www.w3.org) was created in October 1994 to lead the World Wide Web to its full potential by developing common protocols that promote its evolution and ensure its interoperability."

That's what their website says, but what does that really mean? How does that affect you as a web developer? The W3C say that their long-term goals for the web are

- **Universal access**: To make the web accessible to all by promoting technologies that take into account the vast differences in culture, language, education, ability, material resources, access devices, and physical limitations of users on all continents

- **Semantic web**: To develop a software environment that permits each user to make the best use of the resources available on the web

- **Web of trust**: To guide the web's development with careful consideration for the novel legal, commercial, and social issues raised by this technology

In a nutshell, they're trying to ensure that the web has standards and that these standards are adhered to. I mentioned earlier how browsers didn't use to work in the same way as each other. Some would display certain types of CSS, others none. You could use certain code in one browser, but have no chance with the other browser. Most designers would get around this using the methods I described at the start of this chapter, or by creating sites entirely in Flash. While all that Flash work looked very nice, it didn't exactly go down very well in a text-only browser. This wasn't playing fair to people with disabilities either. How could you make the text bigger, if it was all embedded in Flash? How could you navigate the site in the usual way? All Flash sites rendered the browser's Back/Forward buttons pretty much useless, including the keyboard shortcuts for them. This had to stop. Standards were necessary, and soon.

Jeffrey Zeldman (www.zeldman.com) cofounded **The Web Standards Project** (WaSP, at www.webstandards.org) in 1998. Working closely to the W3C's new standards, WaSP aimed to convince Microsoft, Netscape, and other browser developers to make their new browsers comply with these standards, as opposed to each company's individual standards. After all, what's the point of having standards, if nobody sticks to them?

The idea was that by adhering to such standards, a designer could code a page in such a way that it would render correctly in every browser on every platform. That platform could be IE 5.5 on a PC, IE 5 on a Mac, or Lynx on a UNIX system. Even a PDA or a mobile phone should produce the desired result. Standards were in place, but only a handful of designers knew about them or how to implement them.

Even today, probably less than 1 percent of websites are standards compliant. Hopefully, by the time you've read this book, you'll know how to make your sites comply with those standards, as I've tried to make sure all the code included is totally complaint to XHTML and CSS rules (which have possibly been updated somewhat, depending on when you read this book).

Accessibility

"The power of the Web is in its universality. Access by everyone regardless of disability is an essential aspect." Tim Berners-Lee, W3C Director and inventor of the World Wide Web

Accessibility is a word you should be familiar with by now. It's all about opening up the Internet to give everybody access to the same information. With the Internet rapidly replacing more traditional information resources such as libraries, people who are housebound because of a disability now have access to more information than ever before.

Organizations like **W**eb **A**ccessibility **I**nitiative (WAI, at www.w3.org/WAI) are committed to pursuing accessibility, to further opening up the Internet to people with disabilities. Also, the American government introduced something called **Section 508** (www.section508.gov) to deal with accessibility:

"In 1998, Congress amended the Rehabilitation Act to require Federal agencies to make their electronic and information technology accessible to people with disabilities. Inaccessible technology interferes with an individual's ability to obtain and use information quickly and easily. Section 508 was enacted to eliminate barriers in information technology, to make available new

opportunities for people with disabilities, and to encourage development of technologies that will help achieve these goals. The law applies to all Federal agencies when they develop, procure, maintain, or use electronic and information technology. Under Section 508 (29 U.S.C. ' 794d), agencies must give disabled employees and members of the public access to information that is comparable to the access available to others."

I mentioned Flash sites before, and how a visually impaired person couldn't get the same experience out of them. Now, however, Flash MX 2004 has a whole set of accessible components to use, as well as new support materials on accessibility at the Macromedia Accessibility Resource Center for designers and developers (www.macromedia.com/macromedia/accessibility).

If you think you're ready to comply, and you want to test your sites, you can get **Bobby** (http://bobby.watchfire.com) to give them the once-over for you. Bobby will check your site against the latest WAI and/or Section 508 guidelines.

XHTML

What is XHTML, and why are we using it? XHTML (which stands for Extensible Hypertext Markup Language) sounds cool, because it starts with an X. In real life, however, it's just a set of document types to extend HTML, which wasn't really designed for the kinds of things that people ended up using it for. Tags got misused, and people were applying all kinds of hacks to it to get results. It was aging fast, and other technologies were moving faster. With the ability to view web pages on a mobile phone or PDA came the ability to see how badly designed most of the Internet was. Shonky coding meant bad rendering on these new gadgets (if the page rendered at all).

Enter XML

XML (short for Extensible Markup Language) was written with the Internet in mind, yet could be understood by any gadgetry that was XML-savvy. Hailed as the next Best Thing Ever™, it was designed to be completely usable and easy to read, yet powerful and easy to write. Because it used a similar format to HTML (tags, attributes, and so on), it wasn't a completely alien language from the beginning. Open any of your preference files (those `.plist` files in your Preferences folder) and you're reading an XML document. Whereas HTML was limited to a certain number of tags, XML isn't. In fact, people often mistakenly refer to it as *Extendible Markup Language* because there are no such constraints in place. That's not to say it doesn't have rules. It's far stricter than HTML, and you can't bend the rules this time. XML is here to stay, but we're not totally ready for it yet; we need a period of adjustment.

Skip to the end . . .

This isn't a book about XML so let's get on with it. XHTML is a combination of XML and HTML (I bet you never saw that one coming), designed to make things as forward compatible as possible, which means sticking to standards. XHTML documents conform to the same rules as XML, as well as most of the more commonly used HTML rules. You can't just expect modern browsers to display XML output overnight, so "transitional" is the best way of describing the period we're in, hence combining the two to produce XHTML. Even though we're only up to version 1.1 of XHTML, it'll be written in such a way that all future versions *should* be able to read 1.1 forever. As the latest versions of GoLive and Dreamweaver are XHTML compliant, you don't have to worry about your code.

DOCTYPE

Because you're now conforming to XML rules these days, there are certain things you *must* have in place in order for a document to be classed as valid XHTML. The first thing you need is the DOCTYPE declaration. This is one of three varieties:

```
<!DOCTYPE html PUBLIC "-//W3C//DTD XHTML
➥1.0 Strict//EN" "http://www.w3.org/TR/
➥xhtml1/DTD/xhtml1-strict.dtd">
<!DOCTYPE html PUBLIC "-//W3C//DTD XHTML
➥1.0 Transitional//EN" "http://www.w3.org/
➥TR/xhtml1/DTD/xhtml1-strict.dtd">
<!DOCTYPE html PUBLIC "-//W3C//DTD XHTML
➥1.0 Frameset//EN" "http://www.w3.org/TR/
➥xhtml1/DTD/xhtml1-strict.dtd">
```

- XHTML 1.0 Strict is, as the name suggests, strict. You might like to think of it as having to take your driving test again, after all those bad habit-forming years.

- XHTML 1.0 Transitional is far closer to the HTML that makes up the Internet that you're currently used to. This is probably the easiest route to take if you're planning on converting a lot of old files, or if your current design isn't up to Strict standards.

- XHTML 1.0 Frameset speaks for itself. If you're using frames, you *have* to use this DOCTYPE.

Namespace

Next up, you need an `xmlns` (XML namespace) declaration. XML namespaces allow qualifying elements and attribute names used in the document by associating them with namespaces identified at the location shown:

```
<html xmlns="http://www.w3.org/1999/
➥xhtml" xml:lang="en" lang="en">
```

Tags

In XHTML, you *must* write all tags in lowercase. XML is case sensitive; therefore `<div>` is completely different than `<DIV>`, and so on. While in HTML certain tags didn't have a closing tag, XML doesn't allow such reckless behavior. As such, you have to close every tag. For example:

```
<li>this list item needs closing</li>
<p>that goes for paragraph tags too</p>
```

Even the empty tags need to be closed. `<br>` is now `<br />` (note the space before the slash).

```
<img src="artley.jpg" width="320"
➥height="240" alt="artley, looking wobbly"
➥title="the funny thing is, he doesn't
➥know why he said it!" />
```

Be sure to wrap those values in quotes too! Incorrect: `width=320`. Correct: `width="320"`.

Div

A **div** is short for "division." For example, having content grouped together is a division of your HTML document. You'll be meeting the `<div>` tag at the end of this chapter, when you come to lay out some code.

Cascading Style Sheets

They've been around for a while, but Cascading Style Sheets aren't just being used to change a few font colors any more. There is far more to them than that, which I'll briefly touch on here.

Previously, page layout has been driven by the `<table>` tag. If you view source code on an average site, you're likely to see a massive expanse of `<tr>` and `<td>` tags littering the code. Not only did this create some seriously long and often messy code, but technically it was invalid markup, most of the time. Oh, did I mention that you'd have sleepless nights, trying to get the same result in each browser? And then there are the cheap hacks like a transparent `shim.gif` to get a table cell to be a certain width or height.

If you have the desire to become a CSS Grandmaster, I suggest grabbing a book entirely about CSS such as *Cascading Style Sheets: Separating Content from Presentation, Second Edition* by Owen Briggs et al. (Apress, 2004). You can also check out what the W3C have to say at `www.w3.org/TR/REC-CSS1`.

Linkage

Before your XHTML document can read from the style sheet you're going to write, it has to know where to find the style sheet. You can do this in a number of ways.

link

The standard way to link a style sheet is . . . the `link` method!

```
<link rel="stylesheet" type="text/css"
➥href="css/green.css" title="green" />
```

import

The `@import` method only works in browser versions 5.0 and upwards, so using `@import` would effectively "hide" the sheet from 4.0 browsers.

```
<style type="text/css" media="all">
➥@import "fancy_style.css";</style>
```

embed

You might only have a few CSS rules, or you might have a couple that you only need to apply to one page. If this is the case, you can embed them in the head of your XHTML document like this:

```
<style type="text/css">
<!--
h1 {
font-family: verdana, arial, Helvetica,
➥sans-serif;
color: #f00;
font-weight: bold;
}
-->
</style>
```

CSS basics

Let's have a basic look at some CSS styles. With each rule, we're dealing with two parts: a **selector** and a **declaration**. In action, that looks like this:

```
h1 {color: #f00;}
```

h1 is the selector and the contents of the curly braces are the declaration. You've told your document to make all h1 tags red. I could have said color: #red or color: #ff0000, but shorthand saves on typing, and that's always a good thing to get into the swing of.

You can use "shorthand" to save on both typing and file size. As each pair of numbers corresponds to R, G, and B values, you can combine them if a pair is the same. So, for #006633, you can simply use #063 instead. You can't, however, use shorthand for a value such as #5c892e.

The <font> tag has been deprecated. Gone are the days of bloated code, rammed full of lines like

```
<h1><font face="verdana, arial,
➥helvetica, san-serif" size="2" color=
➥"#FF000"> witty line of text!</font></h1>
```

Today, this is simply replaced by a line in your style sheet, like so:

```
h1 {
font-family: verdana, arial, Helvetica,
➥sans-serif;
color: #f00;
   }
```

To add further formatting to this, you could make it bold as follows:

```
h1 {
font-family: verdana, arial, Helvetica,
➥sans-serif;
color: #f00;
font-weight: bold;
   }
```

If you wanted to apply this to all six of the header tags, you could do that simply enough.

```
h1, h2, h3, h4, h5, h6 {
font-family: verdana, arial, Helvetica,
➥sans-serif;
color: #f00;
font-weight: bold;
   }
```

You could then determine the size of each one in individual statements as follows:

```
h1 {
   font-size: 32px;
   }
h2 {
   font-size: 24px;
   }
```

. . . and so on.

The <body> tag in an XHTML document is usually just that: <body>. All your <body> elements are now contained within CSS. Here's an example:

```
body {
background: #ccc url(background.gif)
➥top right no-repeat fixed;
   color: #000;
   margin: 0;
   padding: 0;
   border: 0;
}
```

What you did there was set the body background color to #ccc (a light gray), with any text set to #000 (black). Instead of using leftmargin="0" topmargin="0" marginwidth="0" marginheight="0" to set those margins to zero, you now use margin: 0; (with the same applying to padding).

Back to that first line—notice there's an image there. There's no need to make GIFs about 5000 pixels high now in order for them to seem like they don't scroll (that was always a cheap—but necessary!—hack anyway). Now you can just specify which position you want the image to be in, whether it should be fixed, and whether it should tile. You can even specify x-axis tiling only and likewise for y-axis tiling. Much better than a cheesy old hack job.

Comments in CSS look like this:

```
/* this is a one-line CSS comment */
/* you can also split comments
over a few lines
like this */
```

CSSEdit

Of course, you don't have do all of this by guesswork and straightforward typing. You can use Dreamweaver, GoLive, or a shareware application called CSSEdit ($24.99, from MacRabbit at www.macrabbit.com/cssedit), shown in Figure 3-18. Installing it is child's play, as with a lot of Mac apps. Simply mount the disc image and then drag the icon into the Applications folder. Done.

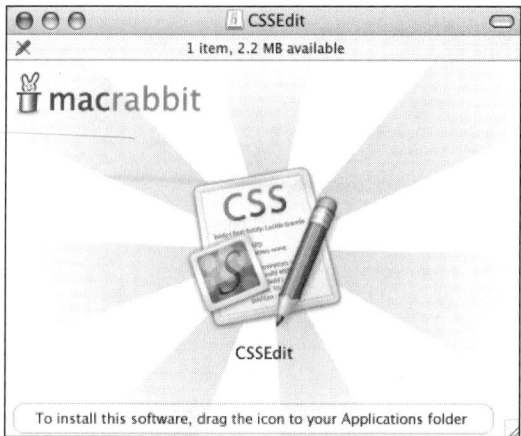

Figure 3-18. CSSEdit is worth its weight in gold.

Point, click, and see a live preview as shown in Figure 3-19. It's a very nice little application, and certainly worth the shareware fee.

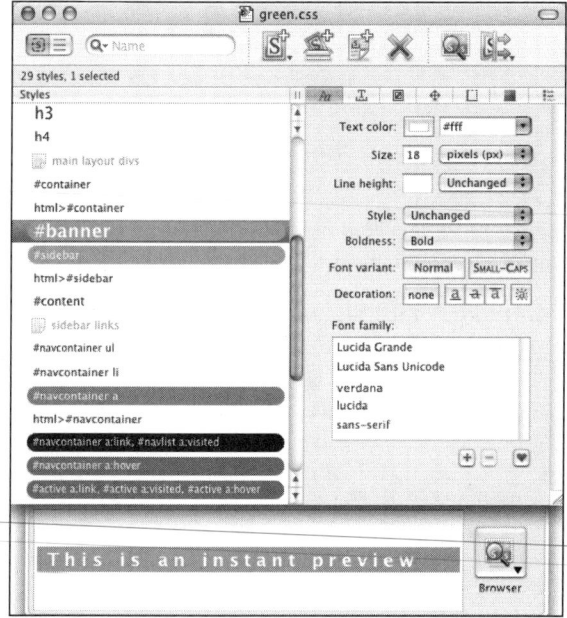

Figure 3-19. As you can see, CSSEdit makes things a lot easier to visualize, as opposed to just "code and hope."

My first style sheet

Now that you've had a quick look at how and why things work, it's time to get stuck into some code. You're not aiming to win any design awards here, just write some valid markup code, learn about the subject matter, and output something that you can feel a little bit proud of. Something like the page in Figure 3-20.

Get your text editor ready for action, open a new Finder window, and let's rattle some ASCII.

1. First, make yourself the following directories, because the files you'll be generating are going to need some form of structure:

   ■ ~/*username*/Sites/chapter3

   ■ ~/*username*/Sites/chapter3/css

   ■ ~/*username*/Sites/chapter3/images

   ■ ~/*username*/Sites/chapter3/js

2. Create a new text file called green.css and save it in the /css directory. Okay, you need some body elements first, so type in the following code:

```
/* green scheme */

body {
  background: #ccc;
  color: #000;
  margin: 0;
  padding: 0;
  border: 0;
}
```

#ccc gives you a gray background, which will be outside of your container, with #000 giving you a black text color should any text escape onto the body.

3. Next, let's tackle the fonts. Carrying on directly underneath the previous code, type the following:

```
/* main page fonts */

p {
  margin-top: 0;
  margin-bottom: 1em;
font: 11px/16px "Lucida Grande",
➥"Lucida Sans Unicode", verdana, lucida,
➥arial, helvetica, sans-serif;
  }
```

code continues

51

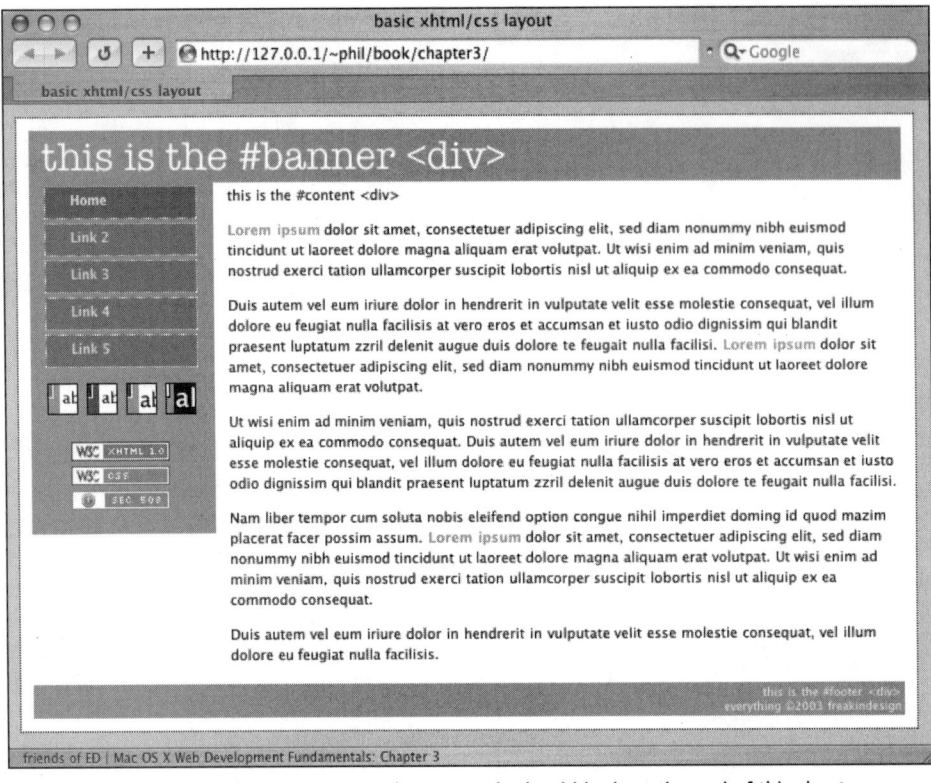

Figure 3-20. This is how the page you are about to code should look, at the end of this chapter.

```
a:link, a:visited {
  font-weight : bold;
  text-decoration : none;
  color: #84a563;
  background: transparent;
  }


a:hover {
  font-weight : bold;
  text-decoration : underline;
  color: #557239;
  background: transparent;
 }


a:active {
  font-weight : bold;
  text-decoration : none;
  color: #5c892e;
  background: transparent;
  }
```

Here, you've specified no underline for links unless the cursor is hovering over it.

4. Now on to the header tags:

```
/* header fonts */

h1, h2, h3, h4, h5, h6  {
  font-weight: normal;
font-family: "American Typewriter",
➥"Trebuchet MS", Trebuchet, Lucida,
➥sans-serif;
  }

h1  {
  margin-top: 0;
  margin-bottom: 0;
  font-size: 32px;
  text-transform: lowercase;
  }
```

```
h2  {
    font-size: 24px;
    margin-top: 25px;
    margin-bottom: 0;
    letter-spacing: 1px;
    }

h3  {
    font-size: 16px;
    margin-top: 0;
    margin-bottom: 0;
    }

h4  {
    font-size: 13px;
    margin: 5px 0;
    padding: 0;
    letter-spacing: 1px;
    }
```

As all of the header tags are using the same font, you can group them all together. After doing that, you specify the individual sizes.

So far, there probably hasn't been too much that you haven't seen before. Fonts, padding, sizes: it's probably all familiar stuff. That feeling of familiarity is about to leave, so wave goodbye.

Positioning

One of the most abused tags in HTML was probably the <table> tag. Created originally to contain tabular data, this poor tag was dragged all over the place. Yes, you could get your layout looking like you wanted it *but* not only was it invalid markup, it was also likely to look awful in whichever browser you forgot to check it in (that just so happens to be the client's favorite browser . . . doh!). This doesn't mean that the <table> tag has gone the same route as the <font> tag, by any means. You can still use it, when used correctly (i.e., for tabular data).

To lay out your document without tables may seem scary at first, if this is what you're used to, but it's nowhere nearly as scary once it's been explained to you. It's just a matter of using a few different lines of CSS.

1. Continuing at the bottom of the same green.css document, let's go wild and make a box on the screen (close the curtains in case the neighbors can see this frenzy of activity, they'll only get jealous).

```
/* main layout divs */

#container {
    background: #fff;
    border: 1px dotted #000;
    margin: 10px;
    padding: 10px;
    width: 700px;
    }
```

Let's dissect that, shall we?

- #container is the name you've given to this element, because it will eventually contain the rest of your content.

- background: #fff; sets the background of the box to white.

- border: 1px dotted #000; gives your box a black dotted border that's 1 pixel wide.

- margin: 10px; sets the space outside of your box.

- padding: 10px; sets the space inside of your box.

- width: 700px; sets the width of the box. (Cunning, eh?)

- margin and padding actually have four values there, but you can utilize a shorthand rule to knock them down to one value of 10 pixels. The longhand version would be

    10px 10px 10px 10px;

The order can be easily remembered, if you think in a clockwise direction starting at 12 o'clock: top, right, bottom, left. So, if you just wanted a margin of 10 pixels on the right, that would be 0px 0px 0px 10px;. Once again, there is a lot more shorthand, but this isn't a 1000-page CSS manual.

> *If you want the container centered, replace* margin:
> 10px *with this line:* margin:10px auto;.

Not so tough to get to grips with, hmm? Hang on; You just need to clear up some Internet Explorer mess. Thanks to Tantek Çelik's Box Model Hack (www .tantek.com), you can do that with a few lines of code.

2. If you head back to that width value (width: 700px), you need to hack it up a bit. Some earlier versions of PC Internet Explorer will make a mess of the padding value. You need to fix that, so use the following new code instead (highlighted in bold):

```
#container {
   background: #fff;
   border: 1px dotted #000;
   margin: 10px;
   padding: 10px;
   width: 722px;          /* false value
     ➥for IE4-5.x/Win, like so: */
   voice-family: "\"}\""";  /* real width
     ➥+ l/r border + l/r padding = false
value */
   voice-family:inherit;    /* end false
     ➥value for IE4-5.x/Win */
   width: 700px;          /* real value
     ➥for compliant browsers */
}
```

What this does is trick IE into thinking that you want your box to be 722 pixels wide (which you do, ultimately). This value is determined by adding together the following: The real value + any left/right borders + left/right padding.

PC IE 5.x doesn't understand voice-family rules, so anything after that will go unnoticed. Once it's been tricked into giving you a workable value, the next two lines get it drunk enough not to notice the real value, which you then state while it's not looking.

3. One final hack needs adding, which is commonly referred to as the "Be nice to Opera" rule. This is just

```
html>#container {
width: 700px;           /* be nice
   ➥to Opera */
}
```

There you have it. You've got a box, ready for content as soon as you start your XHTML document. Let's kick out the rest of the CSS quickly, so we can get on with coding that page.

4. Let's add a banner at the top of the page. You'll lay this out in a similar style to the container you just made.

```
#banner {
   padding: 2px 2px 2px 10px;
   background-color: #84a563;
   font-family: "Lucida Grande", "Lucida
➥Sans Unicode", verdana, lucida,
➥sans-serif;
   font-size: 18px;
   color: #fff;
   font-weight: bold;
   letter-spacing: 0.33em;
   text-align: left;
}
```

5. You're moving down the page, from the left, so it's time to bang that sidebar into position. As you're specifying a width, you need to include those IE/Opera workarounds too.

```
#sidebar {
   float: left;
   margin: 0;
   margin-right: 2px;
   padding: 2px;
   background-color: #84a563;
font-family: "Lucida Grande", "Lucida
➥Sans Unicode", verdana, lucida,
➥sans-serif;
   font-size: 11px;
   font-weight: normal;
   color: #fff;
   text-decoration: none;
width: 149px;                /* false value
➥for IE4-5.x/Win, like so: */
   voice-family: "\"}\"";   /* real width +
➥l/r border + l/r padding = false value */
   voice-family:inherit;      /* end false
➥value for IE4-5.x/Win */
   width: 145px;              /* real value
➥for compliant browsers */
}
```

```
html>#sidebar {
    width: 145px;   /* be nice to Opera */
}
```

6. Moving right from the sidebar, you want somewhere for the actual content to live, so create a <div> for it like this:

```
#content {
    padding: 2px;
    margin-left: 158px;
    background-color: #fff;
font-family: "Lucida Grande", "Lucida
➥Sans Unicode", verdana, lucida,
➥sans-serif;
    color: #000;
    font-size: 12px;
}
```

As you can see, you've told #content <div> to start 158 pixels in from the left, but feel free to experiment with this distance. Use a smaller figure and you'll see some funk occurring. The more you play around with these things, the more you'll understand how they work. Don't just take my word for it; **push things until they break, then fix them**.

Now you have *almost* all of your main areas set out. As well as working from left to right, you've obviously been working from top to bottom too. You do this so that things are easier to read when skimming through the green.css document. You could have the #header <div> detailed at the bottom of the CSS document, but it makes far more sense to be logical and place those elements appearing at the top of the page at the top of your code. With this in mind, you won't be dealing with the page footer for a while.

7. The links in the sidebar are next.

```
/* sidebar links */
#navcontainer ul
{
    margin: 0;
    padding: 0 0 0 10px;
    list-style-type: none;
font: normal 10px/18px "Lucida Grande",
➥"Lucida Sans Unicode", verdana, lucida,
➥sans-serif;
}
```

All you're doing here is simply altering the properties of an unordered list (<ul>). You should be able to tell what's going on by now, apart from one line. Normal lists have bullet points, numbers, and so on, but you don't want any of that stuff here, so you use list-style-type: none; to get rid of that clutter.

8. Now add the list item properties.

```
#navcontainer li { margin: 0 0 3px 0; }
```

This gives you a 3-pixel gap underneath each list item.

> *If you want a rollover image, uncomment the* **background-image** *line in the following* #navcontainer *code in step 9 and make an appropriate image.*

9. Okay, you've specified that your list is going to be unordered, and provided the list items with a nice gap underneath. Next, you'll create the actual containers that the user will click on. Again, you're specifying a width, so it's time to wheel in the IE/Opera show.

```
#navcontainer a
{
    display: block;
    padding: 2px 2px 2px 20px;
    border: 1px dotted #fff;
    width: 100px;
    height: 20px;
    background-color: #5c892e;
/* background-image:
➥url(images/roll_down.jpg); */
    width: 124px;             /* false value
➥for IE4-5.x/Win, like so: */
    voice-family: "\"}\"";    /* real width +
➥l/r border + l/r padding = false value */
    voice-family:inherit;     /* end false
➥value for IE4-5.x/Win */
    width: 100px;             /* real value
➥for compliant browsers */
}

html>#navcontainer {
    width: 100px;             /* be nice
➥to Opera */
}
```

10. Now take care of the fonts:

```
#navcontainer a:link, #navlist a:visited
{
   font-size: 10px;
   color: #eee;
   text-decoration: none;
}
```

11. Let's give the user that "By the power vested in me, I can make things change color!" feeling, and tell things to get excited when the mouse is on the prowl.

```
#navcontainer a:hover
{
   font-size: 10px;
   border: 1px dotted #fff;
   background-color: #557239;
/* background-image:
➥url(images/roll_over.jpg); */
   color: #fff;
}

#active a:link, #active a:visited,
➥#active a:hover
{
   font-size: 10px;
   border: 1px dotted #fff;
   background-color: #557239;
/* background-image:
➥url(images/roll_over.jpg); */
   color: #fff;
}
```

12. As this is to be an all-compliant accessibility exercise, you're going to give the user the opportunity to change some aspects of the page. This will be a change of colors, as well as font sizes, both of which benefit the visually impaired. You'll use some images to show what these buttons will do, but they still need positioning.

```
/* the style selector */

#styletool {
   border: 0;
   margin: 10px 0 15px 0;
   padding: 0 0 0 9px;
}
```

```
#styletool img {
   display: inline;
   border: 0;
   padding: 2px;
}
```

13. Underneath the style selector buttons, you're going to show the majority of the Internet that you are, in fact, compliant with these new web standards. Again, these are to be images, but they're still in need of some layout guidance.

```
/* validation buttons */

#valid {
   border: 0;
   margin: 10px 0 15px 20px;
}

#valid img {
   display: inline;
   border: 0;
   padding: 2px 2px 2px 10px;
}
```

14. Lastly, add the footer, which plays by the same IE/Opera rules as the other main containers.

```
/* footer */

#footer {
   clear: both;
   padding: 2px;
   margin-top: 2px;
   background-color: #84a563;
font-family: "Lucida Grande",
➥"Lucida Sans Unicode", verdana,
➥lucida, sans-serif;
   font-size: 9px;
   font-weight: normal;
   text-transform: lowercase;
   color: #fff;
   text-align: right;
}
```

This file should be saved as /css/green.css. The easiest way to make your alternative color sheet is to then save this file as /css/purple.css, and then use BBEdit to run a find-and-replace operation on the actual colors. You can do the same for the large type and reversed color sheets too, making sure to add a few pixels to those font sizes. Save these sheets as /css/large.css and /css/reverse.css. The following sections detail the schemes that I came up with (included in the download files), but feel free to choose your own colors.

Green color scheme

This file should be saved as /css/green.css (see Figure 3-21).

- #84a563; is used for a:link, a:visited, #banner, #sidebar, and #footer.

- #5c892e; is used for a:active and #navcontainer a.

- #557239; is used for a:hover, #navcontainer a:hover, #active a:link, #active a:visited, and #active a:hover.

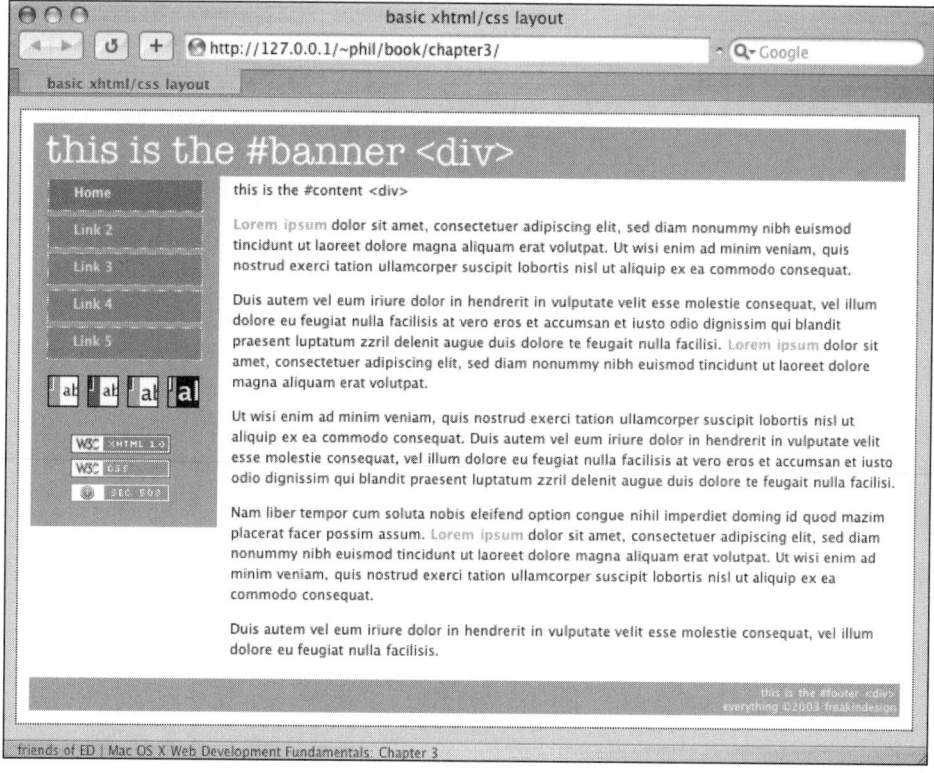

Figure 3-21. If all went according to plan, you should be looking at a page like this now.

Purple color scheme

To create this alternative color scheme style sheet, follow these steps:

1. First save /css/green.css as /css/purple.css.

2. You need to substitute the colors that you used in the green.css file for the following color scheme:

   - #838; for a:link, a:visited, a:hover, #banner, #sidebar, and #footer.

   - #606; for a:active and #navcontainer a.

   - #c6c; for #navcontainer a:hover, #active a:link, #active a:visited, and #active a:hover.

3. The easiest way to do this is with the Find and Replace function in BBEdit. Go to Search ➤ Find to open the Find and Replace window.

4. In the top Search For field, type in the existing color you want to change, and type the new color you want to change it to in the bottom Replace With field. For example, to change a:active and #navcontainer a from the color #5c892e to #606, fill in the window as shown in Figure 3-22.

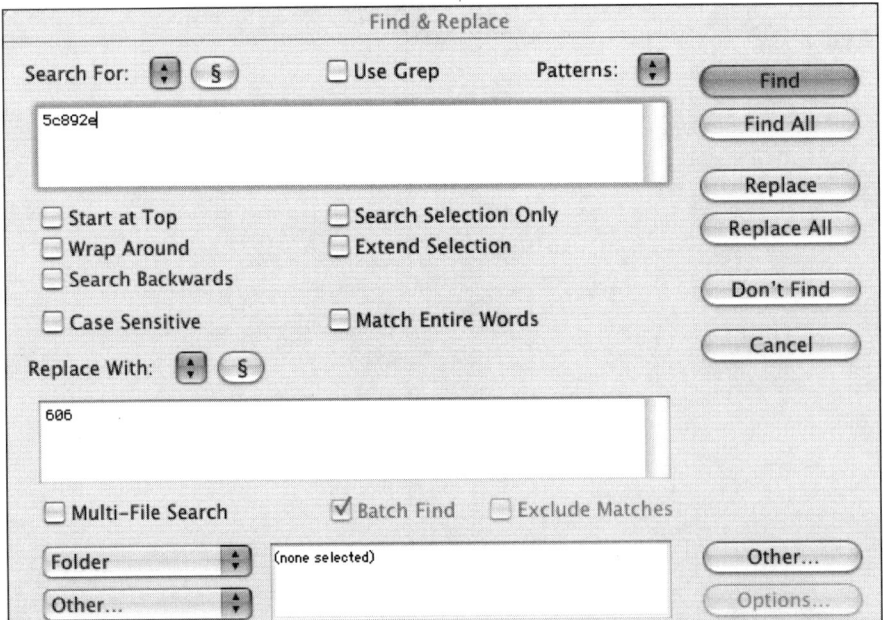

Figure 3-22. Using Find and Replace in BBEdit. Note the Start at Top option!

BBEdit will search the document from wherever the cursor is currently, to the end of the document. To avoid this, place the cursor at the start of the document. You can also select the Start at Top *option in the Search window. To turn this on permanently, open BBEdit's preferences, and then select the Text Search pane. Check the* Remember Find *dialog box's* Start at Top *settings.*

5. Click the Replace All button, and your two instances of the color should be updated in your new purple style sheet (see Figure 3-23).

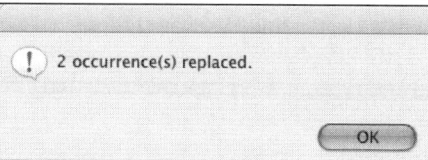

Figure 3-23. The dialog box tells you how many occurrences it replaced.

Figure 3-24 shows what the page will look like with the purple color scheme.

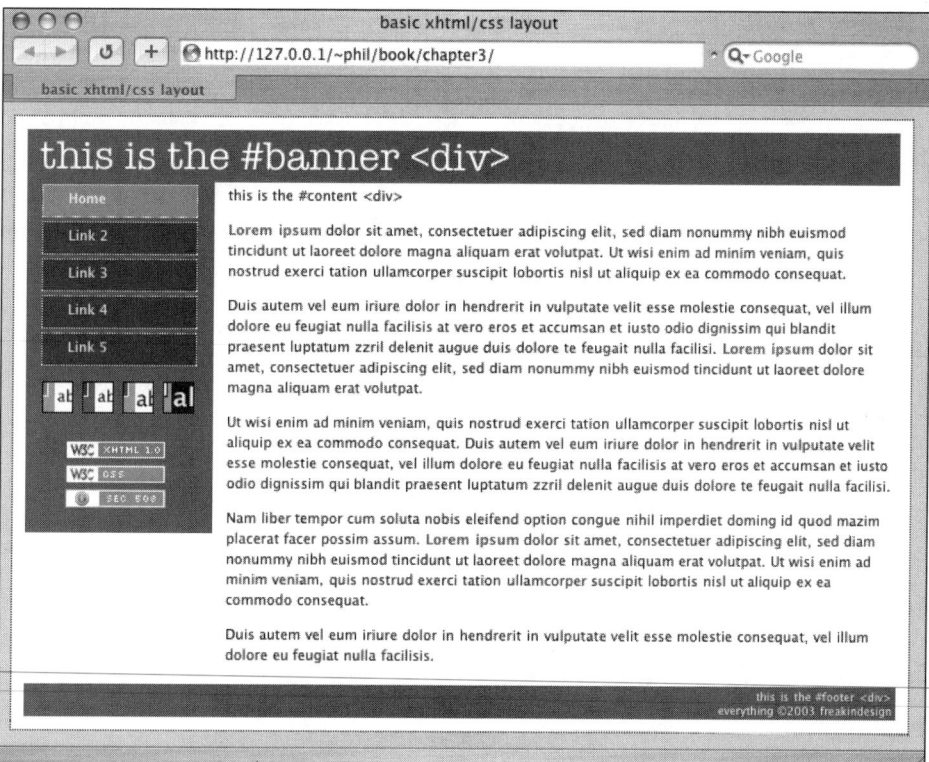

Figure 3-24. Click the purple switcher button, and you get this view.

Large type scheme

Now move on and create the large type scheme style sheet (/css/large.css). Aside from the colors, the only change here is the font size. I've just added 4 pixels to each font size in the document. Here's the new color scheme (see Figure 3-25):

- #999; for a:link, a:visited, #banner, #sidebar, and #footer.

- #666; for a:active and #navcontainer a.

- #333; for a:hover, #navcontainer a:hover, #active a:link, #active a:visited, and #active a:hover.

Reversed color sheet

As you can see, this scheme (/css/large.css) is a bit different. It's for partially sighted people, most of whom feel more comfortable with light text on dark backgrounds. The font size has also been bumped up a few more notches yet again, adding 10 pixels to the original size. The links and text colors are all #ff9, and the grays are the same as the large type scheme. See if you can match them up (refer to Figure 3-26).

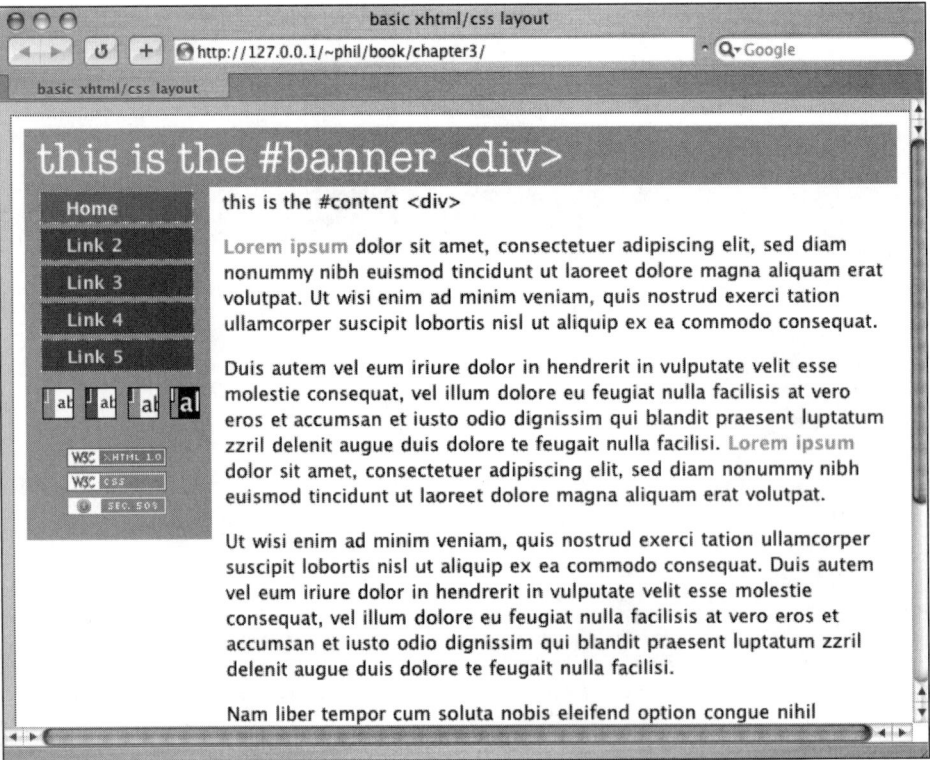

Figure 3-25. Click the large type switcher button, and you get this view.

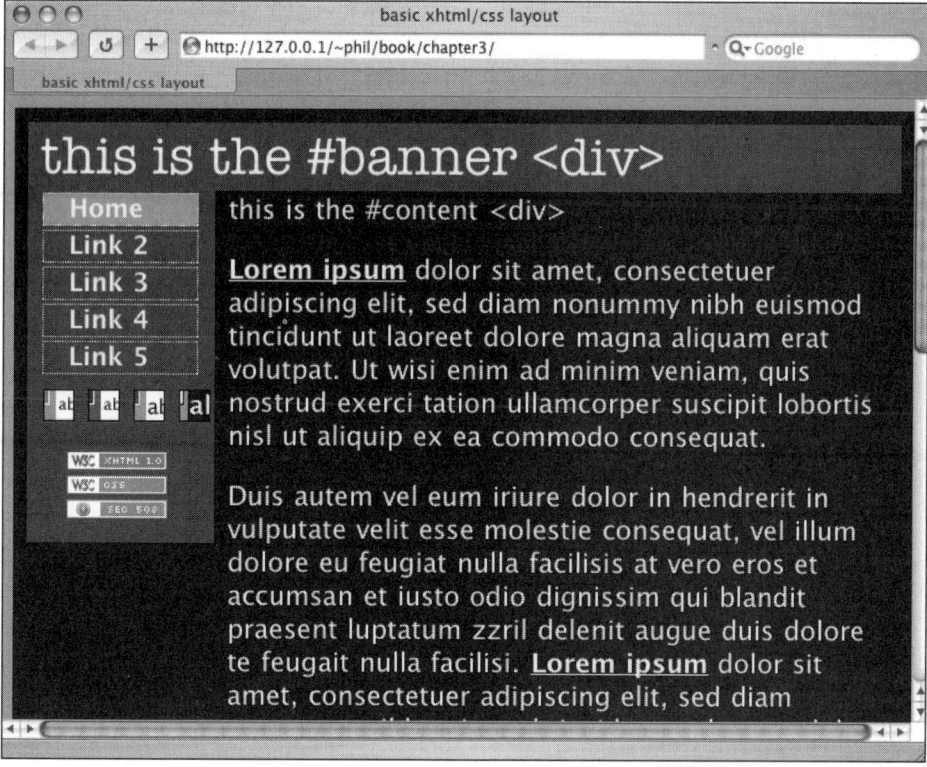

Figure 3-26. Click the reverse colors switcher button, and you get this view.

JavaScript

As with a few things I've mentioned in this chapter, this isn't the time to go into huge details. One thing falling squarely into that category is JavaScript. If you've ever created a rollover, then you've probably used JavaScript. You might have generated that JavaScript via Dreamweaver or Fireworks, but it was there all the same.

Bandwidth usage, and how to save on it, has already been touched on, but there's another way you can cut down on the code bloat. The average Macromedia rollover effect produces something like this in the head of your document:

```
<script language="JavaScript"
➥type="text/JavaScript">
<!--
function MM_preloadImages() { //v3.0
var d=document; if(d.images){
➥if(!d.MM_p) d.MM_p=new Array();
 var i,j=d.MM_p.length,
➥a=MM_preloadImages.arguments;
➥for(i=0; i<a.length; i++)
 if (a[i].indexOf("#")!=0){
➥d.MM_p[j]=new Image;
➥d.MM_p[j++].src=a[i];}}
}
```

(code continues)

```
function MM_swapImgRestore() { //v3.0
var i,x,a=document.MM_sr;
➥for(i=0;a&&i<a.length&&(x=a[i])
➥&&x.oSrc;i++) x.src=x.oSrc;
}

function MM_findObj(n, d) { //v4.01
var p,i,x; if(!d) d=document;
➥if((p=n.indexOf("?"))
➥>0&&parent.frames.length) {
d=parent.frames[n.substring(p+1)]
➥.document; n=n.substring(0,p);}
if(!(x=d[n])&&d.all) x=d.all[n]; for
➥(i=0;!x&&i<d.forms.length;i++)
➥x=d.forms[i][n];
for(i=0;!x&&d.layers&&i
➥<d.layers.length;i++) x=MM_findObj
➥(n,d.layers[i].document);
if(!x && d.getElementById)
➥x=d.getElementById(n); return x;
}

function MM_swapImage() { //v3.0
var i,j=0,x,a=MM_swapImage.arguments;
➥document.MM_sr=new Array;
➥for(i=0;i<(a.length-2);i+=3)
if ((x=MM_findObj(a[i]))!=null)
➥{document.MM_sr[j++]=x;
➥if(!x.oSrc) x.oSrc=x.src; x.src=a[i+2];}
}
//-->
</script>
```

If you have the same rollovers on 50 or more pages of a site, then this is just a ridiculous waste of time and bandwidth. Fortunately, there's an easy way to tackle this.

1. Cut all of this code and paste it into a new document.

2. Save the new document as global.js in your /js directory.

3. Link it in the <head> of all those pages, like this:

```
<script language="JavaScript"
➥type="text/javascript" src=
➥"js/global.js"></script>
```

This way, you're cutting out all the boated code from each page, and the user only has to download the file once. Everybody wins!

While you'll be using a JavaScript style switcher in this example to change the style sheets, I didn't write it myself (gasp) because in the wonderful world of web development, people are nice enough to write things and willingly let you borrow them. That is how I came by the stylesswitcher.js file you'll use in this example. You can download the code with an explanation of what does what from the following sites:

www.alistapart.com/articles/alternate/

www.alistapart.com/d/alternate/stylesswitcher.js

Save this file to your chapter3/js folder. If you want to investigate JavaScript in more depth, there are many resources on the web.

http://javascript.internet.com is a good place to start.

Status bar message

In the bottom left of most browser windows, you can usually see some text whizzing past, as the browser loads a page (Safari breaks with this tradition). This is called the status bar, and you can use JavaScript to have a default status bar message there. Just expand your <body> tag to read like this:

```
<body onload="window.defaultStatus='
➥friends of ED | Mac OS X Web Development
➥Fundamentals: Chapter 3'">
```

Templates and Library Items

When you have a heavy workload, saving time whenever possible is essential. Dreamweaver's templates and Library Items can seriously cut down time in a number of ways. For starters, once you've decided on your page layout, you can just turn that page into a template and keep reusing it for every new page in your site.

But how do these work? Well, you set "editable regions" where your content is going to be changing for each page. Typically, this could be the page title, possibly a banner graphic, and, of course, the page content. This is useful if you're not working alone on a project, as you can rest assured that the rest of the team are all working from the same template. If you use Contribute (as discussed earlier in this chapter), you can rest easy there too. When your client logs onto the server to alter any pages with Contribute, the application honors those same editable regions. There's no way clients can delete anything they're not supposed to.

Library Items are useful if you're designing a site with certain assets on every page, which may be subject to change before the site goes live. Rather than wait for the final assets to turn up, you could use a placeholder image, turn it into a Library Item, and then drag this onto your documents. This way, all you have to do when you get the final assets is update the Library Item, and this will update through all the pages you linked it from. Just make sure to upload the /Library folder to the server or you'll be in big trouble.

XHTML time

Okay, you've got your Cascading Style Sheet all nicely typed out, so let's go ahead and finish coding that page.

1. Start a new text file and save it as index.html in the root directory of your site folder structure. Begin by typing in this basic starting block of code:

```
<!DOCTYPE html PUBLIC "-//W3C//DTD XHTML
➡1.0 Transitional//EN" "http://www.w3.org/
➡TR/xhtml1/DTD/xhtml1-transitional.dtd">
<html xmlns="http://www.w3.org/1999/
➡xhtml" xml:lang="en" lang="en">
<head>
<meta http-equiv="content-type"
➡content="text/html; charset=iso-8859-1"
/>
<title>Chapter 3 Example</title>
<link rel="stylesheet" type="text/css"
➡href="css/green.css"
➡title="green" /></head>
<body>

</body>
</html>
```

As you can see, you're using XHTML 1.0 Transitional rather than Strict 1.0, because it's more than suitable for your needs. Once you've got your head around this, you can venture forth into the world of Strict 1.0 forever. You've also added the CSS document you made earlier in this chapter.

2. Now you need some structure for your content, so position your `<div>` tags. To avoid confusion, these will be added a couple at a time. These go between the `<body>` tags, like so:

```
<body onload="window.defaultStatus='
➡friends of ED | Mac OS X Web Development
➡Fundamentals: Chapter 3'">
<div id="container">
<div id="banner">this is the #banner
➡&lt;div&gt<div>

</div> <!-- end of the container div -->
</body>
```

As you might have guessed, this sets out the main area, which will contain all the content, and the banner `<div>` up at the top. I'll comment the end tags, so you have a clear idea of which tag is doing what. Each `<div id>` corresponds to a section of the style sheet. So, `<div id="container">` gets its instructions from the #container section of the style sheet. You can see how this works by just unlinking the style sheet and watching how the page lays itself out (similar to Netscape 4.x!).

3. Next, add these `<div>`s between the previous pair:

```
<div id="banner">this is the #banner
➡&lt;div&gt<div>
<div id="sidebar">
<div id="navcontainer">

</div> <!-- end of the navcontainer div -->
</div> <!-- end of the sidebar div -->
</div> <!-- end of the container div -->
```

Unsurprisingly, this sets up the sidebar on the left of the page, where your navigation container will sit. Let's add some links to it.

4. Add the following code inside the navcontainer `<div>`:

```
<div id="navcontainer">
<ul id="navlist">
<li id=" active "><a href="index.html"
➥id="current" title="Back to the Home
➥Page">Home</a></li>
<li><a href="link2.html" title="Link 2
➥title">Link 2</a></li>
<li><a href="link3.html" title="Link 3
➥title">Link 3</a></li>
<li><a href="link4.html" title="Link 4
➥title">Link 4</a></li>
<li><a href="link5.html" title="Link 5
➥title">Link 5</a></li></ul>
</div> <!-- end of the navcontainer div -->
```

The first link here has an ID called active. This simply states which page you're on now, so the color for that link is different. On your Link 2 page, you'd move that ID down to Link 2, and so on.

5. Next, let's add those style buttons. As with the `global.js` document mentioned earlier, you first need to attach the JavaScript file to your document. You do this by adding the following line within the `<head>` tags like this:

```
<title>Chapter 3 Example</title>
<link rel="stylesheet" type="text/css"
➥href="css/green.css" title="green" />
<script language="JavaScript"
➥type="text/javascript"
➥src="js/styleswitcher.js"></script>
</head>
```

6. Because you're using alternative style sheets on this job, you need to have those sheets specified as such. Here's how you do it:

```
<title>Chapter 3 Example</title>
<link rel="stylesheet" type="text/css"
➥href="css/green.css" title="green" />
<link rel="alternate stylesheet"
➥type="text/css" media="all" href="css/
➥purple.css" title="purple" />
<link rel="alternate stylesheet"
➥type="text/css" media="all" href="css/
➥large.css" title="large" />
<link rel="alternate stylesheet"
```

```
➥type="text/css" media="all" href="css/
➥reverse.css" title="reverse" />
<!-- the @import method only works from
➥5.0 and upwards -->
<!-- so, using @import would "hide" the
➥more sophisticated sheet
➥from < 5.0 browsers -->
<!-- <style type="text/css" media="all">
➥@import "fancy_style.css";</style> -->
<script language="JavaScript"
➥type="text/javascript"
➥src="js/styleswitcher.js"></script>
</head>
```

The commented-out @import section shows you how you would include a `.css` file that wouldn't work in browsers earlier than version 5.0, so, using this method, those earlier browsers wouldn't even read this line. Maybe you have some cutting edge CSS3 code that you want to show off? Only the very latest browser will be able to handle it, so import it using this method.

Back to the `<body>` of the document, and it's time to code those links. The way you're calling them is as follows:

```
<a href="#" title="Switch Styles: green"
➥onclick="setActiveStyleSheet('green');
➥return false;" accesskey="g">
➥<img src="images/selector_green.gif"
➥alt="Switch Styles: green" /></a>
```

It's a basic href link with both a title and an access key (which will be discussed in the next chapter) in keeping with those standards. The call to the JavaScript is setActiveStyleSheet, which then tells the browser which style sheet to select.

7. Add this to the bottom of your existing code:

```
<li><a href="link5.html"
➥title="Link 5 title">Link 5</a></li>
</ul>
</div> <!-- end of the navcontainer div -->
<div id="styletool">
<a href="#" title="Switch Styles:
➥green" onclick="setActiveStyleSheet
➥('green'); return false;" accesskey="g">
➥<img src="images/selector_green.gif"
➥alt="Switch Styles: green" /></a>
```

```
<a href="#" title="Switch Styles:
➡purple" onclick="setActiveStyleSheet
➡('purple'); return false;" accesskey="p">
➡<img src="images/selector_purple.gif"
➡alt="Switch Styles: purple" /></a>
<a href="#" title="Switch Styles:
➡large type" onclick="setActiveStyleSheet
➡('large'); return false;" accesskey="l">
➡<img src="images/selector_large.gif"
➡alt="Switch Styles: large type" /></a>
<a href="#" title="Switch Styles:
➡reverse colors, large type" onclick="
➡setActiveStyleSheet('reverse');
➡return false;" accesskey="r"><img src="
➡images/selector_large_reverse.gif"
➡alt="Switch Styles: reverse colors,
➡large type" /></a>
</div>
</div> <!-- end of the sidebar div -->
</div> <!-- end of the container div -->
```

The buttons used in this example are from Taylor McKnight's Steal These Buttons site (http://gtmcknight.com/buttons). They are also in the download files for this chapter. To use them in this exercise, copy them to your chapter3/images folder.

8. Immediately beneath the last block of code you typed, you're going to have a set of buttons to show people that all your code validates and meets the new standards.

```
</div>
<div id="valid">
<a href="http://validator.w3.org/check/
➡referer" title="Validated XHTML 1.0">
➡<img src="images/xhtml10.png" alt="XHTML
➡1.0 valid" width="80" height="15"
➡border="0" /></a><br />
<a href="http://jigsaw.w3.org/
➡css-validator/check/referer"
➡title="Validated CSS">
➡<img src="images/css.gif" alt="CSS valid"
➡ width="80" height="15" border="0" />
➡</a><br />
<a href="http://www.contentquality.com/
➡mynewtester/cynthia.exe?Url1=
➡http://www.freakindesign.com/"
➡title="Validated Section 508">
➡<img src="images/sec508a.gif" alt="508
➡valid" width="80" height="15"
➡border="0" /></a>
</div>
</div> <!-- end of the sidebar div -->
</div> <!-- end of the container div -->
```

You can get these buttons from Taylor McKnight's site (http://gtmcknight.com/buttons) or this book's download files. Remember to put them in your chapter3/images folder.

9. If you save and preview this file in your browser now, you'll see things are beginning to shape up (see Figure 3-27)!

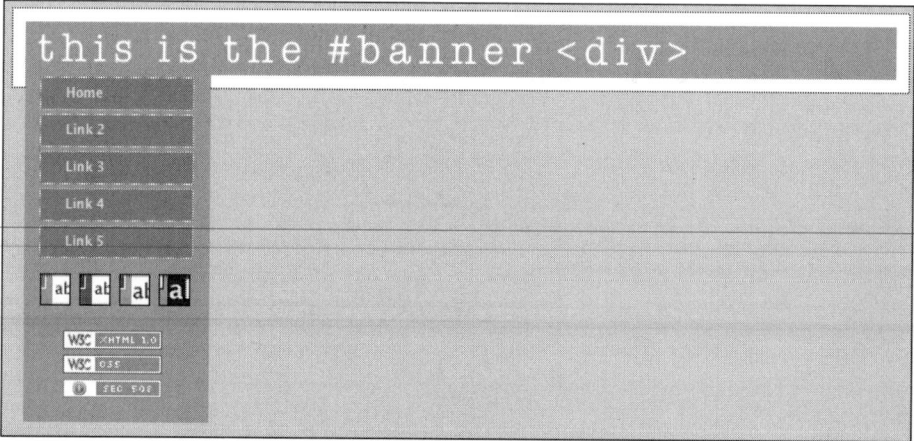

Figure 3-27. A preliminary check, and you should see things starting to take shape.

Well, almost. The container <div> has no height value and no content, other than the banner <div>, so that's all you'll see of that until it gets some content. So without further ado, let's add some content in there, right after the end of the sidebar <div>. Let's use good old Lorem Ipsum for now. You can grab this filler text from www.lipsum.com, and you might want to repeat it a few times, to expand the content <div>, so you can see how things expand.

10. So, immediately after the last block of code, add the following:

```
</div>
</div> <!-- end of the sidebar div -->
<div id="content">
<p>this is the #content &lt;div&gt;</p>
<p><a href="http://www.lipsum.com/"
➥title="why do we use Lorem ipsum?">Lorem
➥ipsum</a> dolor sit amet, consectetuer
➥adipiscing elit, sed diam nonummy nibh
➥euismod tincidunt ut laoreet dolore
➥magna aliquam erat volutpat. Ut wisi
➥enim ad minim veniam, quis nostrud
➥exerci tation ullamcorper suscipit
➥lobortis nisl ut aliquip ex ea commodo
➥consequat.</p>
<p>Duis autem vel eum iriure dolor in
➥hendrerit in vulputate velit esse
➥molestie consequat, vel illum dolore eu
➥feugiat nulla facilisis at vero eros et
➥accumsan et iusto odio dignissim qui
➥blandit praesent luptatum zzril delenit
➥augue duis dolore te feugait nulla
➥facilisi.
➥<a href="http://www.lipsum.com/"
➥title="why do we use Lorem ipsum?">Lorem
➥ipsum</a> dolor sit amet, consectetuer
➥adipiscing elit, sed diam nonummy nibh
➥euismod tincidunt ut laoreet dolore
➥magna aliquam erat volutpat.</p>
<p>Ut wisi enim ad minim veniam, quis
➥nostrud exerci tation ullamcorper
➥suscipit lobortis nisl ut aliquip ex ea
➥commodo consequat. Duis autem vel eum
➥iriure dolor in hendrerit in vulputate
➥velit esse molestie consequat, vel illum
➥dolore eu feugiat nulla facilisis at
➥vero eros et accumsan et iusto odio
➥dignissim qui blandit praesent luptatum
➥zzril delenit augue duis dolore te
➥feugait nulla facilisi.</p></div>
➥<!-- end of the content div -->
```

11. Last but not least, complete the site by adding the footer at the bottom of your code.

```
</div> <!-- end of the content div -->
<div id="footer">this is the #footer
➥&lt;div&gt;<br />everything &copy;2003
➥freakindesign</div>
</div> <!-- end of the container div -->
</body>
</html>
```

12. When you add all this together and preview in your browser, you should see something like the layout in Figure 3-28.

If all went according to plan, you should be able to see similar results in most compliant browsers, although it still won't look like a complete mess either, if you view it in noncompliant browsers.

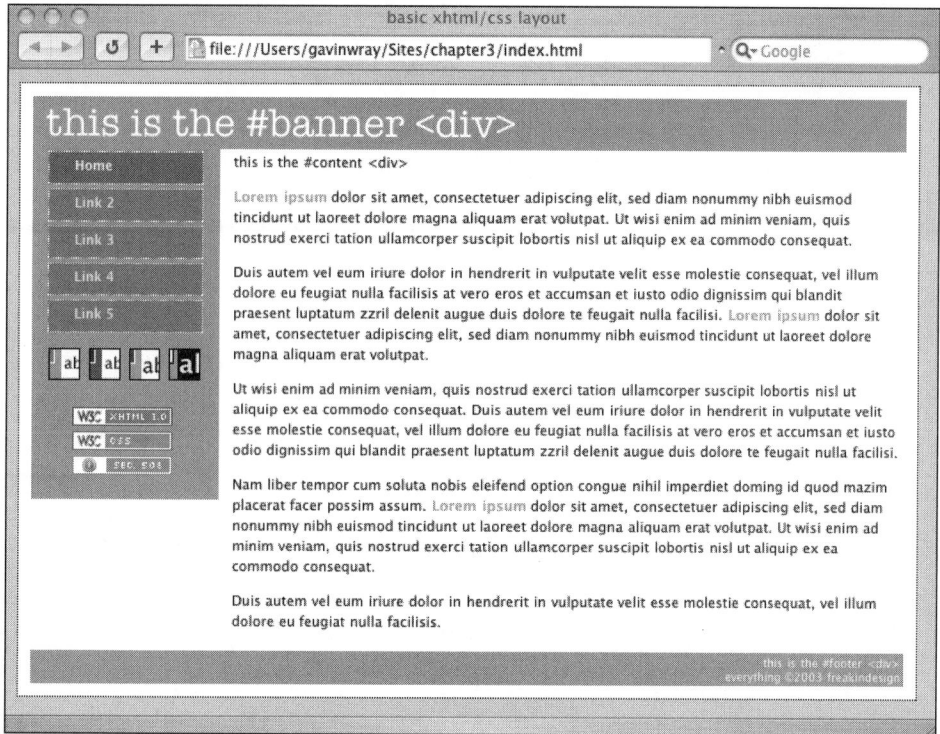

Figure 3-28. The finished page! Success!

Chapter review

Now that you're at the end of the chapter, you should feel like you're actually getting somewhere. You've learned something about web standards and why we have to have them. You should know what all those acronyms actually stand for now!

More importantly, you've actually got some code under your belt, and because you wrote it by hand, you know how each part of it works. Later on, you'll be using Dreamweaver, and you should be able to understand the code.

None of the code from this example is written in stone, of course. Experiment with colors, fonts, etc., but change other things too. If you had to go over a section a few times before it sank in, then experiment with that section, to make doubly sure you understand how and why it works. "Think for yourself. Question authority."

Find the time to check your page in as many different browsers as you can, on different platforms. That should help you appreciate how appearances can change.

Speaking of browsers, let's check into Chapter 4, for a closer look.

Chapter 4

BROWSER ISSUES

What we'll cover in this chapter:

- The history of browser development
- The range of browsers
- The different browser rendering engines
- The `<div>` vs. `<table>` tag
- Frames and iFrames
- Why browsers break

There isn't much point in developing a website if people can't see it. Unfortunately, this means that the end user has to use a browser to view it. I say "unfortunately" because this really isn't as easy as it sounds. If it was, this book would be a chapter shorter, and a hippy like me would feel better about saving a tree.

For starters, there are multiple platforms and multiple screen resolutions, and there is *certainly* more than one browser out there. Some are old, some are new. Some code will break gloriously in older browsers, but render exactly as you intend it in others. Yes, you're developing on the Mac OS X platform, but what will your website look like on Windows 98? It's exactly this kind of question that this chapter tackles.

It's not you, it's me

Life as a web developer would be fantastic if you could guarantee that every user was viewing your sites using the same platform, at the same monitor resolution, and in exactly the same browser. As everybody knows, this is far from the truth and will almost certainly never happen. You spend all your time creating a superb site, but the users and clients go and ruin it all by viewing it in an old-school browser, or at a huge screen resolution that you weren't prepared for. Because of this, bad rendering ensues. The thing is, it's not them. It's you.

As you learned in the last chapter, it doesn't have to be like this any more. You *don't have* to code differently for all those factors. In fact, it's correct *not* to work that way. These days, one size fits all, as it were . . . well, within reason. There is certainly no call for sending all the non-MS/IE users to a page that says something like "Sorry, I couldn't be bothered coding the Internet for your browser, here's a link to Microsoft.com."

Developing sites like that is now looked upon as exclusion because you are effectively excluding people from that site, which doesn't really match up with the whole ideal of accessibility. Not only that, but it's just dumb to exclude people based on what browser they use. Nobody should be excluded from content on the Internet; everyone has a right to access to the same information.

This is where people who have coded for years tell you how lucky you are to arrive into the world of web development at such a time. Everything is much easier these days, thanks to both the standards that are finally in place and the software that conforms to these same standards. Dreamweaver and GoLive make it so quick to create sites that also conform to standards, but don't forget to retain that invaluable hand-coding knowledge. It can get you out of many a scrape.

Browsers are finally beginning to play fair too. Can you remember the Browser Wars? No? Let me fill you in on that then, using the website of "Mr. Usability" himself, Jakob Nielson, for the simple reason that his site is Flash-free and, well . . . pretty much everything-free. This means that you should get a result in each browser.

Browser history

In the beginning, back in 1993, there was a browser called Mosaic. Mosaic was *the* browser, initially for the Unix platform. A version for the Macintosh was developed and released a few months later, making Mosaic the first browser with cross-platform support (see Figure 4-1).

Along came Lynx 2.0 in March 1993, but this was (as it still is today) a text-only browser (see Figure 4-2). Lynx was for geeks then and pretty much is to this day. There was no real competition and neither the content creators nor the browser developers were really trying to outperform anyone. These applications were only really used by people working in academia, and the chances of anyone outside of this circle having heard of them were pretty slim.

> *If you want to see what your site looks like in Lynx but don't have it installed, you can use an online Lynx viewer:* www.delorie.com/web/lynxview.html.

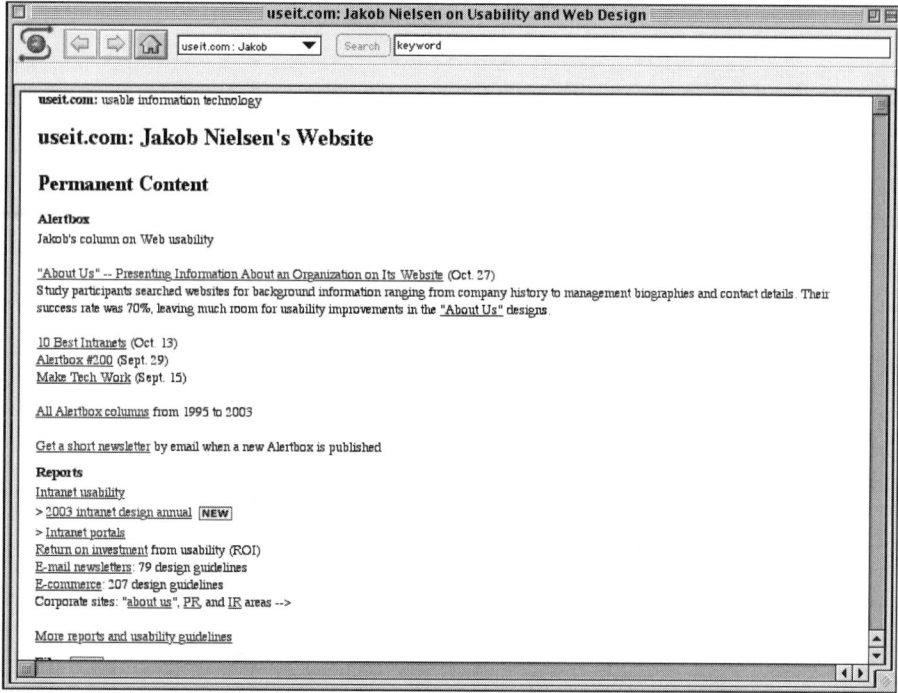

Figure 4-1. Mosaic was the first cross-platform browser, shown here on the Macintosh.

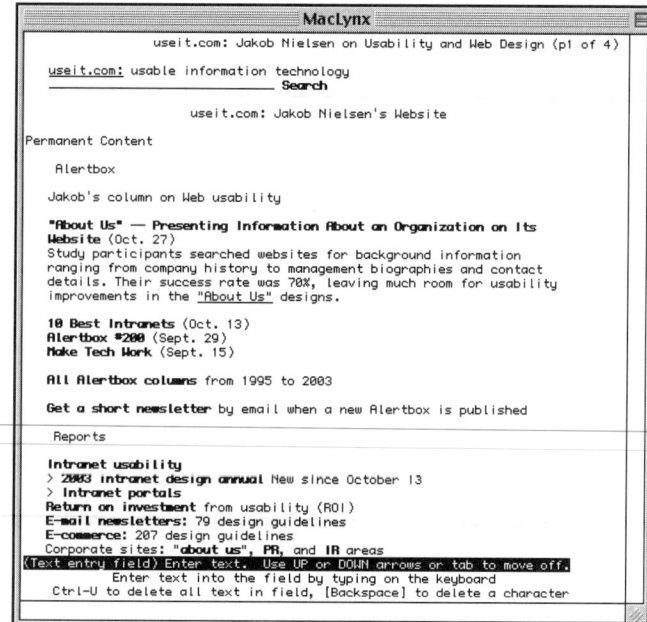

Figure 4-2. An OS 9 Lynx client showing the same site

That was about to change. Members of the Mosaic team got together with some guys from Silicon Graphics and formed a company that was soon to be known as Netscape Communications. In December 1994, Netscape 1.0, shown in Figure 4-3, hit the streets. Boom. Did you feel that? Didn't exactly feel big, did it? It was silent but very significant. Midway through 1995, if you were using a browser, you were probably using Netscape.

Again, competition was minimal, until Internet Explorer for Windows (MS/IE) arrived as part of Windows 95 in August 1995 (which started life as Spyglass Mosaic version 1.0 for Windows). Macintosh users weren't tainted with Internet Explorer until early the next year, a few months after Netscape 2.0 was released. Version 2.0 of Internet Explorer for Macintosh, which was released in April 1996, came bundled with the Eudora Light e-mail application (see Figure 4-4).

This, ladies and gentlemen, was where the smackdown started: Browser Wars was in full effect, and the contenders were both heavyweights.

Seconds out!

When version 2.0 of Netscape was released in the first quarter of 1996, it brought some of the goodies that will be familiar to many web developers, namely frames, Java, JavaScript, and plug-ins (see Figure 4-5). This knocked MS/IE down a peg, and Netscape continued to rule the roost.

Never one to settle for being beaten, the folks at Redmond (that's Microsoft) had other ideas and decided to get themselves some of the same features Netscape had, and anything else they could muster. This meant that MS/IE 3.0 came complete with, yes, you guessed it, frames, Microsoft's own weird version of JavaScript (JScript), and plug-ins. Some CSS action was also beginning to happen. Things looked a lot more like you know them today, in both 3.0 browsers (see Figures 4-6 and 4-7).

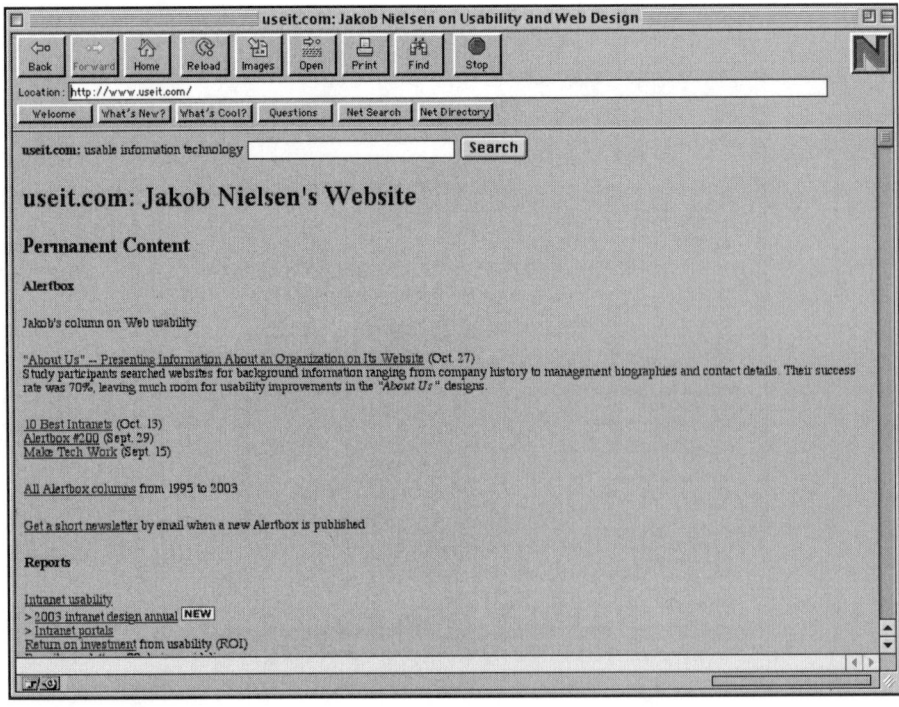

Figure 4-3. Netscape 1.0 was coded by ex-Mosaic programmers.

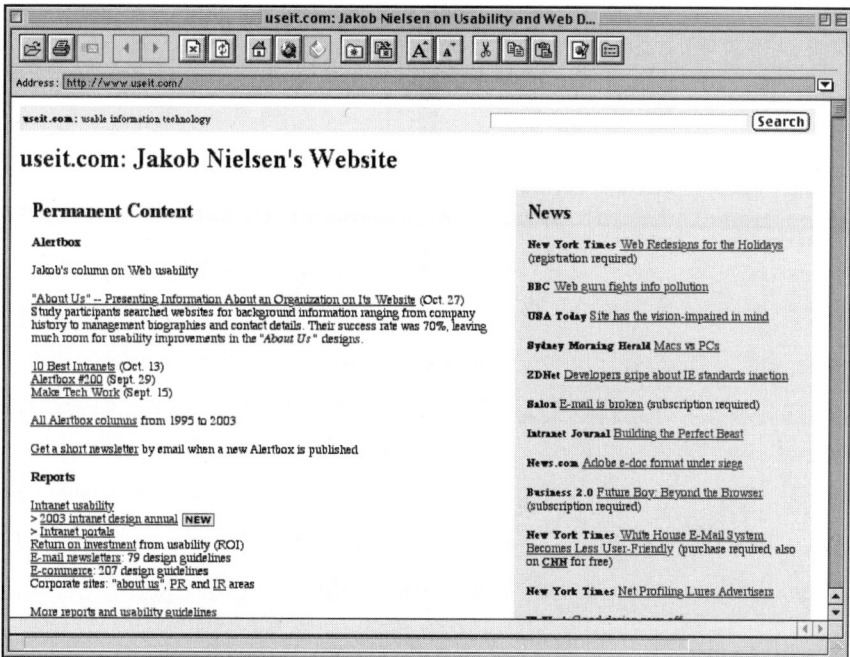

Figure 4-4. Internet Explorer 2.0 for Macintosh made things a bit more exciting.

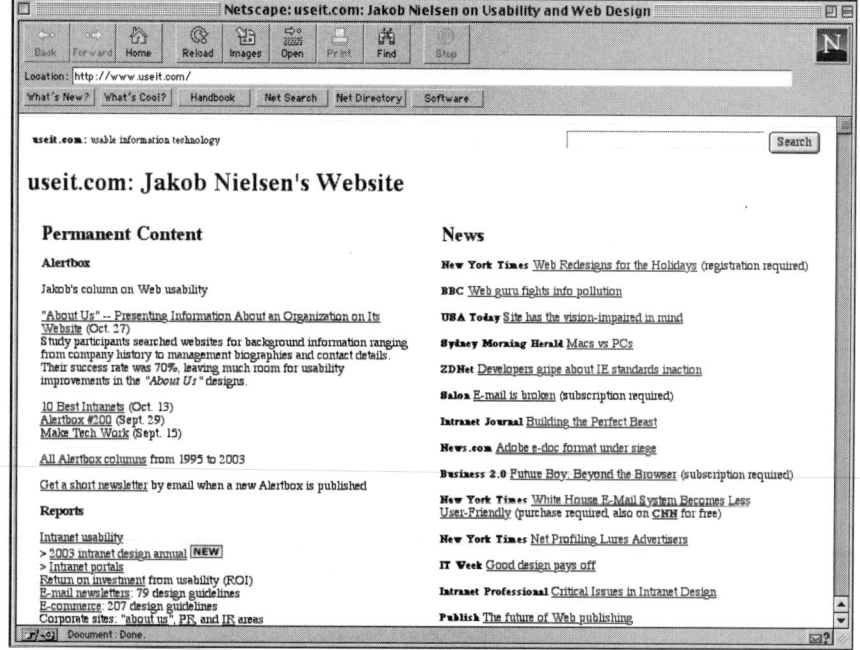

Figure 4-5. Netscape 2.0. What did these guys have against color?

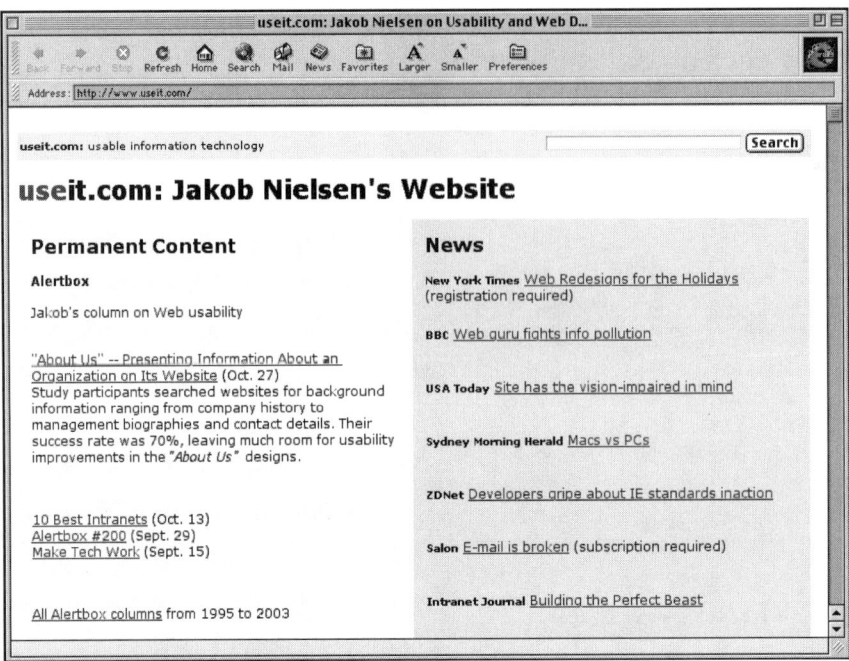

Figure 4-6. Internet Explorer 3.0

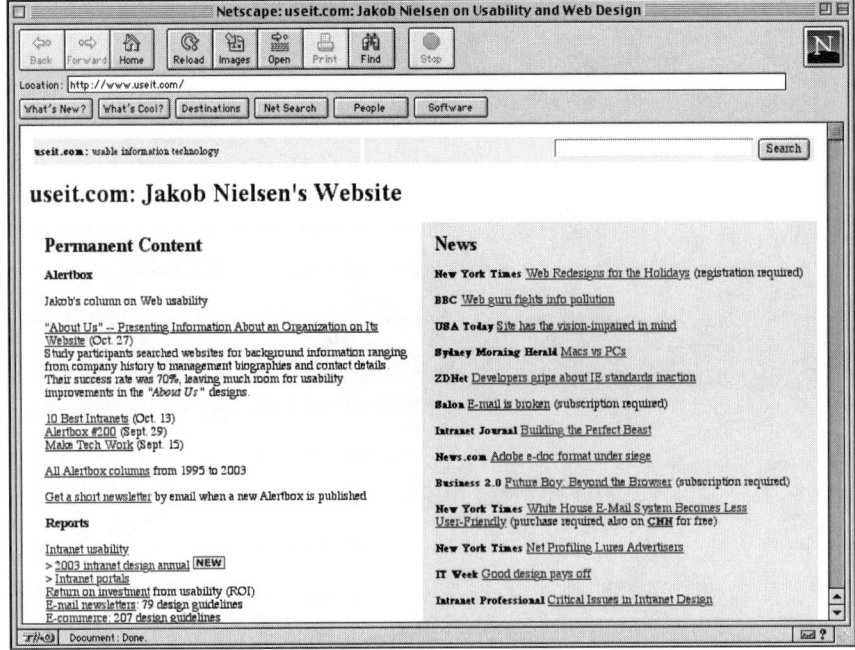

Figure 4-7. Netscape 3.0 finally realizes there are some colors on the page!

Netscape used to be the browser of choice for most people (including this author), but when version 4.0 of both browsers were released in 1997 (see Figures 4-8 and 4-9), MS/IE seemed to have finally surpassed its rival. IE was now seriously integrated into Windows (as opposed to just slightly), and when Joe Homeowner unpacked his brand new PC, there it was just waiting. The chances are that Joe doesn't even know there's a choice . . . even to this day.

Developers were starting to use more CSS than before, now that it was coming of age. They obviously used MS/IE to test everything because Netscape 4.0 handled CSS embarrassingly. No, scratch that. Until version 6.0, Netscape didn't handle CSS *period*. From the little information I haven't blotted out for good, I seem to recall it choked when it got to the line of code where you had the gall to link a style sheet. If you put your CSS inline, it was as effective as writing the lyrics to "Stairway To Heaven" in there: It looked nice in the

code but had little to zero effect on the actual page. Fantastic. If the person in charge of implementing CSS for Netscape before version 6.0 is reading this, write the following sentence 60,000 times, then stand at the back of the class and think about what you've done: "I will make Cascading Style Sheets work correctly."

In August 1997, IE became the default browser on Mac OS after Microsoft invested $150 million in Apple. Mac IE 4.0 was still pretty poor though, it has to be said.

Once the version 5.0 browsers started showing up, some things had changed, but they were still very buggy in some areas, especially when it came to CSS. (As a classic example, see the IE5 CSS workaround in the previous chapter.) Mac IE 5.0, shown in Figure 4-10, was possibly the best browser OS 9 has ever seen. It had good CSS capabilities and is widely acknowledged as the most correct HTML renderer on any platform.

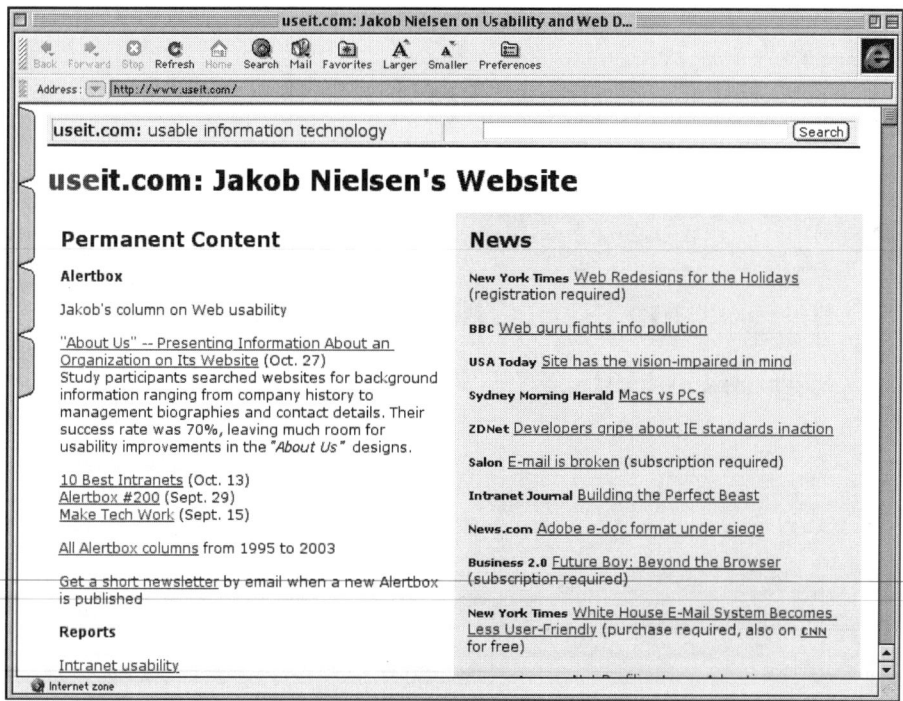

Figure 4-8. Internet Explorer 4.0 renders the page far better, but still has a spot of bother with that Search table.

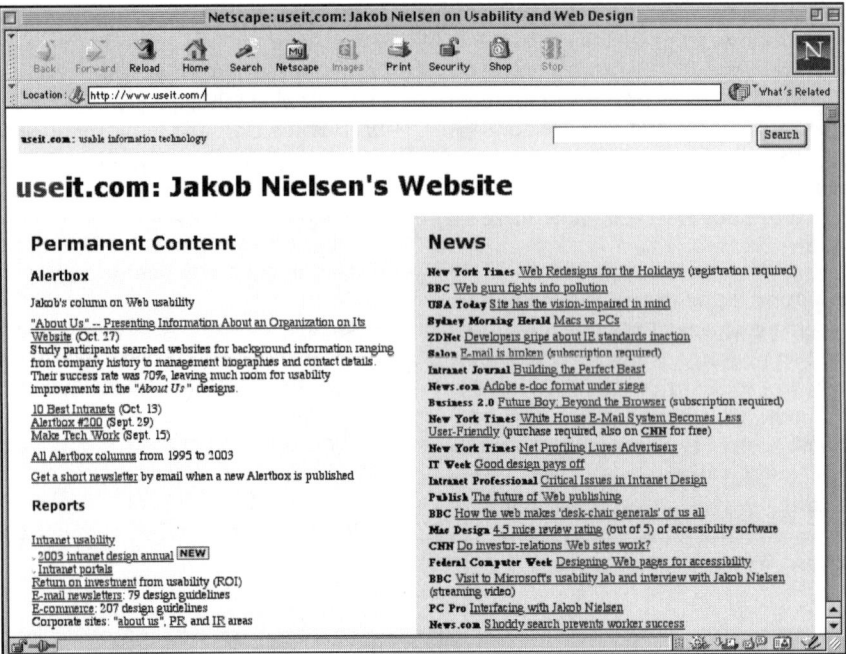

Figure 4-9. Netscape 4.0 finally nails the Header tag.

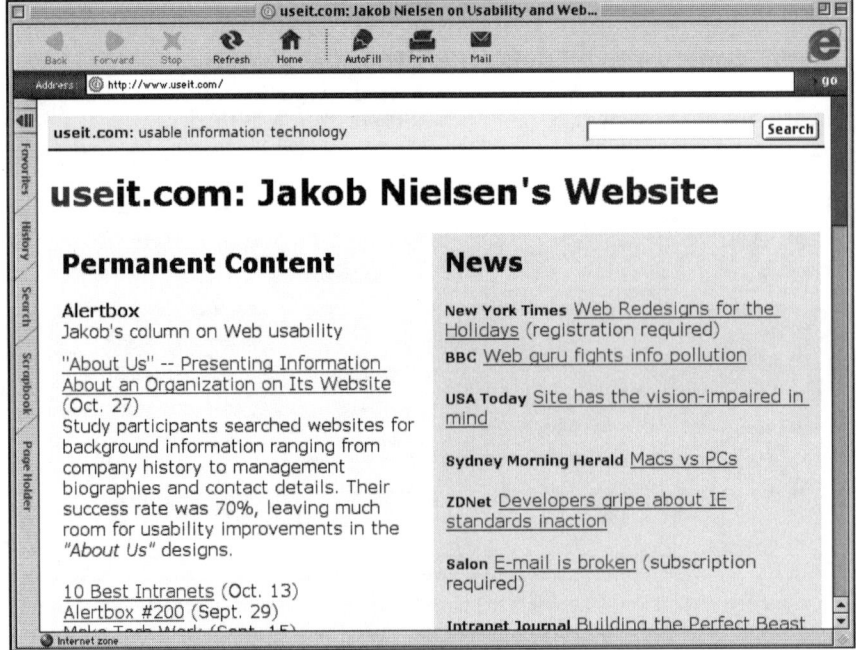

Figure 4-10. Mac IE 5.0

There wasn't even a Netscape 5.0 because Netscape simply couldn't iron out all the bugs in time to release it. AOL had bought Netscape and decided to integrate their Instant Messenger into the browser. Netscape continued working on their new baby and finally released a bloated version 6.0 (version 6.1 was the first Netscape release for Mac OS X), but it was too late. Leaving people struggling with version 4.7 left Microsoft with an open market and a lot of Netscape users jumped ship (ashamedly, including your "I was a PC user at work, during the day" author) to Internet Explorer. Once again, Microsoft beat their opposition to a pulp. Will they be able to retain this position? Who knows?

There can be only one?

While the two giants were slugging it out to take over peoples' browsing habits, other things had started to happen in the Macintosh browser world. For a start, other developers took advantage of the new platform and starting coding things in Cocoa, the native language of OS X.

When OS X was first introduced, it was bundled with Internet Explorer. This was an extremely compliant version of IE, but it rendered pages very slowly. Oh, wait. When Mac OS X was first introduced, *Mac OS X* was

very slow! Was this the major factor in IE's lack of speed? We have 10.3 Panther now, so who cares. In fact, Microsoft themselves gave up caring after Apple introduced their Safari browser, ceasing development of Internet Explorer for the Mac altogether. However, this doesn't mean that you should exclude it from your tests. It's still the most important browser to test your sites in, due to its default status on so many Macs.

As mentioned in Chapter 1, there are currently ten well-known browsers for Mac OS X. You can still use Lynx as a Terminal application (as shown in Figure 4-11), should you feel the need to, but I'm talking about full-on Graphical User Interface (GUI) browsers here.

> To use Lynx, you first need to install it. You can download Lynx and the relevant required libraries (ncurses, gettext, libiconv) as easy package installers, at http://macosx.forked.net.

These different browsers have different rendering engines (the central part that does all the work) and can be grouped into three categories: Gecko, WebCore/KHTML, or proprietary.

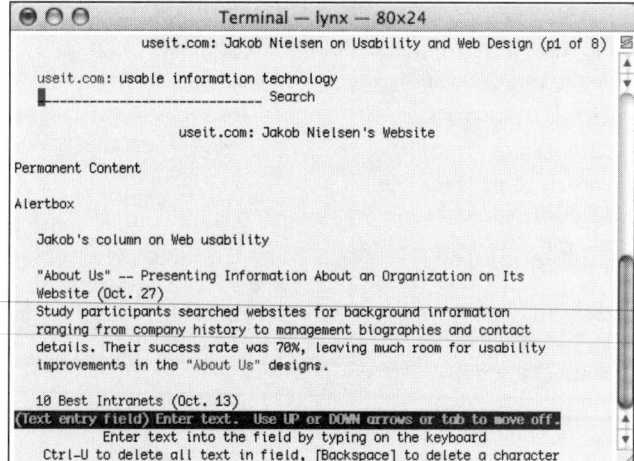

Figure 4-11. Browsing doesn't get any more basic than this.

Gecko

The Gecko browsers are

- Camino
- Firebird
- Mozilla
- Netscape

Developed for Mozilla, Gecko is a fast, standards-compliant rendering engine that implements standards such as HTML 4.0, CSS, the W3C Document Object Model (DOM), XML 1.0, and ECMAscript (JavaScript), and is continuously under development at www .mozilla.org.

WebCore/KHTML

WebCore/KHTML (and the accompanying JavaScript-Core) are used by Safari and OmniWeb (since version 4.5). From http://developer.apple.com/darwin/projects/webcore:

> *"WebCore is a framework for Mac OS X that takes the cross-platform KHTML library (part of the KDE project) and combines it with an adapter library specific to WebCore called KWQ that makes it work with Mac OS X technologies. KHTML is written in C++ and KWQ is written in Objective C++, but WebCore presents an Objective C programming interface. WebCore requires the JavaScriptCore framework. The current version of WebCore is based on the KHTML library from KDE 3.0.2.*
>
> *"JavaScriptCore is a framework for Mac OS X that takes the cross-platform KJS library (part of the KDE project), combines it with the PCRE regular expression library, and makes it work with Mac OS X technologies."*

Proprietary

Proprietary browsers have their own rendering engines: Internet Explorer (whose engine was called Tasman), Opera, and iCab.

With its new Tasman Engine, Internet Explorer was up to 50 percent faster than previous versions of Mac IE, but still not as fast as the PC version. It also rendered differently on Mac than PC. This is because the Tasman Engine was Mac-only. A member of the Tasman team was a certain Tantek Çelik, whom you may recall from the previous chapter. In its day, it was the best and most standards-compliant browser engine out there. It was also the first Mac web browser to render pages at a default setting of 96 dpi, as opposed to the standard 72 dpi screen resolution (96 dpi rendering is standard on the PC).

If you've recently installed any of the Macromedia Studio applications, then it's likely that you already have Opera on your Mac. Macromedia has licensed Opera to use as the rendering engine for their software. But why Opera and not Safari for OS X? For a start, Opera is cross-platform and it makes sense to use the same engine on both platforms. Adobe has signed a similar deal too. However, you may recall the "be nice to Opera" hack from the previous chapter.

iCab is probably the least used out of all these browsers, but it's still in development. In fact, iCab has accessibility functions that none of the other browsers do: **Access Keys**. With the right line of code, users can navigate your site with their keyboard. As you may recall, I showed you how to add such Access Keys in Chapter 3's example:

```
<a href="#" title="Switch Styles: green"
➥onclick="setActiveStyleSheet('green');
➥return false;" accesskey="g">
➥<img src="images/selector_green.gif"
➥alt="Switch Styles: green" /></a>
```

One way to implement these is to allow users to skip to the content if their older browser breaks your page. I first saw this come into play on Mr. Zeldman's site, back when I was investigating this new CSS layout world. Looking at his code, I had no idea what was going on in the following line:

```
<div class="hide">
➥<a href="#primarycontent"
➥title="Skip navigation." accesskey="2">
➥Skip navigation</a>.</div>
```

It wasn't until I saw how the page broke in earlier Netscape browsers that I understood what was going on. In fact, it took iCab to make me realize. That little snippet of code is telling iCab to display a link, or allow the 2 key to be pressed, which skips down the page to where the content starts (see Figure 4-12).

In his CSS file, this was called by the following lines of code:

```
/* Hide earlier versions     */

#primenav, .hide {
    display: none;
}
```

Archive

If you want to download and test any of these browsers, the best source is Evolt's Browser Archive (http://browsers.evolt.org). Evolt has every (and I mean *every*), browser that has ever been coded. PC, Mac, UNIX, etc.—they're all there. Feel free to leave Evolt a bandwidth donation too, so that your download is a guilt-free experience.

```
</history>
```

That's quite enough history for this chapter. If you couldn't see what web developers had to put up with before you started reading this book, you should certainly see it now. Each screenshot of the example site in the chapter so far was of exactly the same code; it was just handled differently by each browser. This is the reason for all those "browser sniffing" JavaScript pages, which send you to the page your browser could handle. Only the MS/IE page would usually have the good content too, with the others lacking in care, detail, and attention. That's because each page was coded separately, by hand, as opposed to pulling in the content from a central resource. (You'll get to these kinds of techniques soon enough.) Also, a lot of browsers these days allow you to change the User Agent details, so that the browser can identify itself as something else. Most commonly (still!), you have to pretend that you're surfing with MS/IE for a page to even display content.

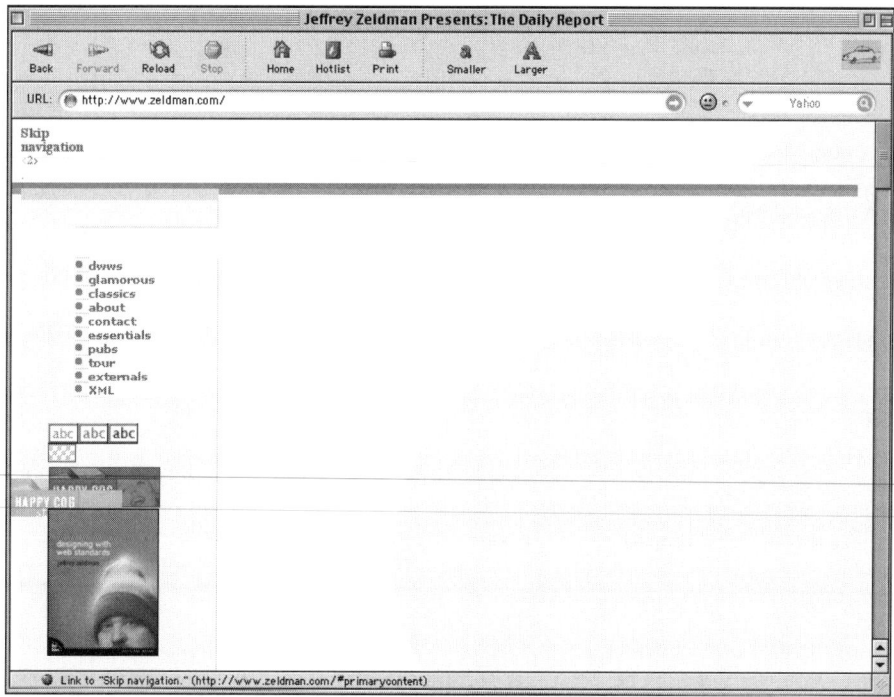

Figure 4-12. iCab shows you how it handles Access Keys.

The <table> tag

One of the things that clearly didn't work in those first version browsers was the <table> tag. HTML was still young back then, so a lot of tags weren't even around. As soon as it appeared for use, it appeared for abuse. It was designed for holding tabular data; that was its function. It wasn't designed to be stretched to 100 percent height, be nested like crazy, incorporate fancy background graphics, and so on. But, as we all know, that's how most developers and bedroom hacks used it. Yes, myself included. It was cheap, but it was necessary to get the job done. Imagine this scenario:

CLIENT: Why didn't you do it like the layout my artist sent you?

DEVELOPER: I'm sorry, that would mean seriously misusing the <table> tag.

CLIENT: Oh, my goodness, I'm sorry. I'll have my artist draw up something lame.

DEVELOPER: Thanks. You're the best client anyone could hope for.

CLIENT: I owe ya one, buddy. (Client pretends to shoot with fingers, winks, and exits.)

Of course, this would *never* happen in a million years. Instead, clients would get the finished result looking exactly as they wanted it . . . along with about 150K of code that probably wasn't even valid HTML 4.0 markup.

<div> vs. <table>

The <table> tag hasn't been sent to bed just yet. I'm sure it will be awhile before it unpacks its bags in the Home For Deprecated Old Tags. Usage of the tag is quite acceptable, as long as you use it correctly: tabular data! Slicing up an image into 182 JPEGs and GIFs, then using a mass of nested tables to reconstruct your masterpiece image map with all those cute rollovers, is likely to have Tim Berners-Lee himself knocking on your door and asking for his Internet back.

Certain aspects *are* deprecated though, like width and height. For a more detailed and up-to-date list, check the W3C's documentation on this subject: www.w3.org/TR/REC-html40/struct/tables.html.

So how are you to survive without this misuse? Simple. You've already tackled that in the last chapter. Remember that <div> tag? Get used to it. It's here to stay. It's been around for a while anyway, but these days it is used more and more to lay out a page.

<div> and <span>

The div and span elements, in conjunction with the id and class attributes, provide a way for you to structure your documents. These elements define content to be either inline (span) or block-level (div).

<id> and <class>

The id attribute assigns a name to an element, and this name must be unique in a document. In the example in the last chapter, you only had one #container, one #sidebar, and so on.

The class attribute assigns a class name or set of class names to an element. Any number of elements may be assigned the same class name or names, and white space characters must separate multiple class names. Define your class like so:

```
.funkyclassname {
  letter-spacing: 0.75em;
  }
```

Then call it like this:

```
<span class="funkyclassname">
I say, do you know the way to
the Garden Party?
</span>
```

Frames and iFrames

To frame or not to frame . . . that used to be the question. These days, far fewer people use frames, despite browsers being able to handle them better. Frames have a lot in common with Flash; most people who dislike them do so because they've seen them used badly far too many times. We've all seen sites where the links don't target the correct frame, and go berserk. Then there are the sites where the designers obviously used every pixel of their 1280×1024 resolution screen to design the site. Viewing this site at 800×600 is going to leave frames looking truncated, if they were defined absolutely with no scrolling.

"Mommy, where did the navigation frame go?"

"Sorry petal, we can only afford 800×600 this week."

Like their love-it-or-hate-it counterpart, Flash, frames can be used to great effect. It's also a personal choice like Flash. One thing is for sure though: The time it takes to construct a quick frame set is minimal, and zero hassle. Both Dreamweaver and GoLive have a whole palette of framesets to choose from (see Figure 4-13). It's as easy as clicking a button, and then designating which content lives in which frame.

Sometimes you might want to use them for a different reason, such as having a domain name point at your ISP or .Mac web space. Load the content into the bottom frame, and people can just remember www .yourdomain.com instead of the http://homepages .somehugecompany.com/users/~yourusername/main .html page, which loads your content.

Maybe you only need a bit of a frame in the middle, but you don't want to dissect the whole page into a huge frameset. One way around this is the <iframe> tag, which stands for **inline frame**, and acts exactly as

its name suggests. It just dumps a frame where you tell it to, but the rest of the page acts just like a normal static page. Normal frame rules apply with regards to scrolling. Most people using an iFrame would have scrolling content in there, with the rest of the page getting on with static life around the edges, as shown in Figure 4-14.

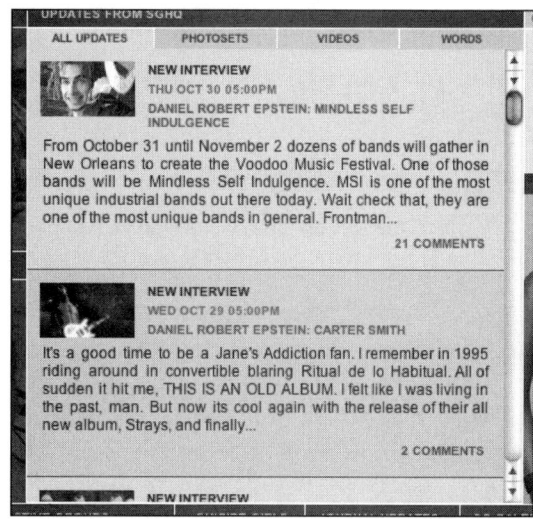

Figure 4-14. The <iframe> tag in use in the middle of a normal page

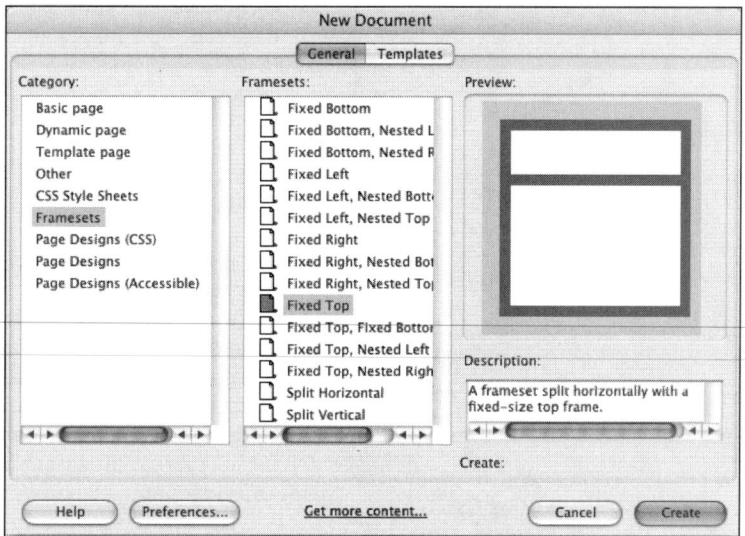

Figure 4-13. Adding framesets in Dreamweaver MX 2004

If you were using a CSS layout, you would add it with code like this:

```
<iframe src="/updates/" frameborder="0"
➥name="updates"></iframe>
```

name="updates" refers to the following <div>, which you would have in your style sheet:

```
#updates iframe
{
  float: left;
  width: 399px;
  height: 354px;
}
```

You saw it in the last chapter, but if you're wondering what the float property is, here's a word from the W3C:

> "Using the 'float' property, an element can be declared to be outside the normal flow of elements and is then formatted as a block-level element. For example, by setting the 'float' property of an image to 'left', the image is moved to the left until the margin, padding, or border of another block-level element is reached. The normal flow will wrap around on the right side. The margins, borders, and padding of the element itself will be honored, and the margins never collapse with the margins of adjacent elements."

How browsers break things

You've seen how different browsers render the most simple of pages, so how do things look with a more complicated CSS layout? Quite simply, some break the Internet. What looks fantastic in one browser will render in such a way that designers will probably break down in tears and start deleting all their design applications, never to design again.

I introduced a friend to PHP once and changed his life forever. Just recently, I introduced him to using CSS as a layout tool . . . and changed his life forever. Again.

A few tech support e-mails and some of those aforementioned tears later (his, not mine), he had a whole new look for the sites he was responsible for. ("Hey look, my name's in the code! I'm famous, Ma!")

Having got the hang of things pretty easily, then forgetting to sleep for a few days while he coded, Scott (as we'll call him from now on, for that is his given name), yelled "Eureka!" Really, he did. I heard him from here. Safari also heard him and quite rightly too, as that was the browser Scott was working in. Then came good old MS/IE time. Round about then is when the tears showed up. Then came the tech support e-mails. If you cast an eye over some of Scott's handy (and not-so-handy) work, it becomes clear how important it is to test in every browser you can get your hands on, and how familiar you need to be with the necessary workarounds.

MS/IE breaks it with ease—where's the right sidebar on the page in Figure 4-15?

Oops, there it is in Figure 4-16, stuck at the bottom.

All it took was five words and the sun was shining again: Box Model and Opera hacks. With those hacks applied, and the code written again from scratch (I find it's often quicker and easier to do that, rather than fix broken code), the page came together nicely. Writing from scratch also helps eliminate any other stray bugs that might have gate-crashed the party. Now everything is in the right place, at last, as you can see in Figure 4-17.

Getting your site to work in MS/IE 5.5 is probably the most critical test over and done with. If it works in this browser, it's 99 percent certain to work in the other MS/IE browsers, as well as the majority of others.

Obviously, if you don't have a PC at hand, you'll have to ask someone to check them for you and provide some screenshots. Another way around this problem is the application mentioned in Chapter 2, called Virtual PC (www.microsoft.com/mac/products/virtualpc/virtualpc.aspx?pid=virtualpc). This really is useful if you don't have a PC in the office. You can load up as many versions of Windows as you want, and all those builds of Linux that you always wanted to play with.

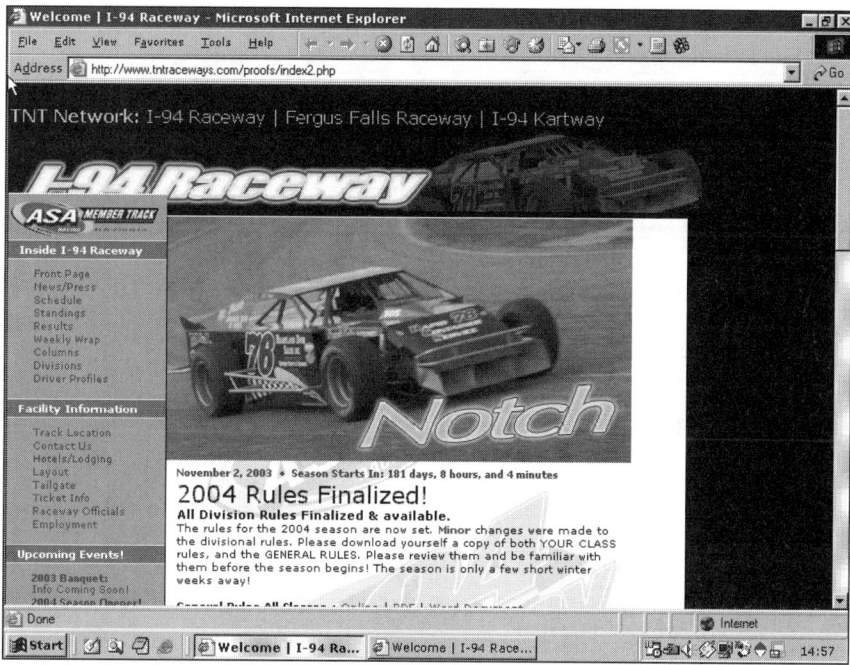

Figure 4-15. Right sidebar, totally absent

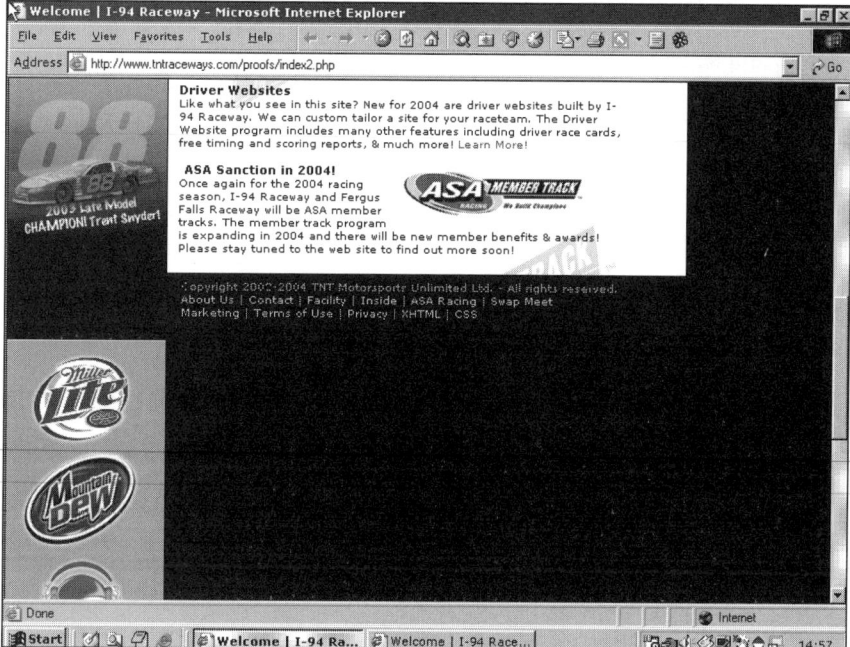

Figure 4-16. The elusive sidebar, hiding under the main content

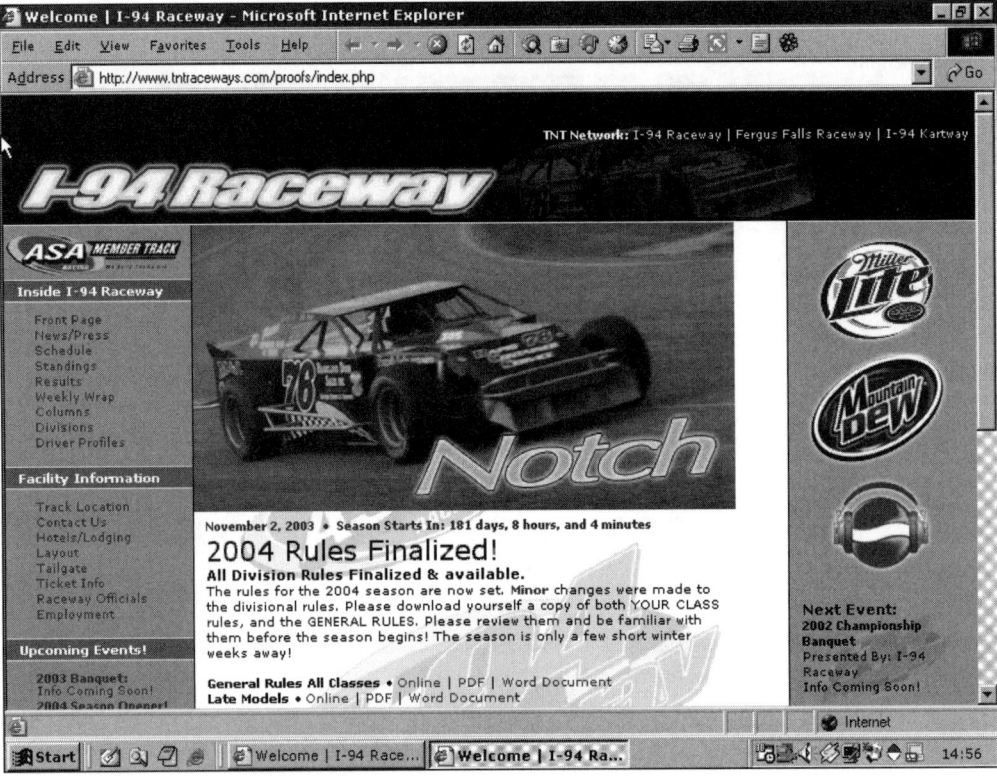

Figure 4-17. How the site should look, with the sidebar on the right

OS 9/Classic

Depending on how new your Macintosh is, you might not have the ability to boot into OS 9. If you have an older Mac lying around, you can just drag the System Folder to the root of the hard disk, and you should then be allowed to run Classic instead.

From an application point of view, this is only really useful to check those old browsers. In the past, Classic mode was essential, as a lot of applications weren't available as native OS X applications. Although pretty much any application of any importance is OS X native now, you'll still need that System Folder to run Classic.

Another way around this is to hit eBay (www.ebay.com), and snag an old Mac just for testing purposes. You can find them here: Home ➤ All Categories ➤ Computers & Electronics ➤ Apple, Macintosh Computers. Hey, a Mac nerd can never have too many Macs. I have five with another in limbo and a seventh on the way, and there's nothing wrong with me. Honest.

Chapter review

Although it's very unlikely that you'll ever have to code for browsers earlier than version 4.0 of "the big two," it helps to be aware of what things look like in very old browsers. Believe it or not, some people out there will still be using some of those real old dusty ones.

You've seen how things can break in one browser, but not in others. Again, this shouldn't be a problem if you code properly, but you can never guarantee what MS/IE is going to do to your site until you try it.

I coded an admin area for a client once, which worked fine in Mac browsers. My clients all used Macs, so there was no problem there. Like a true IT professional, I neglected to test it properly and when I needed to access that area from a Windows XP machine one day, a blank page greeted me whenever I called the URL in the browser. Doh! Scuppered by not paying attention to my own rules.

With all this talk of history and such, you're probably wondering when I'll get round to some more code. So, without further ado, let's head into Chapter 5 and get stuck into some geeky stuff.

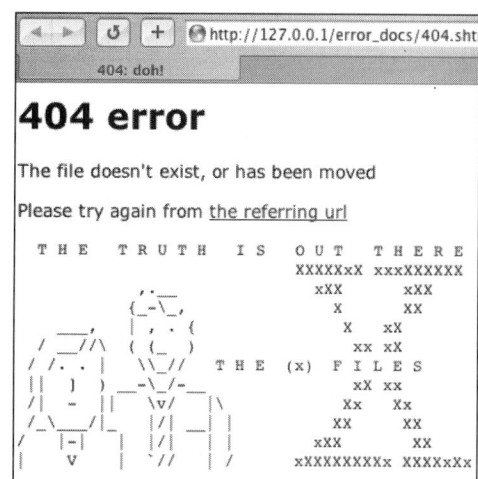

Chapter 5

DYNAMIC WEB PAGE DEVELOPMENT

What we'll cover in this chapter:

- How dynamic sites work
- The dynamic duo: Perl and PHP
- Server-Side Includes (SSI)
- Using the mail() function
- Adding other pages dynamically

Back in Chapter 3, you learned the basics of putting a web page together. In the example you created, everything on the page is there because you specifically coded it to be there. Nothing changes on the page until *you* change the code. If your site isn't going to be updated very often, this might be all you need to know, and you can get on with mowing the lawn (or something exciting like that).

Now, imagine that you're in charge of a large site with a lot of content that changes on a regular basis. Imagine having to code all of it by hand every time the client wanted some content updated. No thank-you, Sir. As well as boring, it's also an inefficient way of working. You could be doing countless other things instead of all that coding. With just a bit more work, you can make things a lot easier, and even enable clients to update the site themselves.

While static web pages do have their place, dynamic pages are very much the way forward. In this chapter, we'll look at some of the methods you can use to make your site dynamic with minimal work.

As this chapter will be more technical than in previous chapters, you'll be using Terminal a bit more, so you might want to drag the Terminal icon to your Dock for easy opening. Terminal is located in `/Applications/Utilities/Terminal` as shown in Figure 5-1.

Choose your weapon

As with most popular things these days, there are a number of different ways you can add dynamic content to a web page. I'm not going to cover each one in serious detail here, just the basics. There's a reason why some of the books on the shelves next to this one are over 1000 pages in size: The topics are very complex! Once you've tried out some of the technologies discussed in this chapter, it's up to you to decide whether you want to know all there is to know about it and buy one of those gigantic tomes.

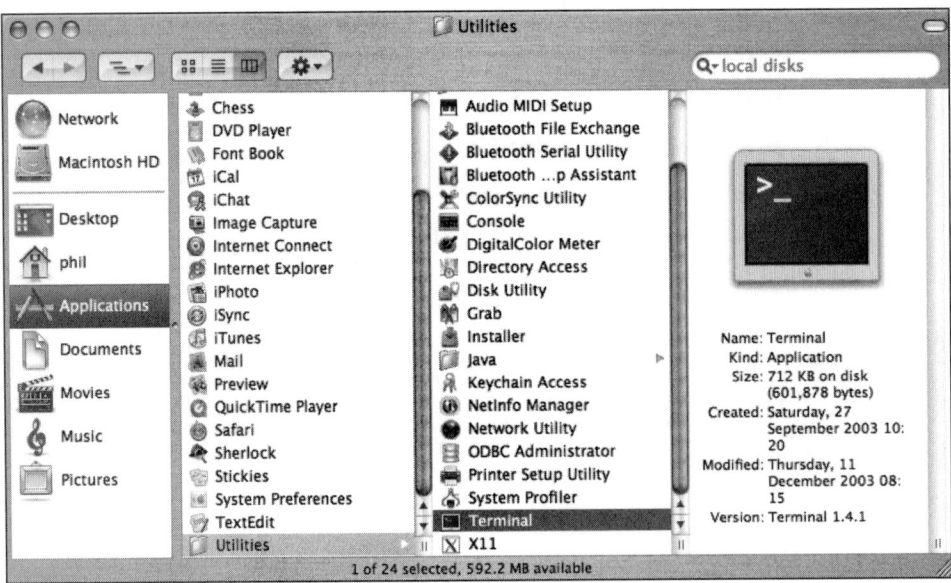

Figure 5-1. Where to find Terminal

How do dynamic sites work?

When you call a normal HTML page via your browser, the request is sent from your machine to the web server, which sends back the requested page. No other process is involved. You get back an exact copy of the HTML page that is sitting on the web server.

With dynamic sites, things are a bit different. For example, say you request a PHP page. The request has to go via the web server application—in this case, Apache—through the PHP engine for processing. Once processed, PHP spits out the page in an HTML format, which is then sent back to the user, as shown in Figure 5-2.

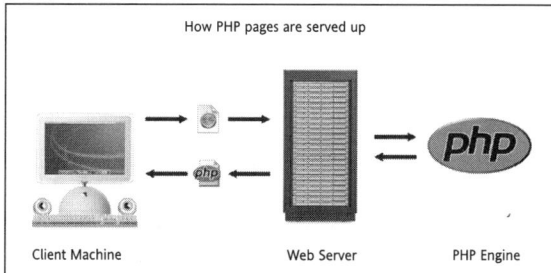

Figure 5-2. The round trip a PHP web page makes

Common Gateway Interfaces

The **C**ommon **G**ateway **I**nterface (CGI) is a standard for interfacing external applications with information servers, such as HTTP or web servers. As covered earlier in Chapter 3, the example page you created was a **static** HTML page. This means that the web server outputs exactly what you originally coded, and nothing more. A CGI program, on the other hand, is executed in real time so that it can output dynamic information. This program can be written in Perl, PHP, C, JavaScript, and a number of other programming languages.

A common use for this is in extracting data from a database. As you won't always know what is in that database, you have to write a program to query the data somehow, and then display the results of this query on a web page. This is how a gateway works, and there are numerous ways of extracting the data.

So, what are the available options? It makes sense to start with the built-in options, so let's have a quick look at what you've got. Straight out of the box, Mac OS X 10.3 comes fully loaded with Perl, PHP, Ruby, and Python.

Perl (.pl/.cgi)

> *"Perl is a stable, cross-platform programming language. It is used for mission critical projects in the public and private sectors and is widely used to program web applications of all needs."* (www.perl.org)

Perl is widely known as "the duct tape of the Internet" because it holds so many sites together. Created by Larry Wall in 1987, it's an abbreviation of "Practical Extraction and Report Language," although Larry himself has often referred to it as being short for "Pathologically Eclectic Rubbish Lister." It's estimated that over one million people use it, and there are whole Perl-dedicated sections in bookstores, full of scary code. If you want to get into the whole dynamic side of things, I'd suggest buying a beginner's book, as knowing some basic Perl is never a bad thing. A small amount will be covered in this chapter, but nothing too mind-blowing.

Perl is ready to roll out of the box and will be covered in more detail later in the chapter in the section "The dynamic duo: Perl and PHP." To use it, you first need to edit the Apache configuration, which will also be tackled in this chapter in the section "Apache configuration."

> .cgi *documents are usually just Perl* (.pl) *documents renamed. This is necessary in order to run them on most Windows servers.*

PHP (.php)

> "PHP (recursive acronym for "PHP: Hypertext Preprocessor") is a widely used Open Source general-purpose scripting language that is especially suited for Web development and can be embedded into HTML." (www.php.net)

PHP is quite different from Perl but can perform a lot of the same tasks. From a complete beginner's point of view, PHP is far easier to learn because you can just drop segments of it into your HTML pages. Even the basics don't look as scary as Perl can. Its syntax is based heavily on C++, and a lot of the functions are the same, so if you know any C++, you should be right at home with PHP.

Like Perl, PHP is also ready to roll out of the box, and it'll be covered more in this chapter in the section "The dynamic duo: Perl and PHP." Again, you need to edit the Apache configuration first in order to use it.

Ruby (.rb)

> "Ruby is the interpreted scripting language for quick and easy object-oriented programming. It has many features to process text files and to do system management tasks (as in Perl). It is simple, straightforward, extensible, and portable." (www.ruby-lang.org)

Relatively new on the scene compared to Perl (Ruby was born in 1993), Ruby is fast becoming the favorite scripting language of geeks. It's similar to Perl in a lot of ways, yet deemed more powerful and flexible than the mighty Perl that it was modeled on. Ruby programs are compact, yet very readable and maintainable; you can get a lot done in a few lines without being as cryptic as with Perl. For a few fun examples of what you can do with a Ruby one-liner, check out Rob's Ruby page at www.rollmop.com/ruby.

Python (.py)

> "Python is an interpreted, interactive, object-oriented programming language. It is often compared to Tcl, Perl, Scheme, or Java. By the way, the language is named after the BBC show 'Monty Python's Flying Circus' and has nothing to do with nasty reptiles." (www.python.org)

Python was born about halfway between Perl and Ruby, and shares more in common with the two of these than it does with PHP in that it looks just as frightening to the complete beginner. One of the main reasons you might come into contact with Python is the Content Management System (CMS) called Zope (www.zope.com). I think it's very much a personal preference as to which you prefer among Perl, Ruby, and Python, as they are all very similar, yet all have individual pros and cons.

Perl, Ruby, and Python scripts need to be kept in a specific place on the web server (usually /cgi-bin) with the right permissions, whereas PHP documents can live anywhere that normal HTML documents can with no special permissions needed. Permissions can be set in a few ways, and you'll learn more about these in the section "File Permissions" later in this chapter once you've written some Perl.

Line breaks

Another thing you must bear in mind with Perl, Ruby, and Python scripts is **line breaks**. Macintosh, DOS, and UNIX systems all have a different line break system. This causes a bit of mayhem with your scripts because, to a UNIX system, a file saved with Mac line breaks has ^M at the end of every line, instead of a physical carriage return, which starts a new line (as shown in Figure 5-3), and DOS breaks cause similar mayhem. This renders the script unreadable, and you'll usually get a 500 Error page from the web server. You can combat this by specifying UNIX Line Breaks in your text editor (both BBEdit and Dreamweaver can do this), or by simply using one of Mac OS X's built-in editors: Vim (shown in Figure 5-4), Pico, or Emacs.

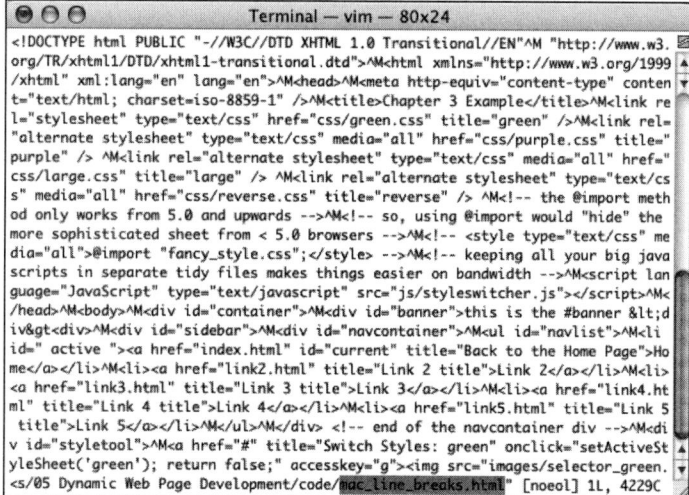

Figure 5-3. You can clearly see the Mac line breaks here.

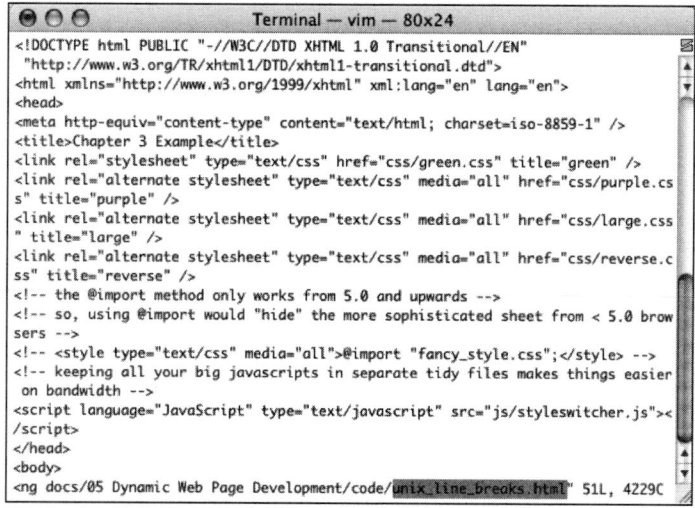

Figure 5-4. UNIX line breaks make things look normal again.

A quick line of Perl can help strip those line breaks and convert your existing documents for you.

1. Open the Terminal application.

2. Type perl -pi -e 's/\r/\n/g' (leave a space at the end, as shown in Figure 5-5).

3. Drag your file(s) onto the Terminal window and hit *Enter*.

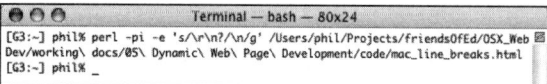

Figure 5-5. Don't expect any output; Perl just gets on with it, and you're back at the command prompt.

4. Reopen your file in Vim (vim filename.html, where filename.html is the name of your file), and you can see the difference that one line of Perl makes to the file in Figure 5-6.

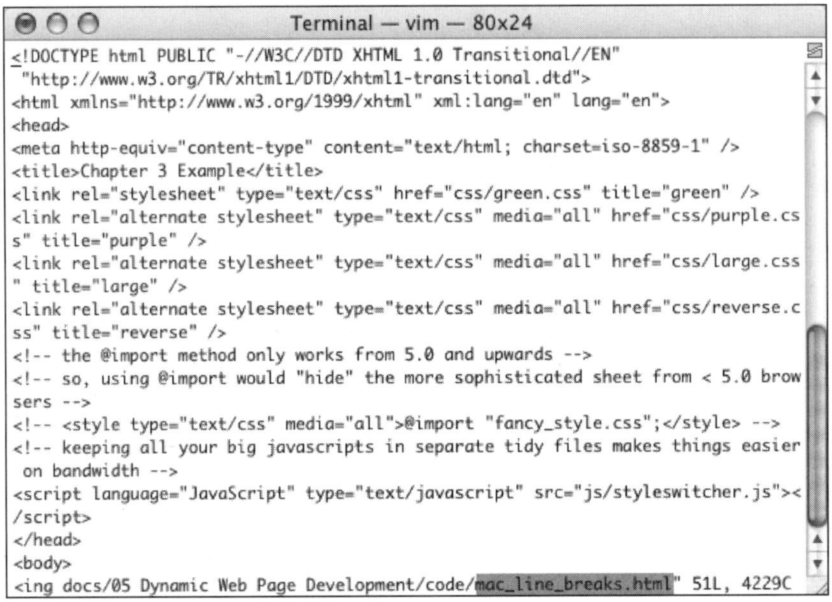

Figure 5-6. Mac line breaks converted to UNIX line breaks

Okay, that's the built-in languages taken care of, but what else is out there?

JavaServer Pages (.jsp)

"JavaServer Pages technology allows web developers and designers to rapidly develop and easily maintain information-rich, dynamic web pages that leverage existing business systems. As part of the Java family, JSP technology enables rapid development of web-based applications that are platform independent. JavaServer Pages technology separates the user interface from content generation, enabling designers to change the overall page layout without altering the underlying dynamic content." (http://java.sun.com/products/jsp/)

JavaServer Pages were developed by Sun Microsystems and will be covered in Chapter 9. To run JSP pages, you need an application server that supports JavaServer Pages. Here are some popular choices:

- **Macromedia JRun for Mac OS X:** You can download a trial version of JRun at www.macromedia.com/go/jrun.

- **Tomcat for UNIX (including Mac OS X):** You can download a copy of Tomcat from the Jakarta Project website (http://jakarta.apache.com/tomcat). For more information on installing Tomcat on a Macintosh, see the Apple website at http://developer.apple.com/internet/java/tomcat1.html.

ColdFusion (.cfm)

> "ColdFusion MX is the solution for building and deploying powerful web applications and web services. Using the proven tag-based scripting and built-in services in ColdFusion MX, web application developers can easily harness the power of the Java platform without the complexity. Available for stand-alone installation or for deployment on industry-leading J2EE application servers, ColdFusion enables over 10,000 customers and hundreds of thousands of developers worldwide to deliver powerful web applications in record time." (www.macromedia.com/software/coldfusion)

ColdFusion is a markup language that looks a lot like HTML but has a lot more functions along the lines of PHP et al. You get database connectivity, you get Flash connectivity, and you get power. You also have to buy the server software from Macromedia for a hefty price and then find yourself a host who offers ColdFusion hosting.

Active Server Pages (.asp)

You may have heard of these. They're a Microsoft invention that run natively on Windows servers. To run ASP, you need an application server that supports Microsoft Active Server Pages 2.0. As this is a book about Mac OS X Web Development, ASP won't be covered.

The dynamic duo: Perl and PHP

Because they are the most widely used languages and the easiest to configure, you'll be using Perl and PHP during this chapter but, by all means, *do* check out the other technologies mentioned previously.

It's always handy to know a little about every technology you might come into contact with. Focus on the one you feel comfortable with, but grant some time to the others, as you may well get clients asking you to fix some of their code urgently. When said with meaning, "I can have a look at that, sure" *always* sounds better than "No, sorry, I don't know how to do that."

However, this certainly isn't a Perl/PHP master class. What you'll get from this chapter are a few real-world solutions to some frequently asked questions, which you should be able to start using straight away.

Configuration

Before you even get to any code, there are a few things you need to do to your Mac. You already have Apache, Perl, and PHP installed, but you need to configure them. As with many features in Mac OS X, they aren't fully enabled by default for security reasons. So, this is what you need to do:

- Configure Apache for Perl and PHP (edit the `httpd.conf` file).
- Restart the web server.

Enabling root access

At some stages during the next few pages, you'll need **root access**. Root is the SuperUser on UNIX systems (don't forget, Mac OS X is a UNIX operating system), and some operations can only be performed by root as a security measure. To enable the root user, you're going to use NetInfo Manager (Applications/ Utilities/NetInfo Manager) as shown in Figure 5-7.

1. Open NetInfo Manager.
2. Click the Click the lock to make changes button and enter your password when prompted.

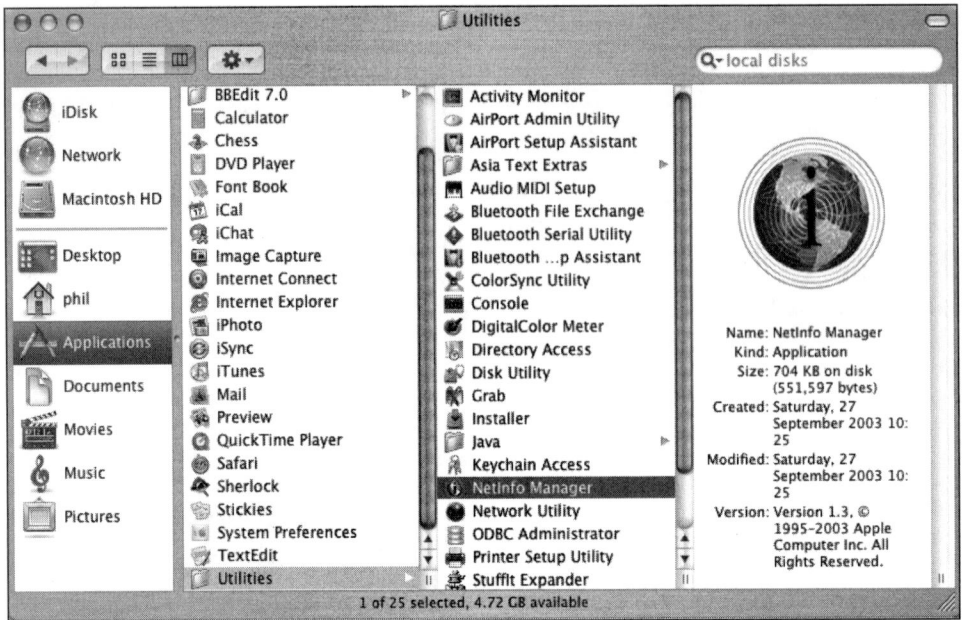

Figure 5-7. Where to find NetInfo Manager

3. Select Security ➤ Enable Root User as shown in Figure 5-8.

Figure 5-8. Selecting Enable Root User

4. Okay the alert, and then enter your password in the bottom two fields shown in Figure 5-9.

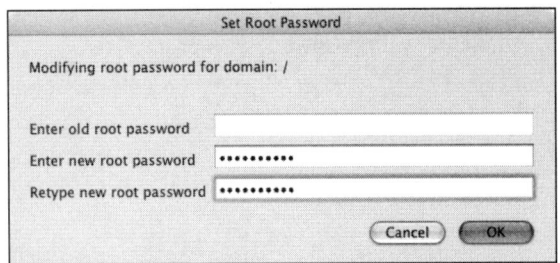

Figure 5-9. Entering the new password twice

5. Authenticate with your password when prompted again.

With that done, you can now move on to editing that configuration file.

Configuring BBEdit

Just a couple of more tweaks, and you're ready to start. To edit BBEdit's Preferences, follow these steps:

1. Select Preferences from the Menu Bar (⌘+;).

2. Select Text Files: Saving from the left-hand pane.

3. Select the Unix radio button option under Default Line Breaks as shown in Figure 5-10.

4. Select Status Bar in the left-hand pane and check Show Line Numbers as shown in Figure 5-11 to make things easier to locate.

5. Click the Save button and close the window.

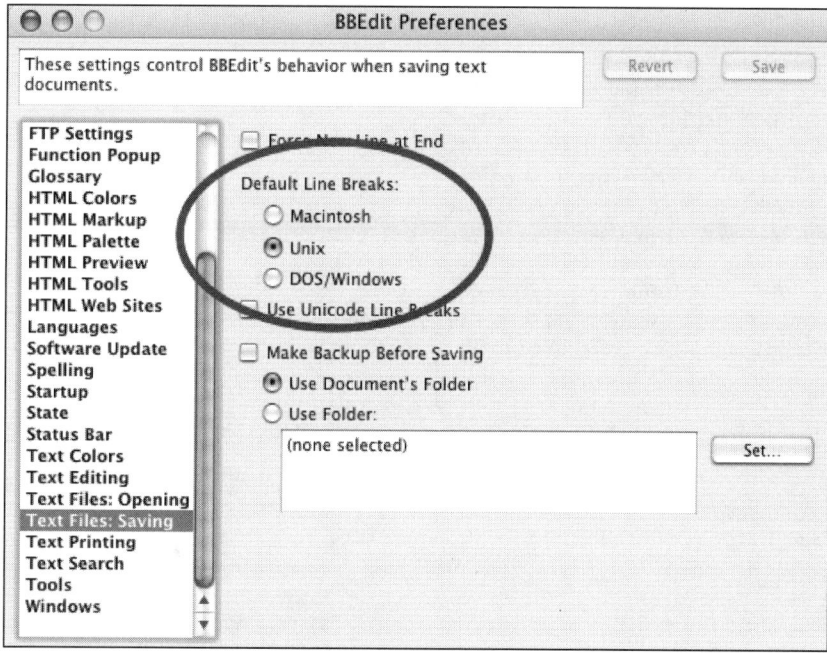

Figure 5-10. Selecting Unix Line Breaks

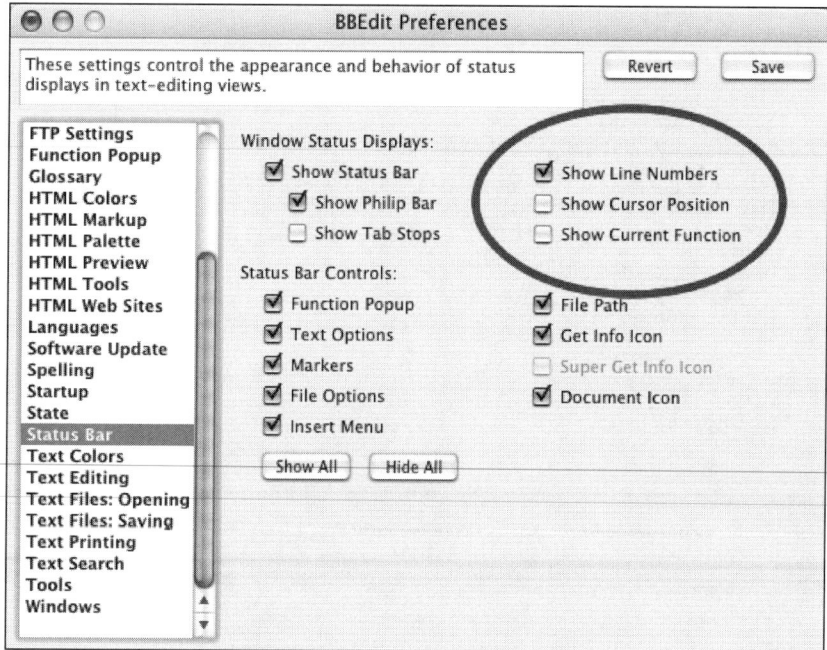

Figure 5-11. Showing line numbers makes things a lot easier.

Apache configuration

To configure Apache to run Perl and PHP, you need to edit the configuration file, which is hidden among the system files. As it's just a text file, you can use a text editor to edit it. However, it's owned by root, so using something like TextEdit won't allow you to save any changes, because you don't have permission to. There are ways around this, as you'll see in a minute.

To find out where the Apache configuration file lives, you can just skip to the next part or type httpd -V into Terminal. You should see an output screen like the one in Figure 5-12.

The only things of interest to you right now are these two lines:

```
Server version: Apache/1.3.28 (Darwin)
-D SERVER_CONFIG_FILE=
➥"/etc/httpd/httpd.conf"
```

Now you know what version of Apache you're running and where your configuration file lives. Later on, while testing, you may encounter some errors. If (or when) you do, you can open the error log. You can see the path now in the Terminal: /var/log/httpd/error_log.

Tip: To easily open a file in TextEdit from the command line, use this command:

```
open -e <filename>
```

For example:

```
open - e /var/log/httpd/error_log
```

Backing up the Apache configuration file

Before you start messing with any files, it's important to make backups. By default, there is already a backup copy of the file you're going to edit, but you might not be starting with a default installation, so always back up your file. Here's how you do it:

1. To navigate to the directory where your file lives, open Terminal, and type

```
cd /etc/httpd
```

2. To see what's in there, you need to list the files using this command:

```
ls -Gal
```

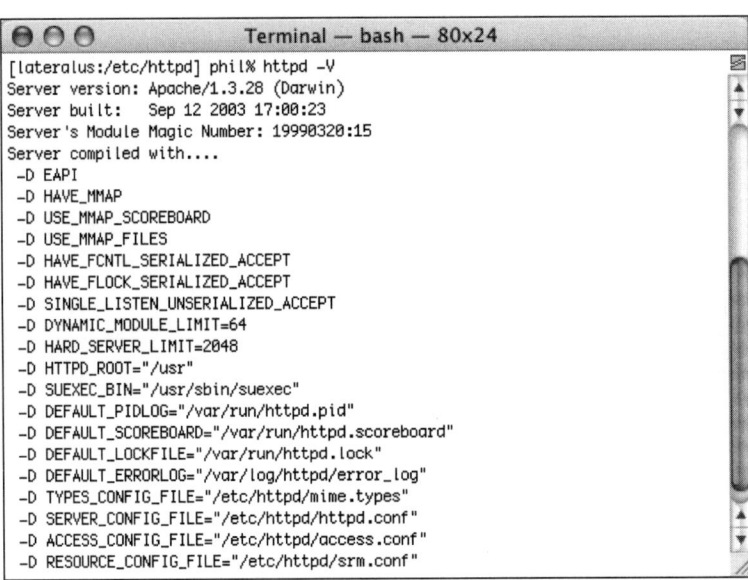

Figure 5-12. Apache's Version output

What does that actually mean? Let's break it down:

- `ls` means list directory contents.
- `-G` enables colorized output (as shown in Figure 5-13).
- `-a` means list directory entries whose names begin with a dot (.). This will be useful later on when dealing with `.htaccess` files.
- `-l` lists the files in long format, so you can see their size and the date they were last modified.

> *You could combine the last two commands with the && (AND) operator, like so:* `cd /etc/httpd && ls -Gal` *as shown in step 2 and Figure 5-13.*

You should now see something like the screen in Figure 5-13.

3. As it's a system file, which is owned by root, that you're trying to back up, you need to execute the following commands with some root muscle:

   `sudo cp httpd.conf httpfd.conf.bak`

```
Terminal — bash — 80x24
iBook:~ phil$ cd /etc/httpd
iBook:/etc/httpd phil$ ls -Gal
total 368
drwxr-xr-x  10 root  wheel    340 13 Sep 03:41 .
drwxr-xr-x  97 root  wheel   3298 20 Jan 19:35 ..
-rw-r--r--   1 root  wheel  38008 13 Sep 01:01 httpd.conf
-rw-r--r--   1 root  wheel  37047 13 Sep 01:01 httpd.conf.bak
-rw-r--r--   1 root  wheel  38008 13 Sep 01:01 httpd.conf.default
-rw-r--r--   1 root  wheel  12965 13 Sep 01:01 magic
-rw-r--r--   1 root  wheel  12965 13 Sep 01:01 magic.default
-rw-r--r--   1 root  wheel  15150 13 Sep 01:01 mime.types
-rw-r--r--   1 root  wheel  15150 13 Sep 01:01 mime.types.default
drwxr-xr-x   3 root  wheel    102 19 Jan 17:07 users
iBook:/etc/httpd phil$ _
```

Figure 5-13. There's your file, highlighted in orange.

sudo (superuser do) lets you issue the command as the root user. cp is the command for copy, and works like this:

```
cp <original filename> <new filename>
```

> *For a full explanation of* sudo, *open Terminal, type* `man sudo`, *and hit* ENTER.

4. If you run `cd /etc/httpd && ls -Gal`, as shown in step 2 and Figure 5-13, again, you'll see that the date stamp has changed on the `httpfd.conf.bak` file.

With your file backed up, you can now edit it.

For the UNIX beginner, I'd always recommend Pico over Vim as a text editing application, *any* day of the week. It's just easier to use for getting a job done for the first time. If you simply have to flex your geek, use Vim, by all means; otherwise use Pico. If you want the *really* easy option (as I'm going to show you how to use here), download a 30-day trial of BBEdit from `www.barebones.com/products/bbedit`.

Editing the Apache configuration file with BBEdit

1. Open BBEdit.
2. Choose File ➤ Open Hidden.
3. Navigate to `Macintosh HD/etc/httpd/httpd.conf` (see Figure 5-14) and click Open.

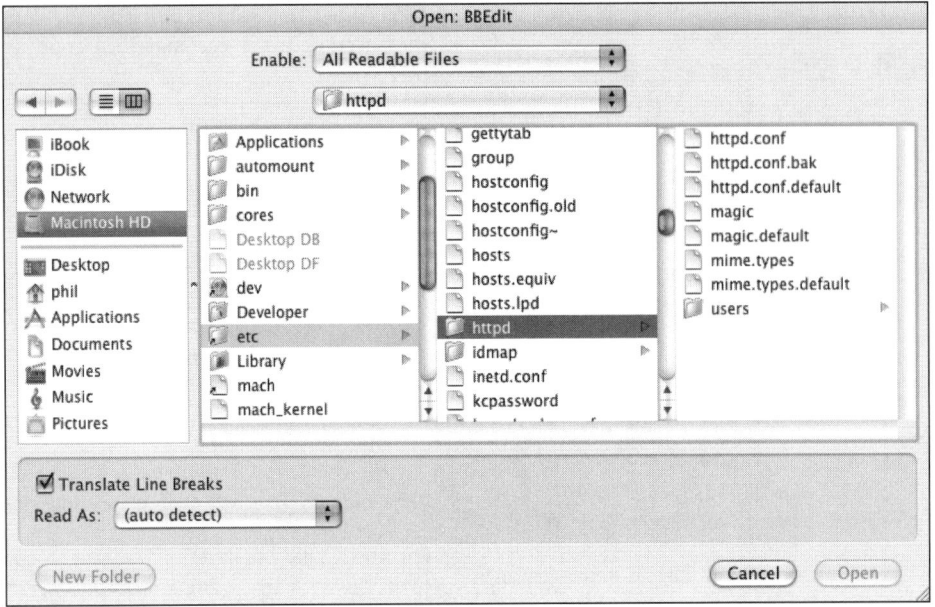

Figure 5-14. Opening a hidden file in BBEdit

---

4. ⌘-click the pencil icon at the top left of the document window, and confirm that you want to unlock the document by clicking Yes (see Figure 5-15).

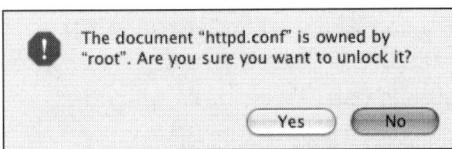

Figure 5-15. Unlocking a document for editing

5. Scroll down to approximately line 239, where you should see the code in Figure 5-16.

6. Lines beginning with a hash (#) are commented out and therefore inactive. You need to use some of them though, so uncomment the php4_module line to make it look like this:

```
#LoadModule perl_module
➥libexec/httpd/libperl.so
LoadModule php4_module
➥libexec/httpd/libphp4.so
LoadModule hfs_apple_module
➥libexec/httpd/mod_hfs_apple.so
LoadModule rendezvous_apple_module
➥ libexec/httpd/mod_rendezvous_apple.so
```

```
238   #LoadModule perl_module          libexec/httpd/libperl.so
239   #LoadModule php4_module          libexec/httpd/libphp4.so
240   LoadModule hfs_apple_module      libexec/httpd/mod_hfs_apple.so
241   LoadModule rendezvous_apple_module libexec/httpd/mod_rendezvous_apple.so
242
243   #   Reconstruction of the complete module list from all available modules
```

Figure 5-16. Scrolling to the end of the LoadModule section

7. Scroll down to approximately line 282, where you should see the code in Figure 5-17.

```
281    #AddModule mod_perl.c
282    #AddModule mod_php4.c
283    AddModule mod_hfs_apple.c
284    AddModule mod_rendezvous_apple.c
```

Figure 5-17. Scrolling to the end of the AddModule section

8. Uncomment the mod_php4.c line so that it looks like this:

#AddModule mod_perl.c
AddModule mod_php4.c
AddModule mod_hfs_apple.c
AddModule mod_rendezvous_apple.c

9. To allow you to run PHP documents from within ~/Sites, locate this block of code at approximately line 422 and uncomment all of the highlighted lines:

```
# Control access to UserDir directories.
➥# The following is an example for a site
➥# where these directories are restricted
➥# to read-only.
#<Directory /Users/*/Sites>
  # AllowOverride FileInfo AuthConfig Limit
  # Options MultiViews Indexes
  ➥SymLinksIfOwnerMatch IncludesNoExec
  # <Limit GET POST OPTIONS PROPFIND>
    # Order allow,deny
    # Allow from all
  # </Limit>
  # <LimitExcept GET POST OPTIONS PROPFIND>
    # Order deny,allow
    # Deny from all
  # </LimitExcept>
#</Directory>
```

That's the PHP part taken care of. Previously, there were a few other things that needed changing in httpd.conf, but Apple kindly configures this document to include those changes now. This means that you don't have to specify index.php as a DirectoryIndex, or AddType the PHP file extension. These changes can be found at the end of the document, roughly between lines 1061–1071.

With PHP configured, you can now pay attention to turning on Server-Side Includes (SSIs), allow use of .htaccess, and tell your server where to find the custom error pages you'll be making later on in this chapter.

10. Scroll to approximately line 390, and add the highlighted code to the last line of the following block:

```
# This may also be "None", "All", or any
➥# combination of "Indexes", "Includes",
➥# "FollowSymLinks", "ExecCGI", or
➥# "MultiViews".
#
# Note that "MultiViews" must be named
➥# *explicitly* --- "Options All" doesn't
➥# give it to you.
#
Options Indexes FollowSymLinks
➥MultiViews ExecCGI +Includes
```

That lets you execute Perl scripts and use SSIs later on, which means you can include dynamic content in your pages, such as the small Perl applications in this chapter.

11. As you'll be using .htaccess files, you need to factor this in, so look for the following code (around line 400) and edit the last line to read as shown here:

```
# This controls which options the
➥.htaccess files in directories can
# override. Can also be "All", or any
➥combination of "Options", "FileInfo",
# "AuthConfig", and "Limit"
#
    AllowOverride All
```

12. Scroll to the following block of code around line 656, and edit the AllowOverride line:

```
# "/Library/WebServer/CGI-Executables"
➥should be changed to whatever your
➥ScriptAliased
# CGI directory exists,
➥if you have that configured.
#
```

(code continues)

```
<Directory
➡"/Library/WebServer/CGI-Executables">
  AllowOverride All
  Options None
  Order allow,deny
  Allow from all
</Directory>
```

Tip: Apache is currently set to execute CGI files when they are in the correct place (/Library/WebServer/CGI-Executables). If you wanted to allow them to be executed anywhere, you would uncomment the next line. This is a potential security risk though, as well as adding strain to your server, so leave this section uncommented for now:

```
# If you want to use server side
➡includes, or CGI outside
# ScriptAliased directories,
➡uncomment the following lines.
#
# To use CGI scripts:
#
#AddHandler cgi-script .cgi
```

13. As you're going to be dealing with SSIs, this means that your files will need to be SHTML documents, so uncomment the .shtml lines highlighted next, found underneath the previous block of code, around line 867:

```
#
# To use server-parsed HTML files
#
AddType text/html .shtml
AddHandler server-parsed .shtml
```

With Perl scripts and SSIs now executable, you'll tell Apache to serve up your own error messages.

14. Apache-generated error messages are boring, so you're going to use a Perl script to lighten yours up a little, and then include that in an SHTML page. You need to tell the server where to find your error documents, so scroll to approximately line 920. You need to uncomment the following highlighted line:

```
# 2) local redirects
#ErrorDocument 404 /missing.html
# to redirect to local URL /missing.html
#ErrorDocument 404
➡/cgi-bin/missing_handler.pl
# N.B.: You can redirect to a script or a
➡document using server-side-includes.
```

15. Once uncommented, add the following three new lines underneath for your other error pages:

```
# 2) local redirects
ErrorDocument 401 /error_docs/401.shtml
ErrorDocument 403 /error_docs/403.shtml
ErrorDocument 404 /error_docs/404.shtml
ErrorDocument 500 /error_docs/500.shtml
# to redirect to local URL /missing.html
#ErrorDocument 404
➡#/cgi-bin/missing_handler.pl
# N.B.: You can redirect to a script or a
➡document using server-side-includes.
```

You've allowed for the four main errors there:

- **401 Unauthorized:** The server is looking for some encryption key from the client and is not getting it, or the wrong password may have been entered.

- **403 Forbidden/Access Denied**: You'll probably see this one before the end of this chapter! This is similar to 401. Special permission is needed to access the site, such as a password and/or user-name if it's a registration issue. At other times, you may not have the proper permissions set up on the server, or you just might not want people to be able to access the site.

- **404 File Not Found**: This most common of errors could be the fault of the user (typing in the wrong address), or your fault by moving files, renaming them, or including a bad link in your code, for example.

- **500 Internal Error**: If there are any errors with your scripts, this error will pop up. If so, check those error logs for a clue as to what the problem is.

16. Save your httpd.conf file, authorizing when asked to do so.

Rebooting Apache

Since you've just made a lot of changes, you have to reboot the web server. Don't worry though, as this can be done without rebooting your machine. You can do this in two ways: via System Preferences or Terminal.

Rebooting via System Preferences

1. Open System Preferences.
2. Click the Sharing icon.
3. Turn Personal Web Sharing off . . . and then back on again (see Figure 5-18).

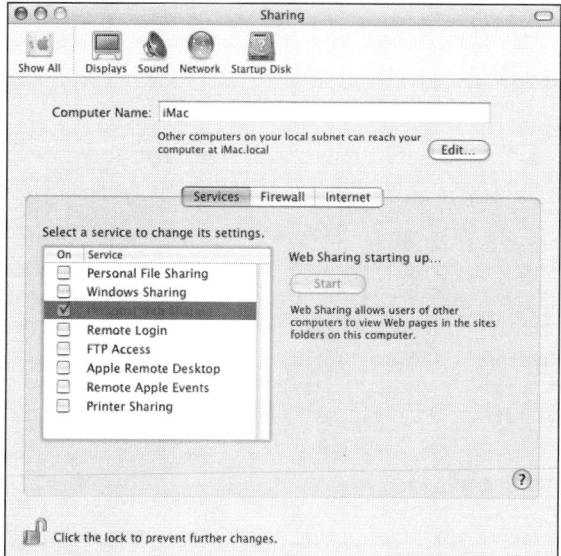

Figure 5-18. Restarting the web server (Apache), via System Preferences

Rebooting via Terminal

1. Open Terminal and type in

   `sudo apachectl restart`

2. Enter your password when prompted and you should see the code shown in Figure 5-19.

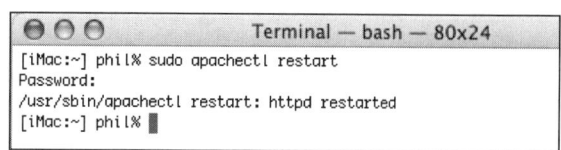

Figure 5-19. Restarting the web server (Apache), via Terminal

Both of these methods do the same thing and the result is exactly the same. Use whichever you feel more comfortable with. Obviously, if you have guests round, use the Terminal to try and look more like a hardcore geek.

Perl or PHP?

You might be wondering why you 're dealing with both Perl and PHP here, rather than one or the other. The answer to this is simple: Just because you have access to both technologies on your Mac, it doesn't mean that you'll always have the same choice in real life. Clients might have their sites hosted on a server with PHP access turned off, but full Perl access, and vice versa. You might need to deal with some simple Perl FormMail or Guestbook scripts for a client, in which case permissions will be an issue you should be aware of. You can never rely on anything when there's a client involved, so once again I shall remind you that it's always good to know a little bit about every technology.

Perl

*"Perl is a language optimized for scanning arbitrary text files, extracting information from those text files, and printing reports based on that information. It's also a good language for many system management tasks. The language is intended to be practical (easy to use, efficient, complete) rather than beautiful (tiny, elegant, minimal)." Taken from Perl's man page (**% man perl**)*

I once saw a dude in a t-shirt with #!/usr/bin/perl written on it. I immediately thought "GEEK!" and wanted one. I didn't know what it meant back then, but I had a feeling it was something I'd be into. Now, of course, I know it's the path to Perl, as found at the top of every Perl script. #! is actually referred to as the "shebang." You got to love that geeky terminology.

> *If your scripts ever end up on a Windows server, you'll have to alter the path to something like this:* #!C:/perl/bin/perl.

Escapology

Perl has commands inside both single and double quotes, so what happens if you need to use quotes? You have to escape them by using a backslash, like this:

```
print "The room was shocked when \"Later,
➥I said!\" came out of his mouth";
```

There are a few of these double-quoted strings, but you'll probably only ever need to know these six:

Construct	Meaning
\n	New line
\r	Return
\t	Tab
\\	Backslash
\'	Single quote
\"	Double quote

You'll now write your first Perl script!

1. Open a new text document, and save it as /Library/WebServer/CGI-Executables/hello.pl.

2. Line 1 specifies the path to Perl, so type

   #!/usr/bin/perl

3. Line 2 gives the program a header line, which specifies the kind of output you're generating. There *must* be a blank line under this line, so specify two line breaks at the end to give it that clear line:

   print "Content-type:text/html\n\n";

4. For line 3, type the following as shown in Figure 5-20:

   print "Hello, Cleveland!\n";

5. Save your file.

6. To view this in your browser, go to http://127.0.0.1/cgi-bin/hello.pl (see Figure 5-21).

Ooops! There's that 403 Error I mentioned back in the section "Editing the Apache configuration file with BBEdit" of this chapter, as well as an additional error, because you haven't actually made your error documents yet. For a script to run properly, it has to have the right permissions. Let's take a look at what that's all about.

File Permissions

With a UNIX system being a multiuser system, every file belongs to a user and a group. The root user can access every file on the system. As a user yourself, you have access to your own files, but not other people's. There are, in fact, 18 different permission classes, which fall into three categories:

- File and directory permissions
- Read, write, and execute permissions
- Owner, group, and public (others) permissions

Figure 5-20. Your first Perl script!

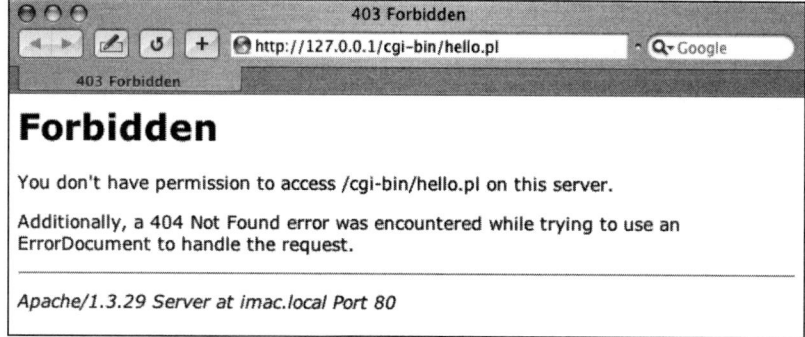

Figure 5-21. Your first Perl error!

You're interested in that middle group. If you run the following command:

```
ls -al /Library/WebServer/
➥CGI-Executables/hello.pl
```

. . . you should see something like the screen in Figure 5-22.

> *Use TAB to auto-complete names, e.g., type /L, hit TAB and /Library will appear. So, all you would have to type to get this line is* ls -al /L *TAB* /W *TAB* /C *TAB* /h *TAB.*

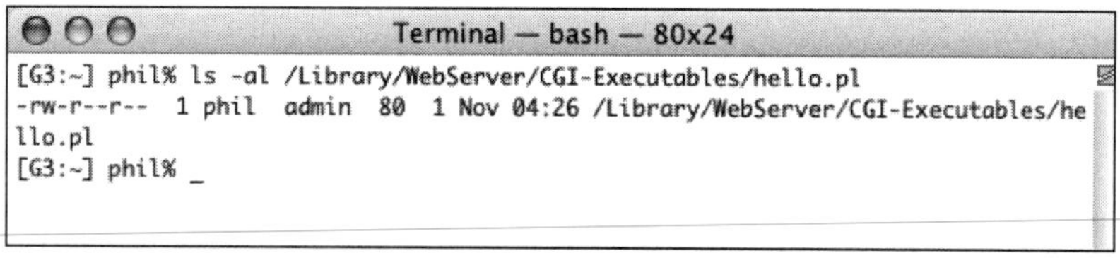

```
000                  Terminal — bash — 80x24
[G3:~] phil% ls -al /Library/WebServer/CGI-Executables/hello.pl
-rw-r--r--  1 phil  admin  80  1 Nov 04:26 /Library/WebServer/CGI-Executables/he
llo.pl
[G3:~] phil% _
```

Figure 5-22. Getting file information from the command line

But what on earth does this mean? Look at the following table, which breaks it down:

Permission	Symbol	Meaning
No permission	-	Permission withheld.
Read	r	Read permission on a file allows access to its contents.
--	--	Read permission on a directory allows the determination of the names and subdirectories (e.g., with ls).
Write	w	Write permission on a file allows change to its contents.
--	--	Write permission on a directory allows change to the contents of that directory by adding or deleting files and subdirectories.
Execute	x	Execute permission on a file allows use of that file as a command.
--	--	Execute permission on a directory allows a search of that directory for a file.

If you examine that listing again, it can be broken down further. -rw-r--r-- can be broken down into -, rw-, r--, and r--, which equate to the following:

- The first symbol tells you that it's a file (a d would signify a directory).
- The first rw- means that the owner (phil) has read and write permissions only.

- The next r-- means that all members of the admin group have read permissions only.
- The last r-- means that the public permissions group has read permissions only.

Field	Description
1	The file only has one link, and is only known as hello.pl.
phil	The file is owned by phil.
admin	The file belongs to the group called admin.
80	The file has 80 bytes.
1 Nov 04:26	The file was last modified when I clearly should have been in bed.
/Library/WebServer/ CGI-Executables/ hello.pl	File name.

You need all three groups to be able to read and execute the file. You own the file, and like the option to write to the file (depending on what the file does). You can now work out the necessary access permissions.

Permission	Numeric Value
-	0
r	4
w	2
x	1

You then add things up like this:

```
rwx = 4 + 2 + 1 = 7
r-x = 4 + 0 + 1 = 5
r-x = 4 + 0 + 1 = 5
```

This gives you 755, so let's get stuck into Terminal and get that script working.

1. To make `hello.pl` work, you need to change its permissions using a command called chmod. Open Terminal and type

cd /Library/WebServer/CGI-Executables

2. Check you can see your file and its permissions as shown in Figure 5-23 with the following:

ls -al

```
000              Terminal — bash — 80x24
[G3:~] phil% cd /Library/WebServer/CGI-Executables
[G3:/Library/WebServer/CGI-Executables] phil% ls -al
total 32
drwxrwxr-x   4 root   admin   136 18 Jan 18:07 .
drwxrwxr-x  10 root   admin   340 18 Jan 18:02 ..
-rw-rw-r--   1 phil   admin  6148 18 Jan 18:07 .DS_Store
-rw-r--r--   1 phil   admin    80  1 Nov 04:26 hello.pl
[G3:/Library/WebServer/CGI-Executables] phil% _
```

Figure 5-23. `hello.pl` has no permission to execute.

3. Change the permissions like so:

chmod 755 hello.pl

4. Check to see the change as shown in Figure 5-24:

ls -al

```
000              Terminal — bash — 80x24
[G3:~] phil% cd /Library/WebServer/CGI-Executables
[G3:/Library/WebServer/CGI-Executables] phil% ls -al
total 32
drwxrwxr-x   4 root   admin   136 18 Jan 18:07 .
drwxrwxr-x  10 root   admin   340 18 Jan 18:02 ..
-rw-rw-r--   1 phil   admin  6148 18 Jan 18:07 .DS_Store
-rw-r--r--   1 phil   admin    80  1 Nov 04:26 hello.pl
[G3:/Library/WebServer/CGI-Executables] phil% chmod 755 hello.pl
[G3:/Library/WebServer/CGI-Executables] phil% ls -al
total 32
drwxrwxr-x   4 root   admin   136 18 Jan 18:07 .
drwxrwxr-x  10 root   admin   340 18 Jan 18:02 ..
-rw-rw-r--   1 phil   admin  6148 18 Jan 18:07 .DS_Store
-rwxr-xr-x   1 phil   admin    80  1 Nov 04:26 hello.pl
[G3:/Library/WebServer/CGI-Executables] phil% _
```

Figure 5-24. You can now execute `hello.pl`.

5. Okay, try running `hello.pl` in your browser, as shown in Figure 5-25, and it should dazzle you with a greeting!

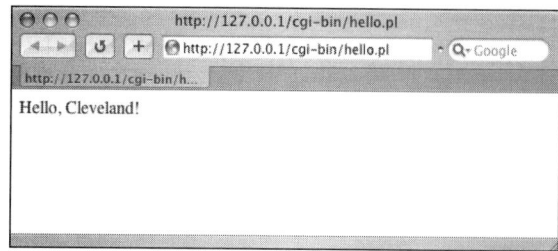

Figure 5-25. Success! The script now works, thanks to the correct permissions.

Phew! And that was the easy version of the script. Here's another (more technically correct) way you could do that:

1. Open a new text document, and save it as /Library/WebServer/CGI-Executables/ hello_proper.pl.

2. Line 1 specifies the path to Perl, so type

#!/usr/bin/perl -wT

You'll notice that something has been added here: -wT. They're called **switches**, and are there to help. This is what they mean:

- -w turns on warnings, and you should always use this switch.

- -T turns on **Taint checking**. With this on, Perl assumes that all data entering the program from outside of itself is tainted. If Perl uses this tainted data to perform any actions that it considers dangerous, it will kill the script. Safe!

For some more information about Perl, open Terminal and type man perl.

3. Line 2 instructs Perl to use the `strict.pm` module, which doesn't stand for any messing about whatsoever. If it considers anything unsafe at all, it shuts you down. Type in

use strict;

4. Line 3 uses CGI.pm, an important module that is part of the standard Perl distribution. There is an awful lot you can do with it, and it can save you lots of time; but there are whole books devoted to CGI.pm, which should give you an idea of how involved the subject matter is. Type the following:

```
use CGI qw(header);
```

5. On line 4, you'll create a new CGI object to access various properties of the CGI module. You can use any variable name you like, as long as you stick to it. In the following example, you use $query as your variable name, all the way through the script:

```
my $query = CGI::->new();
```

6. On the next line, type in the header info you need for the web browser:

```
print $query ->header("text/html"),
```

7. Type in the following lines to give you a page title, background color, and text color:

```
$query ->start_html(-title =>
➡"My first Perl Script", -bgcolor =>
➡"#000",
  -text => "fff",
  ),
```

8. There isn't much on the page yet. It could do with some text, so remedy that by typing the following:

```
$query ->h1("Hello, Cleveland!"),
$query ->p("Rock'n'Roll! Rock And Roll!"),
```

9. To close things up, type

```
$query ->end_html;
```

Figure 5-26 shows what your finished code should look like.

10. Save the file, give the file the correct permissions (chmod 755 as you did before—see Figure 5-27).

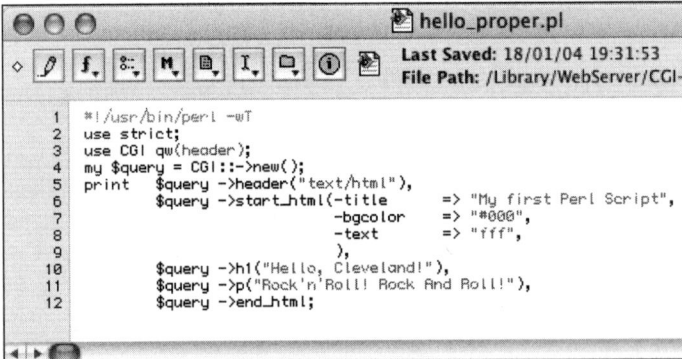

Figure 5-26. A nicely aligned script is easy to read.

```
[G3:/Library/WebServer/CGI-Executables] phil% ls -al
total 48
drwxrwxr-x  5 root  admin   170 18 Jan 18:36 .
drwxrwxr-x 10 root  admin   340 18 Jan 18:02 ..
-rw-rw-r--  1 phil  admin  6148 18 Jan 18:07 .DS_Store
-rwxr-xr-x  1 phil  admin    80  1 Nov 04:26 hello.pl
-rw-r--r--  1 phil  admin   319 18 Jan 18:40 hello_proper.pl
[G3:/Library/WebServer/CGI-Executables] phil% chmod 755 hello_proper.pl
[G3:/Library/WebServer/CGI-Executables] phil% _
```

Figure 5-27. Changing the permissions with chmod

11. Test in your browser as shown in Figure 5-28, and reel in amazement at what you've done.

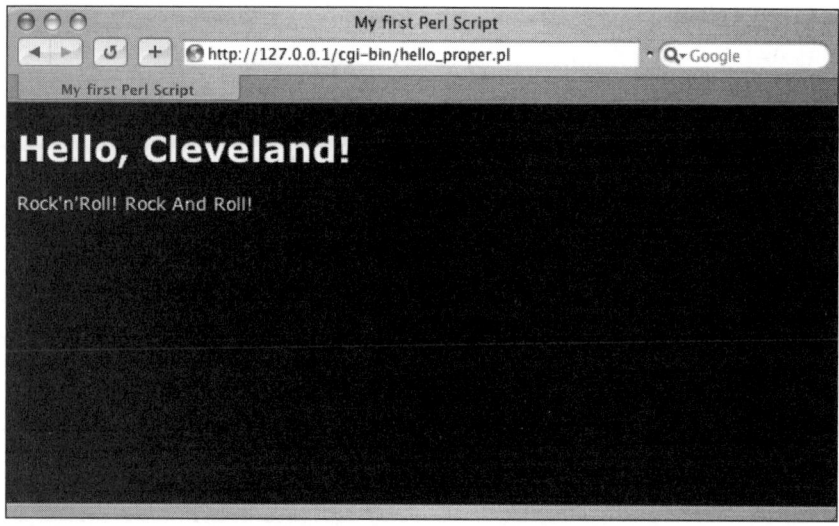

Figure 5-28. More awesome output from your new Perl skills

Random Text

Now that you've set the Perl world on fire with your amazing program, it's time to do something that's more worthwhile. You're going to write a small script to display a random line of text each time the script loads.

1. Open a new text document and save it as /Library/WebServer/CGI-Executables/error.pl.

2. Start with the path and header, as usual.

```
#!/usr/bin/perl -wT
use strict;
use CGI qw(header);
```

3. Print the HTTP header telling the client that plain text follows, and then append a new line to tell the client that the header has ended and content follows.

```
print header("text/plain") . "\n";
```

Use "\n"; to leave a blank line under this header line.

4. You're going to be pulling quotes from another file, so you need to let the script know where that file is (you'll create this file in the next exercise).

```
my $sigfile = '/Library/WebServer
➥/CGI-Executables/random.txt';
```

You have your list of error messages ($sigfile), but you need a way of reading those messages into your program. You do this using something called a **filehandle** (www.perldoc.com/perl5.8.0/lib/FileHandle.html). With the open function, you initialize a filehandle called FILE by associating it with your messages file ($sigfile).

5. Open filehandle to $sigfile and call it FILE (filehandles are generally uppercase).

```
open(FILE, $sigfile);
```

6. The quotes file is really just a text file full of quotes, separated by a field-separator. In this example, use %% as the field-separator as follows:

```
$/ = "%%";
```

7. Create and initialize the variable for holding your line of text by typing

```
my $q = '';
```

8. Iterate over the quote file and choose a line at random.

```
while(<FILE>){
  $q = $_ if(rand($.) < 1);
}
```

9. Each quote in the list will have a line break at the end, so you use the chomp function to get rid of that.

```
chomp($q);
```

10. Lastly, you want to print the actual quote in the browser window and finish the program (see Figure 5-29).

```
print $q;
```

11. Save the file, and then change the permissions by running chmod in Terminal.

```
chmod 755 /Library/WebServer/
➥CGI-Executables/error.pl
```

That's the script taken care of, but it's about as much use as a chocolate teapot without your list of quotes. Let's take care of that now.

Quirky quotes time

1. Open a new document, and save it as /Library/WebServer/CGI-Executables/random.txt.

2. You've already set your field-separator (also referred to as a **delimiter**) as %%, so that is going between each line, as shown in Figure 5-30 (feel free to add your own brand of humor as the random text).

You can spread your error messages over as many lines as you like, as long as you start each message with the delimiter.

3. Save your file.

4. You should now be able to call up http://127.0.0.1/cgi-bin/error.pl and see a random quote every time you reload the page. Obviously, the more quotes you have, the more random it will seem.

```
1   #!/usr/bin/perl -wT
2   use strict;
3   use CGI qw(header);
4
5   print header("text/plain") . "\n";
6
7   my $sigfile = '/Library/WebServer/CGI-Executables/random.txt';
8
9   open(FILE, $sigfile);
10
11  $/ = "%%";
12
13  my $q = '';
14
15  while(<FILE>){
16    $q = $_ if(rand($.) < 1);
17  }
18
19  chomp($q);
20  print $q;
21
```

Figure 5-29. The completed script

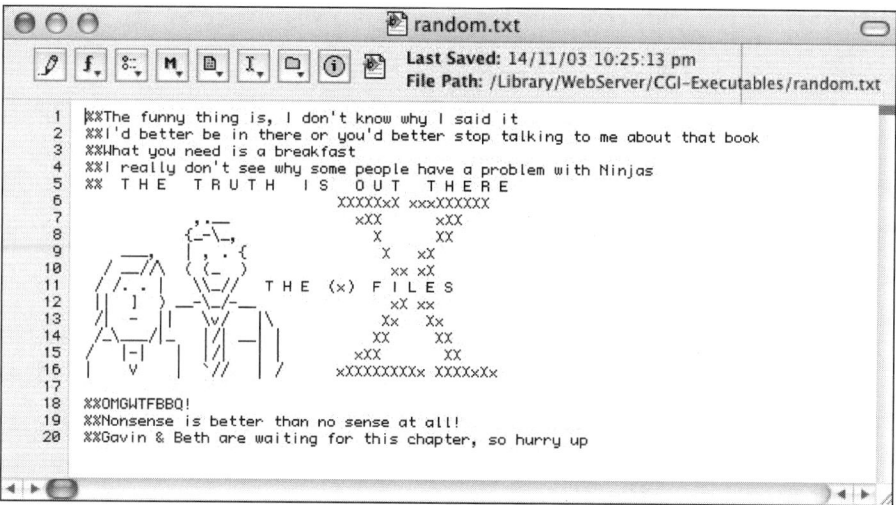

Figure 5-30. Error Page message text shouldn't be boring!

Security

While your file works, there are holes to be exploited. It's good practice to escape any special characters that might appear in the $sigfile document (random.txt). For example, if the $sigfile had a line that said

```
<!-#EXEC "rm -rf /"->
```

(which would execute the command to wipe the drive), then it wouldn't be a good idea to stick that in an HTML page without first escaping it. You can use the function in HTML::Entities called encode_entities() to help you out here by adding the following line of code:

```
use CGI qw(header);
use HTML::Entities qw(encode_entities);
print header("text/plain")
```

and then assign the data back, like this:

```
chomp($q);
$q = encode_entities($q);
print $q;
```

If you do that before printing $q, it'll be nice and safe. However, this safety net isn't automatically available to you in a standard Mac OS X installation. You need a Perl module called Entities.pm, which is part of the HTML::Parser bundle that's usually part of a default UNIX distribution. It's essential for doing CGI or web client coding. Don't panic though! The next chapter explains all about this, and you'll learn how to install these modules in two ways (assuming you've installed the Xcode CD, which was in the OS X box).

Server-Side Includes (SSI)

I mentioned these a few times in the configuration section but what are they? They're an easy way of including other content in your HTML document. Maybe you have a section of code that you want on every page of your site, but they change often. Using a quick SSI, you can just add one line of code to all those pages, and then you only have one document to update. A daily news feature is an example of this, which you would include like so:

```
<!-#include file="news.txt" ->
```

All you or your client then has to do is edit the news.txt file on a daily basis, and each page will parse it (read the file and act on its instructions), including it in the page it serves up to the user.

Another SSI example could be part of a program that lives on the server. That program could be a Perl script of only a few lines long. It could be a lot of PHP. It could be server variables. Whatever it is, you can easily include it with one line of code, similar to the previous example. For instance, if a Perl script automates your news, you would include it like this:

```
<!–#include virtual="/cgi-bin/news.pl" –>
```

> You can also use <!–#exec cgi="/cgi-bin/news.pl"–> on some servers, but this is seen as a security risk by some, and isn't always allowed.

As long as the document is saved as SHTML, you should see the results and not an error. Let's make those error pages, so you can see this in action.

Error pages

1. Open a new document and save it as /Library/WebServer/CGI-Executables/error_docs/404.shtml.

2. Start with a basic HTML page and some basic 404 Error text, which you can make all fancy and compliant once you know things work.

```
<html>
<head>
<title>404: doh!</title>
</head>
<body>
<h1>404 error</h1>
<p>The file doesn't exist, or has been
➥moved</p>
</body>
</html>
```

3. Now you need to add the code that does the work.

```
<body>
<h1>404 error</h1>
<p>The file doesn't exist, or has been
➥moved</p>
<pre><!–#exec cgi=
➥"../cgi-bin/error.pl"–></pre>
</body>
```

This includes the error.pl script you made earlier, which will insert a random line of text for you. Note that you're using the <pre> tag there, in case any of the random messages are ASCII art (like the X-Files example earlier and in Figure 5-31).

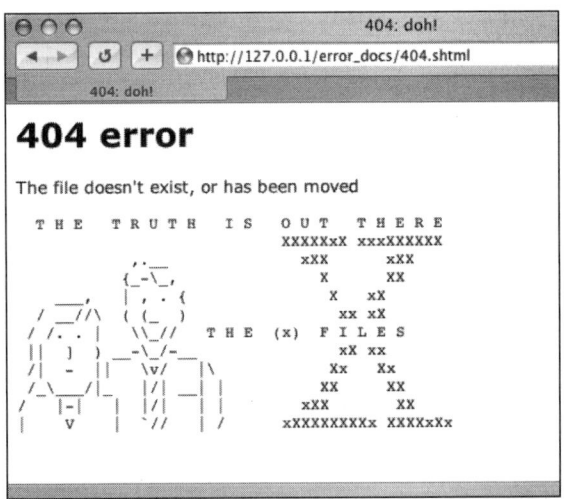

Figure 5-31. Without the <pre> tag, this would look messy.

4. To be a bit more user friendly, you can provide a back button to allow users to get back to the previous page (see Figure 5-32). They already have one on their browser, sure, but it's a nice touch though. Here's how:

```
<p>The file doesn't exist, or has been
➥moved</p>
<p>Please try again from <a href=
➥"<!–#echo var="HTTP_REFERER"–>">the
➥referring url</a></p>
<pre><!–#exec cgi=
➥"../cgi-bin/error.pl"–></pre>
```

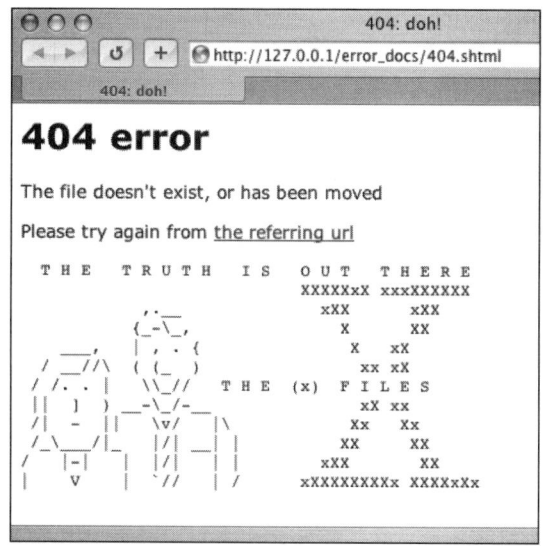

Figure 5-32. The same page, but with referring link

Other environment variables

There are a few more of these environment variables to take a look at, so play around and see what they do. Here's a list:

AUTH_TYPE	Client authorization method, if any.
CONTENT_LENGTH	Size of input posted from client.
CONTENT_TYPE	MIME type of content.
DATE_GMT	The current GMT (Greenwich mean time, UK). Can be formatted using #config.
DATE_LOCAL	The current time/date. Can be formatted using #config.
DOCUMENT_NAME	Document name that was requested.
DOCUMENT_URL	Uniform Resource Locator (URL) of the document.

(continued)

LAST_MODIFIED	Document modified date. Can be formatted using #config.
PAGE_COUNT	Number of accesses to current document since server was brought online.
HTTP_REFERER	URL of the document the client came from.
REMOTE_ADDR	Numeric IP address of the client.
REMOTE_HOST	Domain name of the client (DNS option must be active on server).
REMOTE_USER	ID of user, rarely ever found.
REQUEST_METHOD	HTTP method: GET or POST.
SERVER_NAME	Server hostname (e.g., www.friendsofed.com).
SERVER_PORT	The port used by httpd (80, by default).
SERVER_PROTOCOL	Version of httpd compliance.
SERVER_SOFTWARE	The name of the server software, (e.g., apache 1.2.8).
TOTAL_HITS	Total pages served by server since it was brought online.

For more info on SSIs, check out the Apache manual, which lives on your Mac at http://127.0.0.1/manual/howto/ssi.html.

PHP

PHP is much easier to use if you're familiar with HTML, as you can just drop snippets into your HTML pages. You can still do amazingly complex and powerful things with it, but for the beginner, it's pretty easy to get the hang of things. Whereas Perl scripts need the path to Perl at their start, PHP doesn't.

You merely have to tell the document where your PHP code starts and finishes. You do that like this:

- <?php starts the code.
- ?> ends the code.

You can even reduce that to <? [code here] ?> and it will still work fine, but some servers seem to demand that things are done correctly, so keep this in mind if you get unexpected errors.

Testing PHP

First of all, you need to test that you did actually get PHP working before, when you edited that big configuration file.

1. Create a new file called info.php and save it as ~/Sites/username/book/05/info.php.

2. Add this simple line of code:

   ```
   <? phpinfo(); ?>
   ```

3. Save your file and then open the page in your browser: http://127.0.0.1/~username/book/05/info.php.

Unless something went astray during the configuration section, you should be able to see a screen like the one in Figure 5-33.

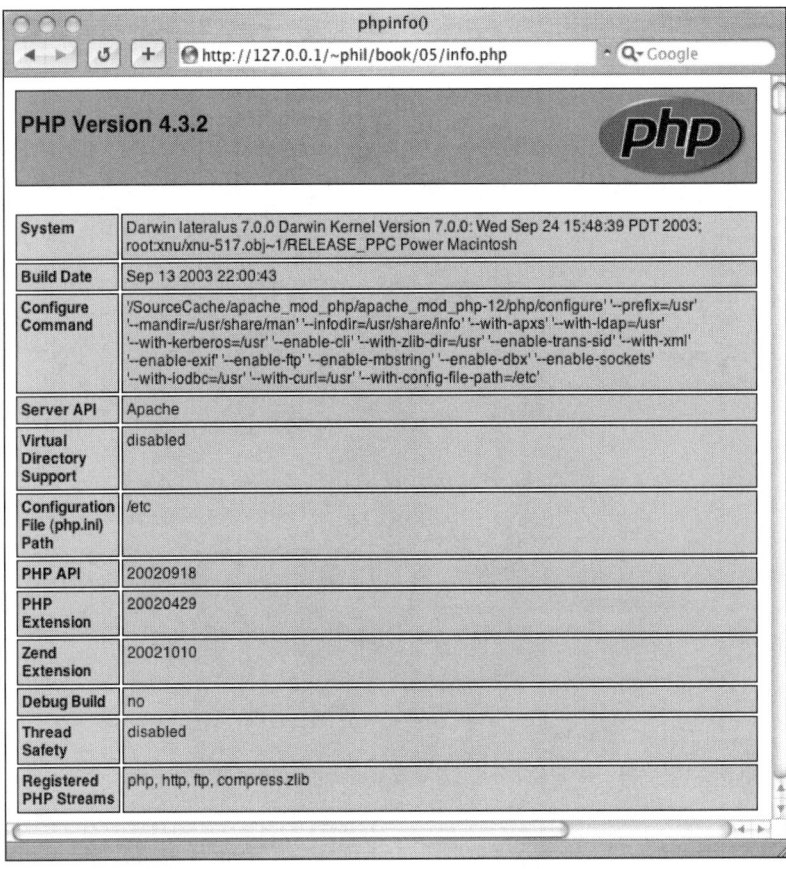

Figure 5-33. PHPINFO gives you a lot of information about the system.

Hello, Cleveland!

Yes folks, it's "Hello, Cleveland!" time again! This time you're dealing with the far easier PHP method.

1. Create a new document and save it as ~/Sites/username/book/05/hello.php.

2. Type in the following content:

```
<html>
<head>
<title>PHP Test</title>
</head>
<body>
<?
echo "<p>Hello, Cleveland!</p>\n";
?>
</body>
</html>
```

You're opening your PHP code and using the echo construct to print whatever is inside the quotes to the screen. To keep the outputted code tidy, you close the line with a break in the same way as you did in Perl. Lastly, you close the code.

3. Save the file and then open the page in your browser (http://127.0.0.1/~username/book/05/hello.php).

If all goes well, you should just see "Hello Cleveland" in the browser window, as shown in Figure 5-34.

4. However, if you view the source, all you'll see is this:

```
<html>
<head>
<title>PHP Test</title>
</head>
<body>
<p>Hello, Cleveland!</p>
</body>
</html>
```

Fantastic. Not only does it work, but it also doesn't show people how you coded it. When you eventually start to write your own scripts, you might want to keep your code to yourself. Okay, let's add more!

5. That was pretty basic, so let's expand on that by adding a server variable to the code and make it look like you're spying on the user. Replace the existing line of PHP with the following new code:

```
<html>
<head>
<title>PHP Test</title>
</head>
<body>
<?
echo "<p>Hello, Cleveland!</p>\n";
echo "You are using " . $_SERVER
➥["HTTP_USER_AGENT"] . "\n";
?>
</body>
</html>
```

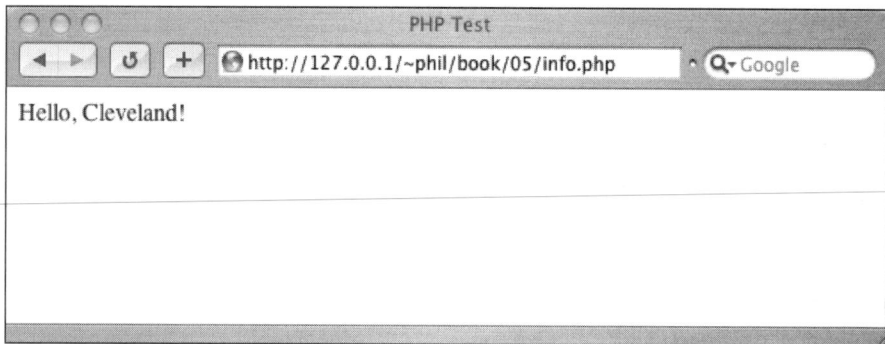

Figure 5-34. It looks just like the Perl version.

6. Save your file, and then reload the page in your browser.

The added line starts echoing your new output, but then you've told it to insert a variable in there. The echo statement is split on either side of that variable, joined together with a period (.) before and after. Each browser identifies itself to the server by a particular User Agent (see Figure 5-35). You just grabbed that variable and echoed it to the page. Neat, eh?

Using the mail() function to send error messages

A really neat feature of PHP is its built-in mail feature. With Perl, you need to send your data to a mail script, which processes the data; with PHP, you use the `mail()` function. Using this function, it's this easy to send mail:

```
mail("name@domain.com", "Subject Line",
➥"Line 1\nLine 2\nLine 3");
```

Let's go back to that dynamic error page and see how to use that example here. You had some server variables in there, which you could get the user to mail to you. However, that still involved user interaction. With PHP, you can have those details e-mailed to the webmaster as soon as that error page loads up.

Setting up Postfix

Previous versions of Mac OS X used Sendmail as the mail server application. This is as time-honored a server application as Apache. However, with the 10.3 release of Mac OS X, Apple has switched to **Postfix** (www.postfix.com). As with Sendmail before it, and the other server applications you've had to configure, Postfix is disabled by default. Luckily for us, Bernard Teo has written an application called **Postfix Enabler** (www.roadstead.com/weblog/Tutorials/PostfixEnabler.html), which does exactly what it says on the tin: enables Postfix. To enable Postfix manually would require configuring a lot of code by hand and gets quite messy. With this Enabler, it's a simple case of filling in some info, pointing, and clicking. Here's how:

1. Download Postfix Enabler from the preceding address, unpack the file, and double-click the application icon.

2. Enter your password when asked to do so (see Figure 5-36).

3. Fill in the domain you are sending mail from, as well as your ISP's mail server details, if you are required to go through that, as shown in Figure 5-37 (otherwise, leave them blank).

4. Hit the Enable Postfix button and watch things happen in the activity log (see Figure 5-38).

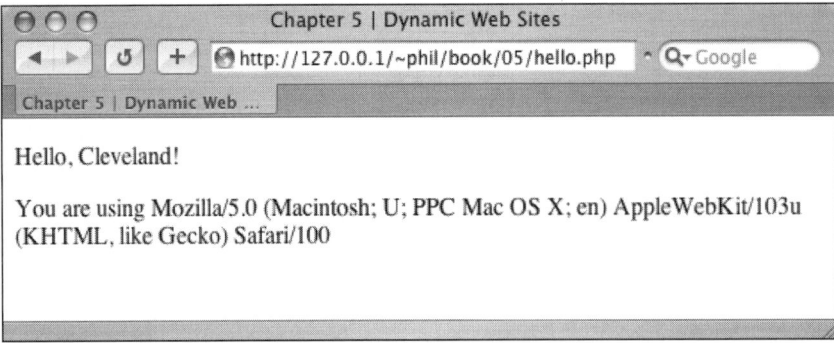

Figure 5-35. Displaying the browser's User Agent

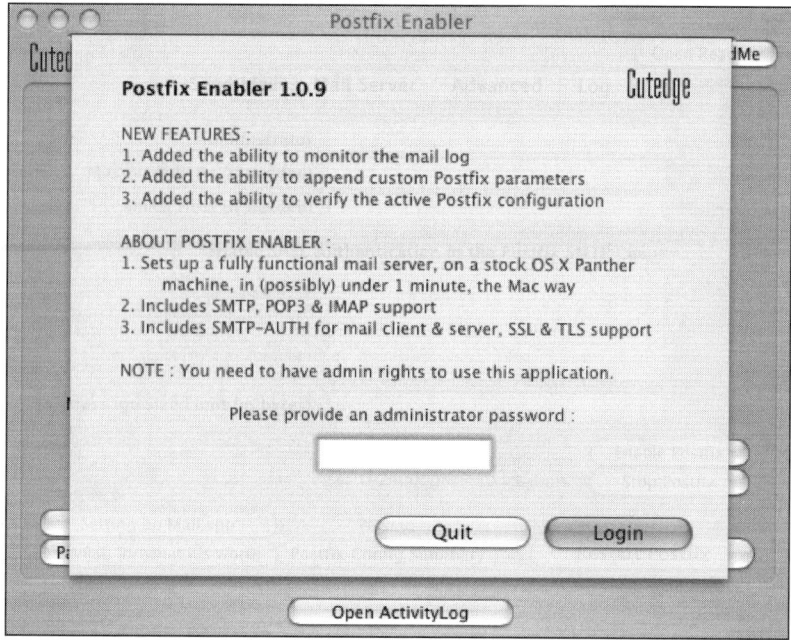

Figure 5-36. Authenticating Postfix Enabler for use

Figure 5-37. Setting up the domain details in Postfix Enabler

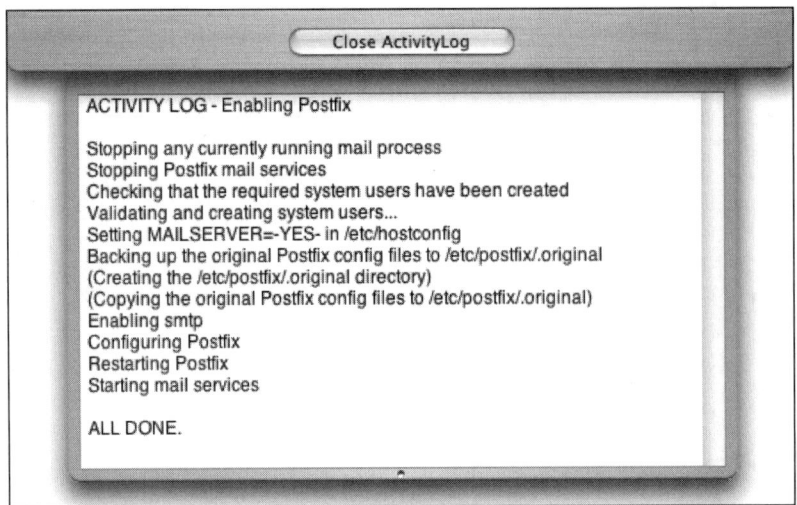

Figure 5-38. The Activity Log lets you know what it has done.

Next, you set up Mail to deal with your new settings, to make sure things work.

5. Open Mail's Preferences from the File menu (or ⌘+,), select the Accounts tab, and click the + at the bottom left to create a new mail account. As you can see in Figure 5-39, I've used the same domain that I filled in during step 3.

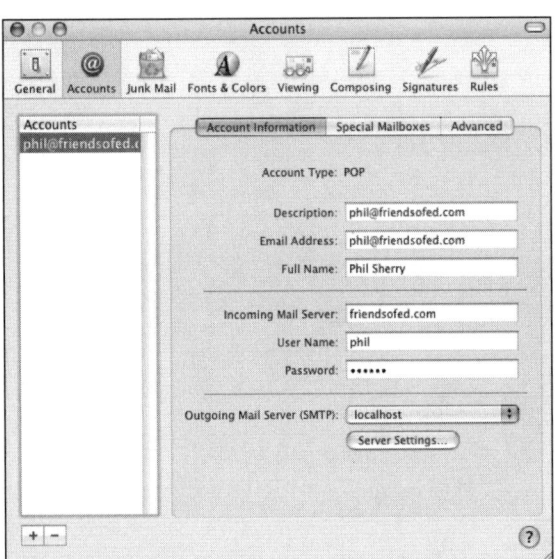

Figure 5-39. Setting up Mail.app to send mail

6. In the Outgoing Mail Server (SMTP) section, select Add Server from the drop-down menu and fill in localhost as the Outgoing Mail Server, as shown in Figure 5-40. If you filled in any ISP settings in step 3, and require authentication settings, fill those in too.

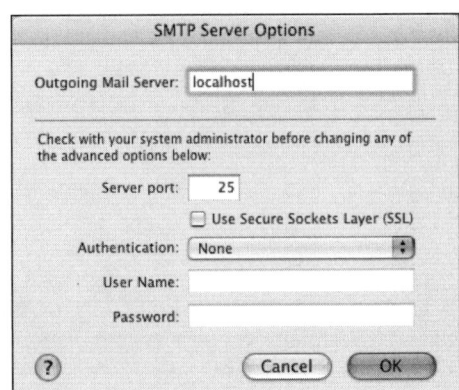

Figure 5-40. SMTP = Simple Mail Transfer Protocol

Fill all that in and the settings will be saved (closing the Accounts window will bring up a dialog box that asks you if you want to save—click Yes).

7. Open a new e-mail (⌘+N) from the new account, and send yourself a test e-mail. If everything went according to plan, you should get it when you check the account you sent it to.

Postfix Enabler has many more settings, including POP3 settings (POP stands for Post Office Protocol, for receiving mail). As this part of the tutorial is only dealing with sending mail, I won't be covering those other settings here.

How to get 404 reports e-mailed automatically

Now that you have Postfix sending e-mail from your Mac, this next exercise will show you how you can have error reports sent by your 404 page.

1. Start a new document and save it as /Library/WebServer/Documents/error_docs/404.php.

2. You're going to declare some variables so you need to open a block of PHP code as follows:

```
<?
```

3. Okay, knowing what time the error occurred is often useful. Maybe someone else was working on those files at a certain time. This might help you pinpoint who is to blame:

```
<?
$timeused = date ("Y-m-d H:i:s" ,time ());
```

Breaking this down, you're declaring a variable ($timeused), then using PHP's date function to give you year-month-day hours:minutes:seconds. You can alter this if you want. Just look up the date function on the PHP site (www.php.net/date).

4. Now specify whom the e-mail is from. In this case, it's from a machine, so let's give it a nerdy name:

```
<?
$timeused = date ("Y-m-d H:i:s" ,time ());
$mailFrom = "From: TRON
➥<admin@freakindesign.com>";
```

5. This is the mail recipient, which is usually whoever looks after the site.

```
<?
$timeused = date ("Y-m-d H:i:s" ,time ());
$mailFrom = "From: TRON
➥<admin@freakindesign.com>";
$mailTo = "webmaster@freakindesign.com";
```

6. An e-mail also needs a real subject line, otherwise it could end up in the junk mail.

```
<?
$timeused = date ("Y-m-d H:i:s" ,time ());
$mailFrom = "From: TRON
➥<admin@freakindesign.com>";
$mailTo = "webmaster@freakindesign.com";
$mailSubject =
➥"404 report from freakindesign.com";
```

7. Next, you need the body of the actual message, complete with some of those server environment variables you met before.

```
<?
...
$mailTo = "webmaster@freakindesign.com";
$mailSubject =
➥"404 report from freakindesign.com";
$mailMessage = "IP: " .
➥$_SERVER["REMOTE_ADDR"] . "\n
Referrer: " .
➥$_SERVER["HTTP_REFERER"] . "\n

Date: $timeused\n
Browser: " .
➥$_SERVER["HTTP_USER_AGENT"] . "\n
\n
THAT IS ALL\n";
```

8. This is the part that actually sends the mail, using the mail() function. Also close your PHP code.

```
<?
...
THAT IS ALL\n";
mail($mailTo, $mailSubject, $mailMessage,
➥$mailFrom);
?>
```

9. Immediately after the PHP code, the rest of the page can be the same as the previous example (see Figure 5-41). You could add something to tell them that you've been alerted to the error, like this:

```
<?
...
mail($mailTo, $mailSubject, $mailMessage,
➥$mailFrom);
?>
<html>
<head>
<title>404: doh!</title>
</head>
<body>
<h1>404 error</h1>
<p>The file doesn't exist, or has been
➥moved</p>
<p>a report has been sent to the
➥webmaster, thanks</p>
</body>
</html>
```

10. If you plan on making and using PHP documents as your error pages, don't forget that you need to specify so on the httpd.conf, in this section:

```
# 2) local redirects
ErrorDocument 401 /error_docs/401.shtml
ErrorDocument 403 /error_docs/403.shtml
ErrorDocument 404 /error_docs/404.shtml
ErrorDocument 500 /error_docs/500.shtml
```

Change the preceding code to this:

```
# 2) local redirects
ErrorDocument 401 /error_docs/401.php
ErrorDocument 403 /error_docs/403.php
ErrorDocument 404 /error_docs/404.php
ErrorDocument 500 /error_docs/500.php
```

Let's take a look at coding this into a page now.

```
                                           404.php

      Last Saved: 22/01/04 17:43:52
      File Path: ~/Projects/friends...ror_docs/404.php

 1    <?
 2    $timeused = date ("Y-m-d H:i:s" ,time ());
 3    $mailFrom = "From: TRON <admin@funkydomain.com>";
 4    $mailTo = "webmaster@funkydomain.com";
 5    $mailSubject = "404 report from funkydomain.com";
 6    $mailMessage = "IP: " . $_SERVER["REMOTE_ADDR"] . "\n\n
 7    Referrer: " . $_SERVER["HTTP_REFERER"] . "\n\n
 8    Date: $timeused\n\n
 9    Browser: " . $_SERVER["HTTP_USER_AGENT"] . "\n\n
10    \n\n
11    THAT IS ALL\n";
12    mail($mailTo, $mailSubject, $mailMessage, $mailFrom);
13    ?>
14    <html>
15    <head>
16    <title>404: doh!</title>
17    </head>
18    <body>
19    <h1>404 error</h1>
20    <p>The file doesn't exist, or has been moved</p>
21    <p>a report has been sent to the webmaster, thanks</p>
22    </body>
23    </html>
24

 12  1
```

Figure 5-41. The finished document

Contact form

Error documents are all very well, but it's not exactly proper content, is it? After you have your new site online, it would be nice to know what visitors think of it. Most websites have some kind of communication form on them these days. You can use your new mail() function knowledge to create something similar for your site.

The basis for a contact form is simple: The visitor fills in some fields on a form, and then clicks a Submit button, which sends their data to, in this case, PHP's mail() function on the web server. The data gets processed, and then sent back to the specified location (usually an e-mail address or a database). Meanwhile, the visitor has been directed to a nice "Thank You" page.

Typically, this would involve visitors going to contact.php, where they click Submit to send the data to form.php for processing, while directing the visitor to thanks.php. That's three documents on your web server. Three documents are still three documents though, however you look at it. Why do it with three, when you can do it with one?

Starting from the example page you made in Chapter 3, you're going to turn that into a dynamic contact form, which will allow visitors to give you some feedback. This one page will have three sections to it:

- The main form to gather the data
- A Thanks section, which actually sends the data too
- An error section, to catch any errors

To do this, you're going to use two statements: if and elseif, which go like this:

```
if ("condition") {
  echo "one thing";
} elseif ("other_condition") {
  echo "other thing";
} elseif ("another_condition") {
  echo "another thing";
}
```

All you're saying here is "If a condition is met, do one thing. If the other condition is met, do the other thing, or else another thing will happen." This example is along the lines of

```
if ("page_is_called") {
  echo "contact form";
} elseif ("form_has_been_submitted") {
  echo "thank you (and send mail)";
} elseif ("NOT page_is_called AND NOT
➡form_has_been_submitted") {
  echo "error message";
}
```

Let's break that apart a bit. Your page is going to be called contact.php, and that is how users will call the page up in their browser. To invoke the other sections, you'll be using something call a "query string," which I'm sure you will have seen before even if you didn't know what it was called. A query string looks like this: contact.php?id=sent (webpage.php?variable_name= variable_value) and usually calls up a specific section of the document that has been coded in (like in this example), or it will pull certain dynamic data from a database. So, you're going to put some PHP code into the content section of your Chapter 3 example page, as follows:

```
if (empty($_GET["id"])) {
/* print the contact form to screen */
} elseif ($_GET["id"] == "sent") {
/* say Thank You and send the data */
}
elseif ((!empty($_GET["id"])) &&
➡($_GET["id"] != "sent")) {
/* print an error message to screen */
}
```

The first line checks to see if the id variable is empty and, if so, prints your contact form. Both contact.php and contact.php?id= are considered empty, so you'll use this to display your form, in order to have a nice tidy URL.

The first `elseif` statement prints your "Thank You" message, and sends the data if the query string variable is equal to (`==`) sent. So, if the URL is contact.php?id=sent, the users' data is sent to you and they see your nice "Thank You" message.

The final `elseif` statement is a bit more complex, and uses characters called **operators**. The first section introduces the logical operator `!`, which means NOT. Next up, you have the `&&` logical operator, which means AND. Finally, you have the comparison operator `!=`, which means NOT EQUAL. If you now look at that line in plain English, it reads as follows:

```
elseif ((id is NOT empty) AND
➡(id is NOT EQUAL TO "sent"))
/* print an error message to screen */
```

This will print your error message to screen, only if the id variable is not empty or not sent. In other words, anything at all, other than those two conditions, will result in an error message.

> *When coding PHP, it's always best to check the actual code works first before adding your real content. Just use some placeholder text until you're satisfied that it works, and then add your real content piece by piece. This can also help locate any bugs that might creep in.*

Stripped-down version

Now you know the basics of how this will work, you'll start coding.

1. Open a new HTML document in BBEdit (File ➤ New ➤ HTML Document), give it the title, and you'll code the stripped-down version, ready to add content to later on. Save this in your Chapter 5 folder, calling it `~/Sites/book/05/contact-stripped.php` (see Figure 5-42).

2. Place the following code between the `<body>` tags:

```
<body>
<?
if (empty($_GET["id"])) {
?>
</body>
```

This opens a section of PHP code, and then starts your `if` statement to determine if the `id` variable is empty, before closing the PHP tags again. You could just use the echo statement to print your output to screen at this point, staying within the PHP tags but this would mean having to escape certain characters (such as quotes, as discussed earlier in this chapter), which is a pain. It's just as easy to close the PHP tag, and then get on with some normal HTML code.

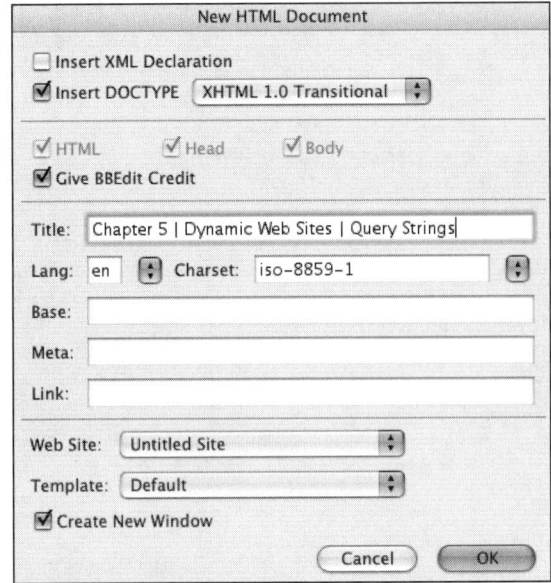

Figure 5-42. Opening a new HTML document in BBEdit

Following on from that, you need some output if the variable is empty. Typically, this is something descriptive, so you could just type empty, and move on through the code. As you're going to be testing three states altogether, you may as well give yourself an easy way of navigating through all three states.

3. The easiest way to do this is to make your placeholder word into a hyperlink to the next state of the test as follows:

```
<body>
<?
if (empty($_GET["id"])) {
?>
<p><a href="?id=sent">empty</a></p>
</body>
```

When the page is called now, you'll have a link to take you through to contact-stripped.php?id=sent, which is the next stage of the page.

4. Immediately after, you opening your PHP tags again and close the statement from step 2 by closing the curly brackets. With an elseif statement, you determine whether the id variable is equal to sent.

```
<body>
<?
if (empty($_GET["id"])) {
?>
<p><a href="?id=sent">empty</a></p>
<?php
} elseif ($_GET["id"] == "sent") {
?>
</body>
```

5. As in step 3, you're just using some placeholder text and linking it up to test the final stage.

```
...
<?php
} elseif ($_GET["id"] == "sent") {
?>
<p><a href="?id=nonsense">sent</a></p>
</body>
```

Here, you'll notice I've used nonsense as the variable name. Obviously, this can be absolutely anything you like, apart from sent, which is the whole idea of this part: to catch anything other than an empty variable or sent.

6. The next line is the slightly more complex code, discussed earlier:

```
...
?>
<p><a href="?id=nonsense">sent</a></p>
<?php }
elseif ((!empty($_GET["id"])) &&
➥($_GET["id"] != "sent")) {
?>
</body>
```

Once again, this should act as a catchall. You should only see this page if the variable is empty or not sent.

7. Your placeholder content for this section doesn't need to be linked to anything, so plain text will do just fine.

```
...
<?php }
elseif ((!empty($_GET["id"])) &&
➥($_GET["id"] != "sent")) {
?>
<p>error</p>
</body>
```

8. The last thing you need to do is open a last set of PHP tags in order to close the curly brackets from the last statement.

```
,,,
?>
<p>error</p>
<? } ?>
</body>
```

With all that done, your final code for the stripped-down version should look like what you see in Figure 5-43.

```
1   <!DOCTYPE html PUBLIC "-//W3C//DTD XHTML 1.0 Transitional//EN"
2       "http://www.w3.org/TR/xhtml1/DTD/xhtml1-transitional.dtd">
3   <html xmlns="http://www.w3.org/1999/xhtml" xml:lang="en" lang="en">
4   <head>
5       <meta http-equiv="content-type" content="text/html; charset=iso-8859-1" />
6       <title>Chapter 5 | Dynamic Web Sites | Query Strings</title>
7       <meta name="generator" content="BBEdit 7.0" />
8   </head>
9   <body>
10  <?
11  if (empty($_GET["id"])) {
12  ?>
13  <p><a href="?id=sent">empty</a></p>
14  <?php
15  } elseif ($_GET["id"] == "sent") {
16  ?>
17  <p><a href="?id=nonsense">sent</a></p>
18  <?php }
19  elseif ((!empty($_GET["id"])) && ($_GET["id"] != "sent")) {
20  ?>
21  <p>error</p>
22  <? } ?>
23  </body>
24  </html>
25
```

Figure 5-43. This bare version of the code will let you know things work correctly.

9. If you call the page up in your browser, you should be able to navigate through all three states, as shown in Figures 5-44, 5-45, and 5-46.

Figure 5-44. The id variable is empty.

Figure 5-45. The id variable is sent.

Figure 5-46. Anything else takes the user to an error page.

Now that you know the code is working, you can get cracking with embedding it into the page you made in Chapter 3.

Embedding the code into a real page

1. Open the finished example from Chapter 3 in Dreamweaver. This is index.html from Chapter 3. If you want to use mine, grab index.html and the site folders from the Chapter 3 download files and paste them in your ~Sites/book/05 folder. Save the document as ~/Sites/book/05/contact.php. Look for the following lines of code:

   ```
   </div> <!- end of the sidebar div ->
   <div id="content">
   Lorem ipsum dolor sit amet...
   </div>
   <div id="footer">
   ```

2. Remove the Lorem Ipsum text, as you won't need that anymore.

3. All of the following code is to be placed within the content <div>. With your page in Split view, start off the PHP you wrote in the stripped-down version.

```
<div id="content">
<?
if (empty($_GET["id"])) {
?>
</div>
```

4. You need some <form> tags, so choose Insert ➤ Form ➤ Form, name the form "comments", and give it an action of contact.php?id=sent, as shown in Figure 5-47.

Tip: Use POST instead of GET. <form> has one required attribute: ACTION. This specifies the URL of the CGI script, which processes the form and sends back feedback. There are two methods to send form data to a server. GET will send the form input in a URL (something like this: http://www.freakindesign.com/contact.php?id=sent&name=your_name&email=name@address.com&website=http://&geek=yes&comments=i+think+it+is+great), whereas POST sends it in the body of the submission. Using POST, you can also send larger amounts of data.

5. Click into the Design Pane, and choose Insert ➤ Table (or click the Table button on the icon bar), filling in the details shown in Figure 5-48.

6. You want a title in the left column and a text field in the right. Obviously, you'll need a larger right column than left, so click your cursor in the middle of the table (as shown in Figures 5-49 and 5-50), and then drag until the left column is 120 pixels wide.

7. Click in the top-left cell of the table and type Your name:.

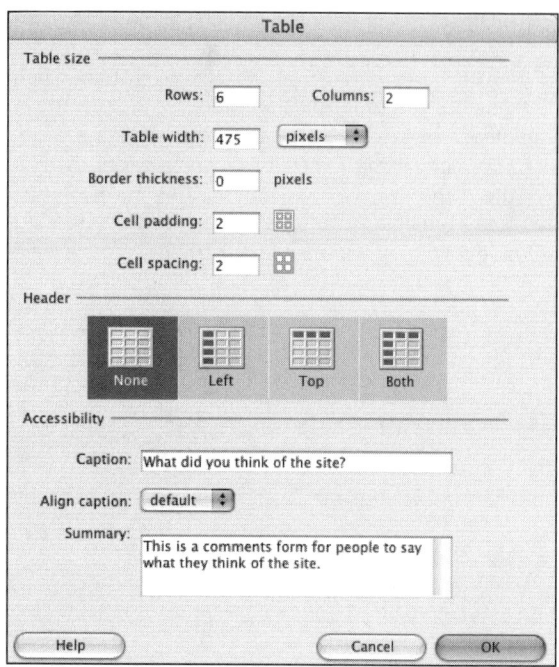

Figure 5-48. Inserting a table, with Accessibility options

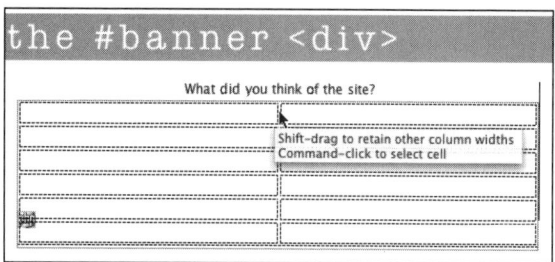

Figure 5-49. Dragging from the middle to the left . . .

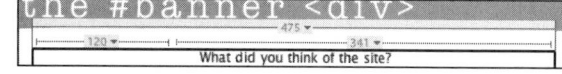

Figure 5-50. . . . until the left column is 120 pixels wide

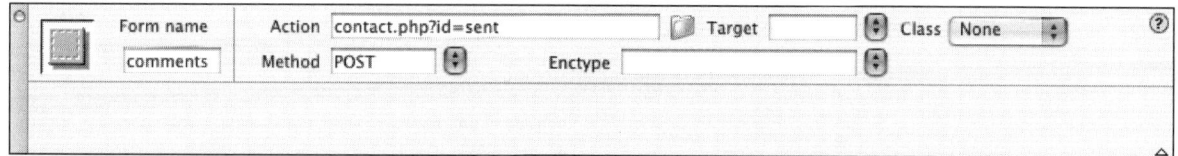

Figure 5-47. Giving the form a name and an action

8. Click in the top-right cell and choose Insert ➤ Form ➤ Text Field (or click the Text Field icon on the Forms Insert bar). As you've already got your field labeled, you can just fill in the Access key and Tab Index, for accessibility reasons (see Figure 5-51). You can set the Accessibility preferences to show the attributes panel when inserting form objects, frames, media, or images. Otherwise *CTRL*-click and select Edit Tag (Input) ➤ Accessibility.

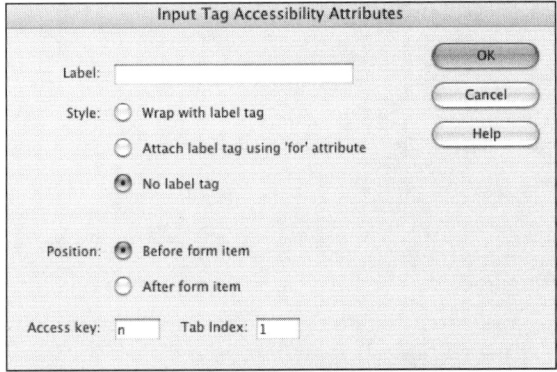

Figure 5-51. More accessibility options in Dreamweaver

This gives you the code shown in Figure 5-52.

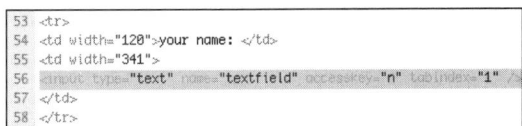

Figure 5-52. The new code in place

9. You want something more descriptive than "textfield" in there, so click in the Properties palette and change it to name, while giving it a Char width of 40 and a Max Chars of 50 (see Figure 5-53).

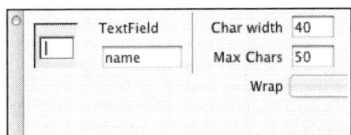

Figure 5-53. Specifying the name of the TextField

10. Go ahead and add the other text fields in the same way. They are quite similar, and here's a table with the properties I set:

TextField	Char Width	Max Chars	Type	Access Key	Index Tab
Name	40	50	Single line	n	1
Email	40	50	Single line	e	2
Web Site	40	50	Single line	w	3
Are you a Geek?	40	50	Single line	g	4
Comments	40	Num Lines 4	Mult line	c	5

The only field where I've added anything extra, is the Web Site field, where I've given it an initial value of `http://` just to let people know I want a URL inputting here, as opposed to just the name of their website (as shown in Figure 5-54).

I find including the question "Are you a Geek?" to lighten the mood, and get some funny answers from people. Feel free to be serious though (Did you finish mowing the lawn yet?). You should now have a table similar to the one in Figure 5-54.

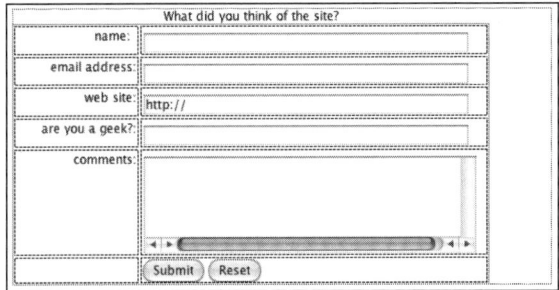

Figure 5-54. The comments table where the users will input their data

11. As you can see, you could do with aligning those text labels a bit better, so click at the top of the left side of the table to select the whole left side. Select Top from the Vert drop-down menu in the Properties palette, and then align the text to the right as in Figure 5-55.

Figure 5-55. Top-right alignment keeps things tidy.

12. Your form isn't much use to you unless you add a Submit button, so click in the bottom-right cell and choose Insert ➤ Form ➤ Button.

13. Add a space next to this Submit button and then insert another button. Change both its Label and Button name to Reset in the Properties palette, and change the action to Reset form as shown in Figure 5-56.

The code for the two buttons should look like that shown in Figure 5-57, which also shows how I named the access key and tab index.

14. With the form section complete, you can now turn to the next section of your page. Click in the code pane and locate the following code at the end of your form:

```
...
</table>
</form>
</div>
<div id="footer">
```

15. Type in the following new code:

```
...
</table>
</form>
<? }
elseif ($_GET["id"] == "sent") {

</div>
<div id="footer">
```

16. Click in the gap after the curly bracket, because it's time to add the code that will actually mail you the details. This is pretty much exactly the same method as in the 404 page, so type in the following code:

```
...
<? }
elseif ($_GET["id"] == "sent") {
$mailFrom = "From: " . $HTTP_POST_VARS
➥['name'] . " <" . $HTTP_POST_VARS
➥['email'] . ">";
```

(code continues)

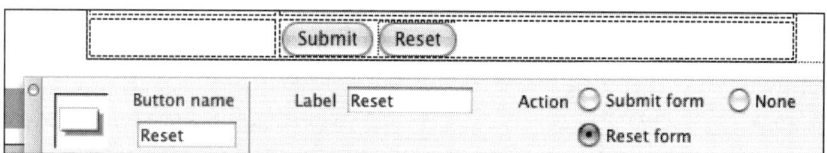

Figure 5-56. Adding buttons to the form

```
97  <td>
98  <input type="submit" name="Submit" value="Submit" accesskey="s" tabindex="6" />
99  <input type="reset" name="Reset" value="Reset" accesskey="r" tabindex="7" />
100 </td>
```

Figure 5-57. The code for the buttons, showing the accessibility options

```
$mailTo = "Freakin Design <phil@
➥freakindesign.com>";
$mailSubject = "form submission from
➥freakindesign.com";
$mailMessage = "Information submitted
➥ from the website, as follows: \n

Name: " . $HTTP_POST_VARS['name'] . "\n
Email: " . $HTTP_POST_VARS['email'] . "\n
Website: " . $HTTP_POST_VARS
➥['website'] . "\n
Geek?: " . $HTTP_POST_VARS['geek'] . "\n
Comments: " . $HTTP_POST_VARS
➥['comments'] . "\n
–EOT\n";
mail($mailTo, $mailSubject,
➥$mailMessage, $mailFrom); ?>


</div>
<div id="footer"
```

The first line is different from the 404 page in that it uses the user's name and e-mail address when it sends the mail. That way, you can just hit Reply in your e-mail program to e-mail the user back directly.

17. Next line, you'll add a "Thank You" message to let users know their details are now flying through the cosmos towards you. So, immediately following on from the last block of code, type

```
...
–EOT\n";
mail($mailTo, $mailSubject,
➥$mailMessage, $mailFrom); ?>

<p>Thank you for your comments.
➥Somebody from Freakin Design will be
➥in touch within 2-3 working days,
➥if you require a reply. </p>


</div>
<div id="footer"
```

18. Following on from that, it's time for the last stage, which is where you'll catch any erroneous id variables.

```
...
2-3 working days, if you required a
➥reply. </p>
<? }
elseif ((!empty($_GET["id"])) &&
➥($_GET["id"] != "sent")) {
?>

</div>
<div id="footer"
```

This code closes the last section, gets a new directive, and then opens up the next section for you.

19. You want your error message to direct people to the correct page, which is your contact page in this case. So, using a simple message and a hyperlink, you'll add the final section of code:

```
...
<? }
elseif ((!empty($_GET["id"])) &&
➥($_GET["id"] != "sent")) {
?>
<p>There appears to have been an error
➥with your form submission. <br />
Please <a href="contact.php">go back</a>
➥and check your details.</p>

<? } ?>
</div>
<div id="footer"
</div>
</body>
</html>
```

20. If you save your document, you should now have a page that looks like Figure 5-58 at the end.

21. All you have to do now is test it (see Figures 5-59 and 5-60).

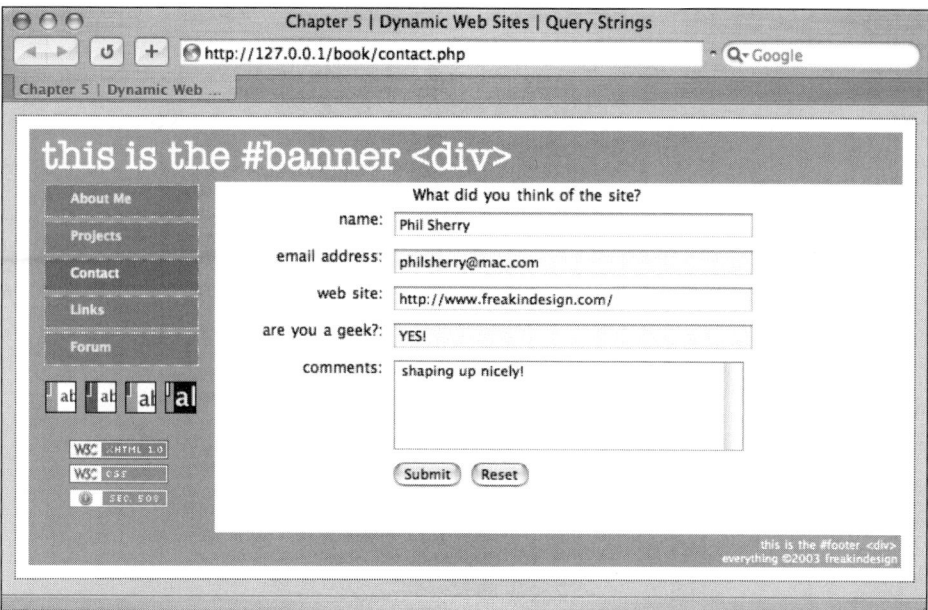

Figure 5-58. Filling in the form

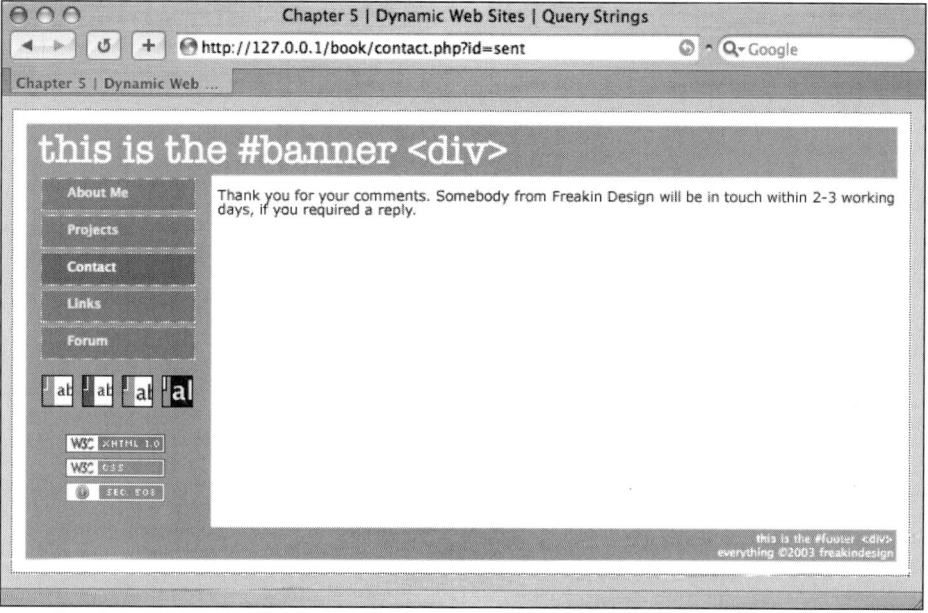

Figure 5-59. Sending the form

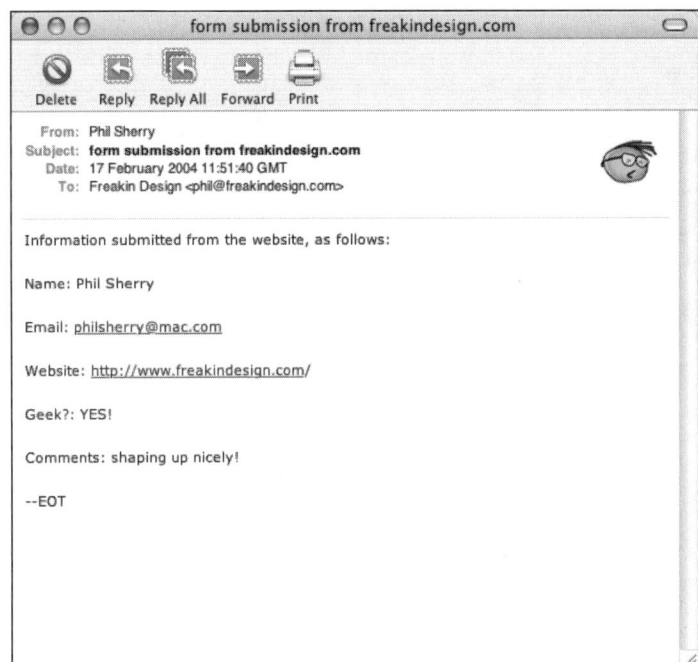

Figure 5-60. And then checking your e-mail

Adding other pages dynamically

As you might have noticed in those last few screenshots of my browser window, my sidebar links are now labeled for real site sections as shown in Figure 5-61.

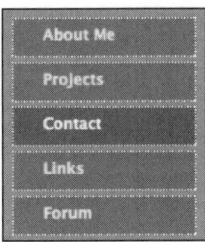

Figure 5-61. The buttons on the contact page, with Contact showing as active

You'll add those sections in a minute, but first, you'll code those links up properly. Here's the code for the buttons:

```
<ul id="navlist">
<li><a href="/index.php"
➥title="Back to the Home Page">
➥About Me</a></li>
<li><a href="/projects.php"
➥title="Projects, past & present">
➥Projects</a></li>
<li id="active"><a href="#"
➥title="Contact me (this Page)">
➥Contact</a></li>
<li><a href="/links.php"
➥title="Explore other sites">
➥Links</a></li>
<li><a href="/forum/index.php"
➥title="Leave a message on the forum">
➥Forum</a></li>

</ul>
```

1. Let's break that down a line at a time. The first link is a link to the index page, which you'll use as the default About Me page, so find the following:

```
<ul id="navlist">
<li id="active"><a href="/index.html"
➥title="Back to the Home Page">
➥Home</a></li>
```

and change that to

```
<ul id="navlist">
<li><a href="/index.php"
➥title="Back to the Home Page">
➥About Me</a></li>
```

2. The second link is the Projects page. This is just a normal link, so change the next line:

```
<li><a href="/link2.html" title="Link 2
➥title">Link 2</a></li>
```

to

```
<li><a href="/projects.php"
➥title="Projects, past & present">
➥Projects</a></li>
```

3. The third link is the Contact page, which has the added id of active to clearly show visitors which page they are on. So, change

```
<li><a href="/link3.html" title="Link 3
➥title">Link 3</a></li>
```

to

```
<li id="active"><a href="#"
➥title="Contact me (this Page)">
➥Contact</a></li>
```

4. The fourth link is to the Links page, which you'll be coding in Chapter 8. Change

```
<li><a href="/link4.html" title="Link 4
➥title">Link 4</a></li>
```

to

```
<li><a href="/links.php"
➥title="Explore other sites">
➥Links</a></li>
```

5. The final link is the Forum, which will also be dealt with in Chapter 8. Change

```
<li><a href="/link5.html" title="Link 5
➥title">Link 5</a></li>
</ul>
```

to

```
<li><a href="/forum/index.php"
➥title="Leave a message on the forum">
➥Forum</a></li>
</ul>
```

Projects page

As I've finished more than one project in my lifetime, I'll need more than one page for my Projects section. To give you an idea of what to aim for here, Figure 5-62 shows a page with some dynamic content pulled in.

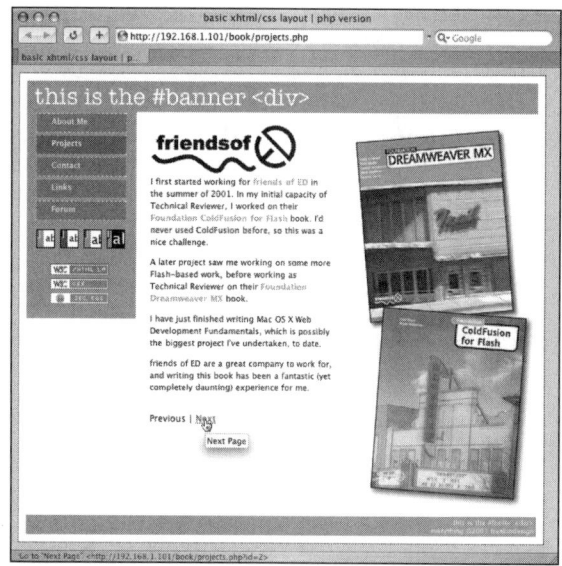

Figure 5-62. Page 1 of the Projects section with CSS columns

As you should be able to see by now, there's no need to totally hard code each individual page when you can just use the same one to pull in some content, based on the query string.

Another way to use the "one page" trick is the **switch method**. The switch statement is similar to a bunch of if statements on the same expression. Quite often, you may want to compare the same variable with a few different values, executing a different piece of code depending on which value it's equal to. This is exactly what the switch statement is for, but it's considered to be faster than the if statement. By using this method, you're specifying each of the files you want to include, rather than relying on the requested URL. Obviously though, if you have 500 files to include, this method might take some time to code! Here's how you do it:

1. Open the completed `index.html` file from Chapter 3 and save it as `~/Sites/book/05/projects.php`. You should also already have the rest of the site folders in this directory from working on the previous Contacts exercise. Be sure to change the links accordingly, so the Projects link is active.

```
...
<ul id="navlist">
<li><a href="index.php" title=
➡"Back to the Home Page">About Me</a></li>
<li><a href="projects.php"
➡title="Projects, past & present">Projects
➡</a></li>
<li id="active"><a href="#"
➡title="Contact me (this Page)">Contact
➡</a></li>
<li><a href="links.php"
➡title="Explore other
sites">Links</a></li>
<li><a href="forum/index.php"
➡title="Leave a message on the forum">
➡Forum</a></li>
</ul>
```

2. As in the previous example, you're adding the content into the content `<div>`, so you can delete that Lorum Ipsum text now. Again, you call your page variable id and use the GET method, like so:

```
...
</div>
<div id="content">
<?
switch ($_GET['id']) {

</div>
```

3. Next, you decide what to do based on the value of the id variable. Use break to break out of the switch statement block and move immediately on to the lines following it. So, in this case, if id = 1, tell $inc to have a value of 1, break, and move on:

```
...
<?
switch ($_GET['id']) {
   case "1": $inc = 'projects/1.inc.php';
   break;

</div>
```

4. Repeat this for a second project page:

```
...
<?
switch ($_GET['id']) {
   case "1": $inc = 'projects/1.inc.php';
   break;
   case "2": $inc = 'projects/2.inc.php';
   break;

</div>
```

5. And the third project page:

```
...
<?
case "1": $inc = 'projects/1.inc.php';
   break;
   case "2": $inc = 'projects/2.inc.php';
   break;
   case "3": $inc = 'projects/3.inc.php';
   break;

</div>
```

6. And the fourth project page:

```
...
<?
case "1": $inc = 'projects/1.inc.php';
   break;
   case "2": $inc = 'projects/2.inc.php';
   break;
   case "3": $inc = 'projects/3.inc.php';
   break;
   case "4": $inc = 'projects/4.inc.php';
   break;

</div>
```

7. You also need a default setting in case no id is specified. Use the first page for this.

```
...
<?
...
  case "4": $inc = 'projects/4.inc.php';
  break;
  default: $inc = 'projects/1.inc.php';
  break;
}

</div>
```

8. With your switch statement complete, all you need to do now is include the relevant file and close the block of PHP code as follows:

```
...
<?
switch ($_GET['id']) {
  case "1": $inc = 'projects/1.inc.php';
  break;
  case "2": $inc = 'projects/2.inc.php';
  break;
  case "3": $inc = 'projects/3.inc.php';
  break;
  case "4": $inc = 'projects/4.inc.php';
  break;
  default: $inc = 'projects/1.inc.php';
  break;
}
include ($inc);
?>

</div>
```

9. Next, you'll make the project pages. Create a new directory called ~/Sites/book/05/projects.

10. Create these four text files:

- ~/Sites/book/05/projects/1.inc.php
- ~/Sites/book/05/projects/2.inc.php
- ~/Sites/book/05/projects/3.inc.php
- ~/Sites/book/05/projects/4.inc.php

11. All you need on these pages for now is some placeholder text, so that you can determine whether your code works or not, and a link to navigate through your pages. You can add some real content once the code is final. So, into 1.inc.php, type

```
<p>Projects page #1</p>
<br />
Previous |
<a href="projects.php?id=2" title="Next
➡Page">Next</a>
```

12. For 2.inc.php, type

```
<p>Projects page #2</p>
<br />
<a href="projects.php?id=1"
➡title="Previous Page">Previous</a> |

<a href="projects.php?id=3" title="Next
➡Page">Next</a>
```

13. For 3.inc.php, type

```
<p>Projects page #3</p>
<br />
<a href="projects.php?id=2"
➡title="Previous Page">Previous</a> |
<a href="projects.php?id=4" title="Next
➡Page">Next</a>
```

14. And finally, for 4.inc.php, type

```
<p>Projects page #4</p>
<br />
<a href="projects.php?id=3"
➡title="Previous Page">Previous</a> |

Next
```

15. You can now navigate through all your pages, so you know that your code works (see Figure 5-63).

Now it's time to add some real content. For this, you'll need to add some more code to your CSS documents first, so let's get on with that.

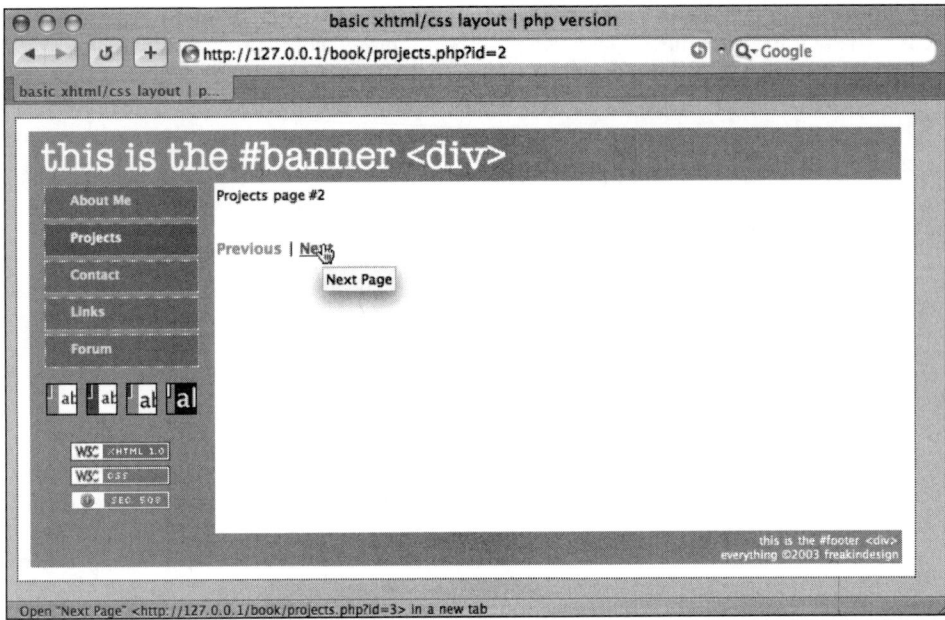

Figure 5-63. Both the Previous and Next links work.

Adding columns to the CSS document

As green.css is your default CSS document, you'll add your new code to that one first. The other style sheets need the same chunk of code added, so don't forget those too.

1. Open ~/Sites/book/05/css/green.css, and then look for the #content code. Immediately underneath, type

```
#content, #contentLeft, #contentRight img {
  display: block;
  border: 0;
  padding: 5px;
}
...
```

This takes care of any images you might have in your content. Telling the image to display as a block-level element (as opposed to an inline element) means you can dispose of a <br /> tag after the image. The border and padding should speak for themselves by now.

2. Now, on to the columns. These are coded in the same way as the sidebar was in Chapter 3, complete with the Box Model Hack and Opera rule. You have a left column, floating to the left.

```
...
#content, #contentLeft, #contentRight img {
  display: block;
  border: 0;
  padding: 5px;
}
#contentLeft {
  float: left;
  padding: 10px 5px 10px 5px;
  margin: 0;
  border: 0;
  background: transparent;
width: 260px;
➡    /* false value for IE4-5.x/Win,
➡like so: */
```

```
  voice-family: "\"}\"";
➡/* real width + l/r border + l/r
➡padding = false value */
  voice-family:inherit;
➡/* end false value for IE4-5.x/Win */
  width: 250px;
➡/* real value for compliant browsers */
}


html>#contentLeft {
width: 250px;      /* be nice to Opera */}
...
```

3. There is also a Right column, floating to the right.

```
...
html>#contentLeft {
  width: 250px;           /* be nice to Opera */
}


#contentRight {
  float: right;
  padding: 10px 5px 10px 5px;
  margin: 0;
  border: 0;
  background: transparent;
width: 260px;
➡/* false value for IE4-5.x/Win,
➡like so: */
  voice-family: "\"}\"";
➡/* real width + l/r border + l/r
➡padding = false value */
  voice-family:inherit;
➡/* end false value for IE4-5.x/Win */
  width: 250px;
➡   /* real value for compliant browsers */


}

html>#contentRight {
width: 250px;      /* be nice to Opera */
}
...
```

With those extra chunks of CSS added to the recipe, you can start to cook up some content—make sure you add the same code to the other three style sheets though!

4. Open up ~/Sites/book/05/projects/1.inc.php again. You're still going to use that link, but you need your new <div> tags in there. So, replace this code:

```
<p>Projects page #1</p>
<br />
Previous |
<a href="projects.php?id=2"
➡title="Next Page">Next</a>
```

with this new code:

```
<div id="contentLeft">
Previous |
<a href="projects.php?id=2"
➡title="Next Page">Next</a></div>
<div id="contentRight">

</div>
```

5. You'll add the images next.

```
<div id="contentLeft">
<img src="images/FoED.gif" width="200"
➡height="69" alt="friends of ED logo" />
Previous |
<a href="projects.php?id=2"
➡title="Next Page">Next</a></div>
<div id="contentRight">
<img src="images/books.jpg" width="250"
➡height="500" alt="friends of ED books" />
</div>
```

6. The next thing you'll add is the copy. Figure 5-64 shows how the code looks in BBEdit.

7. Save your document, grab the images folder from the download files, and place it in your ~Sites/book/05 folder.

8. If you test the page out in your browser, you should see the finished page looking like the one in Figure 5-65.

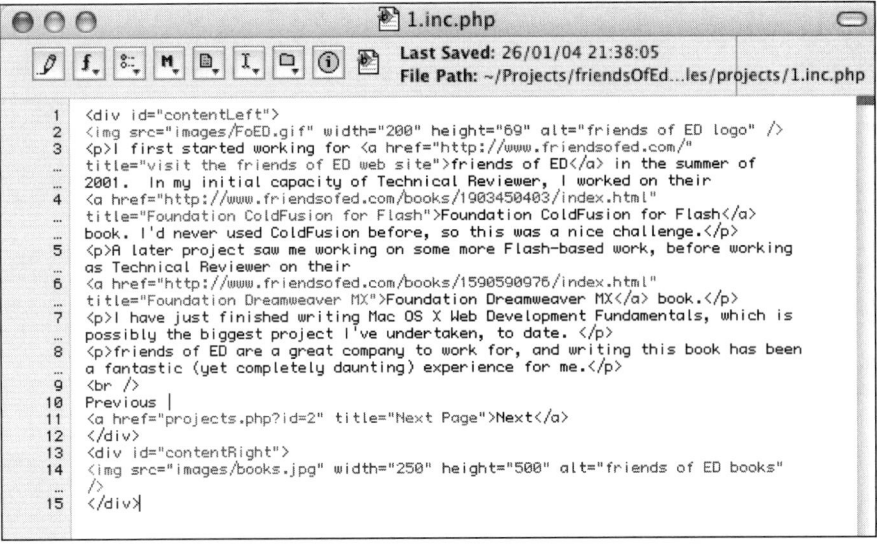

```
1   <div id="contentLeft">
2   <img src="images/FoED.gif" width="200" height="69" alt="friends of ED logo" />
3   <p>I first started working for <a href="http://www.friendsofed.com/"
...  title="visit the friends of ED web site">friends of ED</a> in the summer of
...  2001.  In my initial capacity of Technical Reviewer, I worked on their
4   <a href="http://www.friendsofed.com/books/1903450403/index.html"
...  title="Foundation ColdFusion for Flash">Foundation ColdFusion for Flash</a>
...  book. I'd never used ColdFusion before, so this was a nice challenge.</p>
5   <p>A later project saw me working on some more Flash-based work, before working
...  as Technical Reviewer on their
6   <a href="http://www.friendsofed.com/books/1590590976/index.html"
...  title="Foundation Dreamweaver MX">Foundation Dreamweaver MX</a> book.</p>
7   <p>I have just finished writing Mac OS X Web Development Fundamentals, which is
...  possibly the biggest project I've undertaken, to date. </p>
8   <p>friends of ED are a great company to work for, and writing this book has been
...  a fantastic (yet completely daunting) experience for me.</p>
9   <br />
10  Previous |
11  <a href="projects.php?id=2" title="Next Page">Next</a>
12  </div>
13  <div id="contentRight">
14  <img src="images/books.jpg" width="250" height="500" alt="friends of ED books"
...  />
15  </div>
```

Figure 5-64. I've written a little bit about the work I've done for friends of ED.

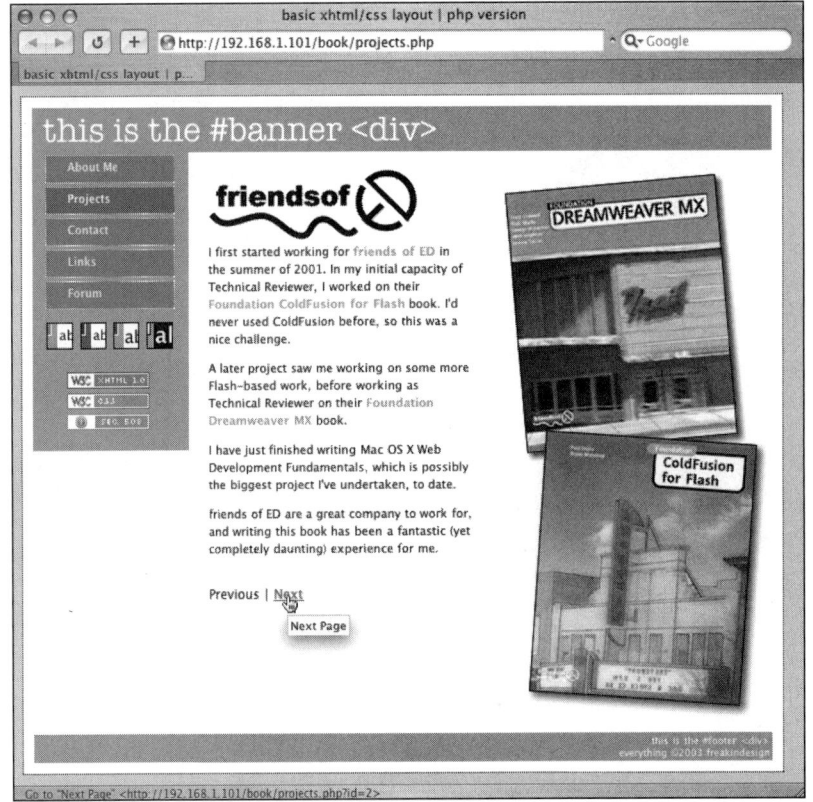

Figure 5-65. The finished Projects page

Chapter review

You've learned a fair bit in this chapter. From plain old static pages in Chapter 3, you now have a nice dynamic page, which you can populate with content at the drop of a hat. You've got some custom error pages to display, in both Perl and PHP formats.

Most importantly, you've tackled the contact page, which will let people tell you what they think of your site. You didn't use a free FormMail script from a site you found on Google; you did it all in one easy page, and you did it yourself.

You're really getting to grips with things now. Having slid down the Batpole and tackled some basic Perl and PHP, you're about ready for anything. Which is a good job, as the next chapter is all about . . . UNIX.

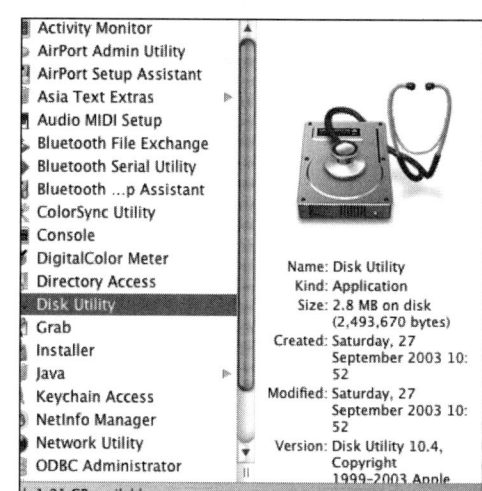

Activity Monitor
AirPort Admin Utility
AirPort Setup Assistant
Asia Text Extras ▶
Audio MIDI Setup
Bluetooth File Exchange
Bluetooth Serial Utility
Bluetooth ...p Assistant
ColorSync Utility
Console
DigitalColor Meter
Directory Access
Disk Utility
Grab
Installer
Java ▶
Keychain Access
NetInfo Manager
Network Utility
ODBC Administrator
1 01 GB available

Name: Disk Utility
Kind: Application
Size: 2.8 MB on disk
(2,493,670 bytes)
Created: Saturday, 27
September 2003 10:
52
Modified: Saturday, 27
September 2003 10:
52
Version: Disk Utility 10.4,
Copyright
1999–2003 Apple

Chapter 6

MAC UNIX ESSENTIALS

What we'll cover in this chapter:

- UNIX
- Open source code
- Darwin
- Multiuser, multitasking system
- Basic UNIX commands
- Using ps and grep
- Remote operations
- Fink and X11

So far, there have been a few mentions of UNIX, but not much has been said in detail. This chapter is set to remedy that and get you a little bit more familiar with how things are working. You'll learn how to do things while you're sitting at your Mac, or while you're logged in from another machine.

For those of you from a UNIX/Linux background, you might want to know how to use your favorite X11 applications in OS X. It's UNIX-based, so you should be able to, right? Right. That's where Fink comes to your rescue. For the uninitiated, you won't be out of your depth, as I'll only be scratching the surface of the X11 world. (X11 is the X Window System, used for running many UNIX applications.)

Permission and security issues are important, especially in a UNIX system. We'll be taking another look at permissions, and introducing .htaccess, which you can use to stop people from seeing certain directories on your web server, as well as much more. .htaccess is the file extension. It isn't `file.htaccess` or `somepage.htaccess`, it's simply named `.htaccess`.

We'll cover some basic but *important* things, to make sure you don't completely hose your system while innocently trying to delete a file. You've already had some exposure to Terminal, but after this chapter, you should be able to handle it like a champ. You'll be using it to locate files, learning how to kill a stubborn application that refuses to quit, and even having some fun. Yes, UNIX can be fun, so don't be scared, let's get in there.

UNIX

UNIX started life as a video game. Okay, so it would be easy to poke holes in that story, but it's not a complete lie, and it sounds infinitely more sexy than saying "UNIX started life as a demonstration of a multiuser file system, command interpreter, and assembler." In 1969, two employees of Bell Laboratories' Computing Science Research Center started work on a project that was later to become UNIX. The original proposals for the project had been either rejected or ignored by Bell Laboratories, but rather than give up on the idea, these

two researchers (Ken Thompson and Dennis Ritchie) tracked down a rather neglected PDP-7 computer and set about developing working versions of some of the features they had been researching.

Two years later, work started on what was to become the C programming language. The stories of C and UNIX are rather intertwined, but to cut a long story short, the UNIX kernel was rewritten in C in 1973.

The upshot of all this is that the UNIX operating system kernel was source-portable, so it could be compiled to run on pretty much any other machine. Consequently, many UNIX applications were also written in C, so they could be compiled on almost any UNIX machine with a C compiler.

It's probably best to point out now that there are a few niggling little implementation details with regards to UNIX, C, and portability. It's not really worth expanding on it all here, but it might be a good idea to take this all with a pinch of salt. Just bear in mind that this is all a slight oversimplification. I'll expand on this a bit more in the next chapter.

Open source code

Unlike Microsoft Windows, or the Mac OS of old, the main engine that drives Mac OS X—the kernel, Darwin—is what's known as **open source**. This means that the actual source code is available to programmers and users, which allows for a unique openness when it comes to writing applications. This approach to operating system development allows developers and students to view the Darwin source code, learn from it, and submit suggestions and modifications to help create better, faster, and more reliable applications. Apple was the first major computer company to make open source development a key part of its ongoing software strategy. To read more about the Darwin open source project, go to the following website: `http://developer.apple.com/darwin/`.

Note: Aqua and Carbon (which is essentially an OS 9 emulation layer) are most definitely *not* open source.

Darwin

When people refer to the "UNIX underpinnings" of Mac OS X, the word "Darwin" will usually pop up (assuming they actually know what they're on about, and not just touting buzz phrases). Darwin isn't OS X though, so what is it? Darwin can be used as a stand-alone, totally independent operating system, but will only function with the most basic of features from Mac OS X. There is a difference evident between the two, so let's look at how they are related and how they differ.

Darwin runs on PowerPC-based Macintosh computers as well as x86-compatible computers. At present, this means that you could actually install it on a PC if you wanted, unlike Mac OS X. How does Darwin figure in with the rest of OS X?

Darwin is the UNIX-based foundation, which is built on technologies such as FreeBSD, Mach, Apache, and GCC. It provides a complete UNIX environment, with X11 and POSIX services comparable to Linux or FreeBSD. This includes all the kernel, libraries, networking, and command-line utilities that most UNIX/Linux users will be familiar with.

Darwin is extremely stable, thanks to its advanced memory protection and management system. It does this by allocating a unique address space for each application or process. This means the entire system won't come crashing down if a lone application freaks out and tries to throw a spanner in the works, as was the case up until and including OS 9.

Let's have a quick look at how the rest of Mac OS X is built on top of Darwin (see Figure 6-1).

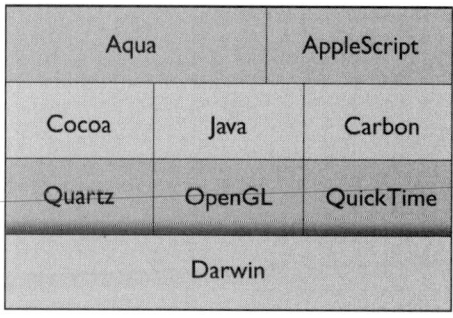

Figure 6-1. How Darwin is related to Mac OS X as a whole

Graphics and media

The Mac OS X graphics system combines 2D (Quartz), 3D (OpenGL), and time-based media standards using an industry-leading compositing window system for a rich yet seamless user experience. Quartz is the primary imaging model for Mac OS X, and is based on the cross-platform Portable Document Format (PDF) standard. Quartz is responsible for the high-quality, anti-aliased text and graphics and provides industry-leading support for OpenType, PostScript, and TrueType fonts (now native on the Macintosh platform). Add a supported video card, and Quartz Extreme totally revs up the Mac OS X graphical experience. OpenGL is the industry standard for visualizing 3D shapes and textures. It does this by enabling high-end 3D graphics on Mac OS X, which makes it the ideal platform for 3D animations and special effects. QuickTime provides a fully standards-based environment for creating, playing, and delivering video, audio (including the new AAC format), and images.

Application frameworks

Mac OS X includes a variety of rich application frameworks, built on top of the traditional UNIX application programming interfaces (APIs), to support developers in many different communities. Using the free CD for Xcode (formerly called Developers' Tools), developers can create Aqua user interfaces for Cocoa, Carbon, AppleScript, and Java applications. Cocoa is a set of object-oriented frameworks designed for rapid application development, making it easy to add rich Aqua interfaces to existing UNIX software or to create entirely new applications. Carbon provides a gentle migration path for developers who have moved their applications from Mac OS 9 to Mac OS X. AppleScript lets you create your own applications that automate application commands, information retrieval, and repetitive tasks. Java 2 Standard Edition v.1.4.1 on Mac OS X is fully compliant, highly optimized, and tightly integrated with the native look and feel, making it easy to run standards-based Java applications right out of the box.

User interface

The face of Mac OS X is the elegant GUI called Aqua. With its drop shadows and transparencies, it's as easy on the eye as it is easy to use. With new features such as Exposé and Fast User Switching, the entire Mac OS X experience is simply stunning.

Multiuser, multitasking system

Most OS X users, like me, are the only people who use their machine on a regular basis. This doesn't mean that you're the only user on the system. You're one of 16 users on a default installation of Mac OS X (see Figure 6-2). All these users belong to groups. You may recall having to set file permissions in Chapter 5, in order to be able to allow certain files to run. This was because the correct group didn't have permission to execute the file. Let's meet all these users and groups now.

Users

Why does the system have all these users? Each one has different rights and privileges. Some have a specific job, and that is their sole purpose in life. They aren't allowed to do anything else. The MySQL user, who we'll be meeting in Chapter 8, runs the MySQL database daemon, which just sits there until it's invoked by another process (as is a daemon's job). The postfix user should be familiar to you, as we met that user in the previous chapter. The www user is in charge of running Apache, by default. A lot of processes run as nobody, to ensure they can cause no malicious damage.

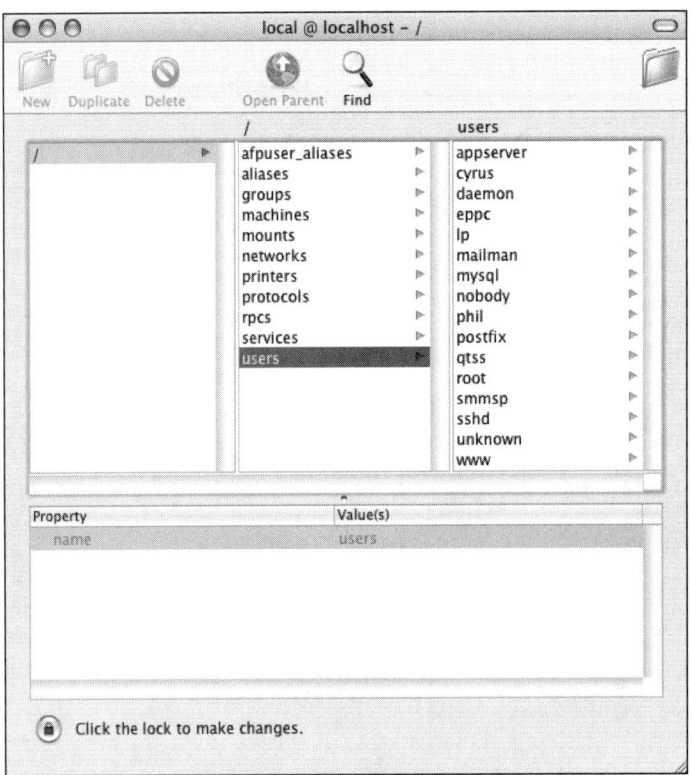

Figure 6-2. Using NetInfo Manager to see all the system's users

It's unlikely you'll ever have to meet all these users, or know what they do. UNIX is a fascinating subject though, so I recommend you get yourself a nice big UNIX book, after you've read this one a few times.

The SuperUser (root) is allowed to do absolutely anything it wants. That is why it's considered dangerous (and a bit stupid, really) to use the root account for daily usage. Strictly speaking, you should only use su to quickly log in as root, do what you have to do, and then exit the su command to return to your normal login. Even safer is the sudo command (SuperUser do), which you would typically prefix onto a command that has to be run at a root level. You saw an example of this in Chapter 5 when editing the httpd.conf.

> *When you open a terminal window, or log in remotely, login displays the system copyright notice, the date and time the user last logged in, the message of the day, as well as other information. If the file* .hushlogin *exists in the user's home directory, all of these messages vanish, and you just go straight to the command prompt. To create this file, open a new terminal window and type* touch .hushlogin.

Groups

All the users you can see in Figure 6-3 are organized into groups. Every user is in at least one group, and may also be in other groups. Group membership gives you access to files and directories that are permitted to that group. As with user permissions, some groups are allowed to do far more than others.

To see which groups you're in, simply type groups in Terminal.

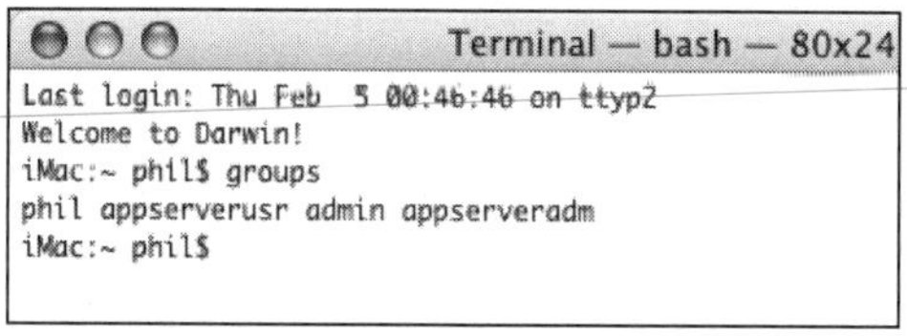

```
○ ○ ○          Terminal — bash — 80x24
Last login: Thu Feb  5 00:46:46 on ttyp2
Welcome to Darwin!
iMac:~ phil$ groups
phil appserverusr admin appserveradm
iMac:~ phil$
```

Figure 6-3. Finding out which groups you are in

As you can see from Figure 6-4, the default number of groups is much higher than the default number of users.

Basic UNIX commands

Now that you've found Terminal, what do you do with it? How do you get around? Here's a list of some of the more useful and important commands you'll need to know, with the most common options. For the full low-down on each command, type man **command** (ie: man ls) in Terminal, which will bring up the manual page.

Listing files

First of all, you'll want to know how to see which files are on the system. You do this using ls, which lists the directory contents. ls has several options, like a lot of UNIX commands. Here's the more commonly used options:

ls -a	Include directory entries whose names begin with a dot (.).
ls -l	List in long format.
ls -G	Enable colorized output.
ls -R	Recursively list subdirectories encountered.
ls -R > files.txt	Output results to a text file.
ls | more	List, pausing for full screens.
ls *.php	List all files ending in .php.

These commands can be used in combinations, too. For example, ls -Gal | more lists items in long format, in color, including dot files, pausing for full screens.

141

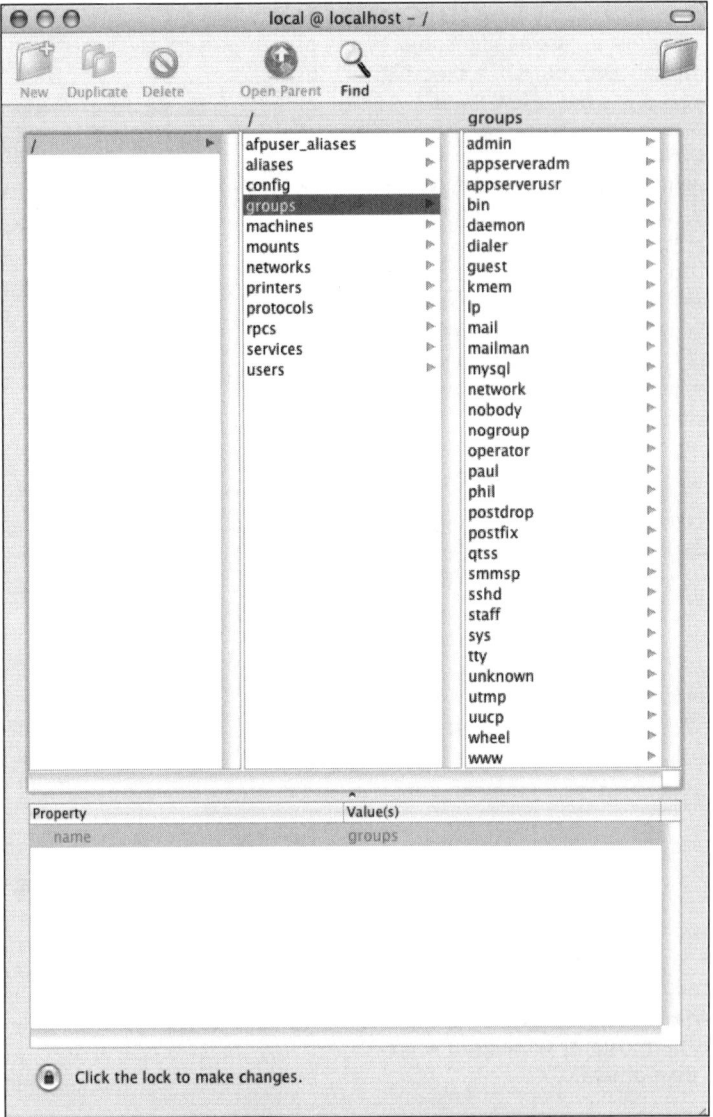

Figure 6-4. Using NetInfo Manager to see all the system's groups

Navigating the file system

Obviously, you're going to want to get around the file system, so you'll need to know how. You do that by using cd (change directory), and a number of options. I've listed some common ones:

pwd	Print working directory—shows the name of the current directory.
cd[space]	Return to the home directory.
cd ..	Move up one directory level.
cd ../..	Move up two directory levels.
cd subdirectory	Move to subdirectory.
cd /usr/bin	Move to an absolute path

> Tip: To read further about the UNIX file system, I recommend you check out the following site: http://www.pathname.com/fhs/.

Creating and deleting files and directories

When it comes to creating and deleting files and directories, you use mkdir and rm; the following are some options.

mkdir	**Make directories.**
mkdir dir_name	Create subdirectory in current directory.
rm	**Remove directory entries.**
rm filename	Delete file.
rm -i filename	Delete file after prompting.
rm -i filename	Delete file without prompting.
rm *	Delete ALL files.
rm /	Delete ALL files from the root directory onwards.

(Continued)

rm -r directory	Delete directory and all contents. (Use with care!)
rmdir directoryname	Delete empty directory.

Warning: The rm command is the equivalent of the big red button that the bad guys have in James Bond movies. You know the one; it blows everything up and there's no stopping it. Unless you use the -i switch, there's no last minute "quick, cut the red wire" to stop it. When you absolutely, positively have to delete every file in a directory, the safest way is to cd into that directory, and *then* use rm.

For example, let's say you have a file in the trash that you can't delete, because you don't have permission to. You guess you should use sudo to override the permissions, but you don't realize you've hit the SPACEBAR by accident, and type this:

    sudo rm -rf / Users/username/.Trash/
    ➥stubbornDirectory.

Wave goodbye to all your files, as you've just told rm to delete everything from / (Macintosh HD) onwards. Do not pass Go; do not collect $200; just cry and slap yourself. This is a far safer way to do it:

    cd /Users/username/.Trash/
    ➥ && rm -rf stubbornDirectory

Moving and copying files

Moving and copying files in Finder is easy. It's actually just as easy at the command line, using mv and cp.

mv	**Move.**
mv file1 newname	Rename file1.
mv directory newname	Rename directory.
mv directory1 directory2	Move directory1 into directory2.
mv file1 file2 directory	Move files into directory.

(Continued)

143

cp	Copy.
cp file1 file2	Copy file1 to file2.
cp file1 subdirectory	Copy file1 into subdirectory.
cp file1 file2 directory	Copy file1 and file2 into directory.
cp -r directory newdir	Copy a directory and all contents.

I had some files on a CD once that I'd burned a long time ago in OS 9. One file's name was ...Art, so OS X wasn't showing it in Finder, because it began with a dot. "Hmm," I thought. Terminal to the rescue! I believe the command went something like

```
cp -R /Volumes/cdName/...Art
➥ /Users/phil/Documents/\342\200\246Art
```

If you're wondering what the \342\200\246 part is, that's what you get when you press *ALT/OPTION*+;. It actually outputs as three dots (. . .). Try it, and go "Whoa!" in your best Keanu Reeves voice.

Displaying files

If you just need to view a file, you can use cat to print it in Terminal. For big files, use more to split the viewing up into screens.

cat	Concatenate and print files.
cat file1	Print file1 in Terminal.
cat file1 file2 > file3	Combine file1 and file2, and save them as file3.
cat file1 >> file2	Append file1 to file2.

(Continued)

more	List by screen.
more filename	Display file one screen at a time.
SPACEBAR	Display next screen.
Q or *CTRL+C*	Cancel listing.

You can also combine these commands with a pipe, as shown here:

```
cat /etc/httpd/httpd.conf | more
```

Links

In Finder, ⌘+*L* makes an alias for you. This is just a shortcut. In UNIX, you use ln.

ln	Make links.
ln -s file1 sym_link	Create symbolic link to file1.

A great use for ln is when you keep all your projects in one place (~/Projects/Book), want to test them on your web server, but don't want to keep copying them there (/Library/WebServer/Documents/Book). However, Apache doesn't know what to do with a Finder alias, so you just see a 404 page. The way around this is to use a symbolic link, which you do like so:

```
ln -s /Users/username/Projects/Book
➥ /Library/WebServer/Documents/book
```

You can now call up http://127.0.0.1/book/ in your browser and get a result.

System info

Here are a few miscellaneous commands that you might find useful for finding out information about your environment:

which	**Locate a program file in the user's path.**
which perl	Show path to perl.
which sendmail	Show path to sendmail.
head / tail	**Display the beginning or end of a file.**
head /etc/httpd/ ➡httpd.conf	Display the beginning of the Apache config file.
tail /etc/httpd/ ➡httpd.conf	Display the end of the Apache config file.
top	Display and update sorted information about processes (see Figure 6-5).
kill	Terminate or signal a process.

top is very a handy process for seeing what is going on behind the nice GUI of Mac OS X. If your Mac is grinding away, or really chugging, running top can often show the culprit. Maybe you'll spot something using a ridiculous amount of RAM or CPU. If you can close the offending application manually, it's always good to do so, so you can determine whether that was indeed to blame. If not, time to save your work, and maybe think about using kill. For a full list if what top's output means, visit the man page: man top.

If you use top to determine the ID of a process (PID), you can then kill the process. This is really useful if something freaks out a bit too much, and a process hangs on your machine, causing the CPU to run at 100 percent. Logging in from another machine (as described later), you can then kill any rogue processes. This is often used with the –9 switch, which means it's nonignorable; for example: kill -9 [PID] (where [PID] is the process number).

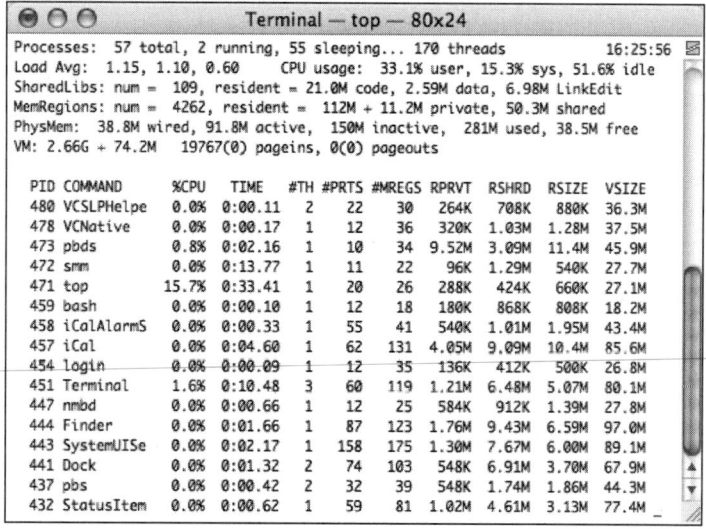

Figure 6-5. Using top to check process activity

> *Tip: As the top process can be a bit more CPU-intensive than it should, it's worth tweaking the command a little, and having an alias for this in your* .bash_profile, *by adding this line*
>
> ```
> alias ttop="top -ocpu -R -F -s 2 -n30"
> ```
>
> *Once you've added that, running* ttop *will only take about 1 percent of your CPU. Check the manual pages* (man top), *for more info.*

chmod

Back in Chapter 5, I covered user permissions to a degree, using the *absolute* chmod (change mode) method. There are several other ways to alter a file's permission, though, so let's cover that before moving on to groups. First, we'll look at using the *relative* or *symbolic* chmod method, in Terminal.

The first argument specifies which permissions you're changing: a for all, u for user, g for group, or o for other.

The second argument says how the permissions should be changed: + to add a permission, – to subtract a permission, or = to assign a permission and remove any others that might be there.

The third argument can be any combination of the permissions symbols we've already used, i.e.: r, w, and x.

Lastly, specify the file or directory to which these changes apply.

Here's how that works in practice:

I have my file, chapter6.txt. I can check the file permissions on it by issuing the command ls –l, which tells me that currently, only I am allowed to read and write to it.

```
-rw——-
```

(I did this by previously running chmod 600 chapter6.txt, to ensure privacy.) This is great while I'm writing Chapter 6, but not so good once I've finished. Seeing as I actually want people to read it, I use the following command when I'm ready to share the file:

```
chmod a+r chapter6.txt
```

As you can see in Figure 6-6, everyone now has permission to read the file, and I still have permission to write to it.

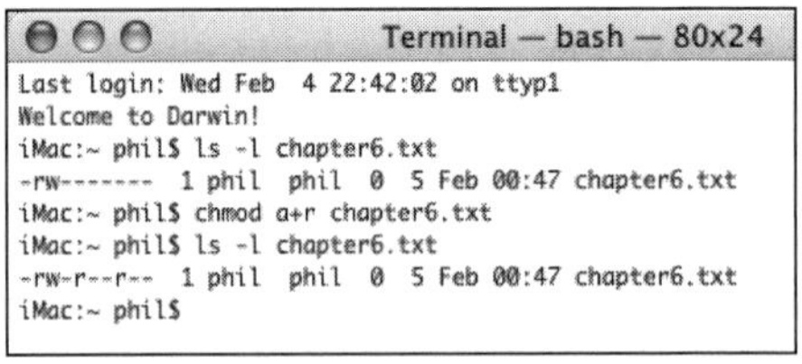

```
Last login: Wed Feb  4 22:42:02 on ttyp1
Welcome to Darwin!
iMac:~ phil$ ls -l chapter6.txt
-rw-------  1 phil  phil  0  5 Feb 00:47 chapter6.txt
iMac:~ phil$ chmod a+r chapter6.txt
iMac:~ phil$ ls -l chapter6.txt
-rw-r--r--  1 phil  phil  0  5 Feb 00:47 chapter6.txt
iMac:~ phil$
```

Figure 6-6. Now everyone can read this chapter!

chown

From time to time, you have to relinquish ownership of a file, or maybe take on ownership of a file from someone else. Now, that person might have given you the file on a CD with 42 witnesses who will swear that you're now the legal owner of the file, but UNIX doesn't know that. In cases like this, we use the chown (change owner) command. With two easy arguments, chown gets to work: the new owner's user name, and the name of the file. So, let's say I've finished with my chapter6.txt document, and my editor has decided it needs no amendments (*cough*). In order to let him take over the file, I would simply type chown gavin chapter6.txt and the file is no longer owned by me.

In order for my editor to change a file which I still owned, he would have to use sudo to override my ownership, like so:

```
sudo chown gavin chapter7.txt
```

chgrp

All files belong to groups, as well as users. Sometimes, more than one person needs to be able to read, write, or execute a file, so they belong to a group that has permission to access the file appropriately. To change which group a file belongs to, you use the chgrp (change group) command, which works exactly the same way as the chown command:

```
chgrp newgroup filename
```

With chmod, chown, and chgrp (and many other commands), you can use the -R (recursive) switch. In the case of these three commands, -R applies the changes to all the files and subdirectories in a directory. Here's how you use it:

```
chown -R us:us yourBase
```

Small applications for small jobs

As time goes on, applications get bigger and bigger, and do all manner of things—whether you personally need those features or not. This bloatware takes up a lot of physical hard disk space, uses a lot of memory, and takes its toll on the CPU. An example of this is Microsoft's Entourage. It's an e-mail application, it's a calendar, it's an address book, etc. Not everybody wants, or needs, all those features. Instead, some people use Apple's Mail, iCal, and Address Book. Each application does one task, and one task only. They pass information on to each other when necessary, but go no further.

UNIX applications tend to work in this way too. They can also be combined at the command line to trigger a few actions in one easy line of code, as you'll see throughout this chapter. Here are a few examples.

cron

Put simply, cron is a daemon to execute scheduled commands. A daemon is program or process that sits idly in the background until it's invoked to perform its task. Let's say you have a script that can deal with certain system commands. cron can be told to automatically kick that script into action on schedule. Classically, cron performs log directory cleaning so that long-lived systems don't end up with excessively old log files. Mac OS X already has this very cron job in place, but it isn't enabled by default. Let's keep the place shipshape and enable it, before moving on to add our own crontab rule.

1. Open a Terminal window and type

   cd /private/etc

2. As I haven't shown you how to do this before (and because it's good practice), you'll first need to back up the existing crontab file (see Figure 6-7). The file is owned by root; you need to use sudo, so type

   sudo cp crontab crontab.bak

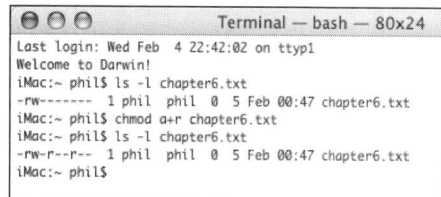

Figure 6-7. Always make a backup, before editing a file.

3. Next, you need to open the crontab file, as root, like so (see Figure 6-8):

   sudo pico crontab

4. Each cron entry begins with five fields, which determine when the command is to be executed, followed by the command to be run. As you can see from Figure 6-8, these fields are minute, hour, day of the month, month of the year, and day of the week.

So, the first line is set to execute at 03:15 every morning. The second line is 04:30 on the sixth day of the week. The third line is 05:30, on the first day of each month.

Obviously, these are all early on in the day. If your Mac is turned off, or in deep sleep, these commands won't be executed. If, like me, you leave your Mac on 24/7, with the monitor turned off, you can just uncomment these lines, if not already uncommented:

```
# Run daily/weekly/monthly jobs.
15  3  *  *  *  root  periodic daily
30  4  *  *  6  root  periodic weekly
30  5  1  *  *  root  periodic monthly
```

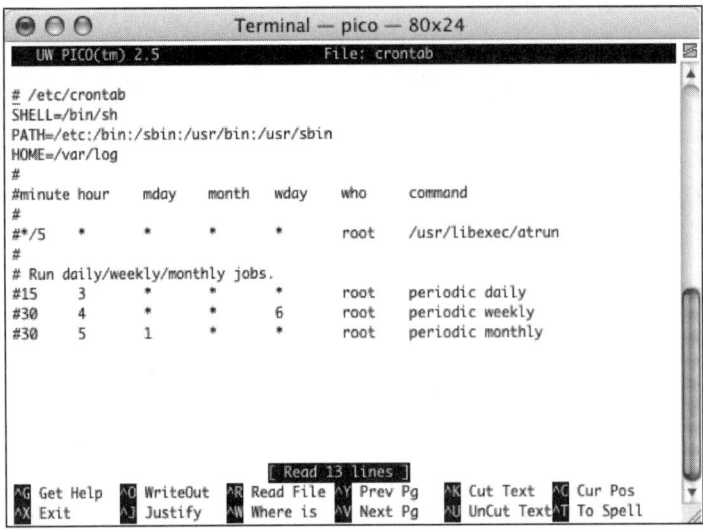

Figure 6-8. The default `crontab` file

You might prefer for all this to happen a bit later in the day, when your Mac is actually turned on. Let's say you get up at 8 a.m. every day, and then turn your Mac on before you get yourself ready for the day. A good time to schedule for would be 08:10–08:30. To do that, you would alter the first line to look like this instead:

```
# Run daily/weekly/monthly jobs.
10  8  *  *  *  root  periodic daily
20  8  *  *  6  root  periodic weekly
30  8  1  *  *  root  periodic monthly
```

5. To save the file, you want ^O WriteOut, which is *CTRL+O*, and then press *ENTER* to okay `crontab` as the file name to write (see Figure 6-9).

6. That's all there is to it. If you want to double-check that cron is actually running, you can issue the following command, ps -auxwww | grep cron (more about this later), and you should get a readout similar to Figure 6-10.

Making a new crontab rule

Using the ready-made crontab rules is all very well, but what if you want to add your own? Maybe you only want the Apache logs rotated? Using a small shell script, here's how you can have the Apache access_log archived using gzip, yet leave the last 30 entries in the new access_log file (just for easy reference).

1. First, you want to create your file, so type

   touch ~/Desktop/log.sh

2. You'll edit this in Pico:

   pico ~/ Desktop/log.sh

3. Like in Perl, shell scripts always start with a path to the shell, so type

   #!/bin/sh

4. The next line changes to the directory where the logs are stored (all these lines are commented, so that you know what's going on when you read them back at a later date).

   cd /private/var/log/httpd
   ➡ # change to the directory

5. To make things a lot easier, you're going to append the date to the file name, so you can see when each file was created. To do this, you'll set today as a variable, to get today's date in YYYYmmdd format (e.g., 20040111 was my birthday this year).

   today=`date +"%Y%m%d"`
   ➡ # get today's date in YYYYmmdd format

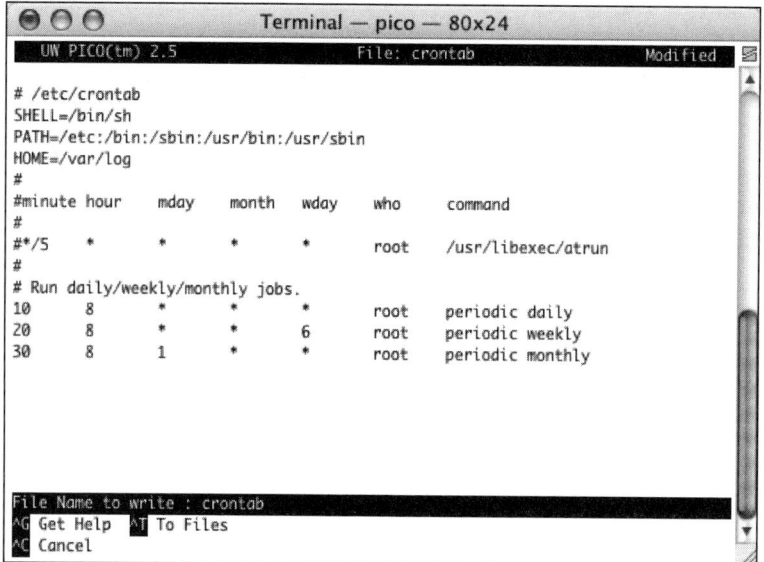

```
 ● ● ●              Terminal — pico — 80x24
 UW PICO(tm) 2.5                  File: crontab                    Modified
# /etc/crontab
SHELL=/bin/sh
PATH=/etc:/bin:/sbin:/usr/bin:/usr/sbin
HOME=/var/log
#
#minute hour    mday    month   wday    who     command
#
#*/5     *       *       *       *       root    /usr/libexec/atrun
#
# Run daily/weekly/monthly jobs.
10      8       *       *       *       root    periodic daily
20      8       *       *       6       root    periodic weekly
30      8       1       *       *       root    periodic monthly




File Name to write : crontab
^G Get Help  ^T To Files
^C Cancel
```

Figure 6-9. The rescheduled crontab file

```
 ● ● ●              Terminal — bash — 80x24
Last login: Sun Feb  8 03:12:31 on ttyp2
Welcome to Darwin!
iMac:~ phil$ ps -auxwww | grep cron
phil    1349  3.0  0.1   18172   344 std  S+   12:47PM   0:00.01 grep cron
root     239  0.0  0.0   27612   156 ??   Ss   Fri01PM   0:01.61 cron
root     546  0.0  0.1   18304   260 p1   S+   Fri10PM   0:00.15 pico crontab
iMac:~ phil$ _
```

Figure 6-10. Confirmation that cron is indeed running

6. Using the mv command, you append today's date to the access log file name, using the today variable you specified in the previous line.

```
mv access_log access.${today}
➡ # append today's date to the access
➡ log filename
```

7. Next, you use tail to read the last 30 lines of the log file, and print it into the new access log.

```
tail -n 30 access.${today} > access_log
➡ # grab the last 30 lines and print it
➡ to the end of the new access log
```

8. Using gzip, you archive the new file. –9 indicates the slowest compression method.

```
gzip -9 access.${today}
➡ # gzip today's access log
```

9. Rather than have to go looking for the new file every month, move it to the desktop as follows:

```
mv access.${today}.gz /Users/username/
➡ Desktop/access.${today}.gz
➡ # move the new file to the desktop
```

149

10. If you want to do the same with the `error_log` file, the process is the same:

```
mv error_log error.${today} # append
➥ today's date to the error log filename
tail -n 30 error.${today} > error_log
➥ # grab the last 30 lines and cat it
➥ to the end of the new error log
gzip -9 error.${today}
➥ # gzip today's error log
mv error.${today}.gz /Users/username/
➥ Desktop/error.${today}.gz
➥ # move the new file to the desktop
```

11. Press *CTRL+O* to save the document.

12. To make the file executable, run chmod 555 on it.

```
chmod 555 ~/Desktop/log.sh
```

13. Finally, move the script to /usr/bin.

```
sudo mv ~/Desktop/log.sh /usr/bin/log.sh
```

With the script written, you can now turn your attention to getting cron to run it for you.

1. Reopen the `crontab` file.

```
sudo pico /private/etc/crontab
```

2. You're going to schedule this to kick off at midday, on the first of every month, run by the root user. If you have a really active web server, you may want to use a weekly schedule instead. So, using your cursor keys, add the following line, as seen in Figure 6-11.

```
*  12  1  *  *  root     /usr/bin/log.sh
```

3. Write out the file with *CTRL+O*.

With just those few lines, you should now have your Apache logs kept nice and trim, with an archived file for reference.

Using ps and grep

Earlier, you saw how to use the command ps -auxwww | grep cron to determine whether cron was running. What that does is take output from one command (ps), pipe (|) it to the next (grep), and then print out the matching results. For the definitive lowdown on both ps and grep, see their man pages (shown in Figures 6-12 and 6-13) by typing man ps and man grep, respectively.

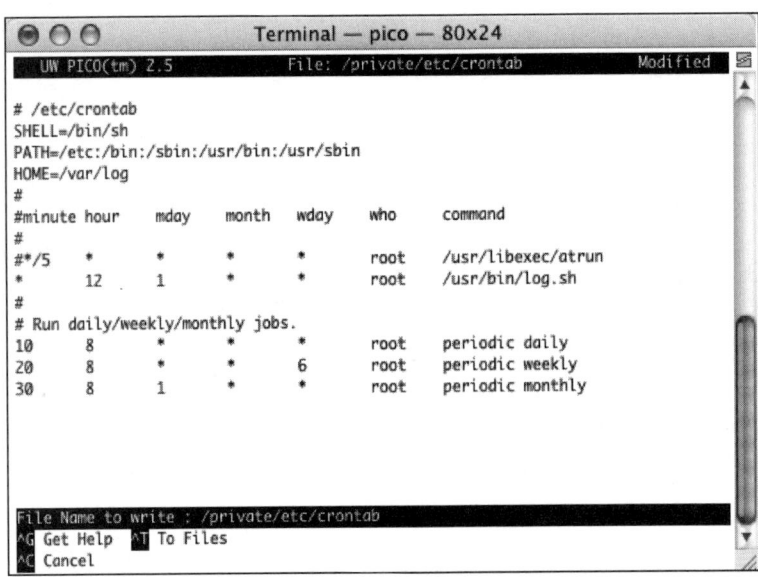

Figure 6-11. `log.sh` is now added to the crontab schedule.

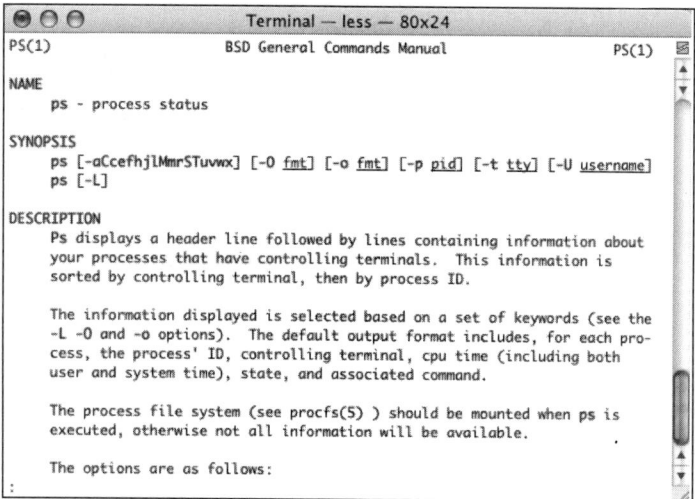

Figure 6-12. man page for ps

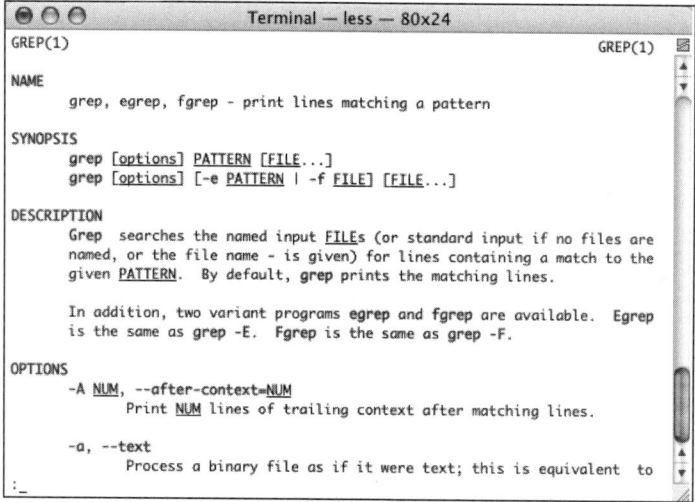

Figure 6-13. man page for grep .

Using pipes

As you saw, the pipe symbol (|) tells the shell to take the output of one command and use it as the input for another command.

To show you how, I'll walk you through combining ps and grep in a simple exercise that is guaranteed to make you feel smug for at *least* 15 seconds. Not quite as good as Andy Warhol's "famous for 15 minutes," but it's a step in the right direction.

By default, the dock is positioned at the bottom, in the middle. Using System Preferences, you can have it on the left of right of your screen, but it's still in the middle, and jumps around a bit.

151

I find it gets in the way less when it's pinned up in the top-right corner. Here's how:

1. You need to edit the dock's preference file, so you'll make a backup first like so:

```
cp /Users/username/Library/Preferences/
➥ com.apple.dock.plist /Users/username/
➥ Library/Preferences/
➥ com.apple.dock.plist.bak
```

2. Next, open the file in your text editor—I'll demonstrate using BBEdit for this:

```
bbedit /Users/phil/Library
➥ /Preferences/com.apple.dock.plist
```

3. Scroll to the bottom, and look for

```
</dict>
</plist>
```

Above them, add the following (see Figure 6-14):

```
<key>orientation</key>
<string>right</string>
<key>pinning</key>
<string>start</string>
</dict>
</plist>
```

```
422    <key>persistent-others</key>
423    <array/>
424    <key>tilesize</key>
425    <real>32</real>
426    <key>trash-full</key>
427    <false/>
428    <key>version</key>
429    <integer>1</integer>
430    <key>orientation</key>
431    <string>right</string>
432    <key>pinning</key>
433    <string>start</string>
434    </dict>
435    </plist>
436

433 | 27
```

Figure 6-14. Adding code in BBEdit

4. Save the file.

5. These changes don't take effect until the next time the dock is launched, so you hunt it down and kill the process, using ps and grep as follows (see Figure 6-15):

```
ps ax | grep Dock.app
```

6. The results tell you the PID of anything with "Dock.app" in the title. As you can see, you have two results: One is the dock itself, the other is the search you've just instigated. You're after killing the lowest number; in my case, this would be 375, so I'd type

```
kill -9 375
```

Your dock should die, and then reappear up in the top-right corner. Marvelous.

Of course, instead of this lengthy method of pinning the dock, you can just type the following in the terminal, and then kill the dock. But you wouldn't have learned much then, would you?

```
defaults write com.apple.dock pinning start
```

UNIX is geeky. Lord of The Rings fans are geekier. This is geekiest (as you can see in Figure 6-16)!

```
cat /usr/share/calendar/calendar.history
➥ | grep "LOTR"
```

Hardly of major use, but it just shows you there's all kinds of things lurking on your system.

```
● ● ●          Terminal — bash — 80x24
Last login: Mon Feb  9 15:46:57 on ttyp3
Welcome to Darwin!
iMac:~ phil$ ps ax | grep Dock.app
  375 ??  S    0:06.26 /System/Library/CoreServices/Dock.app/Contents/MacOS/
 1484 std R+   0:00.01 grep Dock.app
iMac:~ phil$ kill 375
iMac:~ phil$
```

Figure 6-15. Using ps and grep to get the dock's PID

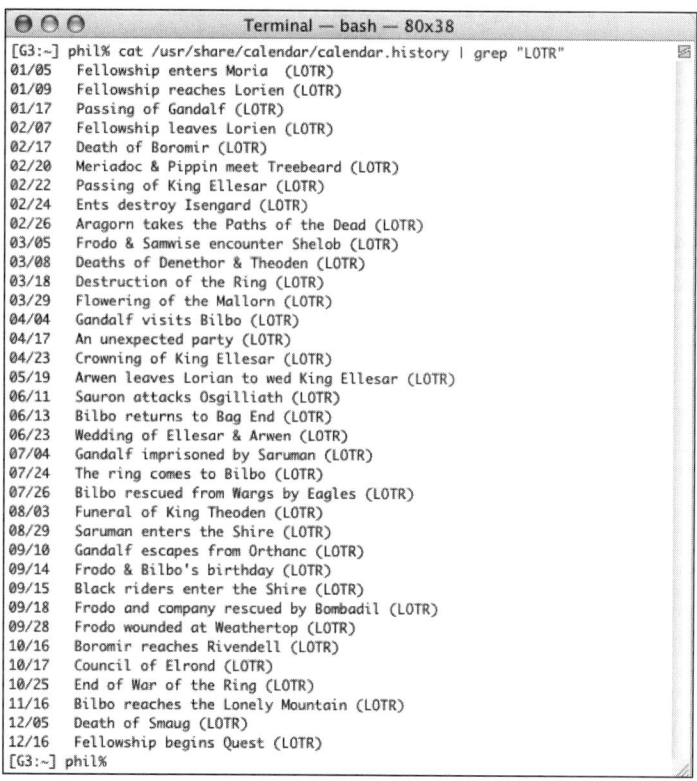

```
 ● ● ●                Terminal — bash — 80x38
[G3:~] phil% cat /usr/share/calendar/calendar.history | grep "LOTR"
01/05   Fellowship enters Moria  (LOTR)
01/09   Fellowship reaches Lorien (LOTR)
01/17   Passing of Gandalf (LOTR)
02/07   Fellowship leaves Lorien (LOTR)
02/17   Death of Boromir (LOTR)
02/20   Meriadoc & Pippin meet Treebeard (LOTR)
02/22   Passing of King Ellesar (LOTR)
02/24   Ents destroy Isengard (LOTR)
02/26   Aragorn takes the Paths of the Dead (LOTR)
03/05   Frodo & Samwise encounter Shelob (LOTR)
03/08   Deaths of Denethor & Theoden (LOTR)
03/18   Destruction of the Ring (LOTR)
03/29   Flowering of the Mallorn (LOTR)
04/04   Gandalf visits Bilbo (LOTR)
04/17   An unexpected party (LOTR)
04/23   Crowning of King Ellesar (LOTR)
05/19   Arwen leaves Lorian to wed King Ellesar (LOTR)
06/11   Sauron attacks Osgilliath (LOTR)
06/13   Bilbo returns to Bag End (LOTR)
06/23   Wedding of Ellesar & Arwen (LOTR)
07/04   Gandalf imprisoned by Saruman (LOTR)
07/24   The ring comes to Bilbo (LOTR)
07/26   Bilbo rescued from Wargs by Eagles (LOTR)
08/03   Funeral of King Theoden (LOTR)
08/29   Saruman enters the Shire (LOTR)
09/10   Gandalf escapes from Orthanc (LOTR)
09/14   Frodo & Bilbo's birthday (LOTR)
09/15   Black riders enter the Shire (LOTR)
09/18   Frodo and company rescued by Bombadil (LOTR)
09/28   Frodo wounded at Weathertop (LOTR)
10/16   Boromir reaches Rivendell (LOTR)
10/17   Council of Elrond (LOTR)
10/25   End of War of the Ring (LOTR)
11/16   Bilbo reaches the Lonely Mountain (LOTR)
12/05   Death of Smaug (LOTR)
12/16   Fellowship begins Quest (LOTR)
[G3:~] phil%
```

Figure 6-16. Checking out the LOTR calendar entries

Disk Utility (fsck)

One of the things you should do from time to time is run Disk Utility to repair any file permissions that have gone wonky. This just keeps things shipshape, and it's always better to prevent than cure. However, Disk Utility can't run properly on a disk with open files, and this includes your startup disk. If you want to run the GUI version (Figure 6-17), you have to boot up from your OS X CD/DVD, and then run it. Alternatively, you can boot into single-user mode. As this is the UNIX chapter, that's what we're going to do.

1. With your Mac powered down, hold down ⌘+S, and then power up with those keys held down until you see some text on your screen.

2. On screen, you're instructed to type fsck –y, but that is incorrect with this release of Mac OS X, because the volume is journaled. The way around

this is to use the –f option to force checking, so type

/sbin/fsck –fy

This will check for any disk errors, and (hopefully) repair them.

3. Run this command until you get the following message:

The volume Macintosh HD appears to be okay

4. Next, you need to mount the disk:

/sbin/mount –uw

5. Finally, exit single-user mode by typing

exit

And you're back to logging in as normal.

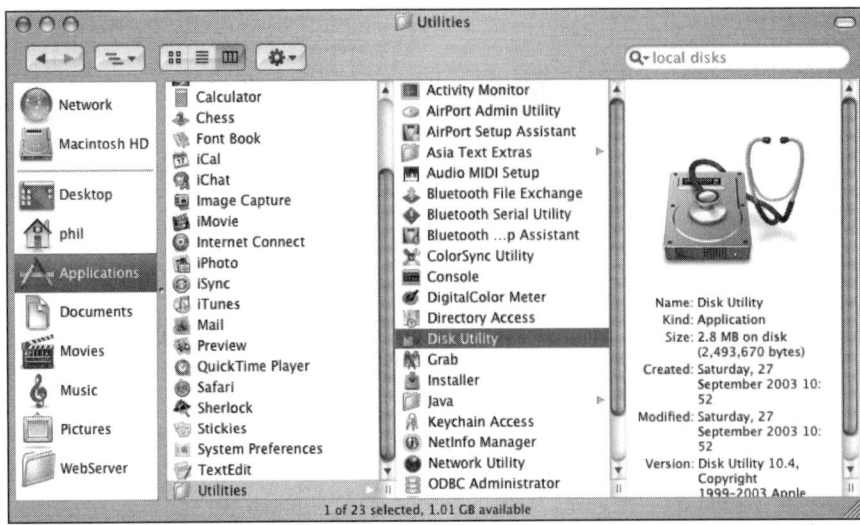

Figure 6-17. Disk Utility

Remote operations

Because Mac OS X is UNIX-based, you don't actually need to be in front of your machine in order to log in and use it. As long as it's powered up, connected to the Internet, and you have the right port open, you can log in from any other machine. This can be another Mac OS X machine, a UNIX/Linux machine, or even a PC (using an application called PuTTY, available at http://www.chiark.greenend.org.uk/~sgtatham/putty/).

Before I show you some of these remote operations, you need to open the relevant port. This is just a matter of opening System Preferences and checking the Remote Login option as shown in Figure 6-18. Easy!

Mac OS X uses the default port for ssh, which is 22. If you have an external firewall and/or router, you may need to forward port 22 to your Mac's IP, depending on how your network is configured.

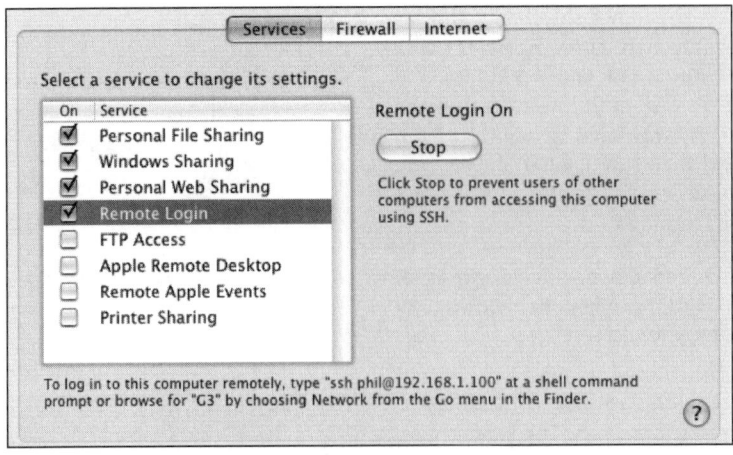

Figure 6-18. Turning Remote Login on in System Preferences

SSH (secure shell)

Previously, logging into a remote machine was done with telnet. Over a telnet connection, your passwords are sent as plain text, which can be read by anyone. This isn't too good, as even an amateur hacker, using sophisticated programs called packet sniffers, can spy on your connection and steal your data. ssh changes this, because it encrypts all your traffic, including well-kept secrets such as passwords.

Once you're logged in, it's just the same as using Terminal while physically sitting at that machine. Using ssh is simple:

```
ssh userid@hostname
```

The first time you log onto a machine, you'll get an RSA key message, as you can see in Figure 6-19. Type yes, and then enter the password. That's it, you're in. You may now use the machine to log in to and administer MySQL, edit the httpd.conf, kill a rogue process that has gone wild, etc.

If, like me, you occasionally play the odd prank, and you have login details for a friend's Mac OS X machine, you can log in, and then run the say command to make the remote machine speak, like so:

```
say "this machine has the artley virus
➡ and all files will be deleted
➡ immediately!"
```

Kinda like in the movie *War Games*, eh? Don't let anyone tell you UNIX can't be fun! You can save that as an .aiff file too, should you need to. All the Radiohead fans in the house, type

```
say -v Fred -o ~/Desktop/fitter.aiff
➡ "fitter. happier. more productive"
```

The file will then be saved to your desktop.

SCP (secure copy)

Transferring files between machines is fairly straightforward using scp—secure copy. The syntax is as follows:

```
scp [remote_file] userid@hostname
➡ :[new_local_path]
```

Put into practice, I would use the following command to grab log.sh from the desktop of my iMac, and dump it in the root of my home directory (see Figure 6-20):

```
scp ~/desktop/log.sh phil@192.168.1.102
➡ :log.sh
```

```
 ● ● ●                    Terminal — ssh — 80x24
[G3:~] phil% ssh phil@192.168.1.102
The authenticity of host '192.168.1.102 (192.168.1.102)' can't be established.
RSA key fingerprint is 0b:a7:fe:0c:93:2c:36:f8:66:16:81:1a:44:84:cb:9e.
Are you sure you want to continue connecting (yes/no)? yes
Warning: Permanently added '192.168.1.102' (RSA) to the list of known hosts.
phil@192.168.1.102's password:
Last login: Mon Feb  9 19:58:13 2004
Welcome to Darwin!
iMac:~ phil$
```

Figure 6-19. Using ssh to log in to another machine on my network

```
[G3:~] phil% scp ~/desktop/log.sh phil@192.168.1.102:log.sh
phil@192.168.1.102's password:
log.sh                              100%  601      36.7KB/s    00:00
[G3:~] phil%
```

Figure 6-20. Using scp to log into another machine on my network

curl and wget

On UNIX systems, there are a number of ways to download a file from an HTTP source. One is installed by default (curl), and another is wget. They both have different merits. To install wget, you can either grab the package installer (http://macosx.forked.net/p/wget-1.8.1.pkg.tgz) or download the source and compile it yourself (http://www.gnu.org/software/wget/wget.html).

Here's a fun example of how to use either of these small applications. I like the Sinfest comic strip (http://www.sinfest.net/). Sometimes I might be too busy to remember to check each day, so I could have the following line as a small shell script, and tell cron to run it on a daily basis:

```
curl -O http://www.sinfest.net/comics/
➥ sf'date +"%Y%m%d"'.gif
```

Broken down, that line simply says to use curl to save a file with the same name as the remote name (-O is the letter "oh," not a zero), from the location we've specified. Each day's comic strip file name is that day's date in YYYYmmdd format, which you should be familiar with from earlier on in this chapter.

With wget, you can use the -r (recursive) switch to grab a whole directory structure, like so:

```
wget -r  http://www.sinfest.net/
```

Because wget is often seen as being a bit harsher on bandwidth, as opposed to just browsing a site, it's only fair that you should send Tatsuya Ishida a bandwidth contribution if you use the preceding example.

SFTP (secure FTP)

For the same security reasons as telnet, **F**ile **T**ransfer **P**rotocol (FTP) has been replaced with **S**ecure **F**ile **T**ransfer **P**rotocol (SFTP). Usage is easy:

1. Turn FTP Access on in System Preferences (see Figure 6-21).
2. Open Terminal and type username@hostname, for example:

   sftp phil@192.168.1.100

   or

   sftp phil@iMac.local

3. Enter your password when prompted, and you're in (see Figure 6-22).
4. To get a file from the server is as easy as it sounds (Figure 6-23).

   get remote_file local_file_name

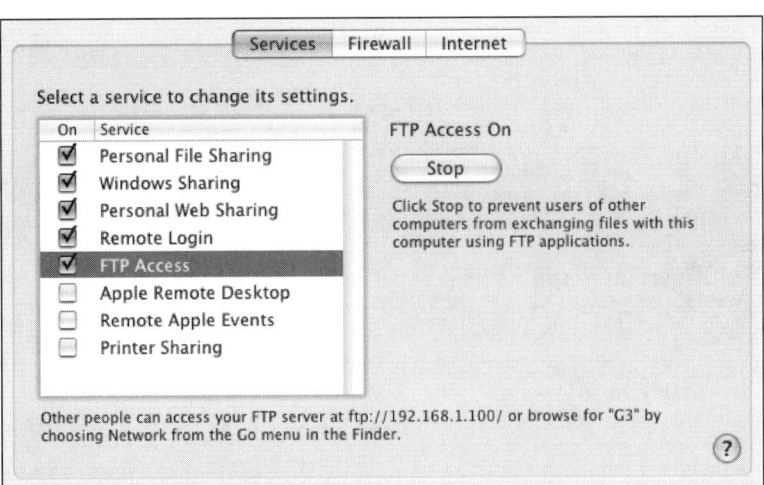

Figure 6-21. Turning FTP access on

156

```
●  ○  ○                    Terminal — ssh — 80x24
[G3:~] phil% sftp phil@iMac.local
Connecting to iMac.local...
The authenticity of host 'imac.local (fe80:4::205:2ff:feb1:9ab5)' can't be estab
lished.
RSA key fingerprint is 0b:a7:fe:0c:93:2c:36:f8:66:16:81:1a:44:84:cb:9e.
Are you sure you want to continue connecting (yes/no)? yes
Warning: Permanently added 'imac.local,fe80:4::205:2ff:feb1:9ab5' (RSA) to the l
ist of known hosts.
phil@imac.local's password:
sftp>
```

Figure 6-22. Logged in via SFTP

```
sftp> get .bash_history bash_history.txt
.bash_history                          100% 2725    296.9KB/s   00:00
sftp>
```

Figure 6-23. Getting a file via SFTP

5. In this instance, I'm getting a dot file. Because OS X sees these files as invisible, I'm renaming it as a .txt file when it lands on my machine. This way, I can see it easily, and the system won't complain about me trying to save what it will refer to as a system file.

6. As you'd expect, to put a file on the server is just as easy.

   put local_file_name remote_file

7. When you're done, type exit to log off the server.

.htaccess and .htpasswd

An .htaccess file is a text file containing Apache directives that apply to the documents in the directory where the .htaccess file is located, and to all subdirectories under it as well. Not everyone has access to the httpd.conf, like you do on your Mac OS X machine. For some people, .htaccess is how they add directives. Note: You turned the ability to use .htaccess on in Chapter 5, when you edited the httpd.conf document.

The .htaccess file can have many uses. Most commonly, it's used as a security measure to keep people out of certain directories; to password protect a Members Only section; for specifying error pages; and for specifying the DirectoryIndex.

For a lot more information, you can check out the .htaccess page in the Apache manual, which lives on your web server: http://127.0.0.1/manual/howto/htaccess.html.

As this manual says,

"In general, you should never use .htaccess files unless you don't have access to the main server configuration file. There is, for example, a prevailing misconception that user authentication should always be done in .htaccess files. This is simply not the case. You can put user authentication configurations in the main server configuration, and this is, in fact, the preferred way to do things."

You obviously *do* have access to the main server configuration file, but maybe you need to know how to add such files. It's possible you're using you Mac OS X machine to host all manner of things for different people who need to be able to configure certain things for themselves, but you don't want them touching your httpd.conf file. You certainly don't want to be constantly rebooting your web server application either.

157

Password protected area

Say you want to be able to create an Admin section on you web server, as I did for my technical reviewer and myself. This area will be http://127.0.0.1/admin/ and only accessible to Jake and me.

1. Open Terminal and change directory to the WebServer root.

   cd /Library/WebServer/Documents

2. To create the admin directory, type

   mkdir admin

3. Next up, cd into the new admin directory.

   cd admin

4. Create the .htaccess file inside the admin directory.

   touch .htaccess

5. Open the .htaccess in the text editor, Vim.

   vim .htaccess

6. Flip into INSERT mode in Vim by pressing *SHIFT+I* and type

   AuthUserFile /Library/WebServer/.htpasswd
   AuthName "Private: Scousers Only"
   AuthType Basic
   require user phil jake

What does all that do?

AuthUserFile is the path to the file where the user names/passwords are stored. You'll create this in a minute.

AuthName is the message that comes up in the authorization box.

AuthType is set to standard Basic authentication.

require user phil jake specifies one of two users only who are allowed access.

7. Exit INSERT mode by pressing *ESCAPE.*

8. Save the file by typing :w (see Figure 6-24), and then exit Vim with :q.

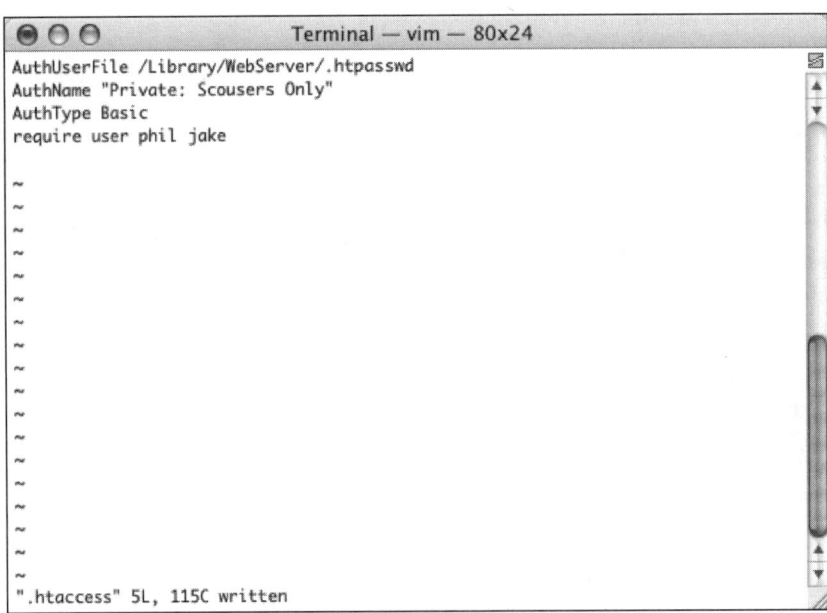

Figure 6-24. Writing the .htaccess file in Vim

With the `.htaccess` file written, you can now turn your attention to the file that stores the user names and passwords: `.htpasswd`.

1. This file should be outside of the web server root directory, for safety. Open a Terminal window and type

htpasswd -c /library/webserver/
➥ **.htpasswd phil**

Here, the –c switch creates the file `.htpasswd` for you, and adds me as a user. Note you have to enter the password twice, when you press *ENTER*.

2. To add another user, you don't need that –c switch. In fact, if you do use it, it will just overwrite the file you just made. So, type

htpasswd /library/webserver/.htpasswd jake

Enter the user's password twice (see Figure 6-25).

3. If you now open that file in Vim, you can see that the passwords are nicely encrypted as shown in Figure 6-26.

4. Close Vim by typing `:q`.

5. Call up http://127.0.0.1/admin/ in your browser, and you should be greeted by the authentication box, as shown in Figure 6-27.

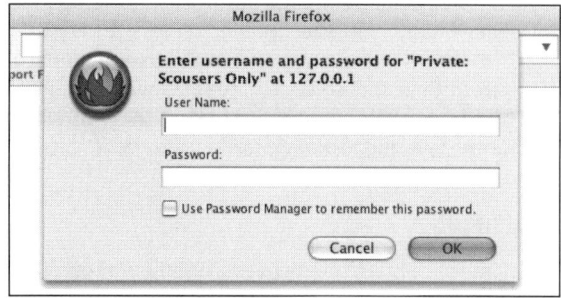

Figure 6-27. If your name's not down, you don't get in!

Obviously, Jake and I aren't likely to be visiting your local machine, so you might want to put your own user name in there. Leave ours in though, just in case . . .

Later on in the book, you'll be adding a lot more to this Admin section; so don't worry about it being empty at the moment.

Figure 6-25. Adding users to the .htpasswd database

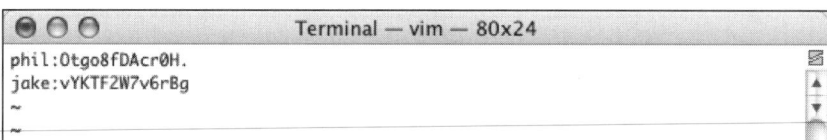

Figure 6-26. Encrypted passwords

159

Fink and X11

With all this talk of a "UNIX-based system," it must be a simple matter of just downloading UNIX applications and installing them, right? Well, not quite. If you installed Xcode from the CD that came with Panther, then you have a head start on installing some applications from their source code. Xcode allows you to run the "configure, make, make install" trinity, of which I'll talk more in the next chapter.

Libraries

In Chapter 5, I mentioned CGI.pm, and how much time it saves to use existing libraries when writing Perl applications. UNIX applications use libraries too, in much the same way. Libraries can be linked with other libraries and other object files to create executable files. Obviously, all these libraries aren't part of the default installation of Mac OS X. Apple has included what they believe to be the minimum set of tools for the job. This is where the trouble lies.

Example: You might want to set about installing the text browser, Lynx, which we discussed in Chapter 4. However, Lynx requires the following libraries: gettext, libiconv, and ncurses. Not any old versions of those libraries, either; it requires a minimum build number of each one. Quite often, libraries need to be installed in a certain order, too. Argh! All you wanted to do was install a simple text-based browser, and it gets out of hand very quickly. Enter Fink.

What is Fink?

Fink is an open source project that lets Mac OS X users run UNIX/Linux software on their OS X machine. No more fumbling around for libraries, or wrestling with configure options—Fink takes care of all dependent files and packages, and installs everything in the right place, in the right order. Installing an application is as simple as typing apt-get install package_name, so let's get to it and download Fink.

1. Download the installer by clicking the appropriate link at http://fink.sourceforge.net/ (see Figure 6-28), and then select the nearest mirror site.

2. When the file is downloaded, double-click the installer and okay everything to install.

3. Towards the end of installation, a Terminal window like the one in Figure 6-29 will pop up and ask to append a line to your .bash_profile, so type yes and press ENTER; once optimizing is complete, Fink is installed.

Fink doesn't interfere with the Mac OS X directory, so there's no need to worry about it breaking any of your nice Mac OS X installation (see Figure 6-30).

Fink Downloads

There are many ways to install or upgrade Fink. For new users, the quick start instructions below are recommended. Otherwise, check out the overview and the upgrade matrix.

Quick Start

New to Fink? These quick start instructions are here to get you up to speed with the binary release.

1. Download the installer disk image:
   Fink 0.6.2 Binary Installer - **19504 KB**
   (10.1 users - use Fink 0.4.1)

Figure 6-28. Click the Fink0.6.2 Binary Installer link, and then select a mirror site.

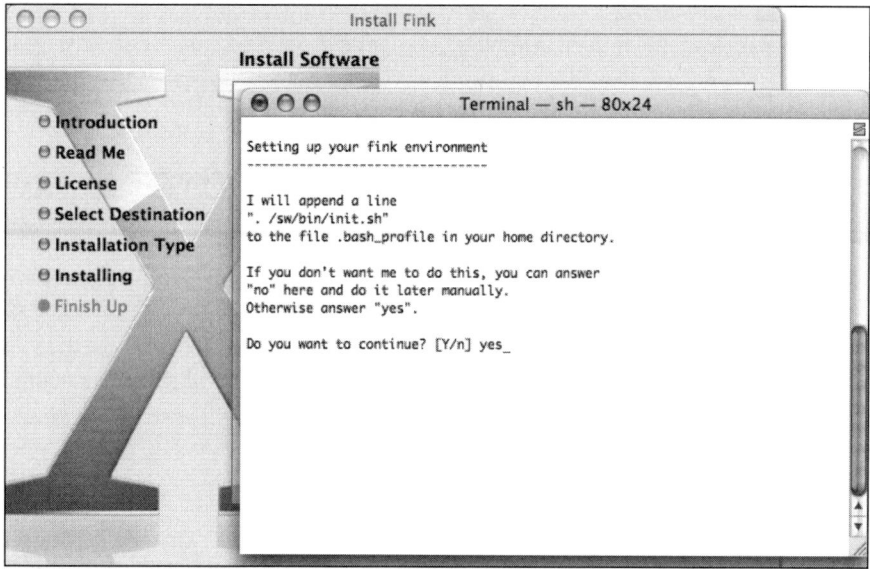

Figure 6-29. Type yes to have the file amendment made.

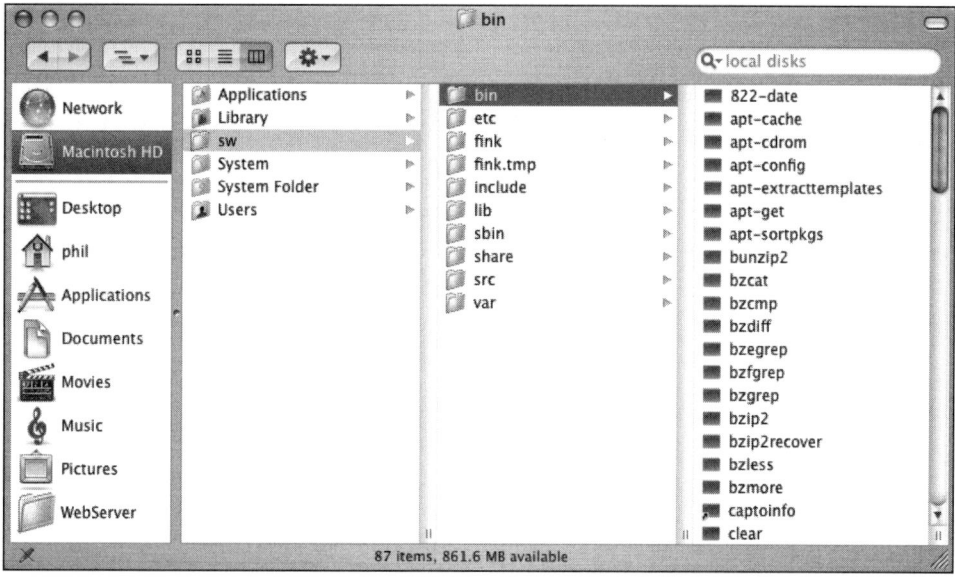

Figure 6-30. Fink installs everything into /sw (Macintosh HD/sw).

If you don't want that /sw directory to be visible, type the following in the terminal, which will make it invisible:

```
sudo /Developer/Tools/SetFile -a V /sw
```

You will need to restart the Finder or log out/in for that to take effect.

To make it visible again, type the following code:

```
sudo /Developer/Tools/SetFile -a v /sw
```

Notice the small v that time. To read more about SetFile, type man SetFile in the terminal.

There are literally hundreds of applications available via Fink. To get a complete list, type fink list (see Figure 6-31).

Update Fink

Once you've installed Fink, you need to update it. This is easy enough. Open a Terminal window and type fink selfupdate.

Many of the binary files for 10.3 have been also been updated. To access the updated files, bring your index of binary files up-to-date by running the command sudo apt-get update.

Installing packages with Fink

There are three ways to install packages with Fink:

- Fink Commander is a GUI, which does things in a very Mac-like way. Just point and click.
- Run apt-get install package_name in Terminal (or the X11 terminal, as I'll mention later).
- Run sudo dselect to invoke Fink's CLI front end.

dselect

As this is the UNIX chapter, it makes sense to ignore the fancy GUI (for now), and head straight for the command-line options, so that's what we're going to do.

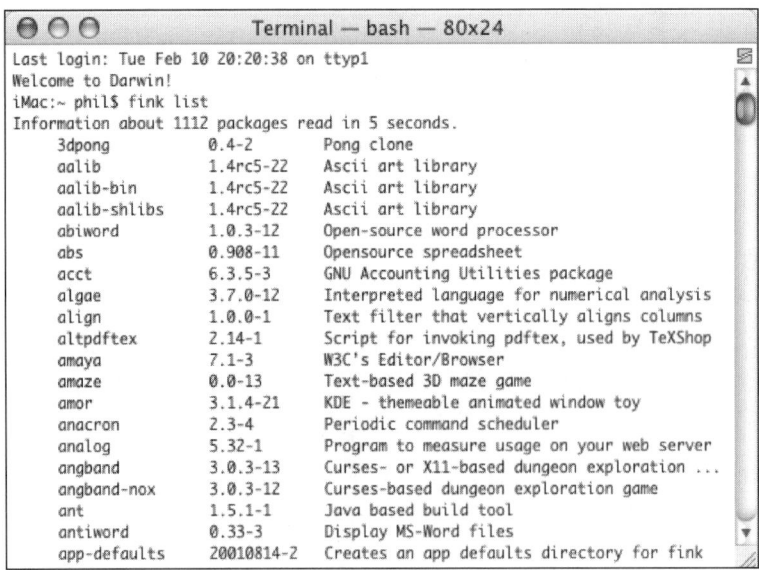

Figure 6-31. Just type fink list to list all the available packages.

1. Open a Terminal window, and type sudo dselect to get the Fink front end on screen (see Figure 6-32).

2. As this is the first time you've run Fink, press *ENTER* to choose the access method to use (see Figure 6-33).

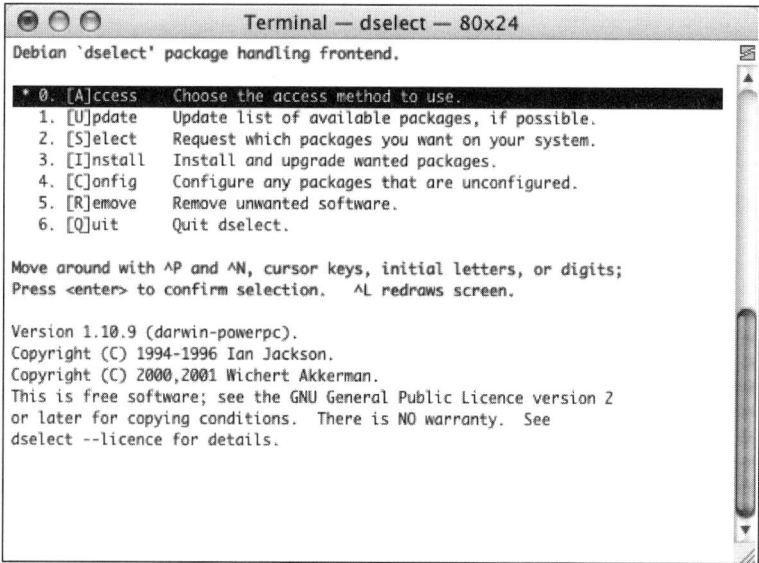

Figure 6-32. Fink's CLI front end

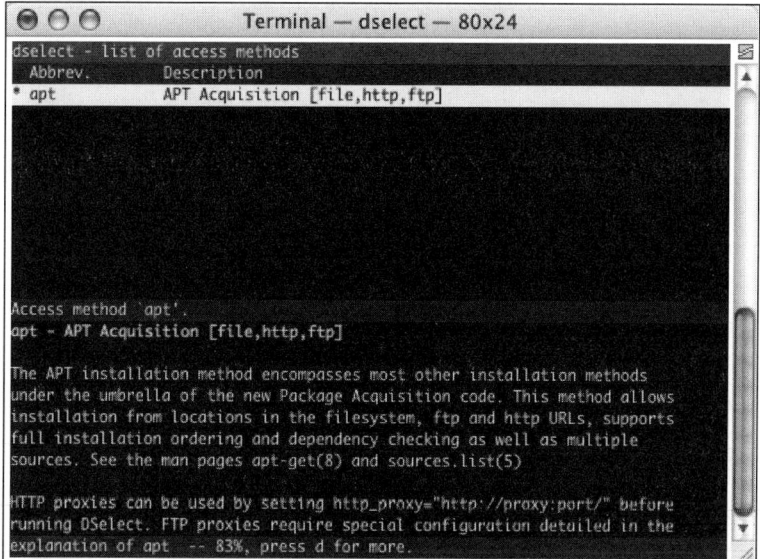

Figure 6-33. Press *ENTER* to select APT.

3. On the next screen (Figure 6-34), you're being advised *not* to overwrite this file, so type N to comply (in case something blows up), and then press ENTER.

4. Next on the menu: Update list of available packages, if possible (see Figures 6-35 and 6-36). Again, with the menu item selected, press ENTER to access it.

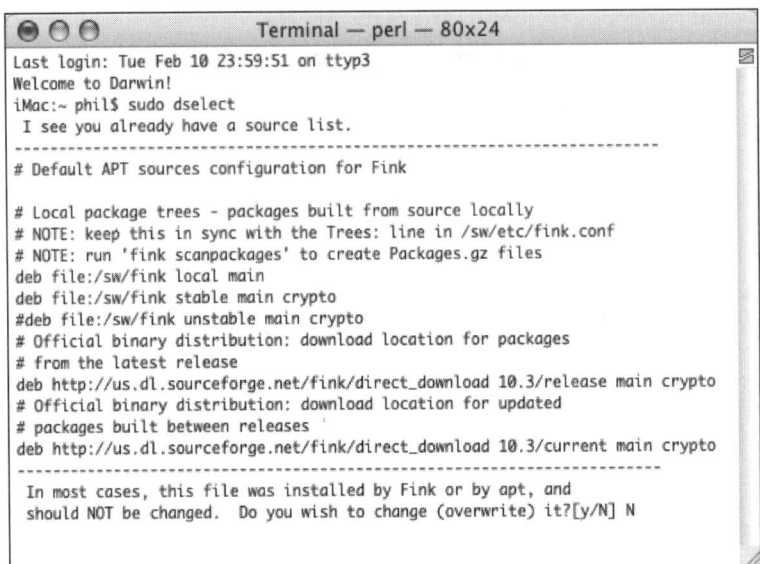

Figure 6-34. Take Fink's advice, and don't overwrite the file.

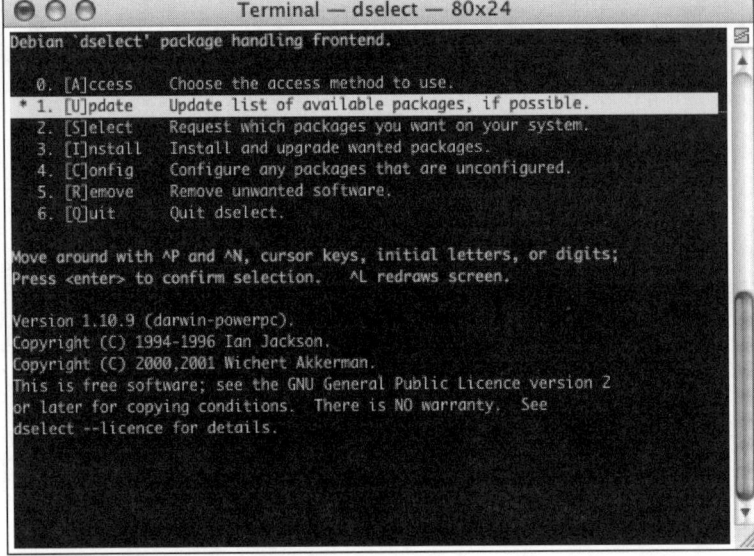

Figure 6-35. Taking the Update option

5. Next, select which packages you want on your system as shown in Figure 6-37.

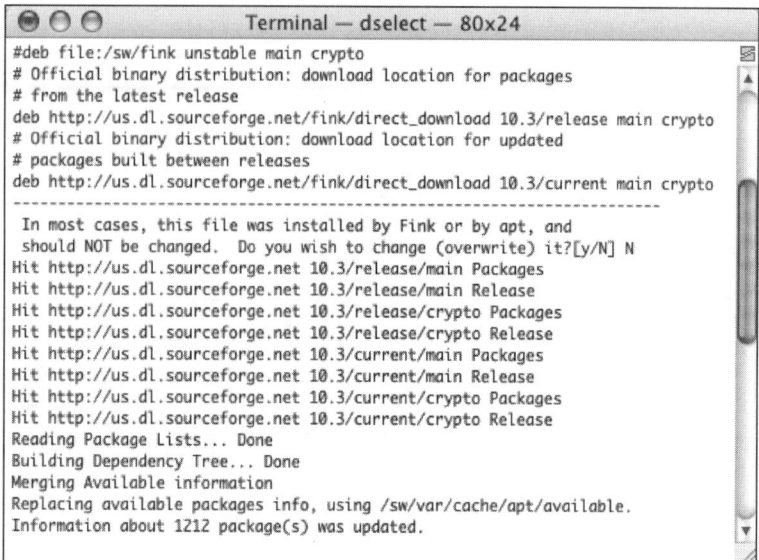

Figure 6-36. Update information is downloaded.

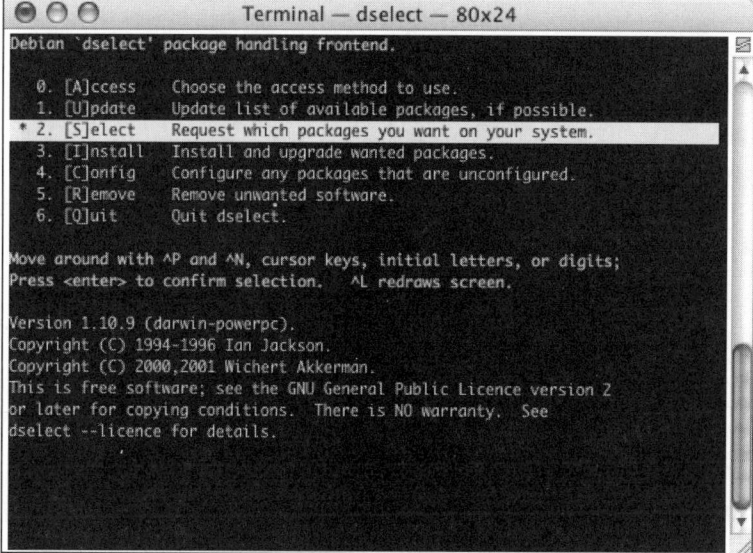

Figure 6-37. Time to select your packages.

6. After you've read the intro text, press *ENTER* to leave help and enter the list (see Figure 6-38).

For now, I'm just going to scroll down and install a text editor called joe, as shown in Figure 6-39, purely

because someone mentioned it to me last night (and it was my granddad's name). Take the time to look through the whole list and see if there are any goodies that you like the sound of.

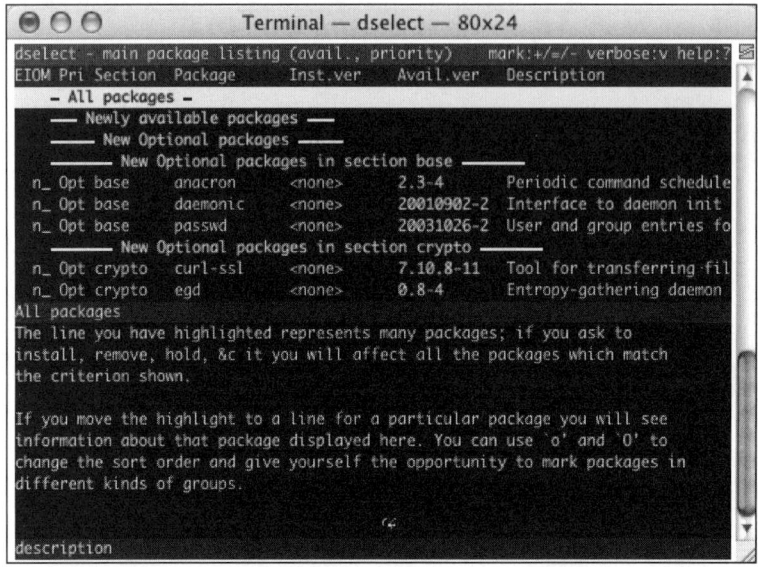

Figure 6-38. There are over 1000 packages in this list.

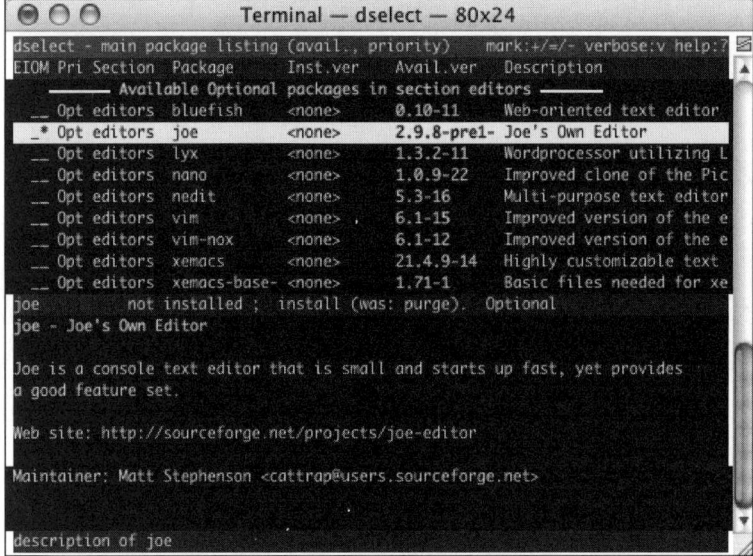

Figure 6-39. joe—Joe's Own Editor

To select a package, simply highlight it with the cursor keys, and press +. If you change your mind, press – to deselect it. I've selected joe now, so I press *Enter* to get back to the main menu.

7. On to menu item 3: Install and upgrade wanted packages. Press *ENTER* to start the installation, as shown in Figure 6-40.

8. Next comes the Config section. Select the option shown in Figure 6-41 and press *ENTER* to start the process, shown in Figure 6-42.

```
Reading Package Lists... Done
Building Dependency Tree... Done
The following NEW packages will be installed:
  joe
0 packages upgraded, 1 newly installed, 0 to remove and 0  not upgraded.
Need to get 282kB of archives. After unpacking 0B will be used.
Do you want to continue? [Y/n] Y
Get:1 http://us.dl.sourceforge.net 10.3/release/main joe 2.9.8-pre1-12 [282kB]
Fetched 282kB in 6s (44.8kB/s)
(Reading database ... 13645 files and directories currently installed.)
Unpacking joe (from .../joe_2.9.8-pre1-12_darwin-powerpc.deb) ...
Setting up joe (2.9.8-pre1-12) ...
Do you want to erase any previously downloaded .deb files? [Y/n] Y
Press enter to continue.
```

Figure 6-40. Installing joe

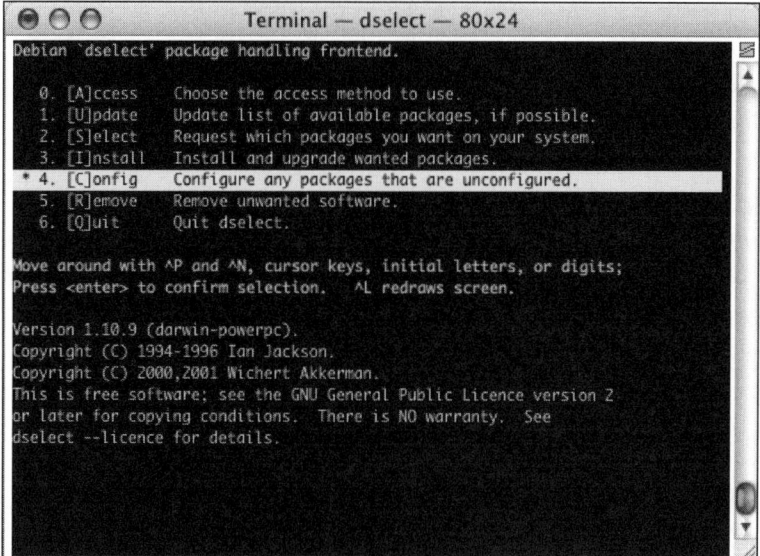

Figure 6-41. Configure, then you're nearly done.

```
running dpkg --pending --configure ...
```

Figure 6-42. The configure process in action

167

9. Lastly, remove unwanted software by selecting the option shown in Figure 6-43.

10. That's it. You can quit dselect now by pressing *ENTER* and selecting menu option 6 (see Figure 6-44).

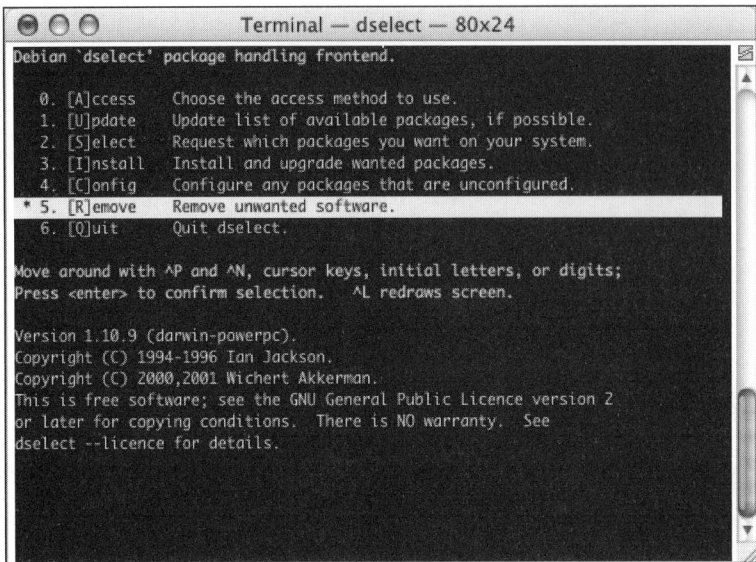

Figure 6-43. Removing unwanted software

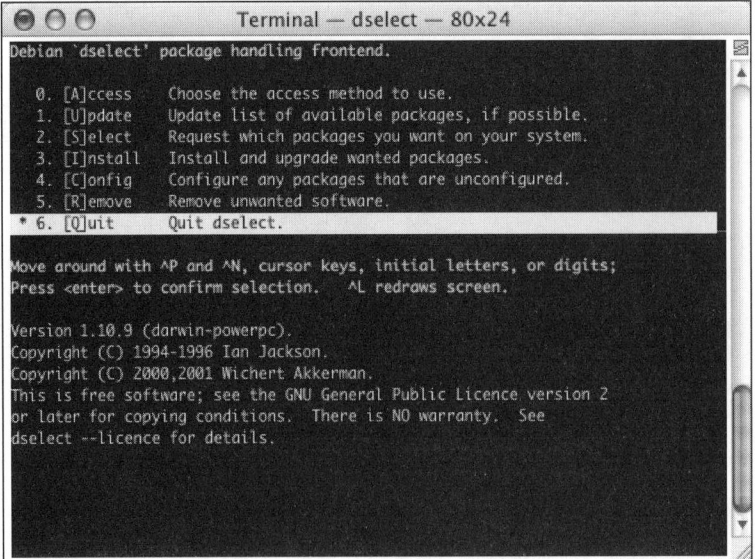

Figure 6-44. Quitting dselect

11. To test joe out, open a file as you would with any other CLI text editor (see Figure 6-45):

```
joe /Library/WebServer/Documents/
➥ 05/index.php
```

Technically, the correct geeky way to open this new application is via the X11 terminal (xterm), as you can see in Figure 6-46. X11 is on CD 3 of Panther and is required to run some of the applications you can download with Fink.

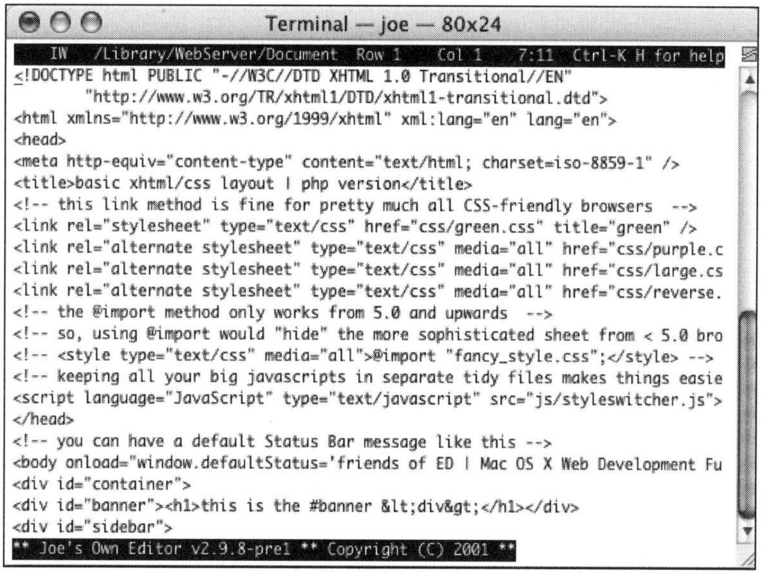

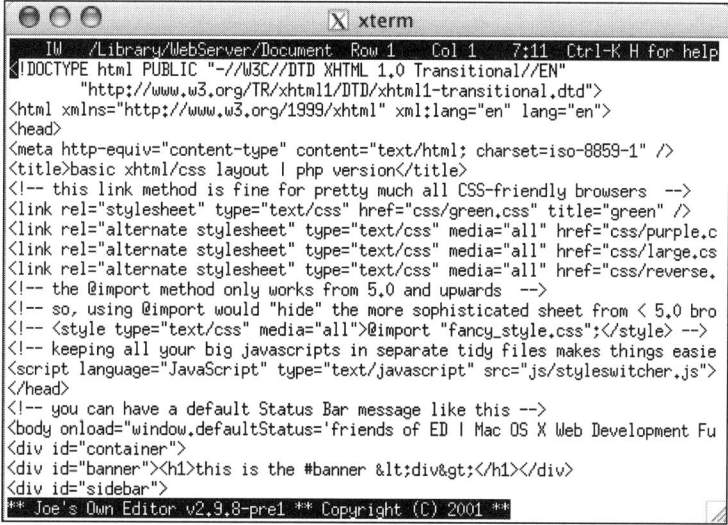

Figure 6-45. Editing a file with joe

Figure 6-46. Running joe in X11

You can find the X11 xterm in /Applications/ Utilities, where it is right next to Terminal, as shown in Figure 6-47.

If you didn't install this when you installed Panther, you can just pop CD 3 in and run the installer. It's recommended that you install the X11 Software Development Kit (SDK), which is on the Xcode CD and isn't installed by default. Insert the CD and double-click the X11SDK.pkg inside the Packages folder, and then follow the usual installation options.

apt-get

Now that you know where the X11 xterm is, open it up and I'll show you the next method. This time, you'll download the wget application I mentioned back in the "Remote operations" section of this chapter.

1. Type sudo apt-get install wget in your xterm window, hit *ENTER*, and then enter your password when prompted (see Figure 6-48).

2. Err, that's it.

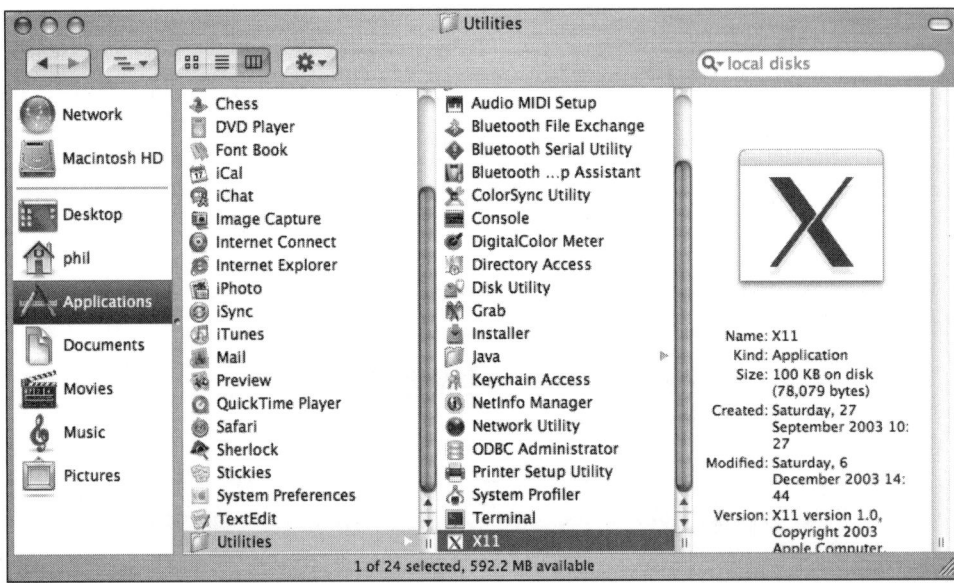

Figure 6-47. Where to locate X11's xterm

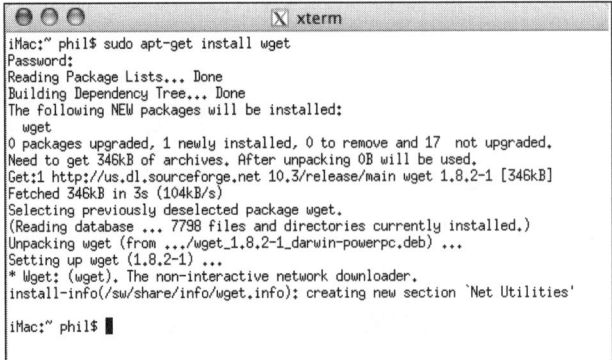

Figure 6-48. Using apt-get to install wget in an xterm window

Fink Commander

You'll use Fink Commander to install the Lynx browser, which I've mentioned a few times in this book.

1. When you mount the Fink disc image to install Fink, you'll see an application called Fink Commander, as shown in Figure 6-49. Once you've dragged the Fink Commander folder into your Applications directory, double-click the icon to launch the application.

2. In the Search box on the top right of Fink Commander, type lynx, and it should show two packages for download (lynx and lynx-ssl), as shown in Figure 6-50.

3. Select the lynx package, choose Source ➤ Install from the File menu, and enter your password when prompted.

4. Sit back while Fink downloads, configures, and compiles Lynx for you.

5. Open an xterm window and check out a website by typing

   lynx http://www.friendsofed.com/

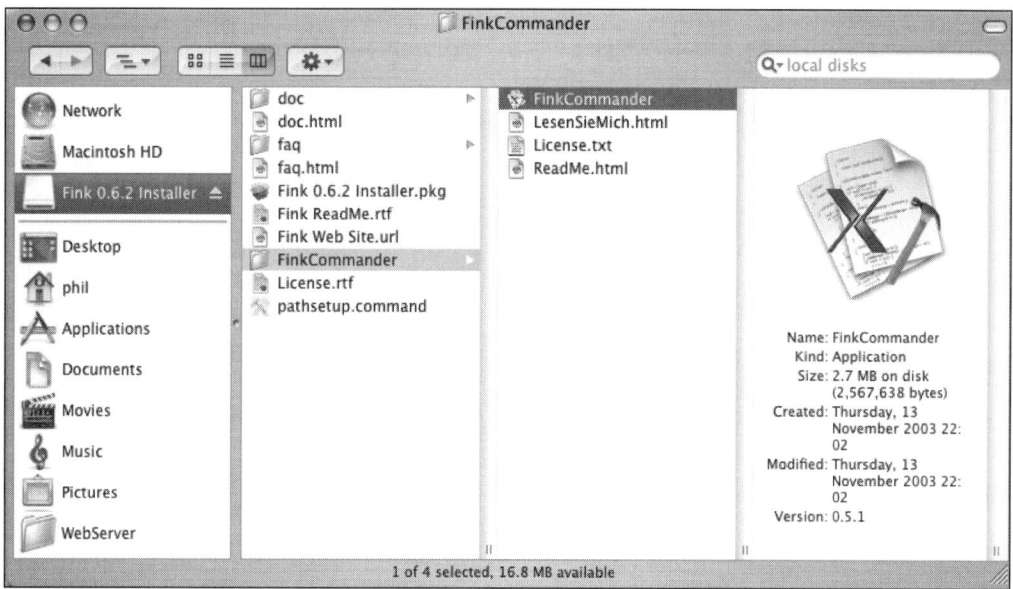

Figure 6-49. Using Fink Commander

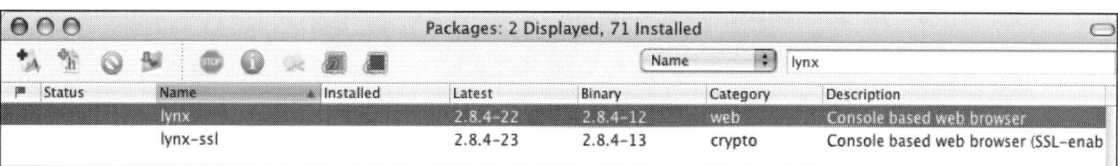

Figure 6-50. Using Fink to install Lynx

Running KDE/Gnome on Panther

If you're from a Linux background, or maybe you just have the urge to see what all the fuss is about, you can install the popular UNIX graphical desktop environments KDE and Gnome on Panther, via Fink. I must warn you, though, this takes long enough on a fast new machine. Tackling the installation from source on a sub-500 MHz G3 Mac is going to take well over 24 hours. (I actually heard a report of an installation taking almost a week!)

If you're interested in learning more about these environments, there is a direct comparison between Windows XP Luna, BeOS 6 (Dano/Zeta), Mac OS X Aqua, and UNIX's KDE and Gnome here: http://www.osnews.com/story.php?news_id=3064.

For the more adventurous of you, there's a guide on how to install KDE on Panther here:

http://homepage.mac.com/sao1/fink/
finpan.html#top19Chapter Review.

Chapter review

It's possible your brain may be hurting by now. It's also possible you read this chapter quite some time after most of the others. Yes, UNIX isn't everybody's cup of tea, but I believe you're missing out if you don't take full advantage of something you've paid for.

As well as knowing some of the background to UNIX, you now know how to get around your Mac via the Terminal, or Command Line Interface (CLI). You're more aware of why the files in the last chapter needed special permissions to run.

You know how to automate tasks with cron, and schedule them to run at a time that suits you. Just as importantly, you know how to run Disk Utility, so that it fixes problems you can't fix when you're logged in via the nice Aqua GUI, as normal.

Knowing how to use your Mac from afar is very useful. With ssh and scp, you never have to miss deadlines due to those vital text/graphics documents you left on your Mac at home.

Finally, the world of Fink showed you just how expandable Mac OS X is.

So, it might have been hard going for you, but I'm sure you feel a lot more confident about using Terminal now. I hope so anyway, because you'll be using it a lot more in the next chapter, which is all about Apache modules.

```
#LoadModule env_module            libexec/httpd/mo
LoadModule config_log_module  libexec/httpd/mod
#LoadModule mime_magic_module  libexec/httpd/mo
LoadModule mime_module            libexec/httpd/mod
LoadModule negotiation_module libexec/httpd/mod
#LoadModule status_module         libexec/httpd/mo
#LoadModule info_module           libexec/httpd/mo
LoadModule includes_module     libexec/httpd/mod
LoadModule autoindex_module    libexec/httpd/mod
LoadModule dir_module             libexec/httpd/mod
LoadModule cgi_module             libexec/httpd/mod
LoadModule asis_module            libexec/httpd/mod
LoadModule imap_module            libexec/httpd/mod
LoadModule action_module          libexec/httpd/mod
#LoadModule speling_module         libexec/httpd/mod
LoadModule userdir_module         libexec/httpd/mod
LoadModule alias_module           libexec/httpd/mod
LoadModule rewrite_module         libexec/httpd/mod
                                [ Read 1097 lines
^G Get Help  ^O WriteOut  ^R Read File  ^Y Prev
^X Exit      ^J Justify   ^W Where is   ^V Next
```

Chapter 7

APACHE MODULES

What we'll cover in this chapter:

- Apache configuration
- The modules
- Xcode
- UNIX

The point of this chapter is to give you a general idea of what an Apache module is and what you're supposed to do with it. To do that, you're going to need to know what Apache is and why it has modules.

Apache shares its origins with those of the first ever web server. In late 1990, two employees at CERN (the European Laboratory for Particle Physics) developed what are widely regarded to be the first HTTP client and server software programs. The original intention was to create a suite of network tools to help scientists and academic institutions share data. Some time later, a group of developers at the **N**ational **C**enter for **S**upercomputing **A**pplications (NCSA) used these ideas in what was later to become the NCSA **H**yper**T**ext **T**ransfer **P**rotocol **D**aemon (or NCSA **HTTPD**).

Work on NCSA HTTPD began to fizzle out in 1994 when its principle maintainer, Rob McCool, abandoned the project. This left the server without a central repository or a point of focus. Developers continued to release patches for the server, but there was nobody to maintain or coordinate them.

A year later, a group of programmers picked up the pieces of NCSA HTTPD and gave it a new home. The core of the web server was redesigned and made tighter, and a module system was implemented to allow new features to be easily added and removed. The end result is something vaguely resembling a web server that we'll call "Apache" out of pure politeness.

Despite the stone-age origins of Apache, it's both relatively stable and feature rich, and best of all, it's open source.

The way Apache is designed means that new features can be loaded into the server software as external modules. People call them "modules," but you might find it easier to think of them as software plug-ins—which they are for most intents and purposes, though there's usually a bit more assembly required, but I'll get to that later.

The ability to load and unload extra features as external modules effectively gives the server administrator complete control over how the web server software behaves. Apache can be a discrete little server that just serves up static pages, or it can be some monstrous database-driven leviathan that eats memory and spits core dumps. It's all down to what modules are included and how they're configured.

Apache configuration

To alter your Apache configuration, follow these simple steps:

1. Load up the terminal in OS X.
2. Type in the following:

   cd /etc/httpd

3. Type

   sudo pico httpd.conf

If you have a quick look at your httpd.conf, you should see detailed comments (lines starting with a # symbol) telling you what each section of the configuration is for.

The Apache configuration is managed using a set of directives that tell the server how to behave. It would be beyond the scope of this book to cover Apache server configuration in any great detail, but I'll cover the configuration directives you'll need to know to make a start on installing and configuring your own modules.

DocumentRoot

The DocumentRoot directive specifies the local directory that Apache will serve files from. As the name suggests, the directory indicated by the DocumentRoot will appear as the root (/) directory of your web server. A default Mac OS X DocumentRoot looks like this:

DocumentRoot /Library/WebServer/Documents

which means that your Apache web server will serve its pages from /Library/WebServer/Documents by default. You can of course change the default directory to whatever you like, for example:

DocumentRoot /Users/YourName/Sites

<VirtualHost>

A <VirtualHost> directive encloses a group of other directives that apply to a virtual host. A virtual host is effectively a running copy of the web server software that has a separate set of configurables to the main web server. A virtual host can be served up when a certain set of criteria are met. For instance, if an HTTP request is made on a specific port (port-based) or if the server is addressed by a certain domain name (name-based), then the directives set out in the relevant <VirtualHost> entry are employed when serving up the files. These might include an alternate server root directory, options to execute CGI scripts, and the like. Virtual hosts are generally used in shared hosting environments; it enables low-cost web hosting as many users can use the IP address and web server.

<Directory>

The <Directory> directive is used to enclose a group of other directives to set configurables for a specified directory or group of directories. Or, to put it in English, you can customize the behavior of directories with this rule.

AddModule

As the name of this directive suggests, the AddModule directive is used to add a module to your web server. So, if you come across a line such as this in your httpd.conf:

```
AddModule mod_speling.so
```

then you can more-or-less tell what it's doing. In this case, it's adding the speling module to the Apache web server. It's also worth mentioning here that you can also include modules with a LoadModule directive. LoadModule has slightly different caveats to the AddModule directive, and AddModule is used by default in the Apache configuration that comes bundled with Panther, so I'll be relying on AddModule directives in the examples to come. I'll be covering AddModule in even more detail very shortly.

<IfModule>

<IfModule> directives enclose a group of configuration options for a specific module. It makes sense if you try reading it as "If such-and-such a module is loaded, then do x, y, z." Most of your module-specific configurations will need to go in the relevant <IfModule> block. You'll see this directive in action later. Now it's time to cover the modules themselves.

The modules

At the time of writing, there are almost 300 modules available for Apache. Some are already part of the default Apache distribution, some are included but not loaded by default, and others are freely available for download. It would be a bit pointless to describe all of them here, but here are a few examples just to give you an idea. A complete list can always be found at http://modules.apache.org/.

mod_dav

mod_dav adds WebDAV facilities to your Apache web server. WebDAV allows you to remotely manage and manipulate files on a web server as if they were mounted as a local volume. If you've used iDisk, you've had exposure to WebDAV. Mac OS X supports WebDAV at the operating system level, so you can quite happily use pretty much any software application with WebDAV. I'll cover WebDAV in more detail, later on in this chapter.

mod_gzip

mod_gzip allows your Apache server to send compressed documents, which can be decompressed and read by the client. This has the advantage of quicker download times for the client, as it would reduce the file size of a requested document. However, it adds the disadvantage of extra memory required to serve the pages and processor time to use the module itself.

177

mod_perl

Normally, when you load up a Perl script, the Apache server has to fork off an extra process for the Perl interpreter, which loads all the required Perl modules into memory before it can start actually executing the script. With mod_perl, the server already has a copy of the interpreter (and any number of specified Perl modules) permanently present in memory. This saves quite a bit of time in the compilation stages of running the script, but at the expense of having a lot of (possibly redundant) data permanently present in memory. In order to save memory, you'll need to disable any modules you aren't using. This module also includes its own API for developing and debugging.

mod_rewrite

This is a rather scary module. It relies on a regular expression engine to dynamically rewrite URLs allowing you to point users to alternate locations depending on any set of given criteria. Not as simple as it sounds, unfortunately. This can get scary, so I'll go over this stuff in a few pages time.

mod_speling

mod_speling is a rather useful module that checks mistyped URLs against what files actually exist and redirects the client to the closest matching pages.

```
243  #  Reconstruction of the complete module list from all available modules
244  #  (static and shared ones) to achieve correct module execution order.
245  #  [WHENEVER YOU CHANGE THE LOADMODULE SECTION ABOVE UPDATE THIS, TOO]
246  ClearModuleList
247  #AddModule mod_vhost_alias.c
248  #AddModule mod_env.c
249  AddModule mod_log_config.c
250  #AddModule mod_mime_magic.c
251  AddModule mod_mime.c
252  AddModule mod_negotiation.c
253  #AddModule mod_status.c
254  #AddModule mod_info.c
255  AddModule mod_include.c
256  AddModule mod_autoindex.c
257  AddModule mod_dir.c
258  AddModule mod_cgi.c
259  AddModule mod_asis.c
260  AddModule mod_imap.c
261  AddModule mod_actions.c
262  #AddModule mod_speling.c
263  AddModule mod_userdir.c
264  AddModule mod_alias.c
265  AddModule mod_rewrite.c
266  AddModule mod_access.c
267  AddModule mod_auth.c
268  #AddModule mod_auth_anon.c
269  #AddModule mod_auth_dbm.c
270  #AddModule mod_digest.c
271  #AddModule mod_proxy.c
272  #AddModule mod_cern_meta.c
273  #AddModule mod_expires.c
274  #AddModule mod_headers.c
275  #AddModule mod_usertrack.c
276  #AddModule mod_unique_id.c
277  AddModule mod_so.c
278  AddModule mod_setenvif.c
279  #AddModule mod_dav.c
280  #AddModule mod_ssl.c
281  #AddModule mod_perl.c
282  AddModule mod_php4.c
283  AddModule mod_hfs_apple.c
284  AddModule mod_rendezvous_apple.c
285
```

Figure 7-1. AddModule directives in the httpd.conf file

mod_ssl

mod_ssl enables Apache to encrypt HTTP transactions using the **S**ecure **S**ocket **L**ayer (SSL). Normally, data is sent via HTTP in an insecure (i.e., easily readable) format, but this module allows you to send and receive data in an encrypted manner over HTTPS.

php

php enables Apache to parse pages for embedded PHP commands and execute them. A full scripting language in its own right, it's available as a loadable module.

Enabling Apache modules

To enable a preinstalled module, you need to edit the httpd.conf file in the conf subdirectory of the Apache installation directory (/etc/httpd/ by default). You just need to remove the comments (# symbols) from the relevant AddModule (Figure 7-1)—just as you did when you edited this same configuration document in Chapter 5—and LoadModule (or <IfModule>) directives (Figure 7-2).

```
189  #
190  # Dynamic Shared Object (DSO) Support
191  #
192  # To be able to use the functionality of a module which was built as a DSO you
193  # have to place corresponding `LoadModule' lines at this location so the
194  # directives contained in it are actually available _before_ they are used.
195  # Please read the file http://httpd.apache.org/docs/dso.html for more
196  # details about the DSO mechanism and run `httpd -l' for the list of already
197  # built-in (statically linked and thus always available) modules in your httpd
198  # binary.
199  #
200  # Note: The order in which modules are loaded is important.  Don't change
201  # the order below without expert advice.
202  #
203  # Example:
204  # LoadModule foo_module libexec/mod_foo.so
205  #LoadModule vhost_alias_module libexec/httpd/mod_vhost_alias.so
206  #LoadModule env_module          libexec/httpd/mod_env.so
207  LoadModule config_log_module   libexec/httpd/mod_log_config.so
208  #LoadModule mime_magic_module   libexec/httpd/mod_mime_magic.so
209  LoadModule mime_module         libexec/httpd/mod_mime.so
210  LoadModule negotiation_module  libexec/httpd/mod_negotiation.so
211  #LoadModule status_module       libexec/httpd/mod_status.so
212  #LoadModule info_module         libexec/httpd/mod_info.so
213  LoadModule includes_module     libexec/httpd/mod_include.so
214  LoadModule autoindex_module    libexec/httpd/mod_autoindex.so
215  LoadModule dir_module          libexec/httpd/mod_dir.so
216  LoadModule cgi_module          libexec/httpd/mod_cgi.so
217  LoadModule asis_module         libexec/httpd/mod_asis.so
218  LoadModule imap_module         libexec/httpd/mod_imap.so
219  LoadModule action_module       libexec/httpd/mod_actions.so
220  #LoadModule speling_module      libexec/httpd/mod_speling.so
221  LoadModule userdir_module      libexec/httpd/mod_userdir.so
222  LoadModule alias_module        libexec/httpd/mod_alias.so
223  LoadModule rewrite_module      libexec/httpd/mod_rewrite.so
224  LoadModule access_module       libexec/httpd/mod_access.so
225  LoadModule auth_module         libexec/httpd/mod_auth.so
226  #LoadModule anon_auth_module    libexec/httpd/mod_auth_anon.so
227  #LoadModule dbm_auth_module     libexec/httpd/mod_auth_dbm.so
228  #LoadModule digest_module       libexec/httpd/mod_digest.so
229  #LoadModule proxy_module        libexec/httpd/libproxy.so
230  #LoadModule cern_meta_module    libexec/httpd/mod_cern_meta.so
231  #LoadModule expires_module      libexec/httpd/mod_expires.so
232  #LoadModule headers_module      libexec/httpd/mod_headers.so
233  #LoadModule usertrack_module    libexec/httpd/mod_usertrack.so
234  #LoadModule unique_id_module    libexec/httpd/mod_unique_id.so
235  LoadModule setenvif_module     libexec/httpd/mod_setenvif.so
236  #LoadModule dav_module          libexec/httpd/libdav.so
237  #LoadModule ssl_module          libexec/httpd/libssl.so
238  #LoadModule perl_module         libexec/httpd/libperl.so
239  LoadModule php4_module         libexec/httpd/libphp4.so
240  LoadModule hfs_apple_module    libexec/httpd/mod_hfs_apple.so
241  LoadModule rendezvous_apple_module libexec/httpd/mod_rendezvous_apple.so
242
```

Figure 7-2. LoadModule directives in the httpd.conf file

A couple of pointers before you start though:

1. When editing a configuration file, you should *always* make a backup just in case things go wrong. That way you can reinstate a known working configuration file rather than try and remember exactly what changes you just made.

2. It's always a good idea to test your updated configurations before loading them into the web server. More about that in a bit.

Okay then, let's enable a module.

1. First of all, you need the actual document open. Use Pico this time. The document is owned by the root user, so you use sudo in your command:

```
sudo pico /etc/httpd/httpd.conf
```

2. For this example, you'll just enable one of the modules that came bundled with Apache, so you just need to remove the comments around the relevant LoadModule directive in the httpd.conf. To find the required line, use *CONTROL+W*. This will give you a search prompt enabling you to perform a search. Search for "#LoadModule speling_module"; this will direct you to the speling_module highlighted in Figure 7-3.

3. This means this directive is ignored and mod_speling doesn't get loaded, but if you remove the comment—place your cursor on the L and press *BACKSPACE* once—then mod_speling gets loaded (see Figure 7-4).

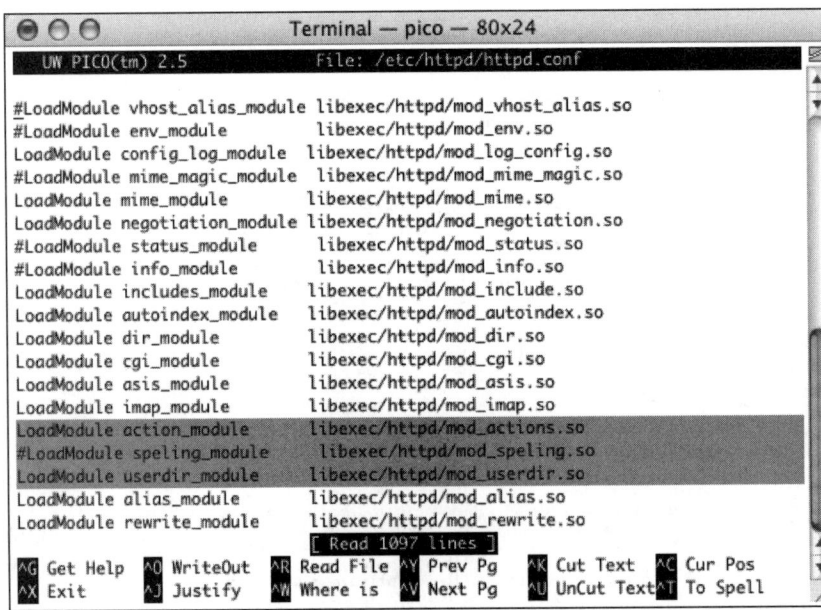

Figure 7-3. I've highlighted the lines you're after, and you can see the commented line in the middle.

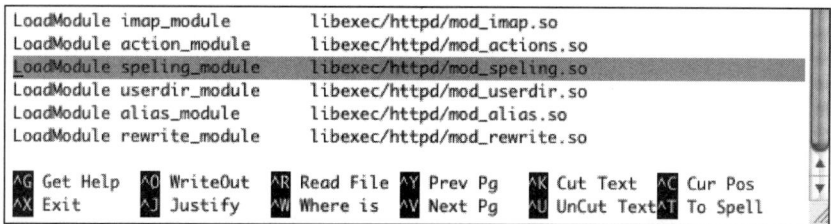

Figure 7-4. Uncommenting the LoadModule directive

4. Now all you need to do is uncomment the relevant AddModule directive for the module to get included (see Figure 7-5). Search again using the same process as previously described for the line "#AddModule mod_speling.c", place your cursor under the A, and hit the *BACKSPACE* key once (see Figure 7-6).

```
AddModule mod_imap.c
AddModule mod_actions.c
#AddModule mod_speling.c
AddModule mod_userdir.c
AddModule mod_alias.c
```

Figure 7-5. Finding the AddModule directive

```
AddModule mod_imap.c
AddModule mod_actions.c
AddModule mod_speling.c
AddModule mod_userdir.c
AddModule mod_alias.c
```

Figure 7-6. Uncommented AddModule directive

5. The next step is to enable the CheckSpelling directive. Find the following line in the httpd.conf file:

<Directory />

then add

CheckSpelling On

before the </Directory> tag.

6. Save the document: press *CONTROL+O*, press *ENTER*, and then press *CONTROL+X* to exit the httpd.conf file.

The changes should be complete and mod_speling will be active when the server next reloads its configuration.

7. To test your configuration, you're best off using the apachectl script that's found in the /usr/sbin/ directory. If you run it through Terminal without any arguments, you should see something like Figure 7-7.

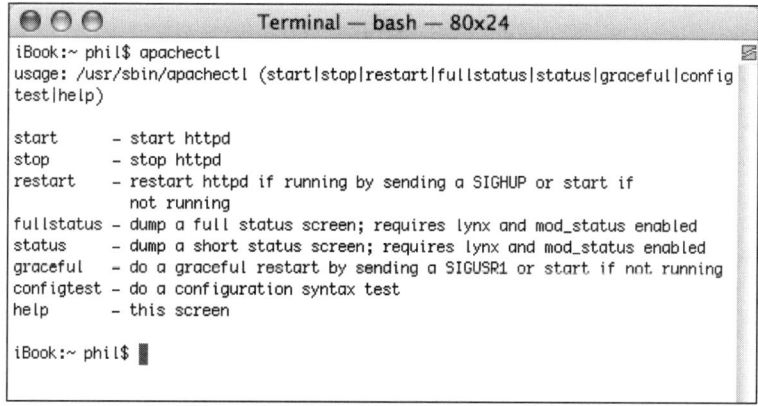

Figure 7-7. apachectl output

8. To test the changes to your Apache configuration, you want to tell apachectl to do a configtest, as shown in Figure 7-8.

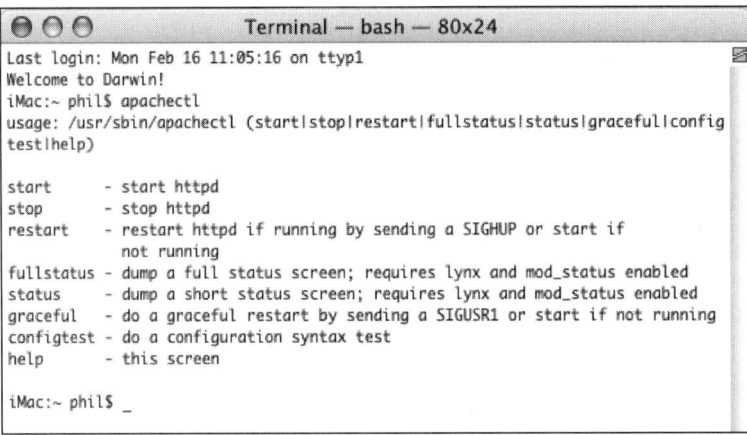

```
Last login: Mon Feb 16 11:05:16 on ttyp1
Welcome to Darwin!
iMac:~ phil$ apachectl
usage: /usr/sbin/apachectl (start|stop|restart|fullstatus|status|graceful|config
test|help)

start     - start httpd
stop      - stop httpd
restart   - restart httpd if running by sending a SIGHUP or start if
            not running
fullstatus - dump a full status screen; requires lynx and mod_status enabled
status    - dump a short status screen; requires lynx and mod_status enabled
graceful  - do a graceful restart by sending a SIGUSR1 or start if not running
configtest - do a configuration syntax test
help      - this screen

iMac:~ phil$ _
```

Figure 7-8. apachectl output

If the Terminal output complains about a syntax error, then you've probably made a slight typo somewhere. You can either correct it, or replace the httpd.conf file with that backup you remembered to make, and start over.

If you see something like Figure 7-9, then it has worked OK.

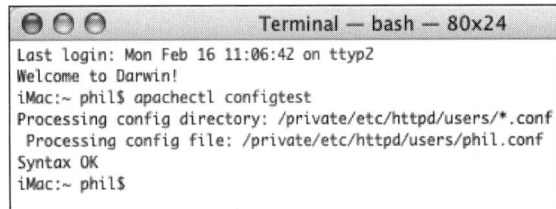

```
Last login: Mon Feb 16 11:06:42 on ttyp2
Welcome to Darwin!
iMac:~ phil$ apachectl configtest
Processing config directory: /private/etc/httpd/users/*.conf
 Processing config file: /private/etc/httpd/users/phil.conf
Syntax OK
iMac:~ phil$
```

Figure 7-9. Everything in working order

9. You can safely reload your server and give yourself a pat on the back. While you're at it, restart the web server, so that the changes you just made will actually have an effect (see Figure 7-10). Remember, you need root permission for this, so the command is

sudo apachectl restart

```
Syntax OK
iMac:~ phil$ sudo apachectl restart
Password:
/usr/sbin/apachectl restart: httpd restarted
iMac:~ phil$
```

Figure 7-10. Restarting the web server

Congratulations, you've just loaded an Apache module. Now, any 404 errors should be caught by the server, which will attempt to redirect the client to the closest matching page.

Xcode

Now is probably a good time to warn you that things will be getting a bit more UNIX-ey from here on in. Mac OS X mostly does a good job of covering up its UNIX internals, but unless you're using Mac OS X Server or Tenon's iTools (www.tenon.com/products/itools-osx), you'll probably need to rely on the command line to do anything more than the most basic of Apache administration tasks. You'll also need to have Xcode installed (formerly called Developers' Tools), which you can download free from Apple's Developer site, http://connect.apple.com/ (you need an Apple ID for this, which is your .mac username, or you can just sign up for an ID there and then), as it's customary to build Apache modules from downloadable source code. To understand why that is, you will need to know a bit more about what UNIX is and where it came from.

UNIX

Because UNIX is essentially a platform-agnostic operating system, it often works out to be slightly more practical to build and install applications from their raw source code rather than to hunt around for precompiled binary distributions of the software for whatever machine architecture you're currently using. Which is (more or less) why it's probably best all around to compile your new Apache modules from their source code. That way, you can happily download the same module as someone running Solaris on a Sparc machine, FreeBSD on a PC, Linux on a DEC Alpha, or NetBSD on a RISC PC, and (fingers crossed) compile and install it on your Mac.

Fortunately, you don't need to know how to program C to build and install Apache modules. You won't even need to directly use the compiler. Most modules will come packaged with all the necessary scripts to configure, compile, and install the modules for you. Provided you've installed the developer's tools and any prerequisite libraries (you haven't got your coffee mug on that Xcode CD, have you?), you should have no problems compiling the modules. Just keep in mind that each Apache module should be treated as an application in its own right. Some require more configuration than others, so it's always a good idea to read the documentation supplied with your new modules.

Downloading and installing Apache modules

Apache modules, or most UNIX source code for that matter, are packed in **tarballs**. A tarball is just a form of file archiving/compression that's a combination of **tar** (tape archive) and **gzip** (a GNU compression utility). Once downloaded, a tarball can be unpacked using either StuffIt (/Applications/Utilities/Stuffit Expander) or the tar and gzip commands like so:

```
$ gzip -dc filename.tar.gz | tar -xvf -
```

where `filename.tar.gz` is the name of the tarball that you're trying to unwrap.

Once unpacked, you'll need to run Terminal and change to the newly created directory with your source code in, and then log in to the Terminal as root using the su command. The easiest way to do this is

1. Type su, hit *ENTER*, and enter your password.
2. Type cd, leaving a trailing space.
3. Drag the directory you want into the Terminal window.
4. Hit *ENTER*.

Much easier than manually hacking away at the keyboard and inputting a long and often complicated path.

Most of the grief is taken out of compiling thanks to the make utility. make is more or less a scripting language specifically designed for managing compile flags for the relevant sources, headers, and libraries of a particular project. To the rest of us, that means that we can practically build and install a source distribution with a few simple commands, which usually goes something like this:

1. Enter cd /path/to/file.
2. Enter su and then enter your password.
3. Type ./configure, after which you'll see a ton of scrolling text.
4. Type make, and then you'll see a ton more scrolling text.
5. Type make install. Woooh, some more scrolling text.
6. Type exit to exit SuperUser mode.

And that's all there is to it. Nine times out of ten, a source distribution can be installed using those few simple commands. There are exceptions though, and many applications and modules need to have some of their features enabled or disabled during the configure phase, which is why it's always a good idea to read the supplied documentation, which can usually be found in either the readme or install files that should be included in the tarball.

There aren't really any strict rules regarding how a source distribution should be bundled and configured, but there are some conventions that you can usually rely on. You can normally find configuration options by asking the configure script for help:

```
./configure –help
```

This should give you a list of options that you can supply to the configure script along with an accompanying explanation. I'll get to that in a minute.

Also, there's often a make rule included to test the software once it's been compiled:

```
make test
```

However, this rule is usually only found included with larger or more critical packages. It's usually a good idea to give it a try before pushing ahead with a make install though.

Once your new Apache module has been installed, all that's left to do is to tell the server that it's there and what to do with it. Again, you do that by adding the relevant LoadModule and AddModule or <IfModule> directives to your httpd.conf file, remembering of course to check the documentation for any configuration directives specific to that module.

Let's look at some examples.

PHP

Let's assume that you want to do a source installation of the latest version of PHP. As I write this, the PHP Group are offering a beta of PHP 5.0 on their site, so let's have a crack at that.

1. Download and unwrap the tarball (http://www.php.net/downloads.php).
2. Change to the source directory in Terminal; for me this is

   ```
   cd /Users/phil/Desktop/php-5.0.0b2
   ```
3. Log in as root:

   ```
   su (enter password)
   ```
4. Run the configure script with the –help switch:

   ```
   ./configure –help
   ```

You should see a whole glut of different configuration options (more than 300 at the last count). Although it should be perfectly possible to configure, compile, and install PHP without any special options, that wouldn't be half as much fun.

The configure script should do a good job of finding out most of the configurables for itself. There are still quite a lot of features of PHP that won't be enabled unless you specifically configure them.

Most configure options will usually be one (or two) of three types: include/exclude a feature (–with/–without), enabling/disabling a feature (–enable/–disable), or setting an element to a value (–item=value). Here is a selection of some of the options you might consider using to configure PHP:

- –enable-ftp Enable support for the FTP protocol.
- –enable-sockets Enable support for sockets.
- –with-apxs[=FILE] Include support for the APache eXtenSion tools, a toolkit for building and installing Apache extensions. It can be optionally supplied with the path to Apache's apxs tool. Use this if you want your module to be dynamically loaded by Apache.
- –with-curl[=DIR] Include support for CURL, a WWW client library.
- –with-iodbc[=DIR] Include support for Independent Open DataBase Connectivity (iODBC). The base installation directory of iODBC can be supplied.
- –with-kerberos[=DIR] Include support for Kerberos, an encrypted network authentication protocol. Can be supplied with the Kerberos installation directory.
- –with-ldap[=DIR] Include support for Lightweight Directory Access Protocol (LDAP), a protocol for looking up user contact details.
- –with-mysql[=DIR] Include support for MySQL. The MySQL base directory can be specified, otherwise the bundled MySQL library is used by default.
- –with-zlib[=DIR] Include support for zlib, a compression library. The location of the zlib libraries can be specified.

A typical configure might look something like

```
./configure –with-curl –with-iodbc
➥ –with-kerberos –with-ldap
➥ –with-mysql –with-zlib
```

The preceding command configures the compiler to use curl, kerberos, ldap, mysql, and zlib and make them available to PHP. In order for the compiler to be able to compile PHP, these applications need to be installed. For this example, you'll exclude any with command, as some of the applications mentioned may not be installed on your computer. Here are some step-by-step instructions on how to compile PHP:

1. You should still be in the directory you untarred PHP to.
2. Type the following into the Terminal: ./configure.
3. Type make.
4. Then type make test.
5. And finally type make install.

Assuming all these steps are successful (and you might have time for a cup of tea during this section, depending on how old your Mac is), then all that's left to do is either add or uncomment the relevant lines in your httpd.conf file. The relevant lines found in the default httpd.conf are used in this example:

```
#LoadModule perl_module
➥ libexec/httpd/libperl.so
#LoadModule php4_module
➥ libexec/httpd/libphp4.so
LoadModule hfs_apple_module
➥ libexec/httpd/mod_hfs_apple.so

#AddModule mod_perl.c
#AddModule mod_php4.c
AddModule mod_hfs_apple.c
```

The earlier versions of OS X made these things a bit more difficult, but with 10.3, you'll find these lines as the default in your httpd.conf.

```
<IfModule mod_php4.c>
# If php is turned on, we respect .php
➥ and .phps files.
AddType application/x-httpd-php .php
```

```
AddType application/x-httpd-php-source
➥ .phps

# Since most users will want index.php
➥ to work we
    # also automatically enable index.php
    <IfModule mod_dir.c>
        DirectoryIndex index.html index.php
    </IfModule>
</IfModule>
```

As with any changes to the .conf doc, you'll just reload the server for them to take effect:

apachectl configtest

apachectl restart

And that should work, assuming that the /libexec/ directory is in the correct place (it can be specified with the –libexecdir[=DIR] option) and that the correct module name is used (PHP4 is currently the stable release version at the time of writing).

mod_rewrite

Another loadable module that comes bundled with Apache is mod_rewrite. As explained earlier, mod_rewrite "rewrites" URLs using regular expressions. This can be used to either simplify complex URLs or redirect clients to alternate pages.

New rewriting rules can be given to mod_rewrite using a RewriteRule directive. To add a new RewriteRule, you'll need to include it in your httpd.conf. Firstly, find the relevant <IfModule> directive:

```
<IfModule mod_rewrite.c>
    RewriteEngine On
    RewriteCond %{REQUEST_METHOD} ^TRACE
    RewriteRule .* - [F]
</IfModule>
```

You'll notice that there are already some directives present. These directives are included in the default Apache 1.3.28 configuration. They'll be covered later on in this section, so feel free to ignore them for the time being. All you need to know now is that new rules for mod_rewrite should be put in this <IfModule> directive.

RewriteRules have three parts:

- The first is an expression to match the requested URI.
- The second is an expression to replace the matched part of the URI.
- The third tells the rewrite engine what to do with the rewritten URI.

I'll take a minute here to explain a few conventions. A **URL** is a **U**niform **R**esource **L**ocation, while a **URI** is a **U**niform **R**esource **I**ndicator. In many situations (especially when you happen to be dealing with rewritten and redirected pages), the page is being referred to by an indicator rather than its actual location, so it's a fair bit more accurate to call it a URI. If any of the other naming conventions being used suddenly appear to change for no good reason, or Apache starts being referred to as "Susan", then there is likely to be an equally boring explanation.

In the simplest cases, a RewriteRule can behave like a **symlink** (symbolic link). Assume that you have a page called foo.html and you want to point the client to a new page called bar.html. To do that, you'd need a RewriteRule that matches foo.html, replaces it with bar.html, and then performs a redirect. Just include something like the following in the relevant <IfModule> directive:

RewriteRule /foo.html /bar.html [R=301]

The [301] in this example is telling mod_rewrite to redirect the client to the new address. The /foo.html is the URI request to match, and the bar.html is the string to replace it with. Of course, it seems a bit pointless to use some almighty rewriting engine just to perform a simple redirect. You can also use mod_rewrite to dynamically alter URIs for you. Say you want to tidy up your URIs so that the arguments to a PHP script look like an actual file name. So you take a URI like this:

http://mydomain/test.php?foo=123&bar=45

and make it look like this:

http://mydomain/test/123/45/

The regular expression engine used in mod_rewrite allows you to capture previously matched parts of the expression. These captured parts of the string can then be used in the substitution phase.

RewriteRule /(test)\.php\?foo=([^&;]*)[&;]
➥ bar=([^&;]*) /%1/%2/%3/ [L]

In this rewrite rule, the name of the script and the first and second arguments are captured, and then used to replace the URI. The [L] (last) flag tells mod_rewrite not to continue applying rewrite rules once this substitution has been performed.

mod_rewrite also lets you do conditional redirecting using RewriteCond (Rewrite Condition) directives. This is useful in situations where you want to perform a conditional redirect determined by environment variables set by the client. In a simple case, you might redirect a client to a page built specifically for their browser:

RewriteCond %{HTTP_USER_AGENT} IE
RewriteRule ^/$ /ie_pages/ [R]

RewriteCond %{HTTP_USER_AGENT} Mozilla
RewriteRule ^/$ /mozilla_pages/ [R]

Hopefully, the preinstalled RewriteRule ought to make sense now:

RewriteCond %{REQUEST_METHOD} ^TRACE
RewriteRule .* - [F]

This will produce a 403 (forbidden) error for any page requested if an HTTP TRACE request is made (TRACE queries are detailed along with the rest of the HTTP specification in RFC 2616). TRACE queries can give away sensitive information about your web server, so it's a good idea to disable this service. Having this rule in mod_rewrite is one of the more practical ways of disabling TRACE queries.

Rewrite rules can also be used to redirect clients to pages on remote servers. Here's a simple rewrite rule that will redirect the client from a user's page to a different web page:

RewriteRule /ferret
➥ http://rollmop.org [301]

Those were just a few simple examples of what mod_rewrite can do. You can also mix some mad combinations. However, mod_rewrite rules can start to eat into your processing time if you use them too recklessly, so it's a good idea to show a bit of discipline when adding new RewriteRules and try not to take them too much for granted.

mod_dav

mod_dav comes already bundled with Apache on Jaguar. You just need to remove them comments to enable it:

1. Open /etc/httpd/httpd.conf and look for

```
LoadModule setenvif_module
➥ libexec/httpd/mod_setenvif.so
#LoadModule dav_module
➥ libexec/httpd/libdav.so
#LoadModule ssl_module
➥ libexec/httpd/libssl.so
```

2. Change this code to

```
LoadModule setenvif_module
➥ libexec/httpd/mod_setenvif.so
LoadModule dav_module
➥ libexec/httpd/libdav.so
#LoadModule ssl_module
➥ libexec/httpd/libssl.so
```

3. Then you need to add the module, so scroll down to find the following:

```
AddModule mod_setenvif.c
#AddModule mod_dav.c
#AddModule mod_ssl.c
```

4. Change this to

```
AddModule mod_setenvif.c
AddModule mod_dav.c
#AddModule mod_ssl.c
```

5. To enable WebDAV, you need to either alter the configuration on an existing /Directory/ or /Location/ directive, or add a new one. Refer to the Apache documentation where appropriate. (Full documentation for Apache is available at http://httpd.apache.org/.) Find these lines:

```
<Directory /webdavstuff>
    Options None
    AllowOverride None
</Directory>
```

And just add the following directive:

```
<Directory /webdavstuff>
    DAV On
    Options None
    AllowOverride None
</Directory>
```

If WebDAV is enabled for a Directory, then that particular directory and all its subdirectories have WebDAV enabled. If WebDAV is enabled for a Location, then WebDAV is enabled for that entire namespace.

Next, you need to add a DAV lock database directive either at the top level of your httpd.conf (i.e., not contained within another directive) or within a VirtualHost directive. This is so that Apache can create a database lock file. The file's name needs to be DAVLock, and it needs to be writable by the effective user ID of the Apache process. Assuming that Apache is installed to /etc/httpd, the DAVLockDB directive should look something like this:

DAVLockDB /etc/httpd/var/DAVLock

To test this, it would be a good idea to first do a config test with apachectl, and then restart Apache and check the httpd error log to see whether the server is complaining about being able to generate the lock file.

For security reasons, it's recommended that you restrict the actions permitted on a WebDAV-enabled location and that you require user authentication rather than let random strangers play about with your files. You'll probably also want to deny overrides so that your carefully thought out security policy can't be compromised with the addition of an .htaccess file:

```
<Directory /webdavstuff>
    Options None
    AllowOverride None
    DAV On
    <LimitExcept GET HEAD OPTIONS>
      require user bob
    </LimitExcept>
</Directory>
```

To connect to a WebDAV server, you can either use the Finder, or download and install Goliath (which is still freely available at the time of writing). To use the Finder, just select Connect to Server from the Finder menu (⌘+*K*), give the location of the server you want to connect to (with the leading `http://`), and supply your user name and password when prompted. You should then see the web folder mounted on your desktop, and you can play with it to your heart's content the same way you would add, remove, edit, and manipulate any local files. If you have an iDisk, try connecting to it like this.

Chapter review

There you have it; we've finally scratched the surface of what Apache modules are and how they work. It's entirely up to you whether you choose to slim down your web server to something smaller and lighter, or to plug in a whole mess of redundant features that slows your computer down to a snail's pace.

You'll probably find that some Apache modules really need some data to work with for you to get the most out of them. This is certainly true of embedded interpreters such as PHP and `mod_perl`. Ideally, you'll need to have a database installed to do that. Some tools, such as the Perl-based site authoring tool Mason, are practically useless without a database. Luckily, I'll be covering databases in the following chapter.

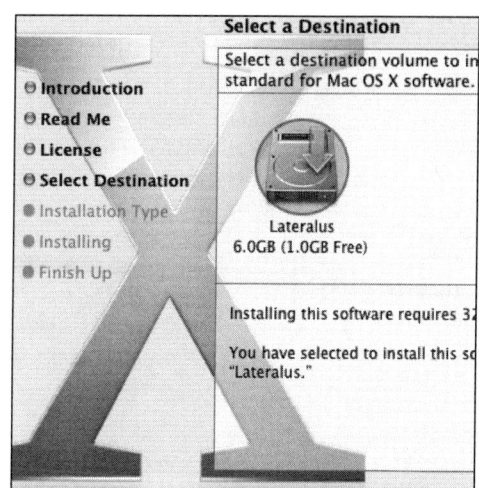

Chapter 8

DATABASES

What we'll cover in this chapter:

- How to install MySQL on your Mac
- How to create and maintain a database from Terminal
- How to get Dreamweaver to connect to MySQL
- Constructing a page in Dreamweaver, which lets you add, edit, and delete data from your database
- How to install phpMyAdmin
- How to install a message board

I think the first commercial database package I came into contact with was Lotus 1-2-3. My dad had just bought a PC, and it came loaded with Lotus SmartSuite. I remember opening it up and thinking, "What on earth is this?" and promptly closing it again. Let's just say it was never exactly the most used piece of software on that machine. A few years later, he bought another new PC. This one had Microsoft Office on it. Again, I investigated all the new stuff. "Access, eh?" Click. "Argh, it's one of those database things again! No fun!" I then proceeded to laugh at all the clip art and forgot all about databases for quite a few years.

When I was a kid, I was a really fussy eater, and wouldn't eat a lot of things (onions, garlic, and so on). When I became a vegetarian over 13 years ago, they were the first things I turned to whenever I'd start cooking a big meal. In the same way, today I wouldn't dream of starting a big site without a database behind the scenes.

As Bob sang, "The times they are a-changin'. . . ."

What is a database?

Data. We all use it. It's all over the place. Left to its own devices, it can get pretty messy. It's like a student, living away from home for the first time: It has no structure on its own. It needs organizing before it sprawls out of control. It needs a system. So what is a database?

> "One or more large structured sets of persistent data, usually associated with software to update and query the data. A simple database might be a single file containing many records, each of which contains the same set of fields where each field is a certain fixed width." The Free On-line Dictionary of Computing (www.instantweb.com/foldoc).

Example: As a developer, you'll most likely have a lot of backup media—spindles of CDs with scribbled writing on them, if you're anything like me. When the time comes to find something off those spindles, it's not always easy to remember which disc you want. As a Mac user, you can use a piece of software called

DiskTracker (www.disktracker.com) that stores each CD's data in a database. This allows you to search for that elusive file and then tells you which disc you need to retrieve. Piece of cake! It's far easier than manually checking each CD for the file you need. And, as we all know, the CD you're looking for is always the last one you check.

You say tom-ay-toe . . .

You might have seen the acronym **SQL** floating around when talk turns to databases. This stands for **S**tructured **Q**uery **L**anguage, and makes up the names of some of the more popular databases (MySQL, PostgreSQL, MS SQL, etc.). SQL is generally pronounced either "sequel" or "ess-cue-ell"—it's really up to you.

How does this chapter benefit me?

As with dynamic sites, if you only have a small 4-page site that gets updated twice a year, it's unlikely that you need a database for your site data. You may now go and wallpaper the house. Or build a fort out of matchsticks. If, on the other hand, you have a lot of data to shove around, or just want to keep up to date with how the Internet works these days, keep on reading. I'll cover how to install MySQL on your Mac, and how to create a MySQL database via Terminal. You'll learn how to connect to that database via PHP, and also how to administer it via a web client called **phpMyAdmin**. You'll learn how to use Dreamweaver to show your data live. This shows you the actual data in place, rather than just some lines of code. With just a few lines of code, you'll be populating your web page with rows of data within minutes.

Database options

I mentioned MySQL would be the database used in this chapter, but let's first look at some of the options that are out there for the budding database wizard:

- **MySQL** (www.mysql.com) calls itself "The world's most popular Open Source database." It's a breeze to install, and you'll be using it in no time at all. It's native to Mac, UNIX, and Windows. This is by far the easiest database to get up and running, and you'll find lots of information about it on the Internet.

- **PostgreSQL** (www.postgresql.org) calls itself "The most advanced Open Source database system in the world." Note the word "advanced" there. For a start, it's a little more complex to install and get running. If you want to check it out, Marc Liyanage has a package installer and some excellent documentation on his site (www.entropy.ch/software/macosx/postgresql).

- **Oracle** (www.oracle.com) is the king of databases. As their site states, "The world's largest commercial data warehouse runs Oracle, with **30 terabytes** of data" (www.oracle.com/solutions/performance_scalability/index.html?winter2003.html). They claim that it's the world's most popular database. It's also expensive (over $1000). At the end of 2002, Oracle released a Developers Release for OS X.

- **Access/Microsoft SQL Server** (www.microsoft.com). I'm including Access here because, although it's not a native Mac application (and never will be, according to Microsoft), it's possible you've heard of it or will be asked to deal with an MDB file (the native Access format) by a client. MS SQL Server is a way of using those files online.

- **FileMaker Pro** (www.filemaker.com). This database application is stated to be the reason why Microsoft will never release Access on the Mac platform. It's a solid database and is available on both Windows and Mac platforms, although at a hefty price.

- **Flat file** (text file). Perhaps the simplest form of database is the flat file database usually in the form of **c**omma-**s**eparated **v**ariables (**CSVs**). All of the databases listed here can import data in this format. Most common spreadsheet packages can export CSV data, which you may then need to import into one of the preceding databases.

As you can see, there's more than one choice, especially for the Windows user. Again, because this book isn't called *Become a Guru in 24 Hours*, we'll take the sensible easy option of MySQL. First, you need to install it and get it running, so charge that coffee mug and don your geek hat. We're going in!

Setting up MySQL

Unlike PHP, MySQL isn't already built into OS X. You have to download and install it.

1. To do this, go to http://mysql.com/downloads/ and select the latest Production release. Once you're on the right page, you need to select the correct package. Scroll down to Mac OS X Package Installer Downloads (see Figure 8-1).

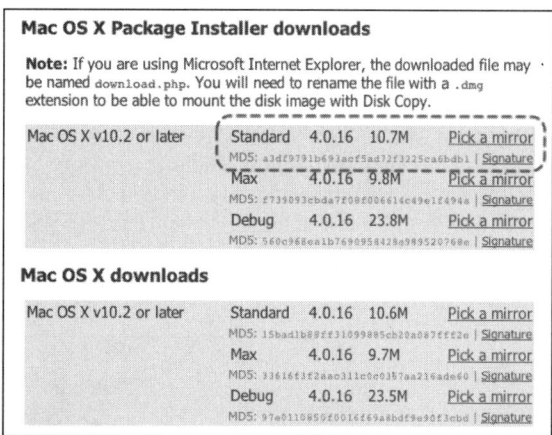

Figure 8-1. Selecting the right version's download page

2. Pick a mirror to select the nearest mirror site to you (see Figure 8-2).

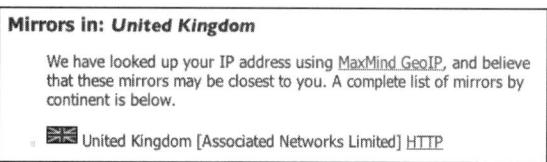

Figure 8-2. Selecting a mirror site

3. Once the disk image has downloaded and mounted, you should have two package files and a text file. Double-click the mysql-standard installer, shown in Figure 8-3.

Figure 8-3. Selecting the standard package first

4. Select the startup drive (or startup partition, if your drive is partitioned), and authorize when required (see Figure 8-4).

Okay, once you've finished the rest of the Installer, MySQL is installed and almost ready to run, but you need to have it run automatically when your Mac boots up, so you need to install the MySQLStartupItem package too.

5. Double-click the installer from the same mounted image, authorize when asked, and you're done.

6. Open a Terminal window and type in the following commands:

```
cd /usr/local/mysql
sudo chown -R mysql data/
```

Authorize with your password when asked for it.

7. To start the server, type

```
sudo echo
```

press *ENTER*, and then type

```
sudo ./bin/mysqld_safe &
```

8. To see some action, as shown in Figure 8-5, type in

```
/usr/local/mysql/bin/mysql test
```

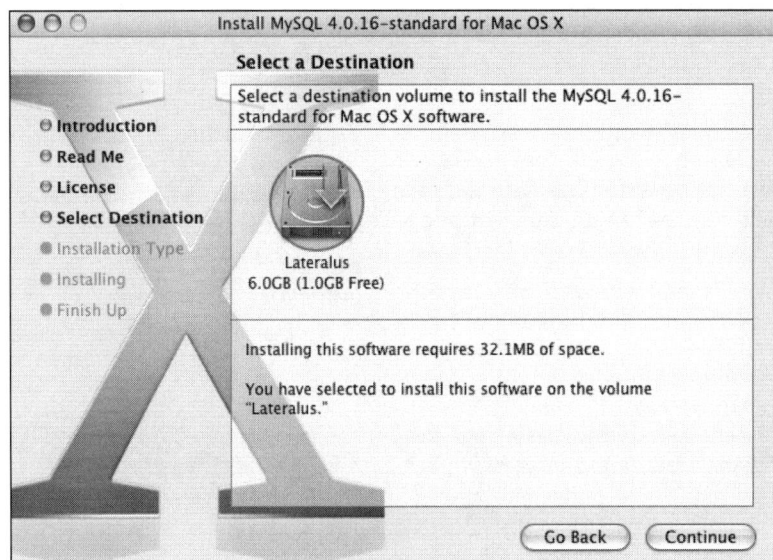

Figure 8-4. Selecting the startup disk

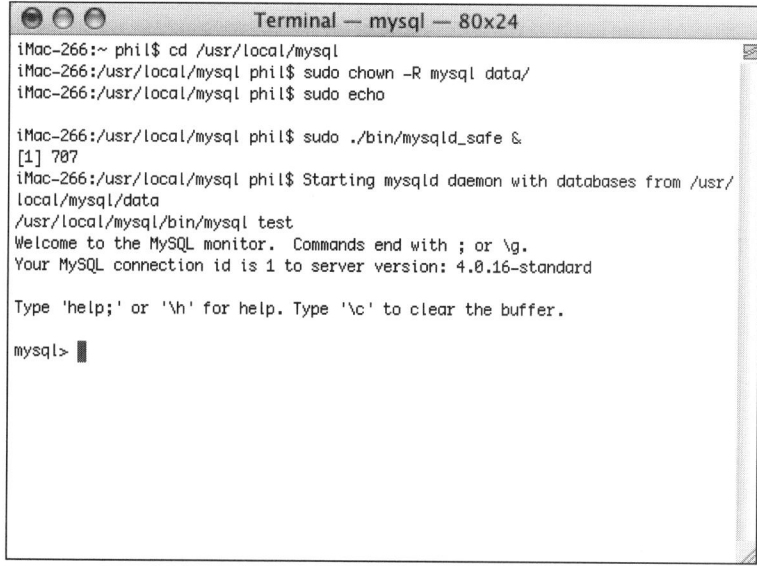

```
●●●               Terminal — mysql — 80x24
iMac-266:~ phil$ cd /usr/local/mysql
iMac-266:/usr/local/mysql phil$ sudo chown -R mysql data/
iMac-266:/usr/local/mysql phil$ sudo echo

iMac-266:/usr/local/mysql phil$ sudo ./bin/mysqld_safe &
[1] 707
iMac-266:/usr/local/mysql phil$ Starting mysqld daemon with databases from /usr/
local/mysql/data
/usr/local/mysql/bin/mysql test
Welcome to the MySQL monitor.  Commands end with ; or \g.
Your MySQL connection id is 1 to server version: 4.0.16-standard

Type 'help;' or '\h' for help. Type '\c' to clear the buffer.

mysql> █
```

Figure 8-5. Welcome to MySQL!

9. Now that you can see the mysql> prompt, you're in the mysql shell. This is where you control MySQL from. You can add, delete, edit, and so on, all from this shell prompt. To exit the mysql shell, type

exit

.bashrc and .bash_profile

If you don't want to have to type /usr/local/mysql/bin in front of every single MySQL-related command you issue, then you have to add the /usr/local/mysql/bin directory to your PATH environment variable in your shell's login script.

1. Mac OS X 10.3 uses the **bash** shell, and the command is

echo 'export PATH=/usr/local/mysql/bin:
➥ $PATH' >> ~/.bashrc

If you're using a version of Mac OS X prior to 10.3, or you prefer to use the tcsh *shell, you can do the same thing by running this command instead:*

echo 'setenv PATH /usr/local/mysql/bin:
➥ $PATH' >> ~/.tcshrc

If you already have a .tcshrc *file, just add* /usr/local/mysql/bin *to your path. You need to close and reopen the Terminal window for the changes to take effect.*

2. You need one more file in place before the bash shell will recognize your path. You need to create a file called .bash_profile, which, as you can see, starts with a period (.). By this stage in the book, you should be comfortable enough with Terminal, so you're going to use Vim to edit your file! First, create the file by typing the following line:

touch .bash_profile

```
000                  Terminal — bash — 80x24
iBook:~ phil$ touch .bash_profile
iBook:~ phil$ ls -Gal
total 48
drwxr-xr-x  18 phil   phil     612 20 Jan 16:22 .
drwxrwxr-t   5 root   admin    170 19 Jan 17:07 ..
-rw-r--r--   1 phil   phil       3 19 Jan 17:07 .CFUserTextEncoding
-rw-r--r--   1 phil   phil    6148 20 Jan 15:16 .DS_Store
drwx------   6 phil   phil     204 20 Jan 15:16 .Trash
-rw-------   1 phil   phil     429 20 Jan 16:21 .bash_history
-rw-r--r--   1 phil   phil       0 20 Jan 16:22 .bash_profile
-rw-r--r--   1 phil   phil      38 20 Jan 15:59 .bashrc
-rw-r--r--   1 phil   phil       0 20 Jan 16:01 .hushlogin
-rw-------   1 phil   phil     525 20 Jan 16:21 .viminfo
drwx------   4 phil   phil     136 20 Jan 15:16 Desktop
drwx------   7 phil   phil     238 20 Jan 13:52 Documents
drwx------  23 phil   phil     782 19 Jan 17:46 Library
drwx------   3 phil   phil     102 19 Jan 17:07 Movies
drwx------   3 phil   phil     102 19 Jan 17:07 Music
drwx------   3 phil   phil     102 19 Jan 17:07 Pictures
drwxr-xr-x   4 phil   phil     136 19 Jan 17:07 Public
drwxr-xr-x   5 phil   phil     170 19 Jan 17:07 Sites
iBook:~ phil$
```

Figure 8-6. I've highlighted the file in orange.

You can see that your file has been created by typing the following (see Figure 8-6):

```
ls -Gal
```

3. Open this file in Vim:

```
vim ~/.bash_profile
```

4. Enter INSERT mode by typing I (an uppercase i), and you'll see the status bar change as shown in Figure 8-7.

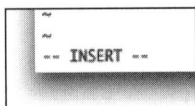

Figure 8-7. Vim in INSERT mode

5. Now that you're in INSERT mode, type the following:

```
. ~/.bashrc
ENV=$HOME/.bashrc
export ENV
```

6. To leave INPUT mode, press the *Esc* key.

7. To save the file, type

```
:w
```

and then press *ENTER*. You should now see a screen like the one in Figure 8-8, telling you that the file has been written (saved).

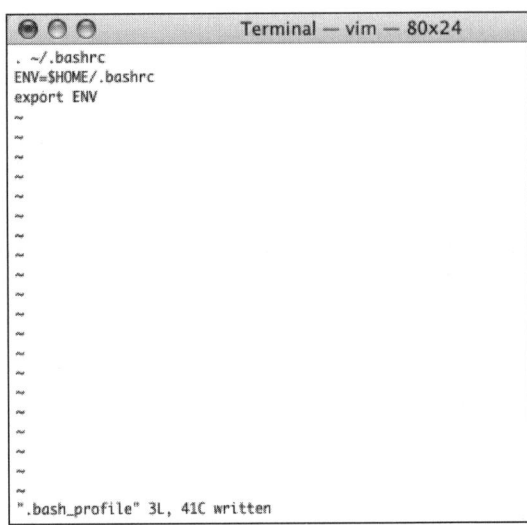

Figure 8-8. Vim's status bar shows you that the file has been written.

8. To exit Vim, type

`:q`

and then hit ENTER.

9. The MySQL server is alive and kicking now, but you should nail a master password onto this thing. If your password is going to be "THRaKaTTak", then you would type

`mysqladmin -u root password THRaKaTTak`

Whatever you choose, try and make it case sensitive (thus, making it harder to crack) and *don't forget it!*

10. Now that your path and password are set, you can log back onto the `mysql` shell with the following command:

`mysql -h localhost -u root -p`

On Mac OS X, the MySQL process is run by an invisible user called MySQL, as shown in Figure 8-9.

11. The MySQL user is almost ready to play ball, but as with any worthwhile party, you need permission to gain access to all the good stuff. Type

`GRANT ALL PRIVILEGES ON *.* TO`
`➥ mysql@localhost IDENTIFIED BY`
`➥ 'THRaKaTTak';`

12. Replace `'THRaKaTTak'` with whichever password you chose, but keep the single quote marks as shown in Figure 8-10. This ensures your MySQL user can read/write data.

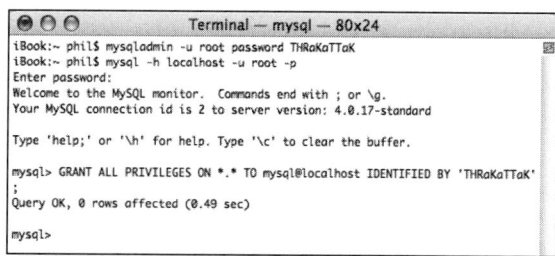

Figure 8-10. Granting privileges to the MySQL user

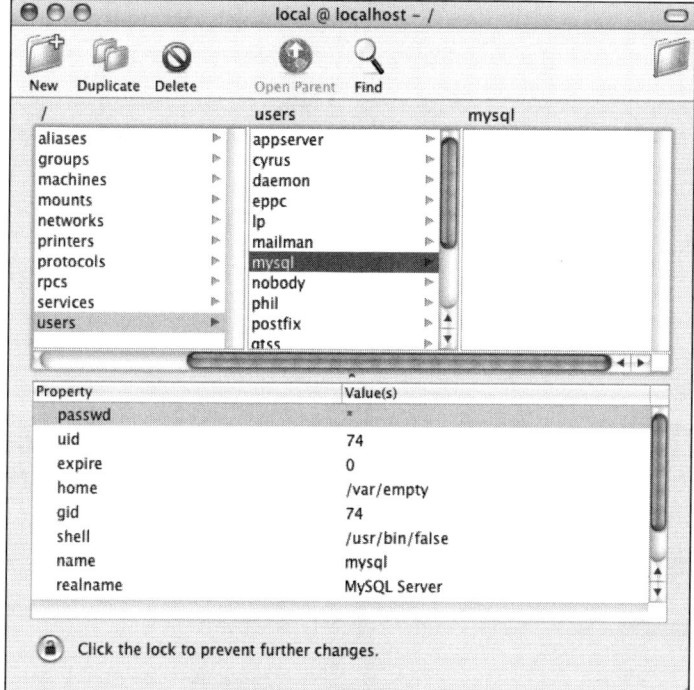

Figure 8-9. NetInfo Manager shows you the MySQL user's info.

First steps with MySQL

Okay, MySQL is running. Now what? You're going to make a database for the links page of your website, as mentioned back in Chapter 5. What do you have to play with then? How do you see what's going on in there? You've got a mysql shell prompt just sitting there, so you should do something to amuse it.

> *Generally, commands are in shown in uppercase, just to make clear which are actual MySQL commands. Apart from entering the password earlier, MySQL isn't exclusively case sensitive.*

1. You can find out what databases are in there by typing

   SHOW DATABASES;

That should show you something like what you see in Figure 8-11.

```
mysql> show databases;
+-----------+
| Database  |
+-----------+
| mysql     |
| test      |
+-----------+
2 rows in set (0.00 sec)
```

Figure 8-11. You should find two databases in waiting.

Remember though, if you miss the semicolon (;) from the end of your command, you'll just get thrown back to the prompt, until you enter that semicolon, like so:

```
mysql> SHOW DATABASES
    -> ;
```

As you can see, the prompt is different (->). This is handy when you need to write long lines of code, but need a visual break to see where you're up to.

2. To see what's inside the test database (or **db**, for short), you need to select it first. Type the following, and get the result shown in Figure 8-12:

   USE test;

```
mysql> use test;
Database changed
```

Figure 8-12. You might not have changed history, but you changed the database.

3. Now you can issue the following command to show the contents of the tables in the selected database (see Figure 8-13):

   SHOW TABLES;

```
mysql> show tables;
Empty set (0.00 sec)
```

Figure 8-13. Showing all the tables in the test database

4. As you can see, it's empty! You could keep it there for fun, or you could drop-kick that thing right out of sight, like this (see also Figure 8-14):

   DROP DATABASE test;

If you run SHOW DATABASES; now, you'll only see the actual mysql database, which holds user info and the like.

```
mysql> drop database test;
Query OK, 0 rows affected (0.01 sec)
```

Figure 8-14. Dropping the test database

5. As you're going to be making a database to hold links for your website, let's call the database **sitelinks**. After you enter the following command, you should see the result shown in Figure 8-15.

   CREATE DATABASE sitelinks;

```
mysql> create database sitelinks;
Query OK, 1 row affected (0.00 sec)
```

Figure 8-15. Creating a new database

6. You can't use a database without having selected it, so you need to specify that you're using it (otherwise, you'll see Error 1046) as follows:

USE sitelinks;

```
mysql> use sitelinks;
Database changed
```

Figure 8-16. Selecting the new database

7. Once you have your database selected, you can do things with it. In fact, it's pretty much useless until you do things to it. You first need to create a table in it, so that it may contain data, using this command:

CREATE TABLE links (

8. Your table will have three columns, so let's take those one by one.

id INT NOT NULL AUTO_INCREMENT PRIMARY KEY,

You've specified that the column is to be called id, which will contain an integer (INT). You don't want the column left empty (NOT NULL), but you want a value that's automatically higher than the highest value already in this column (AUTO_INCREMENT). Lastly, you have PRIMARY KEY. The primary key of a table uniquely identifies each record in the table.

9. The text that will be displayed as the link will be character strings of variable length, and you really don't need them to be much longer than 100 characters. So, use VARCHAR(100) for these fields:

description VARCHAR (100) NOT NULL,

10. The actual address of the site is pretty much the same as the description field.

address VARCHAR (100) NOT NULL

11. That's the main part done, so you can close your brackets up now, to close the statement (see also Figure 8-17):

);

```
mysql> create table links (
    -> id int not null auto_increment primary key,
    -> description varchar (100) not null,
    -> address varchar (100) not null
    -> );
Query OK, 0 rows affected (0.42 sec)
```

Figure 8-17. Creating a table

12. You can check up on that by typing

DESCRIBE links;

You should get an output like what you see in Figure 8-18.

```
mysql> describe links;
+-------------+--------------+------+-----+---------+----------------+
| Field       | Type         | Null | Key | Default | Extra          |
+-------------+--------------+------+-----+---------+----------------+
| id          | int(11)      |      | PRI | NULL    | auto_increment |
| description | varchar(100) |      |     |         |                |
| address     | varchar(100) |      |     |         |                |
+-------------+--------------+------+-----+---------+----------------+
3 rows in set (0.43 sec)
```

Figure 8-18. This is what your table looks like.

199

This should give you a clearer idea of what is actually going on in there.

13. Now that you have your table, you need to populate it with data. Ultimately, this is going to be done via a web page, but here is how you add data via the command line (with the returned result shown in Figure 8-19):

```
INSERT INTO links (id, description,
➡ address) VALUES (NULL, "Apple\'s
➡ Website", "http://www.apple.com/");
```

You want to insert data into a particular table (INSERT INTO links), in a certain order (id, description, address), with certain values (VALUES (NULL, "Apple\'s Website", "http://www.apple.com/")). You'll notice that the apostrophe is escaped (Apple\'s), so that it doesn't cause any calamity.

14. Add a few more links, like so (see also Figure 8-20):

```
INSERT INTO links (link, description,
➡ address) VALUES (NULL, "friends of ED",
➡ "http://www.friendsofed.com/");

INSERT INTO links (link, description,
➡ address) VALUES (NULL, "Macromedia",
➡ "http://www.macromedia.com/");

INSERT INTO links (link, description,
➡ address) VALUES (NULL, "Adobe",
➡ "http://www.adobe.com/");

INSERT INTO links (link, description,
➡ address) VALUES (NULL, "Mac OS X Hints",
➡ "http://www.macosxhints.com/");
```

```
mysql> INSERT INTO links (id, description, address) VALUES (NULL, "Apple\'s Webs
ite", "http://www.apple.com/");
Query OK, 1 row affected (0.00 sec)
```

Figure 8-19. Inserting data into the fields

```
mysql> INSERT INTO links (id, description, address) VALUES (NULL, "friends of ED
", "http://www.friendsofed.com/");
Query OK, 1 row affected (0.00 sec)

mysql> INSERT INTO links (id, description, address) VALUES (NULL, "Macromedia",
"http://www.macromedia.com/");
Query OK, 1 row affected (0.01 sec)

mysql> INSERT INTO links (id, description, address) VALUES (NULL, "Adobe", "http
://www.adobe.com/");
Query OK, 1 row affected (0.00 sec)

mysql> INSERT INTO links (id, description, address) VALUES (NULL, "Mac OS X Hint
s", "http://www.macosxhints.com/");
Query OK, 1 row affected (0.00 sec)

mysql> INSERT INTO links (id, description, address) VALUES (NULL, "MacNN", "http
://www.macnn.com/");
Query OK, 1 row affected (0.00 sec)

mysql> INSERT INTO links (id, description, address) VALUES (NULL, "Speak\'n\'Spe
ll", "http://www.speaknspell.co.uk/");
Query OK, 1 row affected (0.00 sec)
```

Figure 8-20. Adding a load more data to the data, via the shell

```
INSERT INTO links (link, description,
➥ address) VALUES (NULL, "MacNN",
➥ "http://www.macnn.com/");

INSERT INTO links (link, description,
➥address) VALUES (NULL, "Speak\'n\'Spell",
➥ "http://www.speaknspell.co.uk/");
```

15. You can test that data is now living in the database by typing

```
SELECT * FROM links;
```

You should see results similar to what appears in Figure 8-21.

```
mysql> select * from links;
+----+-----------------+-----------------------------+
| id | description     | address                     |
+----+-----------------+-----------------------------+
|  1 | Apple's Website | http://www.apple.com/       |
|  2 | friends of ED   | http://www.friendsofed.com/ |
|  3 | Macromedia      | http://www.macromedia.com/  |
|  4 | Adobe           | http://www.adobe.com/       |
|  5 | Mac OS X Hints  | http://www.macosxhints.com/ |
|  6 | MacNN           | http://www.macnn.com/       |
|  7 | Speak 'n'Spell  | http://www.speaknspell.co.uk/ |
+----+-----------------+-----------------------------+
7 rows in set (0.00 sec)
```

Figure 8-21. Your table with data in it.

16. If you only want to check one column, you would type the following to get the result shown in Figure 8-22:

```
SELECT description FROM links;
```

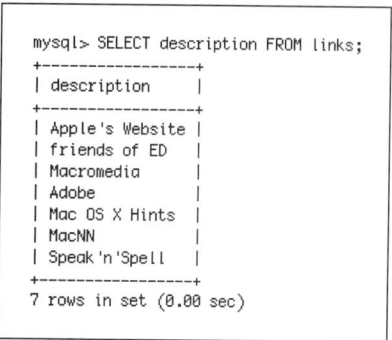

```
mysql> SELECT description FROM links;
+-----------------+
| description     |
+-----------------+
| Apple's Website |
| friends of ED   |
| Macromedia      |
| Adobe           |
| Mac OS X Hints  |
| MacNN           |
| Speak 'n'Spell  |
+-----------------+
7 rows in set (0.00 sec)
```

Figure 8-22. Just one column chosen

Alrighty then. You've established that your table is indeed populated with data goodness. Now what? Well, you're going to leave Terminal for a while, open Dreamweaver, and connect to the database from a web page.

Dynamic links page

You're going to make the links page now, so copy the whole directory structure so far, which is everything you've done since Chapter 5 (Chapter 6 didn't add to the main section of the site), to ~/Sites/book/08. This is so that each chapter still has its files in separate directories, just to avoid confusion.

1. Open the completed index.php file from Chapter 5 and save it as ~/Sites/book/08/links.php. Be sure to change the links accordingly, as shown in Figure 8-23, so the Links link is active (change the id tag).

```
24 <ul id="navlist">
25 <li><a href="index.php" title="Back to the Home Page">About Me</a></li>
26 <li><a href="projects.php" title="Projects, past & present">Projects</a></li>
27 <li><a href="contact.php" title="Contact me">Contact</a></li>
28 <li id="active"><a href="#" title="Explore other sites">Links</a></li>
29 <li><a href="forum/index.php" title="leave a message on the forum">Forum</a></li>
30 </ul>
```

Figure 8-23. Remember to change the active link.

2. Next, you have to delete the PHP code that currently occupies the content `<div>`, so delete the block highlighted in Figure 8-24.

```
43  </div>
44  <div id="content">
45  <?
46  if (empty($_GET["id"])) {
47  $page_name = 'pages/about_me.inc.php';
48  } else {
49  $page_name = 'pages/' . $_GET["id"] . '.inc.php';
50  }
51
52  include($page_name);
53  ?>
54  </div>
55  <div id="footer">this is the #footer &lt;div&gt;<br /
56  </div>
```

Figure 8-24. Clear the content `<div>`, ready for action.

3. There are a few steps you need to take now in order to be able to connect to your database, as you can see in the **Databases** palette (part of the **Application** palette, as shown in Figure 8-25). If you can't see it (and it often disappears all by itself), just open it with Window ➤ Databases (*SHIFT*+⌘+*F10*).

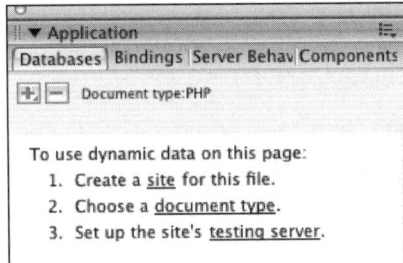

Figure 8-25. Your first meeting with the Applications window

4. Click the first step to create a site, which you should be familiar with doing by now. Call the site "Chapter 8".

5. You do want to use a server technology, so select PHP MySQL from the Which server technology? drop-down menu shown in Figure 8-26.

6. You'll be editing and testing locally, so select the top option, and find the path to your home drive by clicking the folder icon. You should then see something like what appears in Figure 8-27, where you should fill in the relevant path to your files.

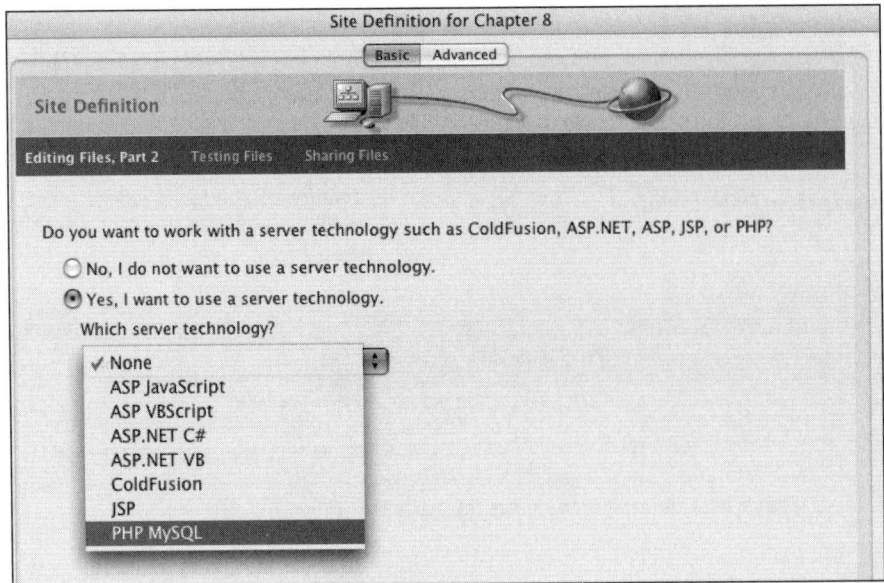

Figure 8-26. Choosing PHP/MySQL as the server technology

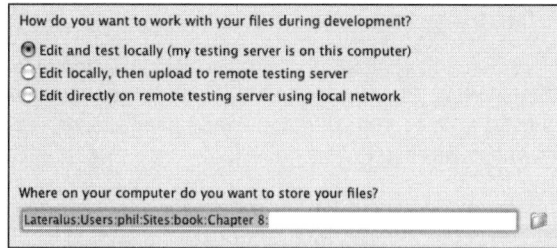

Figure 8-27. Locating the path to your files

7. Enter the root URL as shown in Figure 8-28, which should be something like http://127.0.0.1/~username/book/08/, depending on where your files are stored.

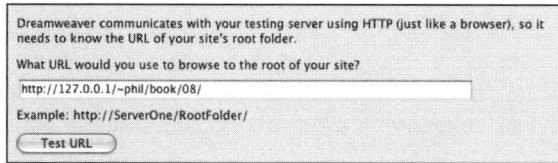

Figure 8-28. Entering the local URL for your files

You can click the Test URL button to confirm things work.

8. Select Local/Network from the drop-down menu and then specify the Chapter 8 files directory again, as shown in Figure 8-29.

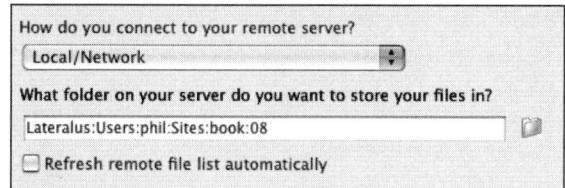

Figure 8-29. Selecting your files again

Whether you Enable Check In/Out or not is very much up to you. If you're working on these files by yourself, there really isn't much need for it. Once you confirm all those details, all three items in the Databases palette should be checked. This means that you can now proceed with linking to your database.

9. Step 4 on the Databases palette tells you what to do. Click that + in the corner, and then select MySQL Connection from the menu as shown in Figure 8-30.

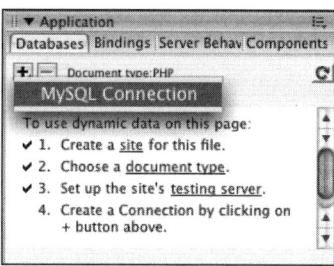

Figure 8-30. Creating the connection

10. MySQL connection time! The connection name (which you enter in the text field shown in Figure 8-31) can be any word you like (but no spaces). Keep it simple and call it conn. On a more complex site where you may be talking to various databases on the same page, you might want to give this a more specific name.

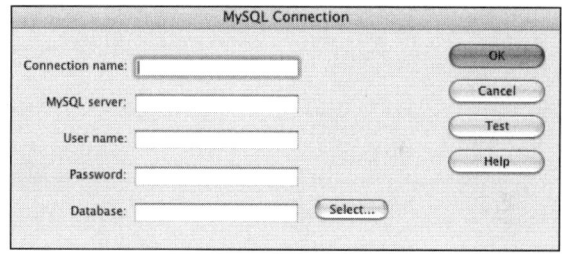

Figure 8-31. Entering the connection name

11. Fill in the rest of the MySQL Connection settings as follows:

- MySQL server: localhost
- User name: mysql
- Password: your_password
- Database: Click the Select button and choose sitelinks from the resulting menu (see Figure 8-32).

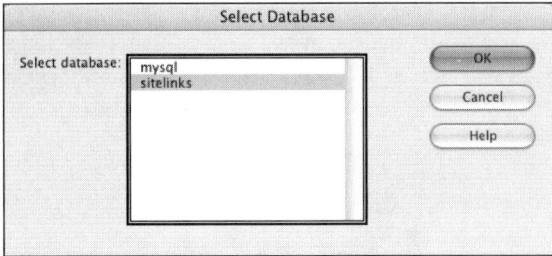

Figure 8-32. Choosing the database your links are in

Once that's done, your Databases palette should look like what appears in Figure 8-33.

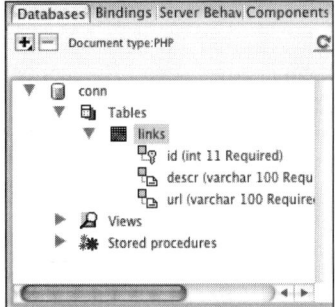

Figure 8-33. Database selected and active

Grabbing that recordset

Now that you've made that connection, let's do something with it. The data will be displayed in a table, a few lines at a time, with the data being pulled dynamically from the database.

1. To do this, you need to first create a **recordset** (a recordset is basically a set of rows containing data), so click the Bindings tab on the Application palette, click +, and then choose Recordset (Query) as shown in Figure 8-34.

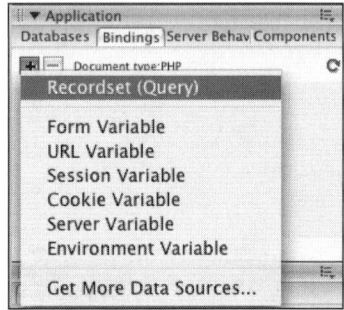

Figure 8-34. Creating a recordset

2. Call the recordset links, select conn from the Connection drop-down menu, and you should see your column titles appear as shown in Figure 8-35.

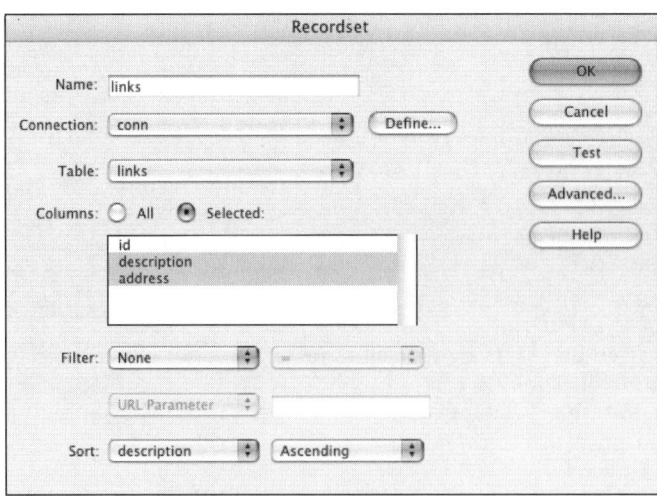

Figure 8-35. Only select description and address.

3. You don't need to show the id column on your web page, so click the Selected button and select description and address. (Click description, hold ⌘, and then click address.)

4. Next, sort by description, ascending. This just puts the recordset data in a nice alphabetical order on the page. Click OK to return to the page.

5. Click into the content <div>, and select Insert ➤ Application Object ➤ Dynamic Data ➤ Dynamic Table.

6. Select the links recordset and choose five records. You're planning ahead here, just in case your links database gets ridiculously huge.

7. You don't really want an ugly border on the table, so give that a value of 0, add a value of 2 for padding and spacing, and then OK it (see Figure 8-36).

8. Now that you have the code in place, click the Live Data button, which should show something like what you see in Figure 8-37.

9. Now, you might be wondering how people are going to see the rest of the links. You're going to add pagination next. Select Application Objects ➤ Recordset Paging ➤ Recordset Navigation Bar from the menu.

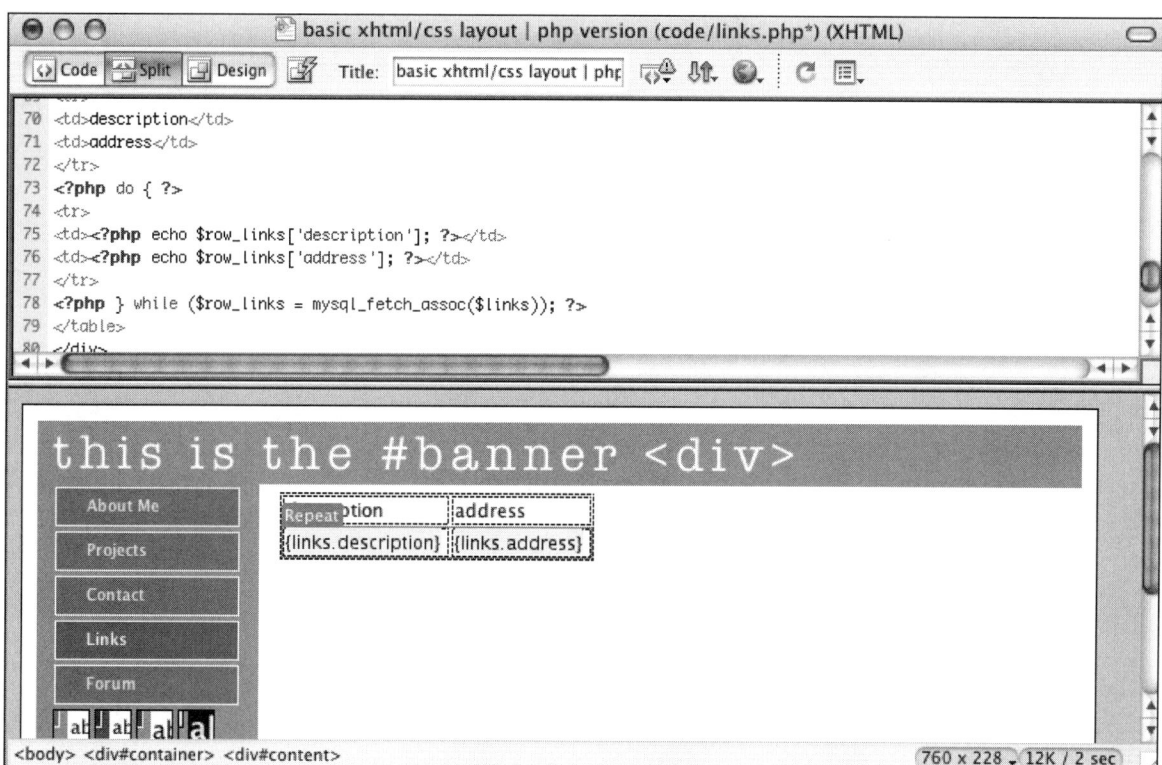

Figure 8-36. There's your code in place.

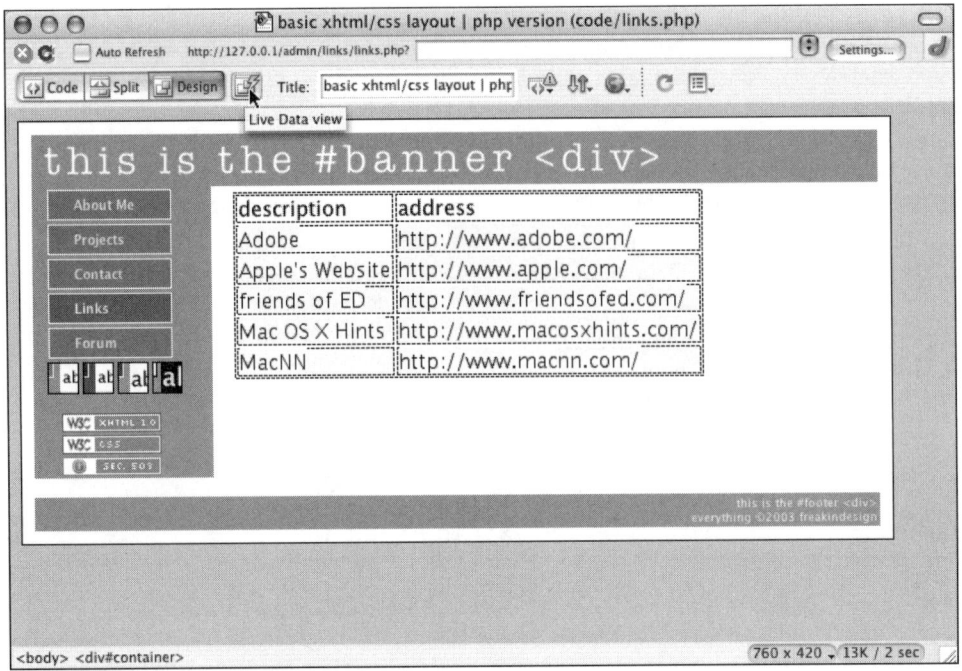

Figure 8-37. Live Data view shows you your links.

10. The choice of text links or images is entirely up to you, but I've gone with text links (see Figure 8-38). This will be governed by the CSS rules of whichever style sheet the user is currently using, whereas images would stay the same.

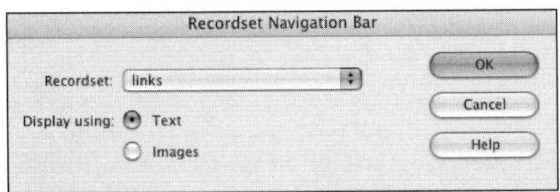

Figure 8-38. Text or images? It's up to you.

11. Once the pagination links are in place, select the table and align it to the left to match the data table as shown in Figure 8-39, and then save the document.

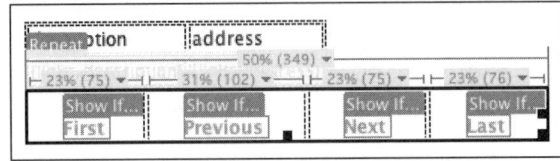

Figure 8-39. Aligning the links

12. Because there are no records lower than id 1, the code doesn't display any back links. Press *F12* to preview in your browser and agree to save any unsaved documents. As you can see in Figure 8-40, you can now move back and forth between the pages of data.

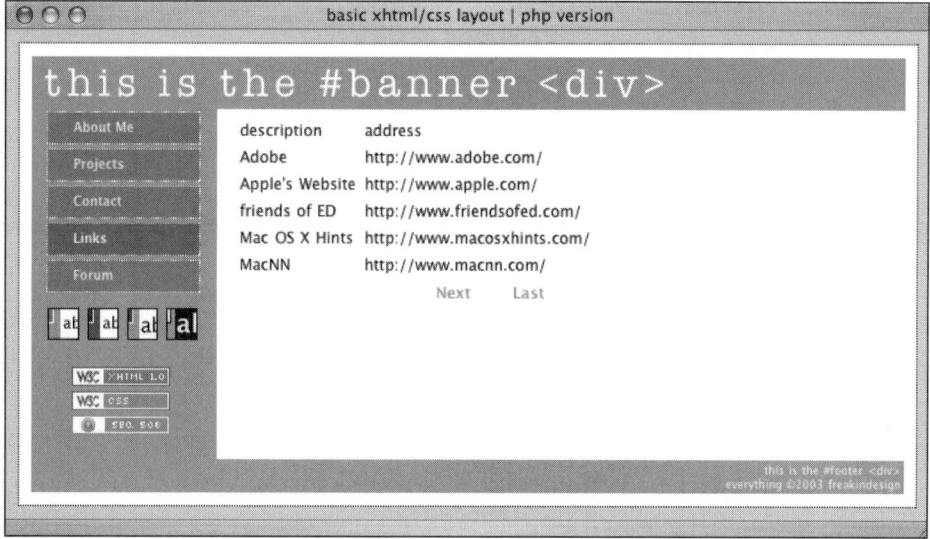

Figure 8-40. Almost finished

Adding dynamic hyperlinks

This is all very cool, but those links aren't very hyper at the moment. You need to connect the actual link with the contents of the field.

1. That's easy enough. Highlight the {links.address} field as shown in Figure 8-41.

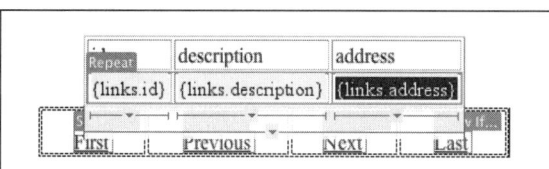

Figure 8-41. A single click will highlight the {links.address} field.

2. Click the blue folder on the Properties inspector, next to the Link field (see Figure 8-42).

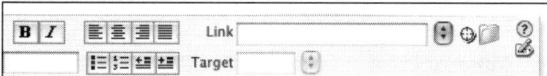

Figure 8-42. Clicking the blue folder

3. Now click the Data Sources button, shown in Figure 8-43.

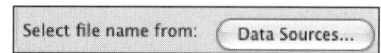

Figure 8-43. Selecting data sources

4. Select the address column, shown in Figure 8-44, from the recordset and click OK.

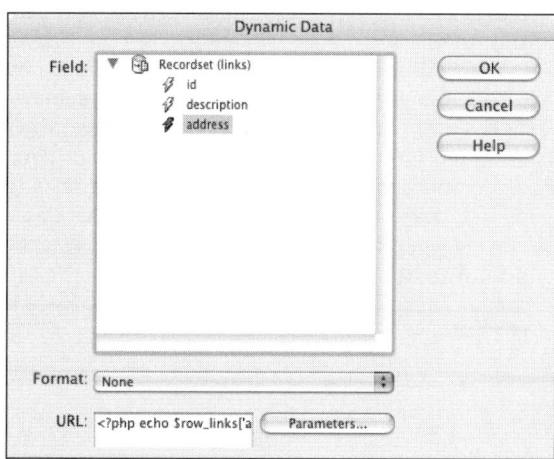

Figure 8-44. Clicking address

207

Your links field should now be real hyperlinks, as you can see in the Code view in Figure 8-45 . . .

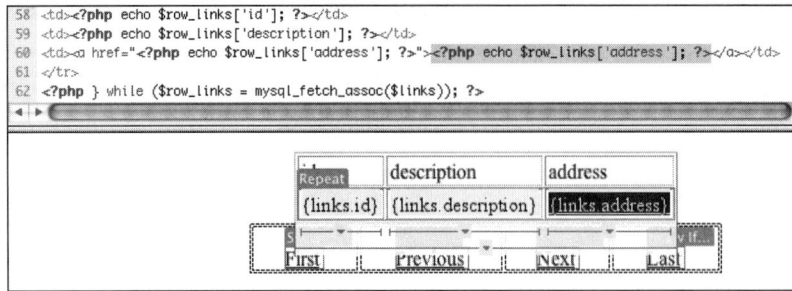

Figure 8-45. Notice the query string in the code pane.

. . . and in the Properties palette as shown in Figure 8-46.

Figure 8-46. The query string in the Properties inspector

Adding links to the database

Using Terminal to add links is all very well and nerdy, but it's hardly practical is it? You could do with a way of adding links via a web page. At the start of this chapter, I mentioned phpMyAdmin. This is a web-based application for administering MySQL databases. It's pretty serious at what it does and is very easy to set up. It gives you a full GUI for creating and editing your databases, and comes in very handy for larger database administration. Another way you could do this is by writing a page with a form on it that writes links to your database. As you don't want just anybody adding links to your web page, you can have this page in the admin area you made in Chapter 6. While you're at it, you can add a link to delete links too.

phpMyAdmin

Let's go back to the first option though: phpMyAdmin. The first thing you have to do is download phpMyAdmin from www.phpmyadmin.net.

1. Download the latest stable release (see Figure 8-47), which should be something like phpMyAdmin-2.5.4-php.tar.gz.

2. To unpack the file, double-click it. phpMyAdmin-2.5.4 is a bit of a handful to type into the address bar, so rename the unarchived directory "db".

3. You want this in your admin area, so drag it over to /Library/WebServer/Documents/admin/db.

4. There is only one file you need to alter (config.inc.php), so let's get on with that. Open the file in your text editor and look for this code (around line 40):

   $cfg['PmaAbsoluteUri'] = ' ';

5. You need to have the absolute URL to phpMyAdmin in there, as shown in Figure 8-48. Type

   $cfg['PmaAbsoluteUri'] =
   ➥ 'http://127.0.0.1/admin/db';

6. Scroll down to about line 80, where you'll find the block of code in Figure 8-49.

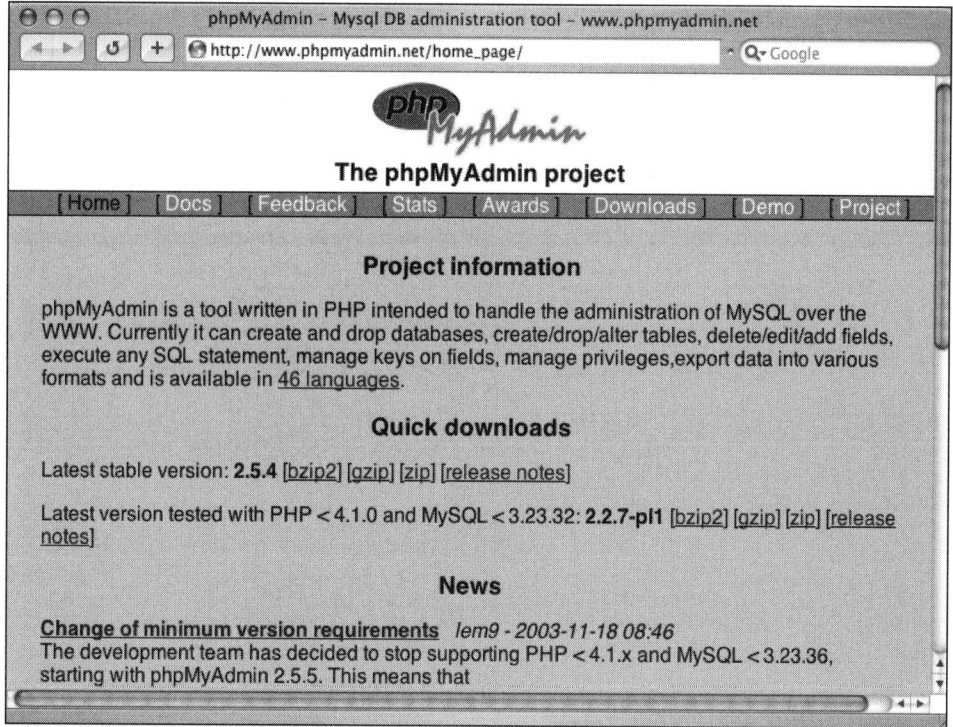

Figure 8-47. The phpMyAdmin website

```
21  /**
22   *  Your phpMyAdmin url
23   *
24   *  Complete the variable below with the full url ie
25   *      http://www.your_web.net/path_to_your_phpMyAdmin_directory/
26   *
27   *  It must contain characters that are valid for a URL, and the path is
28   *  case sensitive on some Web servers, for example Unix-based servers.
29   *
30   *  In most cases you can leave this variable empty, as the correct value
31   *  will be detected automatically. However, we recommend that you do
32   *  test to see that the auto-detection code works in your system. A good
33   *  test is to browse a table, then edit a row and save it.  There will be
34   *  an error message if phpMyAdmin cannot auto-detect the correct value.
35   *
36   *  If the auto-detection code does work properly, you can set to TRUE the
37   *  $cfg['PmaAbsoluteUri_DisableWarning'] variable below.
38   */
39  $cfg['PmaAbsoluteUri'] = 'http://127.0.0.1/admin/db/';
40
```

Figure 8-48. Entering the URL for your phpMyAdmin directory

```
78                                               //  and "mysql/db" tables)
79  $cfg['Servers'][$i]['auth_type']  = 'config';  //  Authentication method (config, http or
80  $cfg['Servers'][$i]['user']       = 'root';    //  MySQL user
81  $cfg['Servers'][$i]['password']   = '';        //  MySQL password (only needed
82                                               //  with 'config' auth_type)
```

Figure 8-49. Entering your MySQL user name and password

7. Because you're creating an admin area for adding links to your database, and you don't want just anybody adding things, this is going to be in your admin area, which is already password protected. Because of this, you can use **config** authentication, changing the code as follows:

```
$cfg['Servers'][$i]['auth_type']     = 'config';

$cfg['Servers'][$i]['user']          = 'mysql';

$cfg['Servers'][$i]['password']      = 'your_
                                        password';
```

'your_password' is whatever you used in the earlier stages. (You did make a note of it, didn't you?)

8. Save and close this file.

9. If you now go to http://127.0.0.1/admin/db and enter the admin area password, you'll see the phpMyAdmin welcome screen.

10. Select sitelinks from the drop-down menu at the top left (see Figure 8-50).

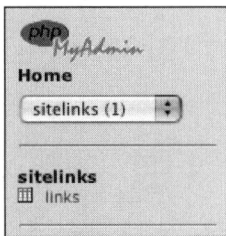

Figure 8-50. Selecting your database

11. Click the small table icon to the left of links, and there's your data, all laid out nicely as shown in Figure 8-51.

Figure 8-51. The links data, nicely laid out in a GUI format

12. To add a link, you need to insert a new row. You do that by selecting the fifth tab along called **Insert** (see Figure 8-52).

Figure 8-52. Clicking the Insert tab

13. Add your link description and address, but leave the id blank as shown in Figure 8-53, and then click Go.

14. You can check that was added by clicking the Browse tab . . . and there's your new link, as you see in Figure 8-54.

Figure 8-54. You added another link!

That was easy enough. You can use phpMyAdmin to empty the database of data, alter the columns, delete rows, and so on. It's really useful, so take some time out to experiment with it.

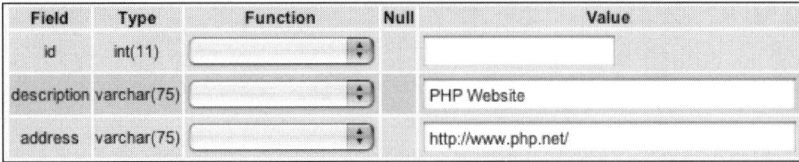

Figure 8-53. Leave the id field blank, as it auto-increments.

Links admin section

While phpMyAdmin is easy enough to use, it still has too many fields and options for just a simple links page. Maybe you have other users whom you'd like to be able to add links, but you don't want to give them access to the whole database. It would make sense to have a section where you could add/edit/delete links, but not access any other databases. Here's how you do it:

1. Select the Admin Site from the Files palette.
2. Create four new dynamic pages in Dreamweaver, and save them as follows:
   - /Library/WebServer/Documents/admin/ links/index.php
   - /Library/WebServer/Documents/admin/ links/insert.php
   - /Library/WebServer/Documents/admin/ links/edit.php
   - /Library/WebServer/Documents/admin/ links/delete.php
3. I gave my pages the following title tags:
   - index.php links admin | index.
   - insert.php links admin | insert.
   - edit.php links admin | edit.
   - delete.php links admin | delete.
4. Open index.php and follow the same steps as you did for links_table.php from the previous exercise, so you have the data displaying in a table, and save the document. Remaking the document from scratch ensures that the database connection is functioning properly.
5. CTRL-click in the address field, and select Insert Rows or Columns from the pop-up menu as shown in Figure 8-55.

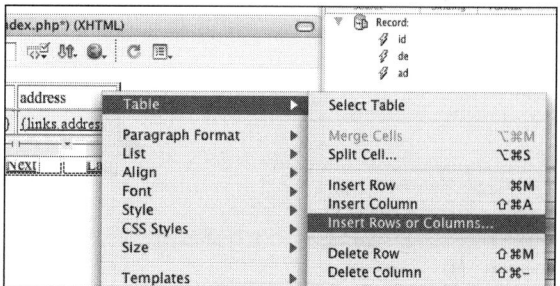

Figure 8-55. Inserting columns in Dreamweaver

6. Add two columns after the current column by selecting the option After current Column (see Figure 8-56). These will contain the links for editing and deleting rows from the database.

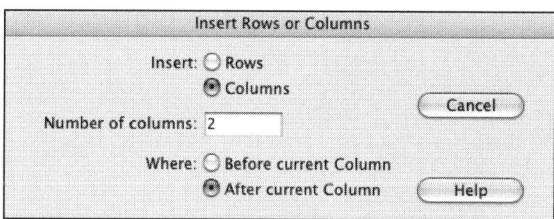

Figure 8-56. Adding the columns after the current column

7. Type in some column headers, like I've done in Figure 8-57.

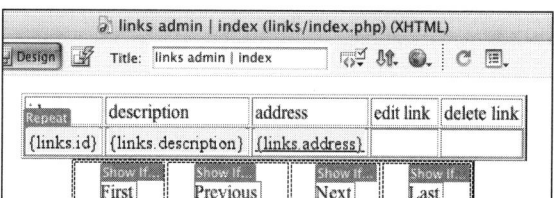

Figure 8-57. Adding your Edit/Delete headers

211

8. You need some text for the links, so add some underneath the column headers, like I've done in Figure 8-58. I also centered them, just to make things look a bit better.

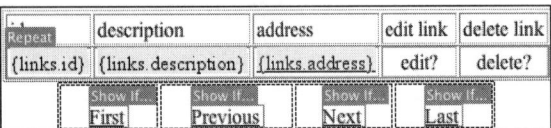

Figure 8-58. Adding an appropriate piece of text for each column

9. Highlight the edit? text that you just added as shown in Figure 8-59, and then click the blue folder on the Properties palette to bring up the links window.

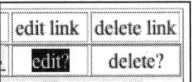

Figure 8-59. Highlighting the text for linking

10. Point the link towards `edit.php` and click the Parameters button as shown in Figure 8-60.

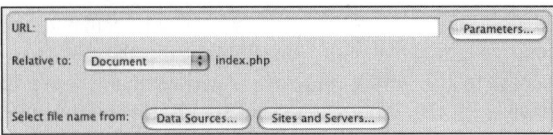

Figure 8-60. Clicking the Parameters button

11. Type id into the Name field as shown in Figure 8-61.

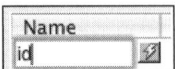

Figure 8-61. Naming the field id

12. In the Value field, click the thunderbolt, and then select id from the recordset in the Dynamic Data window, as shown in Figure 8-62. Okay all of the windows until you're back at your Code window.

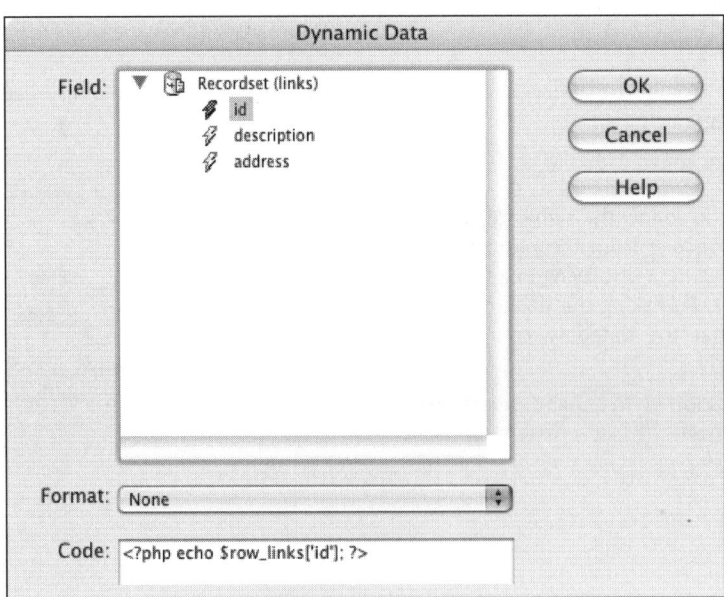

Figure 8-62. Notice the code appear in the bottom pane.

You should now be able to see the new query string in the Code pane of the window (see Figure 8-63).

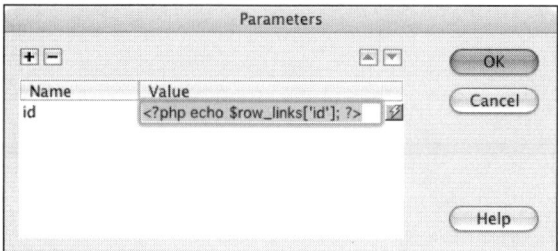

Figure 8-63. Click OK to return to the Code view.

13. You follow a similar procedure for the delete link. Highlight delete? and click the blue folder in the Properties inspector.

14. Select delete.php and click Parameters.

15. Type id in the Name field.

16. In the Value field, click the thunderbolt, and then select id from the recordset in the Dynamic Data window, as shown in Figure 8-64. Okay all of the windows until you're back at your Code window. Your code should now look like the code in Figure 8-64, with the string query links in place.

For each row, the link will be dynamically created using the id column as the reference point. So, the Delete Record server behavior will use this ID to find the requested record in the database and delete it.

17. Lastly, you'll add a link to get to the Insert page. Click to the left of the links table and insert a carriage return with the *ENTER* key.

18. Click in the gap you just made, align to center, and type in add a link.

19. Highlight the new text, click the blue folder on the Properties inspector, select insert.php as the link, and then save the file. Your results should match Figure 8-65.

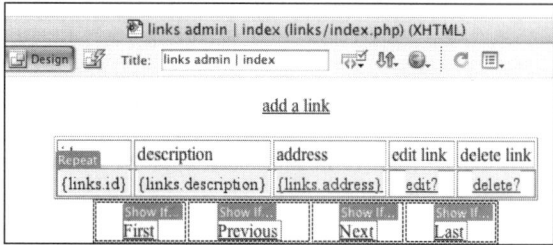

Figure 8-65. All linked up and ready to go.

20. If you reload the page in your browser now, you should see the screen in Figure 8-66.

Figure 8-66. Finished index.php with links

21. Close index.php.

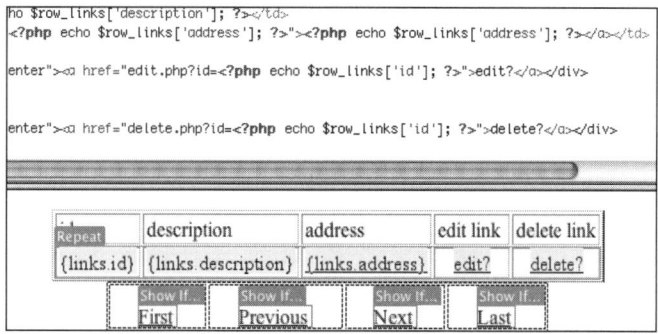

Figure 8-64. Dynamic links in place, for editing and deleting

Add a link

1. Open `insert.php`.

2. Next, select the recordset as before (click the + in the Bindings panel), name it "links," and sort by `id`, ascending.

3. You know how to make the table manually, so let's cheat and use the wizard this time. Choose Insert ➤ Application Objects ➤ Insert Record ➤ Record Insertion Form Wizard.

4. Select your `conn` connection from the Connection drop-down menu, and you should see your table columns appear. Table has already filled in links for you, so move on.

5. Click the Browse button next to the After Inserting, go to field and select the `index.php` you saved in the last section (see Figure 8-67).

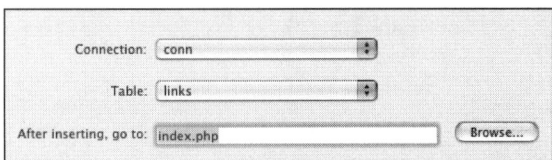

Figure 8-67. Directing the page to `index.php`

6. With id selected in the Form fields window, select Hidden field from the Display as drop-down menu (see Figure 8-68). This field is the auto-increment field, so you don't need to enter a value here. Click OK to return to the insert form.

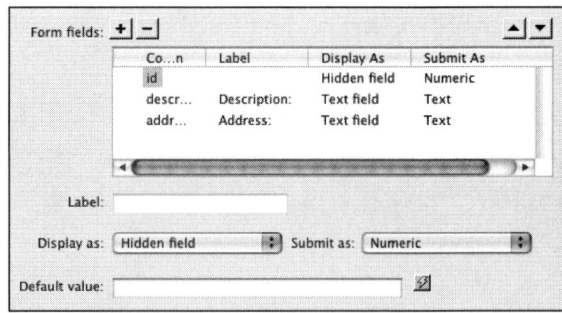

Figure 8-68. Making id a hidden field

7. Click in the Description TextField. Set the Char width to 40 and Max Chars to 100 in the Properties inspector as shown in Figure 8-69.

8. Click in the Address TextField and assign the following values in the Properties inspector (see also Figure 8-70):

   - Char width: 40
   - Max Chars: 100
   - Init Val: http://

9. Click the Insert Record button and make the following changes in the Properties palette: change Label to insert link and the Button name to add (see Figure 8-71).

10. Save the document and preview it in your browser (`http://127.0.0.1/admin/links/index.php`). Add a link and then hit the insert link button as shown in Figure 8-72.

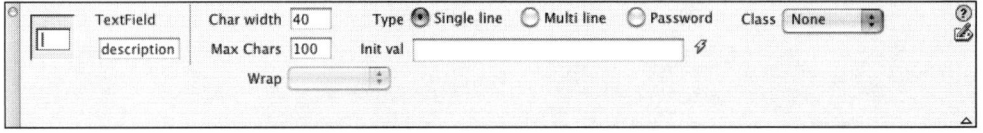

Figure 8-69. Adding properties to the Description field

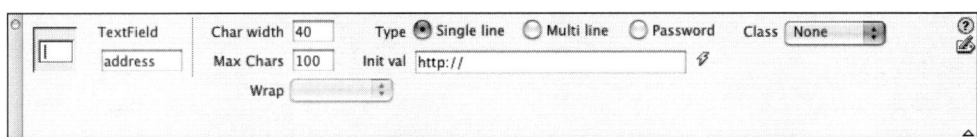

Figure 8-70. Adding properties to the Address field

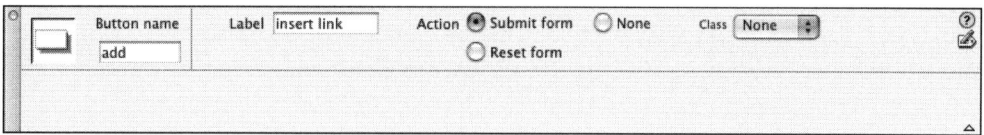

Figure 8-71. Adding properties to the Submit button

Figure 8-72. Adding another link

11. Click the Next button to page 2, where, as shown in Figure 8-73, you should finally see the link you added!

id	description	address	edit link	delete link
6	MacNN	http://www.macnn.com/	edit?	delete?
7	Speak'n'Spell	http://www.speaknspell.co.uk/	edit?	delete?
8	PHP Website	http://www.php.net/	edit?	delete?
9	MySQL Website	http://www.mysql.com/	edit?	delete?
	First	Previous		

Figure 8-73. There's your new link, added at the bottom.

Editing a link

1. Open edit.php.

2. Add your recordset from the Server Behaviors palette, calling it "links" as you did previously.

3. This time you want to use the Filter menu so that you only select the link you're after (as opposed to all of them). For Filter, select id and =, and id for the URL Parameter (see Figure 8-74). Click OK to return to the code.

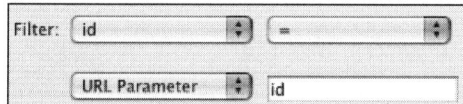

Figure 8-74. Setting the filter

4. To insert your edit form, go to Insert ➤ Application Objects ➤ Update Record ➤ Record Update Form Wizard.

5. Select the conn connection and tell it to go to index.php after updating (see Figure 8-75).

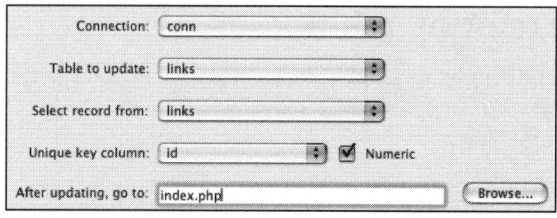

Figure 8-75. Sending the link back to the index page

6. Now make id a hidden field as shown in Figure 8-76.

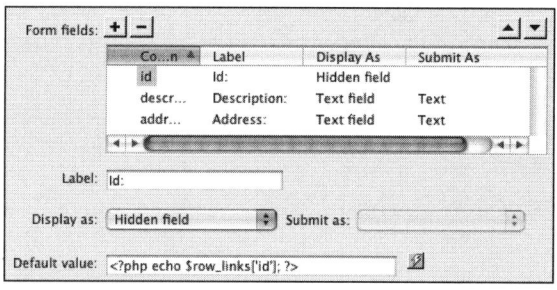

Figure 8-76. id is a hidden field

7. If you save the document and call up index.php in your browser, you should now be able to edit the links (see Figure 8-77).

Description:	Adobe EDITED!
Address:	http://www.adobe.com/
	Update record

Figure 8-77. Editing a link

215

8. You then get thrown back to the index page, where you can inspect your edited link (see Figure 8-78). Winner!

id	description	address	edit link	delete link
1	Apple's Website	http://www.apple.com/	edit?	delete?
2	friends of ED	http://www.friendsofed.com/	edit?	delete?
3	Macromedia	http://www.macromedia.com/	edit?	delete?
4	Adobe EDITED!	http://www.adobe.com/	edit?	delete?
5	Mac OS X Hints	http://www.macosxhints.com/	edit?	delete?

Next   Last

Figure 8-78. Link—edited!

Deleting a link

In the same way that you added an edit column in the previous exercise, let's move on and add a delete column.

1. Open delete.php.

2. As there is no wizard for this part, you'll be creating the form manually. You need to insert some form tags before you go any further, so choose Insert ➤ Form ➤ Form.

3. Click into the form tags (with the red border), and insert a table (either using the Insert menu or through the Insert panel) using the settings shown in Figure 8-79. Center it on the page.

4. Next, you need to bind your recordset to the page. Click the + in the Bindings panel and choose Recordset (Query).

5. You don't want to delete everything; you're only deleting one link. To do this, you use the Filter. The primary ID is used to identify each link, so select that from the Filter drop-down menu, and keep the = selected in the menu to the right of Filter as shown in Figure 8-80.

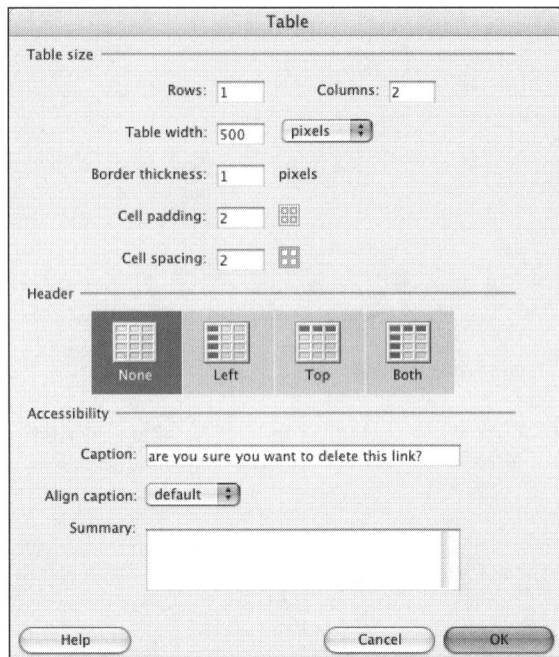

Figure 8-79. Adding a table to hold the dynamic data to be deleted

6. Underneath that, select URL Parameter. id has already been selected for you, which is fine. Okay that.

7. The Bindings panel shows the recordset now. Expand the recordset by clicking the triangle, and then click and drag the description record into the left cell of your table as shown in Figure 8-81.

8. Next, drag the address record to the right cell, in the same way (see Figure 8-82).

9. That's two of the fields taken care of, but you need a hidden field to hold the link ID. Click to the right of the table and choose Insert ➤ Form ➤ Hidden Field (see Figure 8-83).

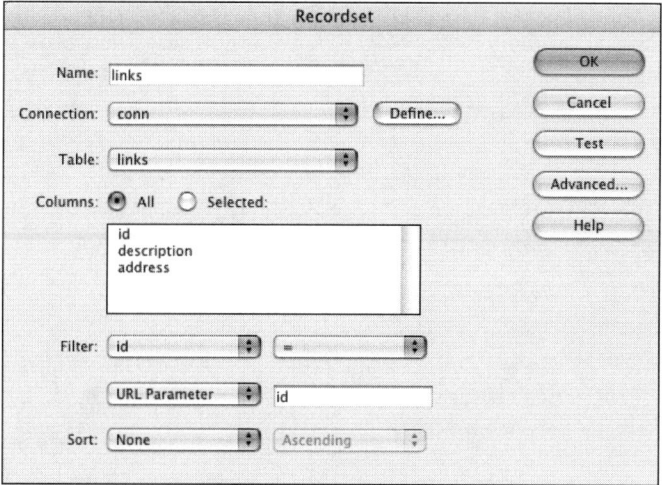

Figure 8-80. Filtering the link out for deletion

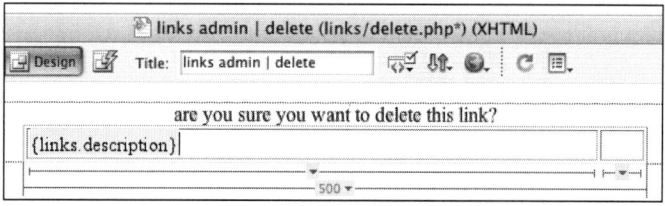

Figure 8-81. Dynamic placeholder text for the description

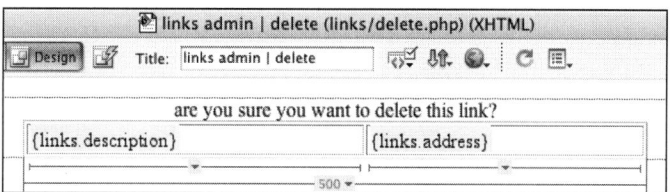

Figure 8-82. Dynamic placeholder text for the address

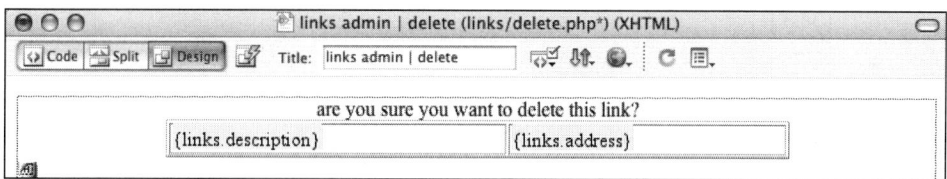

Figure 8-83. The hidden field shows up as a yellow icon.

10. Click the Hidden Field icon and name it "deleteID" in the Properties inspector as shown in Figure 8-84.

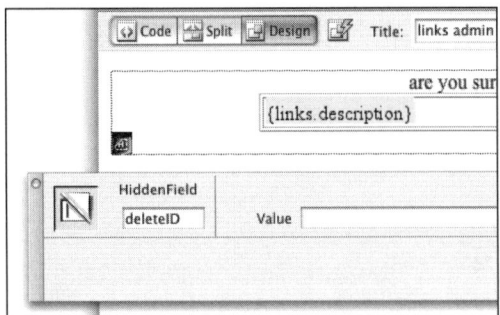

Figure 8-84. Naming the hidden field

11. You need to bind the hidden field to the id record column, so drag the ID record from the Bindings panel and drop it on the icon. This should populate the Value field in the Properties inspector as shown in Figure 8-85.

12. Your form isn't much good without a Submit button, so click to the right of the hidden field and insert a button (Insert ➤ Form ➤ Button or click the button on the Insert panel). Center the button.

13. You're almost there, but you need to add the action that deletes the link. Choose Delete Record from the Server Behaviors panel.

14. The first value is correct, so leave Primary key value as it is, and select your connection from the Connection drop-down menu (see Figure 8-86).

15. The Primary key column is also correct, so move on to Primary key value. Select Form Variable from the drop-down menu and name it "deleteID".

16. You want to return to the index page after deleting the link, so click the Browse button, and select index.php in the After deleting, go to field.

17. Save the document.

18. Reload the index page in your browser, select a link to delete, and you should see the confirmation page shown in Figure 8-87.

Figure 8-87. Confirmation page

That's all there is to it. You now have a nice little section to administer your links from.

Figure 8-85. The hidden field is now bound to the recordset.

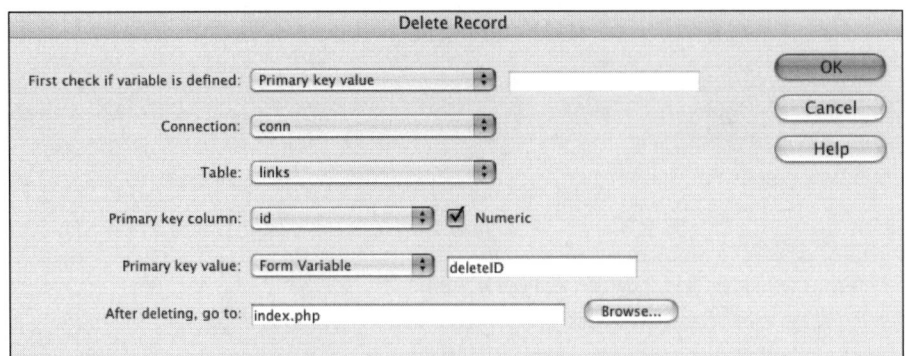

Figure 8-86. Delete Record configuration

Message boards

One thing you might want to add to your site is a message board. Message boards help build a sense of community and provide more feedback than a simple contact form. There are all kinds of packages you can get these days for this purpose. The two main types of boards are Perl and PHP/MySQL.

Back in the day, the two main Perl-based boards were Ultimate Bulletin Board (UBB), which was expensive, and the free iKonboard. I used to have great fun hacking away at iKonboard, adding new features and teaching myself Perl at the same time. These days, however, the PHP/MySQL boards have come to overshadow the Perl-based boards.

The undisputed heavyweight champ of the PHP Boards is **vBulletin** (www.vbulletin.com), which weighs in at around $160. The main contender in this bout has to be **phpBB** (www.phpbb.com), which is free. They are both great boards to work with. Both have a solid set of features, some of them unique. From an administrator's point of view, I have to say I prefer working with vBulletin. You can do so much more with it. A downside has to be paying to change the look of the board (unless you make a theme yourself), as opposed to the large amount of free themes available for phpBB.

Let's go right ahead and install phpBB.

Setting up phpBB

1. Download phpBB from www.phpbb.com/downloads.php. From there, you need to decide which format you want (see Figure 8-88). As you're just installing this on a local Mac, you can use the ZIP file. Unzip the file and move it to /Library/WebServer/Documents/phpBB2.

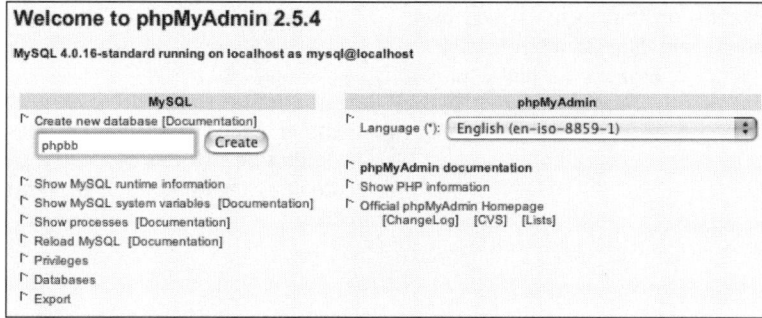

Figure 8-88. Download the full package.

2. Before you can install the board, you need to create a database for it. You can do this via phpMyAdmin or Terminal. Let's use phpMyAdmin this time, so call it up in your browser with http://127.0.0.1/admin/db/.

3. Type phpbb in the Create new database field and click the Create button (see Figures 8-89 and 8-90).

4. With your database created, you can now run the installer in your browser: http://127.0.0.1/phpBB2/. As you'll see, it detects that you haven't installed it already, and sends you to the install page.

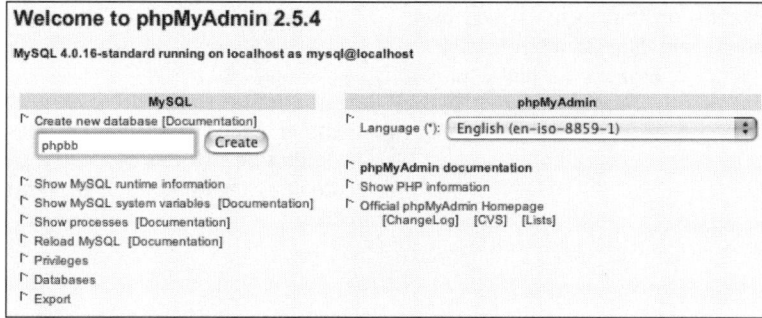

Figure 8-89. Using phpMyAdmin to create a new database

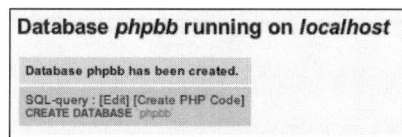

Figure 8-90. Your new database has been created.

219

5. Select the correct Database Type from the drop-down menu shown in Figure 8-91. You should be using **MySQL 4.x**.

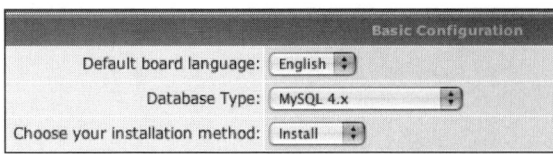

Figure 8-91. phpBB installer screen

6. Next, move on to the Database Configuration section. The Hostname will be localhost, but make sure you use the same database name and mysql password that you chose in the exercise named "Setting up MySQL" earlier on in this chapter (see Figure 8-92).

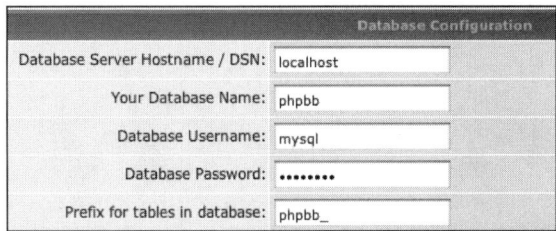

Figure 8-92. Entering your database configuration information

7. The board needs an admin user, which you configure in the final section on that page. As you can see, some fields are already filled in for you, so just add your e-mail address, user name, and a password for the admin user as shown in Figure 8-93.

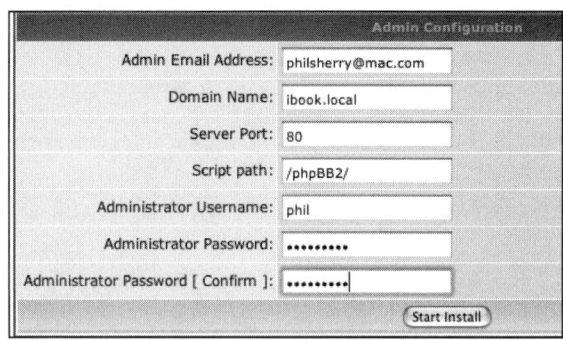

Figure 8-93. Setting up the phpBB admin user account

8. Click the Start Install button and that's it, you're done.

9. When you click Finish Installation, you'll see a message telling you to remove some directories from the phpBB2 folder as shown in Figure 8-94. You can't progress any further until you do this, so throw them in the trash.

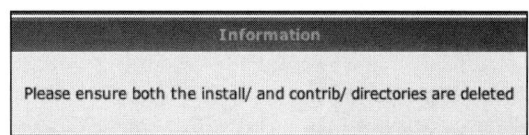

Figure 8-94. phpBB tells you to delete directories so that it can proceed.

10. If you now go back to phpMyAdmin and select the **phpBB** database, you'll see the advantage of using phpMyAdmin (as demonstrated in Figure 8-95).

That message board database is *slightly* more comprehensive than those you've tackled so far, and it wouldn't be my idea of a fun night in to have to navigate my way through it in Terminal. I'm sure you'll agree.

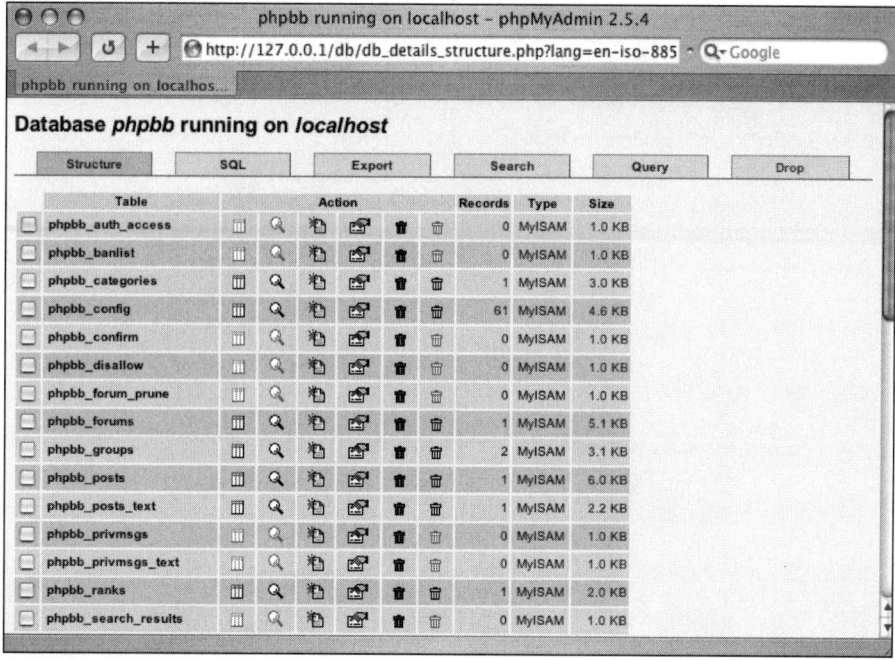

Figure 8-95. The friendly GUI version of the phpBB database

Chapter review

As you can see, using a database to power your site isn't anywhere nearly as hard as it may have seemed. In fact, it's very easy these days when you employ Dreamweaver to do all the hard work for you. I find a lot of the code seems unnecessary—twice the page length, sometimes—but that's certainly worth it when you can create your pages in a fraction of the time you would otherwise spend coding them by hand.

Another great time-saver, phpMyAdmin, means that you can get entire sites up and running in no time at all. You can import data from a previous database too, which is pretty much just a point-and-click operation. All headaches previously associated with database-driven sites are slowly becoming a thing of the past.

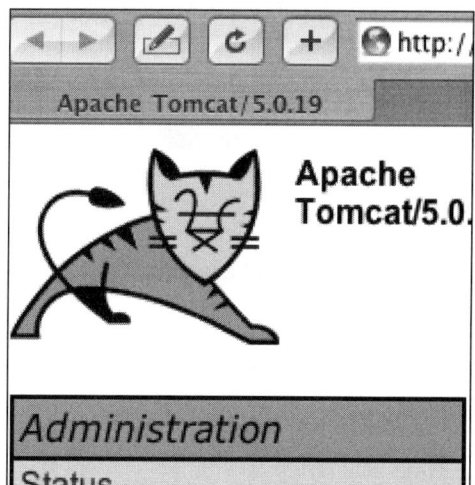

Chapter 9

SERVER-SIDE LANGUAGE ENVIRONMENTS

What we'll cover in this chapter:

- Perl
- PHP
- JSP
- Language examples
- Security considerations of server-side languages
- How to avoid security problems using functions

In this chapter, you'll learn the various server-side languages available for OS X and how to use and implement them in real-world situations. Numerous options are available for budding young developers to learn, each offering advantages and, of course, disadvantages; this chapter covers the pros and cons of each language in turn.

I won't attempt to teach you all the languages in this chapter, but I will give you a taste of what each can do and how they can be used. You can then decide for yourself if the language is your kettle of fish.

Server-side languages are different from client-side languages in that the code is executed on the server not the web browser. A client-side language such as JavaScript receives the content from the web server, and then any actions are performed and executed on the client. With a server-side language, the web browser requests the content; the server then executes the server-side code and then returns the document back to the client. Let's have a look at a few of the options now.

Perl

Perl, or **P**ractical **R**eport and **E**xtraction **L**anguage, is tailored for parsing text but also offers much more than that. It was one of the first languages I used, and still one of my favorites, because it's easy to pick up but offers complexity if you need it. What I like about Perl is the fact that you can code a useful script with a couple lines of code, which would normally take twice the amount in another language. Take the following example, which compares C with Perl performing the same task:

```
C Code:-
#include <stdio.h>
main()
{
    printf("Hello World\n");
}


Perl Code:-
print "Hello World\n";
```

As you can see, Perl provides built-in functions that handle repetitive tasks easily. I think Perl grows on you and stays with you, and even if you move on to another language, you can always come back to Perl to create the quick script that will save your hide when deadlines are tight.

Advantages

1. Perl is easy to learn.
2. It's flexible.
3. Language shortcuts save time.
4. Large collections of Perl modules are available.
5. It's free.

Disadvantages

1. Perl executable overhead is high.
2. Objects and more complex parts of the language are more difficult to pick up.
3. Web integration could be improved.
4. Its built-in functions are limited compared to other languages such as PHP.

PHP

PHP, which stands for **H**ypertext **P**re-**P**rocessor (a reverse acronym), is an ideal language for beginners and advanced programmers alike. The syntax is similar to Perl but offers easy web-oriented features and plenty of useful functions. PHP also borrows from other languages, so you'll find familiar functions from other languages you may have mastered; this proves useful in the learning process. PHP has to be my favorite language for web development because of not only the fast development time, but also the higher-end functionality.

Advantages

1. PHP is quick and easy to learn.
2. It comes with a large array of functions.
3. A large community provides plenty of resources to help you learn.
4. It's flexible.

5. Development time is fast.

6. It's free.

Disadvantages

1. Certain aspects of the language feel unfinished, for example, objects. (These issues are addressed in PHP 5.)

2. The language can be inconsistent. For example, variables are case sensitive but functions are not.

ASP

Active Server Pages (ASP) is the Microsoft implementation of a server-side programming language. It supports Visual Basic and JavaScript syntax but is only available in its full form on the Windows platform. You can get it to run under OS X and Linux using a third-party module for Apache, but this only includes basic support.

Advantages

1. ASP provides familiar syntax for JavaScript or Visual Basic programmers.

2. COM objects offer advanced programmers the opportunity to produce their own DLL using C++ or Visual Basic, which can be used within ASP.

3. It includes plenty of resources and functions.

Disadvantages

1. Certain functionality is only available on Microsoft platforms.

2. It's more expensive to host due to licensing of software.

ASP.NET

The .NET incarnation of ASP basically infuses the client side with the server side, allowing the programmer more control over the dynamic document. This works using the .NET Framework, which includes custom form element objects that the client displays and interact with the server. It also supports a wide variety of programming languages. It's Microsoft's answer to Java, but obviously restricted to the Microsoft platforms.

Advantages

1. ASP.NET supports a wide variety of languages.

2. Client-side controls can be controlled from the server side using the .NET Framework.

3. It includes a large selection of components and resources.

4. ASP.NET provides an object-oriented environment.

5. Compiled scripts increase speed.

Disadvantages

1. ASP.NET is restricted to the Microsoft platforms, and therefore not available for OS X.

2. It's more difficult to learn than ASP due to the complications of the .NET Framework and implementing it.

3. It's slower to develop code with ASP.NET.

4. You need the .NET Framework in order to use ASP.NET to its full potential.

JSP

Java Server Pages (JSP) was created by Sun Microsystems; anyone familiar with Java will be at home with JSP. It's similar to ASP, but isn't restricted to the platform, and offers extensibility in the form of Java Beans, which are reusable software programs that you can develop and assemble easily to create sophisticated applications.

Advantages

1. JSP is extendable.

2. It's not restricted to one platform.

3. It provides support for exceptions and other high-end programming concepts.

4. It's free on OS X.

Disadvantages

1. JSP is complex to learn.

2. Development time can take longer than with loosely typed languages.

ColdFusion

Macromedia purchased ColdFusion from Allaire as a replacement for Generator to create dynamic Flash sites and server-side scripts. Because the syntax is similar to HTML, it's popular with beginners.

Advantages

1. ColdFusion's syntax is easy.
2. It's familiar.
3. It provides good resources.

Disadvantages

1. Many experienced programmers don't like the syntax.
2. It's not as flexible as modern programming languages.
3. ColdFusion server is expensive.
4. It's slower than other languages, as the page needs to be converted twice before returning to the client.

Language examples

Okay, so now that you've seen the various pros and cons of each language, let's go through a couple of examples and dive straight in. In my experience, the best way to learn is when you're presented with a task rather than an example that doesn't really show a real-world situation. I'll walk you through three server-side language environments, Perl, PHP, and JSP; all installations for these environments are completely free, so you don't need to purchase any client or server-side software in order to get them to work.

Perl—the replacer script

Imagine you need a script to perform a find-and-replace operation on all the text files in a directory. The script you'll see in this section performs that operation in just 21 lines of code. That is the power of Perl! This is a command-line script, not a web script, which means it doesn't need to be in the WebServer directory. In fact, it could cause some security issues in there, so

you're going to create a new directory in your home directory, called bin, that you'll also use later on in this chapter. Make the directory by typing the following command in Terminal: mkdir /Users/*username*/bin (replacing *username* with your user name). Next, open a new text file in BBEdit, save it as /Users/username/bin/replacer.pl, and start typing into it the code described in the following steps:

1. As with the examples in Chapter 5, the first line of code tells FreeBSD (the UNIX portion of OS X) that the script you're running is using the Perl interpreter. This is used if the script is executed through the Terminal directly, in the same way that OS X knows to open Word when you double-click a Word document.

   ```
   #!/usr/bin/perl
   ```

2. Immediately after the first line, type

   ```
   $directory = $ARGV[0];
   $find = $ARGV[1];
   $replace = $ARGV[2];
   ```

   @ARGV holds the arguments you pass your program. @ARGV[0] is the first argument, which is the directory the files are in. @ARGV[1] holds the text the program should search for. @ARGV[2] holds the text the program is replacing.

3. Next, you want to open up the directory you specified in the program arguments, but if the program can't open the directory, you want the program to quit and inform you of this. To do this, you use the opendir()and die() functions. In the middle of these two functions, you include the logical operator OR (||). By now, your brain should be twitching and thinking back to Chapter 5, where you briefly met functions and logical operators. The pseudo code for this would look something like opendir (SOMETHING, $somewhere) OR die("error message related to $somewhere");. Now that you know how it works, let's code it. Following on from the last line, type

   ```
   opendir(DIRECTORYHANDLE, $directory)
   ➥ || die
   ➥("Unable to open directory $directory");
   ```

4. The following line basically means run this block of code until you have each file in the directory.

   ```
   while($file = readdir(DIRECTORYHANDLE)) {
   ```

5. As the directory in question may have files other than .txt files in it, it would be nice to ignore those. The next line you need to enter tells your program to skip the file if it doesn't contain .txt at the end of the file name:

```
next if $file !~ /\.txt$/;
```

6. Next, you create a container (a Perl array) to hold the lines of the current file by typing

```
@textlines = ();
```

7. Now you want to open the current file in the directory, or quit if the program fails. You do this in a similar way to step 3, except you use the open() function, which you learned how to use back in Chapter 5.

```
open(FILE, "$directory/$file")
➥ || die ("Unable to open file!");
```

8. Now that the program is in the right directory and reading through the files, you need it to read through all the lines of the current file until it reaches the end. You're going to use while again, so type

```
while(<FILE>) {
```

9. $_ is Perl's variable shortcut for holding the text of the current line. You want to take the original word, give it a nice friendly variable name, and then pass it to this shortcut. Do this by typing the following:

```
$replacedText = $_;
```

10. The next line is where the action happens. You tell Perl to substitute (s) the original text ($find) for the replacement text ($replace), and do it throughout (g). All quite sensible, really, so type

```
$replacedText =~ s/$find/$replace/g;
```

11. You have to add the replaced text into the array you created in step 6. You do this with the push() function by typing

```
push(@textlines, $replacedText);
```

12. In step 8, you started a loop that searches through the current file. It's now time to close that loop by typing a right brace:

```
}
```

13. Now that your program has searched the file, it's time to close it, so type

```
close(FILE);
```

14. The replaced text is still in the array and needs to come out. Now you have to open the current file for writing and add each line that was replaced back into the file. First of all, you open or quit the file in a manner similar to steps 3 and 7, except you use OUTFILE now as follows:

```
open(OUTFILE, ">$directory/$file")
➥ || die
➥("Unable to open file for writing!");
```

15. Now, you need to perform a quick loop to find each occurrence of the original word in the file and print the replacement word in its place. To do so, type the following:

```
foreach $line(@textlines) {
    print OUTFILE $line;
}
```

16. As in step 13, you need to close the file, so type

```
close(OUTFILE);
```

17. Finally, you end the loop that has been searching through the directory by typing

```
}
```

When you've finished, your code should resemble that shown in Figure 9-1 (shown on the following page). If you want to find out more about Perl, there is much more information available, right at your fingertips. Type man perlintro in Terminal for a beginner's guide.

Now that you have your script coded, it would be a good idea to put it to the test.

1. Open up Terminal and use the cd command to change to the directory containing your replacer.pl file by typing cd bin.

2. Now that you're in the bin directory, you can use Perl to check that the code you've typed is correct. In the same Terminal window, type perl -c replacer.pl. -c causes Perl to check the syntax of the program and then exit without executing it. For more information on such matters, check man perlrun.

227

```
    1   #!/usr/bin/perl
    2   $directory = $ARGV[0];
    3   $find = $ARGV[1];
    4   $replace = $ARGV[2];
    5   opendir(DIRECTORYHANDLE, $directory) || die("Unable to open directory $directory");
    6   while($file = readdir(DIRECTORYHANDLE)) {
    7       next if $file !~ /\.txt$/;
    8       @textlines = ();
    9       open(FILE, "$directory/$file") || die ("Unable to open file!");
   10       while(<FILE>) {
   11           $replacedText = $_;
   12           $replacedText =~ s/$find/$replace/g;
   13           push(@textlines, $replacedText);
   14       }
   15       close(FILE);
   16       open(OUTFILE, ">$directory/$file") || die ("Unable to open file for writing!");
   17       foreach $line(@textlines) {
   18           print OUTFILE $line;
   19       }
   20       close(OUTFILE);
   21   }
```

Figure 9-1. The finished `replacer.pl` script

3. If step 2 went according to plan, your Terminal window will output `replacer.pl` syntax OK, as you can see in Figure 9-2. If not, check through the code and run the command again until you get no syntax errors.

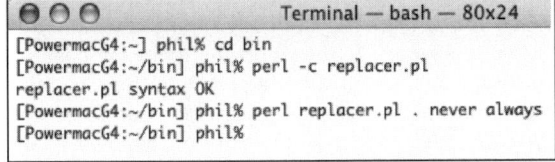

```
000            Terminal — bash — 80x24
[PowermacG4:~] phil% cd bin
[PowermacG4:~/bin] phil% perl -c replacer.pl
replacer.pl syntax OK
[PowermacG4:~/bin] phil% perl replacer.pl . never always
[PowermacG4:~/bin] phil%
```

Figure 9-2. Steps 1 through 3 in action

4. So, your code matches up and you're feeling confident; let's see the code in action. Before you go any further, though, you'll need a test file to perform the find-and-replace operation. Open a new text file in BBEdit, save it as `test.txt` in your new bin directory, and then type the following text (Figure 9-3 shows how the test file should look):

> You tried your best and you failed
> ➥ miserably. The lesson is 'never try'
> ➥ –Homer Simpson

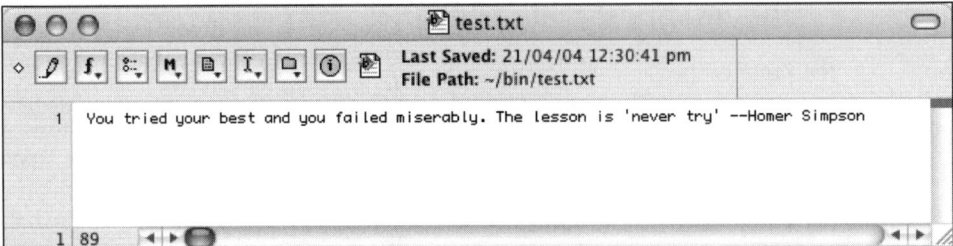

Figure 9-3. `test.txt` before the script is run

5. You then need to run your program to see if it works by using the following command in Terminal:

```
perl replacer.pl . never always
```

If you've coded your program perfectly, the text should have changed in your document, as I have shown in Figure 9-4. Congratulations and welcome back to Perl!

You may have guessed what was going on with the last command, but if not, here is an explanation: Perl comes with OS X at the command line preinstalled, so using the command `perl replacer.pl` invokes the Perl interpreter to run your program. The dot tells your program to look in the current directory for the .txt files, and the next argument tells your program to search for `never` and replace it with the next argument, `always`.

PHP image gallery

Now that you've sunk your teeth into a bit more Perl, it's time for you to chew on some PHP and find out why it's one of the most popular server-side web languages on the Internet. Like in the previous section on

Perl, I'll give you a practical example of creating a script in PHP that you can actually use in the real world.

Imagine you need a script to produce a page of pictures from a directory for your website. Normally, you would have to manually insert the images on the page every time you wanted to add a picture—wouldn't it be much easier to automatically insert the images? The PHP page you'll create will search through a directory and insert the images from that directory with a caption of each image based on the file name.

Open up a Terminal window and a new BBEdit HTML document, get some images ready, and let's get coding.

1. Using Terminal, create a directory on your web server called `imagegallery`; the directory should exist in the root-level directory of your web server: `mkdir /Library/WebServer/Documents/imagegallery`.

2. Create a directory within your imagegallery directory called pictures as follows: `mkdir /Library/WebServer/Documents/imagegallery/pictures` (see Figure 9-5).

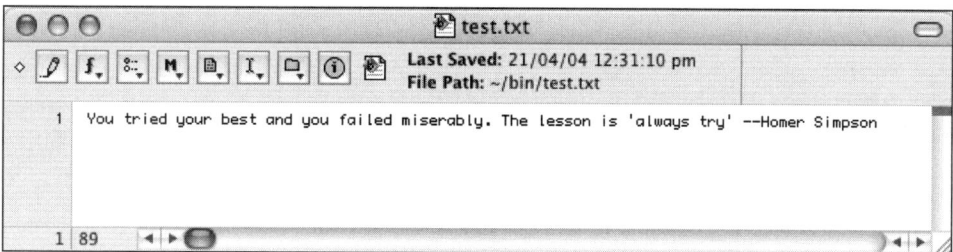

Figure 9-4. test.txt after the script is run

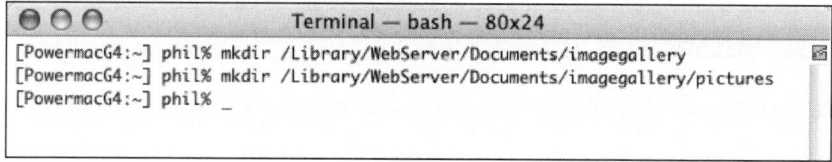

Figure 9-5. Using Terminal to create the new directories

3. Place a couple of test images (in .jpg format) in your new pictures directory. I've just thrown three kitty images in mine, as you can see in Figure 9-6.

4. Open your new BBEdit HTML document, and title it "Image Gallery." Save this as /Library/WebServer/Documents/imagegallery/index.php.

5. Add your <php> tags in between the body tags, to tell the PHP parser that you're going to include some PHP code, as you can see in Figure 9-7.

Okay, that's the easy part out of the way; now you're going to get add the PHP code line by line in between those <php> tags.

6. You need to specify the directory in which your script should look for pictures, so type

```
$directoryName = "pictures";
```

7. Next, give the web address that your script should use to display the images by typing the following:

```
$address = "http://localhost/imagegallery";
```

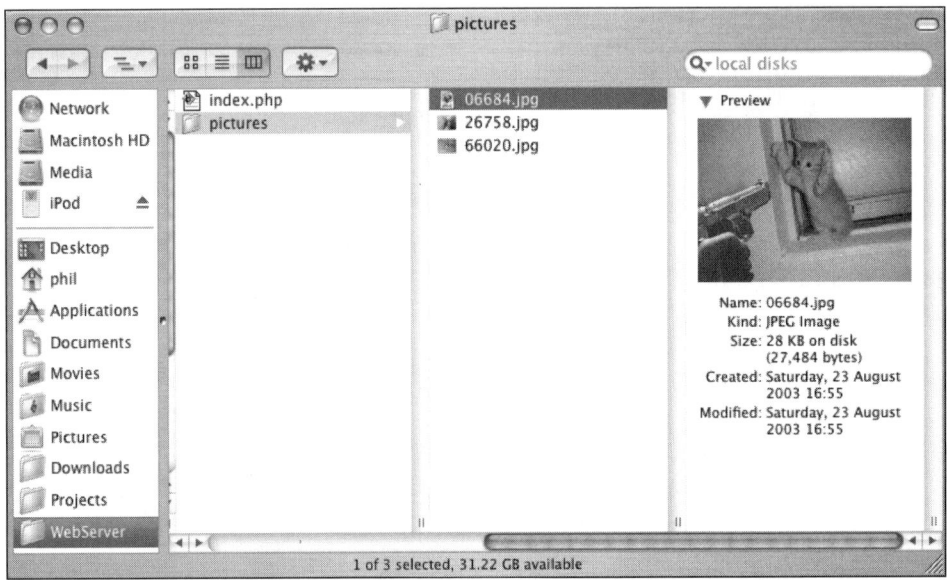

Figure 9-6. Finder shows my images in the pictures directory.

```
1   <!DOCTYPE html PUBLIC "-//W3C//DTD XHTML 1.0 Transitional//EN"
2       "http://www.w3.org/TR/xhtml1/DTD/xhtml1-transitional.dtd">
3   <html xmlns="http://www.w3.org/1999/xhtml" xml:lang="en" lang="en">
4   <head>
5       <meta http-equiv="content-type" content="text/html; charset=iso-8859-1" />
6       <title>Image Gallery</title>
7   </head>
8   <body>
9   <?php
10
11  ?>
12  </body>
13  </html>
14
```

Figure 9-7. <php> tags in place, ready for adding code

8. Once those two variables are set, you can then combine the web address with your directory name so the images can be found by typing

```
$url = "$address/$directoryName/";
```

9. PHP likes a full path to work with, so give it one. You can get the full path to your directory by using getcwd(), which means "Get current working directory." If you were never going to run this script from any other directory, you could hard code this variable to be /Library/WebServer/Documents/imagegallery, but that involves far more typing, and it makes the script less portable. PHP makes a variety of convenient functions available, so let's use them! Type the following on your next line:

```
$directory = getcwd() . "/"
➡ . $directoryName . "/";
```

10. Next, you need to check if the directory you supplied is actually a directory and not a file. You can use a PHP function called is_dir to do this. You're also starting an if loop, which is going to contain most of the working code. So, on the next line, type

```
if(is_dir($directory)) {
```

11. Next, you create a directory handle to store the directory you specified (think of it as a pointer to your directory name) or give an error, much the same as Perl did in the previous section's example, by typing the following:

```
$dHandle = opendir($directory) or
➡ die("Unable to open directory!");
```

12. The next line you need to enter should also look familiar to you from the previous Perl example. It assigns the file name for each file in turn, until it has read all the files, and then opens another if loop.

```
while($file = readdir($dHandle)) {
```

13. Next, type the following line:

```
if(eregi("\.jpg$", $file)) {
```

Using the eregi statement, the program checks the file name to see if it's a JPEG file, and then opens some brackets to contain the code that will print the images out.

14. So if the file is a JPEG, the program prints out the current image and an <alt> tag based on the file name, and also inserts a break.

```
echo '<p><img src="'. $url .
➡ $file . '" alt="' . $file . '"><br />';
```

15. You want a caption under each image, so you're going to use eregi_replace to remove .jpg from the file name and convert it to lowercase, and then use ucwords to change the first letter in each word to uppercase. Don't forget you opened a paragraph tag on the previous line, so close that and add a new line to keep the outputted code tidy. Okay, this is a bit more complex than previous lines; type in the following:

```
echo eregi_replace("\.jpg$", "",
➡ ucwords(strtolower($file))) . "</p>\n";
```

16. Next, end the if statement that checks the file is a JPEG by typing

```
    }
```

17. Then end the while loop that reads all the files in the directory with another closing curly bracket:

```
}
```

18. The last part of this if loop closes the directory handle, freeing memory on the server:

```
closedir($dHandle);
```

19. That's the main part done. Now you need an else statement that indicates if the directory can't be read, it will quit and display an error message. Firstly, close step 10's if statement, and then open the else statement by typing

```
    } else {
```

20. Next, add the error message, which should be completely familiar to you by now:

```
die("Unable to open directory!");
```

21. Finally, close that else statement with a closing brace:

```
}
```

Save your `index.php` file, which should look similar to Figure 9-8.

If you've been successful, you should be ready to test your image gallery by opening http://localhost/imagegallery/ in your browser. You should see all your pictures on your web page from the directory, similar to what's shown in Figure 9-9. If you don't, PHP will display an error and tell you which line number has a problem.

Of course, this script could be greatly improved and customized, but it should have given you a further taste of what PHP can do. Within a few lines of code, you have a script that displays all the JPEGs contained in a directory and formats the file names.

Introducing JavaServer Pages

In the next section of this chapter, you'll be looking at JSP and learning how to use it within OS X. In order to use JSP under OS X, you're going to employ a program called Tomcat (no relation to the cats in the previous example). Tomcat is a stand-alone web server that serves JSP pages. You'll be running Tomcat as a separate web server alongside your Apache web server. The Tomcat server runs on port 8080; by default, your Apache web server runs on port 80. A port is basically a channel that a program uses to communicate with clients. A good example of this is the typical e-mail application. When you check your e-mail, the e-mail client connects to your mail server on port 110. Using this port, the mail server can send the e-mail client information.

Installing Tomcat

First things first: You need to get the current version of Tomcat, which at the time of writing is 5.0.19. You can find Tomcat at the following URL: http://jakarta.apache.org/site/binindex.cgi. The file you want should be named something like `jakarta-tomcat-5.0.19.tar.gz`—as you can see in Figure 9-10—depending on when you're reading this book and how many revisions the file has seen.

```
1  <!DOCTYPE html PUBLIC "-//W3C//DTD XHTML 1.0 Transitional//EN"
2      "http://www.w3.org/TR/xhtml1/DTD/xhtml1-transitional.dtd">
3  <html xmlns="http://www.w3.org/1999/xhtml" xml:lang="en" lang="en">
4  <head>
5      <meta http-equiv="content-type" content="text/html; charset=iso-8859-1" />
6      <title>Image Gallery</title>
7  </head>
8  <body>
9  <?
10 $directoryName = "pictures";
11 $address = "http://localhost/imagegallery";
12 $url = "$address/$directoryName/";
13 $directory = getcwd() . "/" . $directoryName . "/";
14 if(is_dir($directory)) {
15 $dHandle = opendir($directory) or die("Unable to open directory!");
16 while($file = readdir($dHandle)) {
17     if(eregi("\.jpg$", $file)) {
18         echo '<p><img src="' . $url . $file . '" alt="' . $file . '"><br />';
19         echo eregi_replace("\.jpg$", "", ucwords(strtolower($file))) . "</p>\n";
20     }
21 }
22 closedir($dHandle);
23 } else {
24 die("Unable to open directory!");
25 }
26 ?>
27 </body>
28 </html>
29
```

Figure 9-8. The completed `index.php` script

Figure 9-9. Ooooh, look at the kitties! I mean, uhh, the script works!

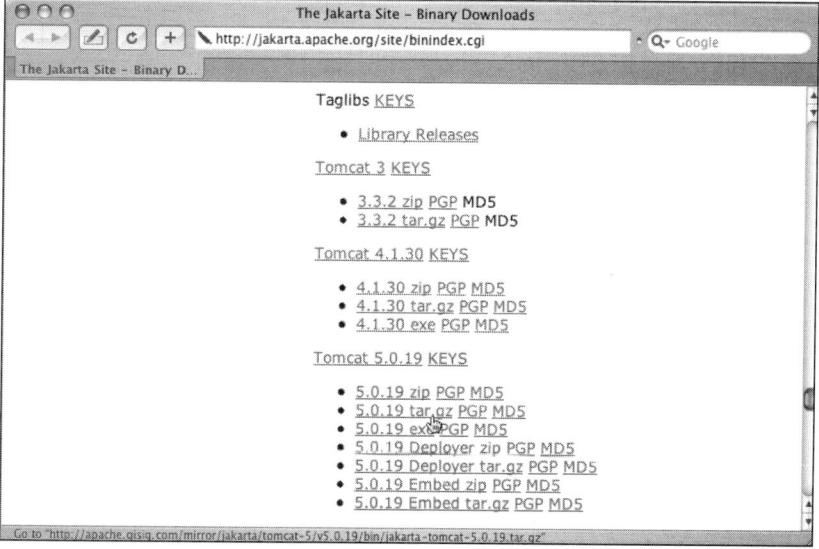

Figure 9-10. Selecting the right Tomcat file

Once the file has been downloaded, StuffIt Expander should automatically extract the file. The file would normally be downloaded to your desktop if you used Safari (unless you changed your default download directory), so that's where the code in this example is expecting to find it. If your default download directory is elsewhere, then just drag the file to the desktop for this example.

1. Open up Terminal and type sudo su to change to the SuperUser. OS X should ask you for your admin password.

2. Next, use the cd command to point to the Tomcat directory. As a shortcut, you can drag the folder into the Terminal window to get the directory path. As you can see from Figure 9-11, I typed cd desktop.

3. You need to move the directory you extracted to the /usr/local/ directory. Type mv jakarta-tomcat-5.0.19 /usr/local/ in Terminal. The file name may be different depending on whether you downloaded the same version or not.

4. Now you need to change the directory to the /usr/local/ directory using the following command:

   cd /usr/local/

5. Next up, the permissions of the directory need to match the account you use in OS X, using the chown command you learned in Chapter 6. For example, I would issue the command chown –R phil:staff /usr/local/jakarta-tomcat-5.0.19, but you'll use your own user name.

6. To exit the root user shell, simply type exit.

7. You need to create some shell scripts to start and stop the Tomcat server. These are going to be kept in the ~/bin directory, which you made back in the Perl replacer script example of this chapter. Use the cd command to change to your bin directory by typing cd /users/phil/bin or just cd ~/bin.

8. In Terminal, type pico start_tomcat to open up the Pico editor with a new file called start_tomcat. In the file, type the following text:

   ```
   #!/bin/sh
   export CATALINA_HOME=
   ➥/usr/local/jakarta-tomcat-5.0.19
   export JAVA_HOME=/usr
   $CATALINA_HOME/bin/startup.sh
   ```

Don't forget to change the line with the directory name jakarta-tomcat-5.0.19 to match the version you downloaded (see Figure 9-12).

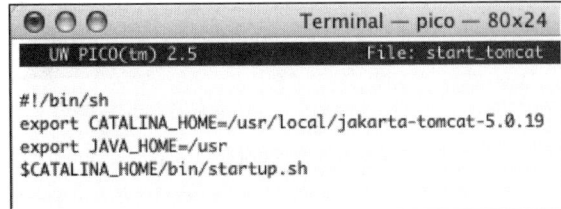

Figure 9-12. Using Pico to create the start_tomcat script

9. Save the file by pressing CTRL+O (^O for Write Out) and confirming the file name, and then exit Pico by pressing CTRL+X (^X for Exit).

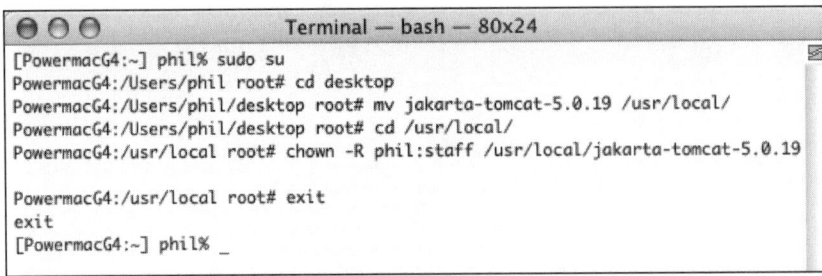

Figure 9-11. Moving Tomcat into place

10. Next you're going to create the stop script in the same directory as the previous step. Use Pico again by entering the command pico stop_tomcat, and when the Pico editor opens, enter the following:

```
#!/bin/sh
export CATALINA_HOME=
➥/usr/local/jakarta-tomcat-5.0.19
export JAVA_HOME=/usr
$CATALINA_HOME/bin/shutdown.sh
```

Again, don't forget to change the line jakarta-tomcat-5.0.19 to correspond with the version you downloaded (see Figure 9-13).

```
● ● ●              Terminal — pico — 80x24
  UW PICO(tm) 2.5              File: stop_tomcat

#!/bin/sh
export CATALINA_HOME=/usr/local/jakarta-tomcat-5.0.19
export JAVA_HOME=/usr
$CATALINA_HOME/bin/shutdown.sh
_
```

Figure 9-13. Using Pico to create the stop_tomcat script

11. That's it with the scripting, but those scripts need to be executable, and you can clearly see in Figure 9-14 that they aren't. Make sure you're in the right directory by opening a new Terminal window and typing cd bin, and then run the chmod command on both files at once by typing chmod 755 start_tomcat stop_tomcat (see Figure 9-14).

12. That's all there is to it! To start your Tomcat server, you simply execute the new start_tomcat file from your bin directory. Because you've exited the root shell, you should type sudo ./start_tomcat as shown in Figure 9-15; otherwise the service won't start correctly.

```
● ● ●              Terminal — bash — 80x24
[PowermacG4:~] phil% cd bin
[PowermacG4:~/bin] phil% ll
total 64
drwxr-xr-x   7 phil  phil    238 21 Apr 15:19 .
drwxr-xr-x  37 phil  phil   1258 21 Apr 15:19 ..
-rw-r--r--   1 phil  phil   6148 21 Apr 15:19 .DS_Store
-rw-r--r--   1 phil  phil    654 19 Apr 15:27 replacer.pl
-rw-r--r--   1 phil  phil    117 21 Apr 15:18 start_tomcat
-rw-r--r--   1 phil  phil    118 21 Apr 15:19 stop_tomcat
-rw-r--r--   1 phil  phil     89 21 Apr 12:31 test.txt
[PowermacG4:~/bin] phil% chmod 755 start_tomcat stop_tomcat
[PowermacG4:~/bin] phil% ll
total 64
drwxr-xr-x   7 phil  phil    238 21 Apr 15:19 .
drwxr-xr-x  37 phil  phil   1258 21 Apr 15:19 ..
-rw-r--r--   1 phil  phil   6148 21 Apr 15:19 .DS_Store
-rw-r--r--   1 phil  phil    654 19 Apr 15:27 replacer.pl
-rwxr-xr-x   1 phil  phil    117 21 Apr 15:18 start_tomcat
-rwxr-xr-x   1 phil  phil    118 21 Apr 15:19 stop_tomcat
-rw-r--r--   1 phil  phil     89 21 Apr 12:31 test.txt
[PowermacG4:~/bin] phil%
```

Figure 9-14. Making the files executable with the chmod command

```
● ● ●              Terminal — bash — 80x24
[PowermacG4:~] phil% cd bin
[PowermacG4:~/bin] phil% sudo ./start_tomcat
Password:
Using CATALINA_BASE:   /usr/local/jakarta-tomcat-5.0.19
Using CATALINA_HOME:   /usr/local/jakarta-tomcat-5.0.19
Using CATALINA_TMPDIR: /usr/local/jakarta-tomcat-5.0.19/temp
Using JAVA_HOME:       /usr
[PowermacG4:~/bin] phil% _
```

Figure 9-15. Running the command to start Tomcat

Your server should now be running on port 8080 of your computer. To display the Tomcat startup screen, shown in Figure 9-16, enter this address into your web browser: http://localhost:8080. You may need to change the address to match your server address if required.

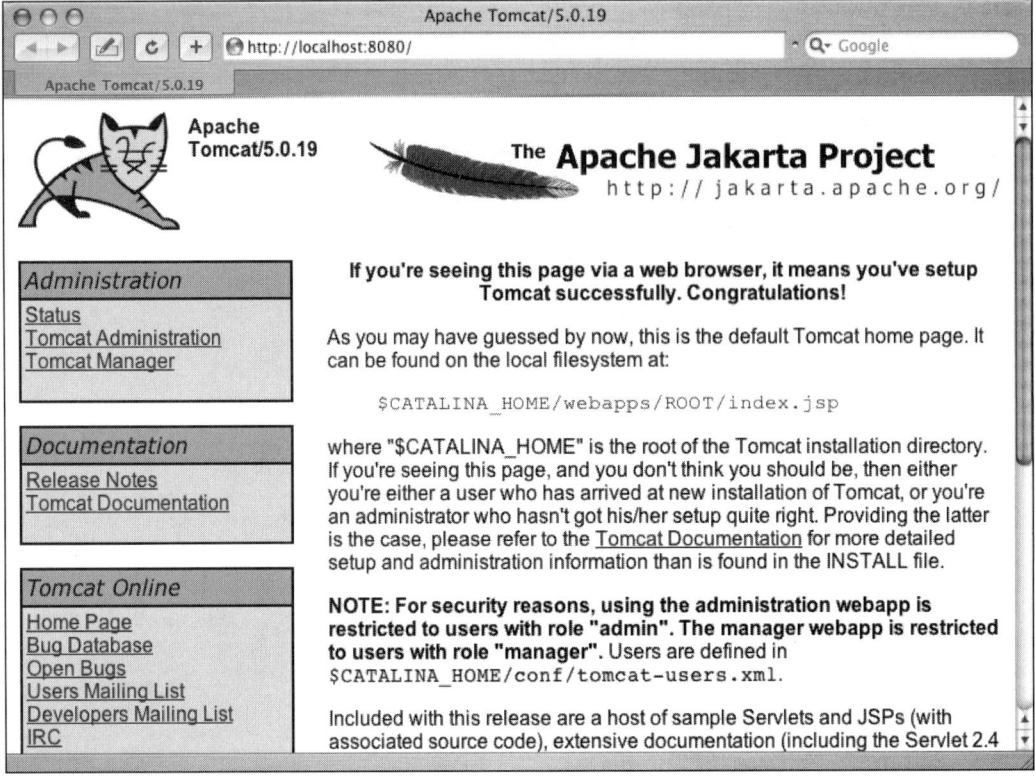

Figure 9-16. The Tomcat startup screen

JSP browser detection script

As with the previous languages, I am going to show JSP in action and give you a chance to try it out for yourself. You'll create a simple script that will detect which browser you're using and direct you to a different set of pages. Although many alternatives exist for performing the same function, this should give you a good introduction to the JSP language and instantly see it in action.

1. The first step is to change the working directory to your JSP web server root (the directory where all your JSP files are served). Type cd /usr/local/jakarta-tomcat-5.0.19/webapps/ROOT. (The Jakarta version may differ, depending on which version you installed.)

2. Next, create a directory to perform our detection script by typing the following:

   mkdir detect

3. Change to that directory by typing

   cd detect

   Your screen should look similar to Figure 9-17.

4. Type pico index.jsp.

5. You should now have a new file open within the Pico editor, so let's take the code line by line. First, the execution of a JSP page relies on special tags, similar to the PHP <? ?> tags, so open the tag by typing the following:

   <%

6. Next, you declare the urlLoc variable as a string.

   String urlLoc;

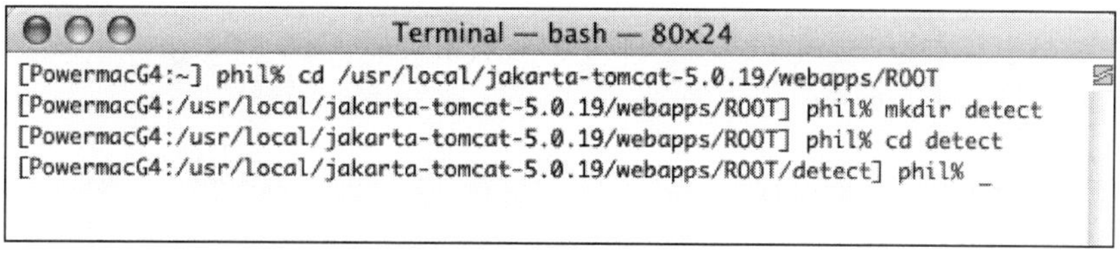

```
● ● ●                    Terminal — bash — 80x24
[PowermacG4:~] phil% cd /usr/local/jakarta-tomcat-5.0.19/webapps/ROOT
[PowermacG4:/usr/local/jakarta-tomcat-5.0.19/webapps/ROOT] phil% mkdir detect
[PowermacG4:/usr/local/jakarta-tomcat-5.0.19/webapps/ROOT] phil% cd detect
[PowermacG4:/usr/local/jakarta-tomcat-5.0.19/webapps/ROOT/detect] phil% _
```

Figure 9-17. Locating Tomcat's documents directory

7. Using the request object and USER-AGENT, the next line stores the visitor's browser within the browserType variable.

```
String browserType =
➥ request.getHeader("USER-AGENT");
```

8. The next line checks the browserType variable to see if it contains the string MSIE, which identifies the Internet Explorer browser. IndexOf will return the position of the string; however, if the string doesn't exist, it will return –1. Start this if statement by typing

```
if(browserType.indexOf("MSIE") != -1) {
```

9. If the preceding line is true, you assign the URL to the urlLoc variable for the Internet Explorer users with the following code:

```
urlLoc = "ie.html";
```

10. If the statement is false (i.e., the user is *not* using Internet Explorer), then the else statement performs an alternative action. So, close the if statement and open the else statement:

```
} else {
```

11. The alternative URL to the urlLoc variable is assigned to anyone who isn't using Internet Explorer. You do this in the same manner as step 9 by typing

```
urlLoc = "others.html";
```

12. Next, you have to end that if statement by typing a closing brace:

```
}
```

13. You then redirect the user using the response object to the URL specified in the urlLoc variable by typing

```
response.sendRedirect(urlLoc);
```

14. Lastly, end the JSP execution by closing the tag as shown here and in Figure 9-18:

```
%>
```

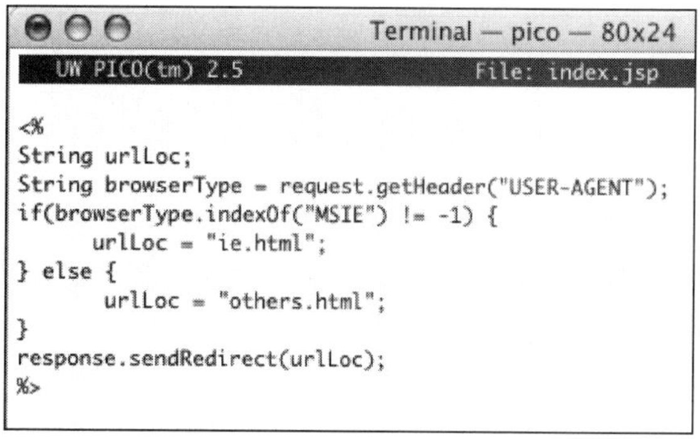

```
● ● ●                        Terminal — pico — 80x24
  UW PICO(tm) 2.5                            File: index.jsp

<%
String urlLoc;
String browserType = request.getHeader("USER-AGENT");
if(browserType.indexOf("MSIE") != -1) {
        urlLoc = "ie.html";
} else {
        urlLoc = "others.html";
}
response.sendRedirect(urlLoc);
%>
```

Figure 9-18. Using Pico to create the detection script

Viewing your masterpiece

Viewing the new script as things stand isn't going to get much of a result other than showing you what a Tomcat 404 Error page looks like, as you can see from Figure 9-19. This is because I'm using a browser other than Internet Explorer, and it can't find others.html.

In order to see your code in action, you need to create two HTML files within your detect directory: one HTML file called ie.html and another called others.html. In your IE file, you could include a welcome message for Internet Explorer users and an alternative message for users of other browsers. Rather than leave these files to your imagination, just copy the code from Figures 9-20 and 9-21. Then, once you've created them, simply go to http://localhost:8080/detect/ your browser.

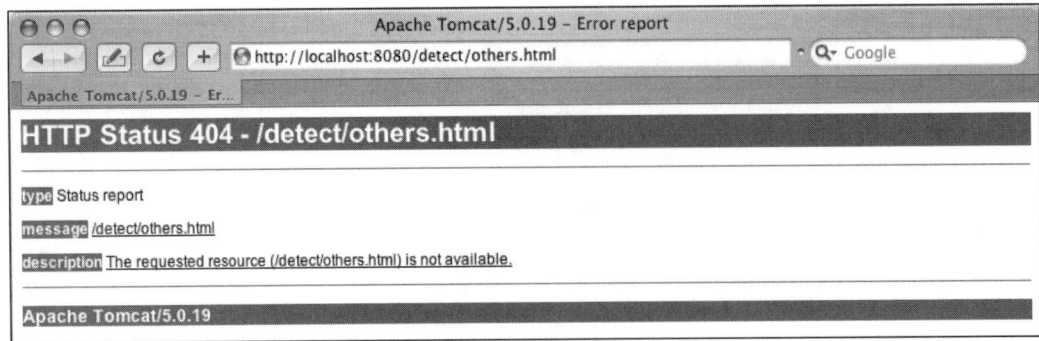

Figure 9-19. Unable to find `others.html`, Tomcat displays a 404 page.

```
000                              ie.html
                        Last Saved: 06/04/04 08:44:15 pm
                        File Path: /usr/local/jakarta-tomcat...pps/ROOT/detect/ie.html

1   <!DOCTYPE html PUBLIC "-//W3C//DTD XHTML 1.0 Transitional//EN"
2         "http://www.w3.org/TR/xhtml1/DTD/xhtml1-transitional.dtd">
3   <html xmlns="http://www.w3.org/1999/xhtml" xml:lang="en" lang="en">
4   <head>
5       <meta http-equiv="content-type" content="text/html; charset=iso-8859-1" />
6       <title>Welcome, IE users</title>
7       <meta name="generator" content="BBEdit 7.0" />
8   </head>
9   <body>
10  Welcome, IE users.  This is chapter 9 of Foundation Mac OS X Web Development.
11  </body>
12  </html>
13
```

Figure 9-20. A very basic page for IE users

```
000                              others.html
                        Last Saved: 06/04/04 08:44:45 pm
                        File Path: /usr/local/jakarta-tomcat...ROOT/detect/others.html

1   <!DOCTYPE html PUBLIC "-//W3C//DTD XHTML 1.0 Transitional//EN"
2         "http://www.w3.org/TR/xhtml1/DTD/xhtml1-transitional.dtd">
3   <html xmlns="http://www.w3.org/1999/xhtml" xml:lang="en" lang="en">
4   <head>
5       <meta http-equiv="content-type" content="text/html; charset=iso-8859-1" />
6       <title>Welcome</title>
7       <meta name="generator" content="BBEdit 7.0" />
8   </head>
9   <body>
10  Welcome.  This is chapter 9 of Foundation Mac OS X Web Development.
11  </body>
12  </html>
13
```

Figure 9-21. A very basic page for users of other browsers

If everything goes well, your script should successfully detect your browser and redirect you to the correct page, as shown in Figures 9-22 and 9-23.

Tip: As the default Tomcat directory is a bit awkward to get to in Finder, use a symbolic link in your home directory, as shown in Figure 9-24. You do this by typing

```
ln -s /usr/local/jakarta-tomcat-5.0.19/
➥webapps/ROOT /users/username/Tomcat.
```

Code summary

The JSP language isn't a loosely typed language like the previous languages discussed in this chapter. You must declare any variables you wish to use; for example, if you want to use the variable urlLoc, you need to tell JSP what type of variable it is. In this instance, because the variable contains a text string, you need to declare the variable with the String keyword.

I kept the JSP example as simple as possible because of the complexities of the language. I hope you followed the code and enjoyed your introduction to JSP. A good book to check out if you're interested in learning more about JSP is *Beginning JSP 2: From Novice to Professional* (Peter den Haan et al., Apress, 2004).

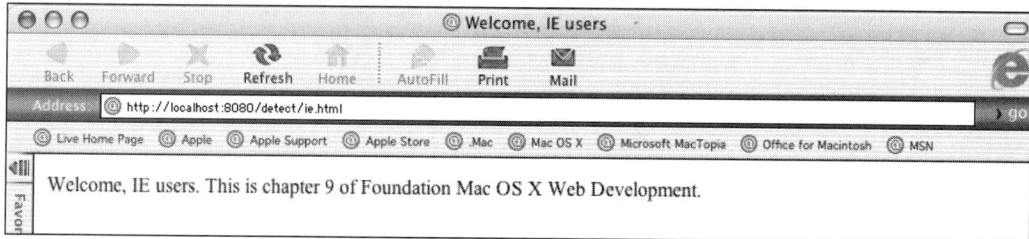

Figure 9-22. Here, the detection script shows the IE page.

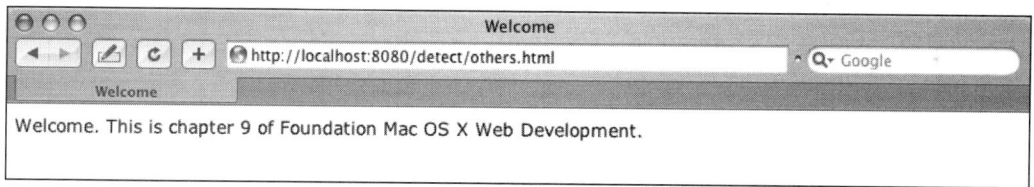

Figure 9-23. Here, the detection script shows the Others page.

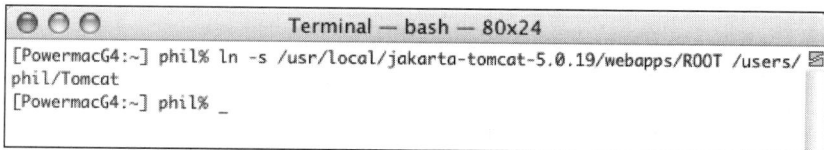

Figure 9-24. Using a symbolic link makes things much easier.

Security considerations of server-side languages

When you develop applications in any server-side language, you must consider the security implications of any action your script may take. As you may be aware, the world is finally starting to take security seriously (and about time too). With so many viruses in the wild, most of the responsibility comes down to sloppy or careless programming.

In order to avoid security problems, you must understand how these problems can be exploited. Imagine you've created an online guest book for your local pizza place. Your guest book allows people to submit their comments about the site and improve the site popularity by encouraging interaction. The site owners are extremely pleased with the comments from the visitors, but one particular user decides to have a little fun with your guest book.

The simple guest book works by displaying the e-mail address of a user and comments made. A simple HTML form is used to ask the user for this information and then submitted to a server-side script. The malicious user decides, instead of entering their e-mail address and comments, they would include some HTML code. The result is you have an angry client complaining that the guest book page has yellow text with a blue table background and a huge image advertising the main competitor. Although this may not be a serious issue, it could have been worse; for example, a competitor may decide to redirect all the users who visit the guest book to their own site using JavaScript.

Taking your code seriously

You can avoid attacks similar to the preceding by filtering any user input. This means anything you ask from the user must be checked for validity. Remove anything that shouldn't be allowed; for example, remove < and > tags and replace them with their HTML entities, which are > and <. Paranoia is your best asset when developing secure web applications. Think of the worst scenario and plan for worse than that (one louder). You'll become a better coder for it, and you'll find, although you generally won't be rewarded for your efforts, you won't be criticized for your security errors.

Understanding other attacks

A magnitude of attacks is available to the would-be hacker. Your job is to eliminate all the possibilities to the best of your knowledge. Following are a few of the possible attacks you may encounter.

XSS

XSS, or cross-site scripting, is an extremely dangerous form of attack. It enables an attacker to retrieve credentials from a user or manipulate a user session. It works by injecting code (usually JavaScript) within server-side code that hasn't been filtered. For example, an attacker may include a JavaScript redirect command that sends the user's cookies to the attacker's server-side script on the attacker's server.

SQL injection

Structured Query Language (SQL) injection works by manipulating SQL queries that haven't filtered user-supplied input. Imagine you have an SQL query that gets a certain record from a table. It might look something like SELECT * FROM table WHERE id = $id. If a hacker decided to pass some SQL commands to the variable $id instead of a number, it could result in deleted data or a compromised server at worst.

Cookie manipulation

Many developers have the naive assumption that they can trust cookie information. They think if they set the cookie, the content can be trusted. This couldn't be further from the truth; it's quite easy to manipulate cookie information. Take a real-world example that I encountered: A developer had created a script that checks a user name and password and then sets a cookie called authorized to equal 1; the problem is that anyone could bypass the authentication by manually creating the authorized cookie.

Session manipulation

Another avenue for a hacker to exploit is user sessions. Programmers often use sessions as a means to store information about the current user. A session ID is usually assigned to a user to identify their session. If a hacker can find out a visitor's session ID, the hacker could hijack the user's session, thereby retrieving the information contained within that session.

Program execution exploits

Sometimes using a server-side language isn't enough. A programmer may decide to call another program on the server or get a directory listing from the server, as demonstrated earlier with the user input in the PHP example in this chapter. This itself isn't a problem; it becomes a problem when you allow the user to choose which program to execute or which directory to access—for example, a script is created to list certain file types within the current directory using the Unix ls command, with a filetype parameter that is requested from the user. The problem is that the user could enter their own commands rather than *.jpg simply by passing the Unix metacharacter ;. This could result in revealing source code or even critical operating system files.

How to avoid security problems using functions

In this next section, I'll discuss how you can plan against security exploits using some simple examples that you should be able to improve and expand upon. In order to understand the examples, you must understand the concept of **functions**.

Functions allow you to encapsulate pieces of code in a reusable statement. Rather than typing the same code ten times, you can type the code once and call it ten times. The next few examples show you how to use functions in each language previously discussed in this chapter. You'll then apply these foundations to create functions that will provide you with useful security tools.

A Perl example

Functions in Perl are called **subroutines**, and although the syntax varies from other languages, you can perform the same actions. Following is an example of a Perl subroutine, with the completed version shown in Figure 9-22.

1. As with the other scripts in this chapter, you want to save this function to the bin directory (in my case, that would be /Users/phil/bin/perl_function.pl), so open a new Terminal window and type cd bin && pico perl_function.pl.

2. As this is a Perl script, you need to tell the shell that, as shown in the following line:

   ```
   #!/usr/bin/perl
   ```

3. The sub command creates a function. In this instance, call it perlFunction by typing

   ```
   sub perlFunction {
   ```

4. Next, you want to return the parameters you've sent to the function. @_ is a special Perl variable that contains the arguments passed to a function, in this case Hello from a perl function.

   ```
   return(@_);
   ```

5. Then end the subroutine by adding a closing brace:

   ```
   }
   ```

6. Lastly, you want to call the function and send the text Hello from a perl function to your function, with a new line at the end (\n), as shown here and in Figure 9-25:

   ```
   print &perlFunction("Hello
   ➥ from a perl function\n");
   ```

```
#!/usr/bin/perl
sub perlFunction {
        return(@_);
}
print &perlFunction("Hello from a perl function\n");
```

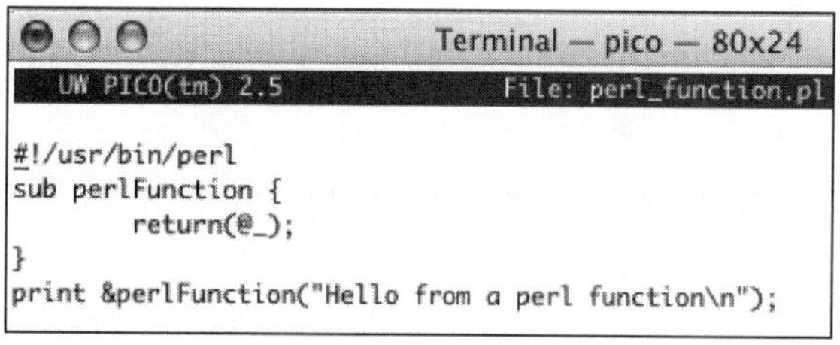

Figure 9-25. Your new Perl function

To test this new function out, open a Terminal window and aim for the result shown in Figure 9-26. (If Terminal isn't in your Dock by now, you're making things too hard for yourself. This is a geek's chapter, and geeks do anything for an easy life!)

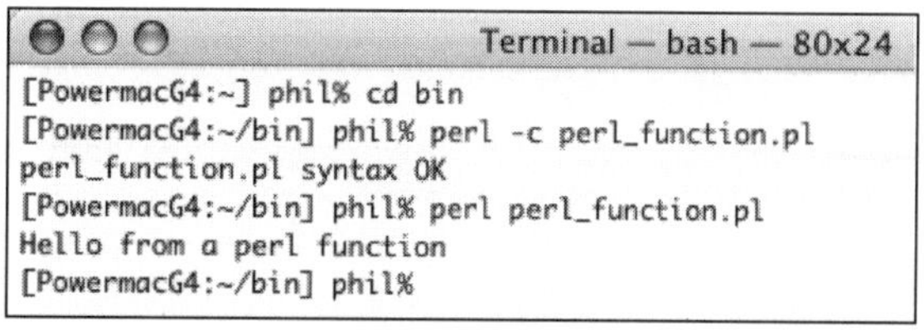

```
[PowermacG4:~] phil% cd bin
[PowermacG4:~/bin] phil% perl -c perl_function.pl
perl_function.pl syntax OK
[PowermacG4:~/bin] phil% perl perl_function.pl
Hello from a perl function
[PowermacG4:~/bin] phil%
```

Figure 9-26. Your new Perl function, running in Terminal

241

7. Type cd bin.

8. Check the syntax is in order by typing

perl -c perl_function.pl

9. If all is well, tell Perl to run the file as follows:

perl perl_function.pl

PHP functions

Functions in PHP are similar to those in JavaScript, so you should be very comfortable with PHP functions if you've used functions in JavaScript. Open a new Terminal window, type cd bin && pico php_function.php and follow these steps:

1. Start the execution of the PHP document by typing

<?php

2. Next, you declare a function called phpFunction. The $text part of the code is used as a parameter passed to the function. It basically holds the text information you send to your function.

function phpFunction($text) {

3. You want the next line to return the parameters supplied by the function call, so type

return($text);

4. Next, end the PHP function by closing with a curly bracket:

}

5. This code needs some output so that you know it has worked. Do this by using PHP's echo function, which prints out the output of the function—in this case, "Hello from a php function" with a line break at the end.

echo phpFunction("Hello
➡ from a php function\n");

6. Lastly, end the execution of the PHP document:

?>

Figure 9-27 shows your PHP code.

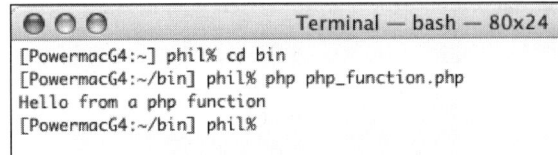

Figure 9-27. The finished PHP function code

As with the Perl example, you can see the results right in your Terminal window. Open a new window and type cd bin.

Issue the command php php_function.php, and you should see something similar to Figure 9-28.

Figure 9-28. The finished PHP function in Terminal

Using JSP functions

JSP functions are slightly more complex than the PHP function you've just dealt with. When declaring JSP functions, you need to specify the data type used, String in this case, and the scope of the function, which is public in this example.

1. Navigate to the Tomcat directory in Terminal with cd /usr/local/jakarta-tomcat-5.0.19/webapps/ROOT (remember, the version may differ, depending on which one you've installed).

2. Next, create your JSP file using pico jsp_function .jsp.

3. The first line starts a JSP class or function declaration. In order to define a function. You must use this tag:

<%!

4. Next, you want to create a function called jspFunction that returns text, so type

public String jspFunction(String text) {

5. To return the parameter text supplied to the function, type

```
return text;
```

6. That's the end of the function, so insert a right brace:

```
}
```

7. Then, end the class/function declaration by closing the tag:

```
%>
```

8. The next line starts a new section of JSP execution:

```
<%
```

9. Now you want to output the text returned by the function with the following line:

```
out.println(jspFunction("Hello
➥ from a jsp function"));
```

You could have also used `<%=jspFunction("Hello from a jsp function")%>` as a shortcut. But I thought it would be useful for you to know how to print from JSP using the out object.

10. Lastly, end the JSP execution by closing the tags:

```
%>
```

Your finished code should look the same as that shown in Figure 9-29.

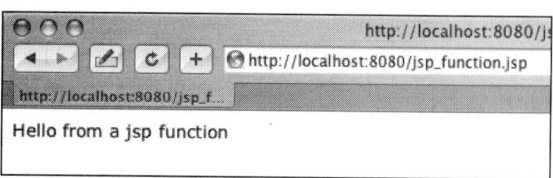

Figure 9-30. The finished JSP function in the browser

Creating a user input function

Before I show you how to create your functions in the various languages, I would just like to point out that there are either prebuilt modules or even language functions that could accomplish the same task, but where's the fun in that? I mention these alternatives later in the chapter, but obviously you'll learn a lot more by writing your own function rather than using a prebuilt one. Let's get it on with Perl.

User input with Perl

As in the preceding sections, I'll start with by walking you through a Perl example. You're going to make a simple form that takes user input and replaces < and > with > and <, as discussed back in the "Taking your code seriously" section.

1. Open a new document in BBEdit and save it as

```
/Library/WebServer/CGI-Executables/
➥perl_input_function.pl.
```

2. As you should now by know, the first line of your Perl script instructs the shell that this is a Perl document.

```
#!/usr/bin/perl
```

3. Next, you use the CGI.pm module to get your HTML input. You should remember this module from an example in Chapter 5.

```
use CGI;
```

4. Now you need to start the htmlEscape function, so type the following:

```
sub htmlEscape {
```

5. The next line assigns the first parameter passed to your function to a userInput variable:

```
$userInput = @_[0];
```

```
<%!
public String jspFunction(String text) {
        return text;
}
%>
<%
out.println(jspFunction("Hello from a jsp function"));
%>
```

Figure 9-29. The finished JSP function code

Time to test that code, so open http://localhost:8080/jsp_function.jsp in your browser (see Figure 9-30).

6. Now you're going to perform a find-and-replace operation on the text using a Perl regular expression.

```
$userInput =~ s/>/&gt;/g;
```

=~ defines the regular expression, and s/ means substitute. So, with the preceding line you're telling the program to find > and replace it with the > HTML entity, which displays the greater than sign but won't allow HTML code to work. /g ends the expression. The g means global, and if you didn't include this, the expression would only find and replace the first > character.

7. The following does the same as the preceding line but instead of replacing the greater than (>) symbol, it replaces the less than (<) symbol:

```
$userInput =~ s/</&lt;/g;
```

8. The last line of this function returns the escaped text.

```
return($userInput);
```

9. You can now end the Perl function by closing with a right brace:

```
}
```

10. Okay, next up is a new CGI object to use for collecting your form data. To create this object, type

```
$query = CGI->new( );
```

11. The next line calls the function, and passes it the HTML you entered in the form. If you've arrived at the page for the first time, it will just pass blank information, and no message will be printed to the web page. Type the following:

```
$message = &htmlEscape
➥($query->param("message"));
```

12. Now you need to print the HTML content type header required by CGI programs in order to display HTML output:

```
print $query->header(-type
➥ => 'text/plain');
```

13. qq is a very useful Perl in-built function that allows you to print out nicely formatted text and also to use quotes. Perfect for HTML! To start using it, type

```
print qq(
```

14. Within the qq function, you just need a very basic HTML form to test. The message variable is used to print out your newly formatted HTML.

```
<html>
<head>
<title>Perl HTML escape example</title>
</head>
<body>
<form action="perl_input_function.pl"
➥ method="post">
<input type="text" name="message">
 
<input type="submit" value="Submit">
</form>
<p>Message: $message </p>
</body>
</html>
```

15. Lastly, you want to end your output of HTML and finish the qq command by typing

```
);
```

Your finished code should resemble what you see in Figure 9-31, if all went according to plan.

16. The very last thing to do to this script is give it executable permissions; otherwise, you'll get a 403 error when you try and run it. Do this by typing

```
chmod 755 /Library/WebServer/
➥CGI-Executables/perl_input_function.pl.
```

If you now go to http://localhost/cgi-bin/ perl_input_function.pl in your browser, you'll hopefully see a tidy little form awaiting input. As this is designed to replace < and > with > and <, it makes sense to test it with those characters, as I've done in Figure 9-32, by typing a malicious command in there. Figure 9-33 shows the results.

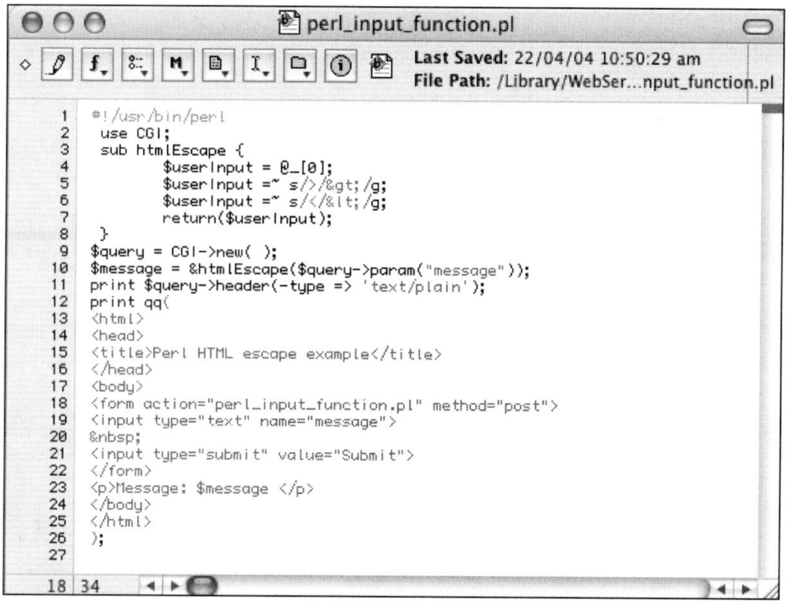

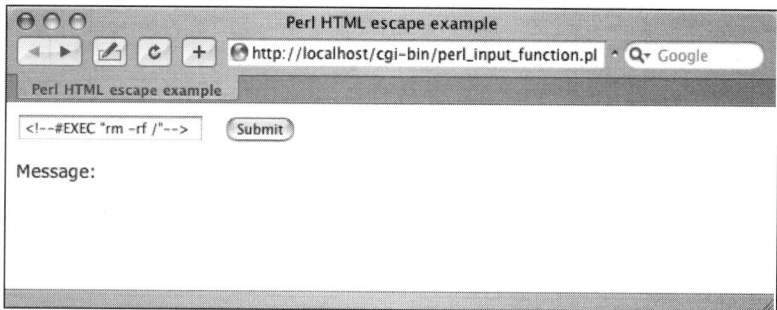

```perl
#!/usr/bin/perl
use CGI;
sub htmlEscape {
        $userInput = @_[0];
        $userInput =~ s/>/&gt;/g;
        $userInput =~ s/</&lt;/g;
        return($userInput);
}
$query = CGI->new( );
$message = &htmlEscape($query->param("message"));
print $query->header(-type => 'text/plain');
print qq(
<html>
<head>
<title>Perl HTML escape example</title>
</head>
<body>
<form action="perl_input_function.pl" method="post">
<input type="text" name="message">
 
<input type="submit" value="Submit">
</form>
<p>Message: $message </p>
</body>
</html>
);
```

Figure 9-31. The finished Perl input function code

Figure 9-32. The finished Perl input function, ready to perform its task

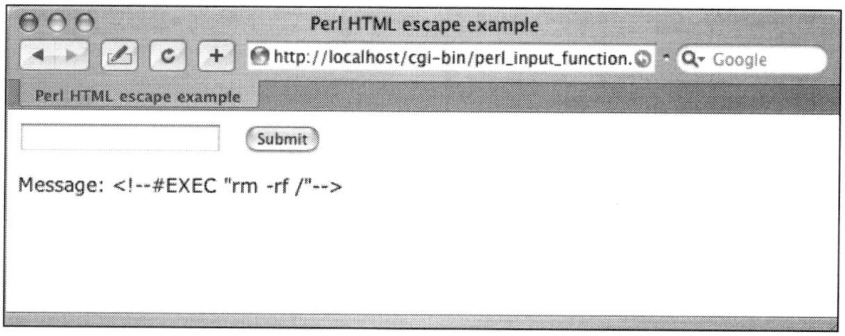

Figure 9-33. Output: code replaced, security risk minimized

245

This is only a basic Perl function, but it should give you an idea how to implement other functions. If you don't want to reinvent the wheel, Perl has a massive array of useful modules that you can use in your Perl scripts, and these can be found at www.cpan.org.

As you can see from Figure 9-31, syntax coloring is very handy. Quite often, just something being the wrong color is enough to alert me that something is wrong with my code. You may be thinking this is a drawback to using a command-line text editor, such as Vim. Think again. You can have full syntax coloring in Vim, as you can see in Figure 9-34. All you have to do is add a few lines to a file called ~/.vimrc.

This actually got me out of a scrape when I had to work on a remote Linux server to fix something that someone else had botched up. Straight away, I could see the problem, and all because of the coloring. Very handy, indeed.

The contents of my ~/.vimrc file are shown in Figure 9-35, which you can customize to your own needs. I also have my Terminal screen set to green on black (when I'm not writing books).

```
syntax on
set shiftwidth=1
set cindent
map <F1> <esc>
set showmatch

set comments+=s:/*,mb:**,ex:*/

highlight Comment term=bold ctermfg=green ctermbg=none
highlight Constant ctermfg=white ctermbg=none
highlight Identifier ctermfg=cyan ctermbg=none
highlight Statement ctermfg=yellow ctermbg=none
highlight Type ctermfg=red ctermbg=none
highlight Todo ctermfg=white ctermbg=red
```

Figure 9-35. The contents of my ~/.vimrc file

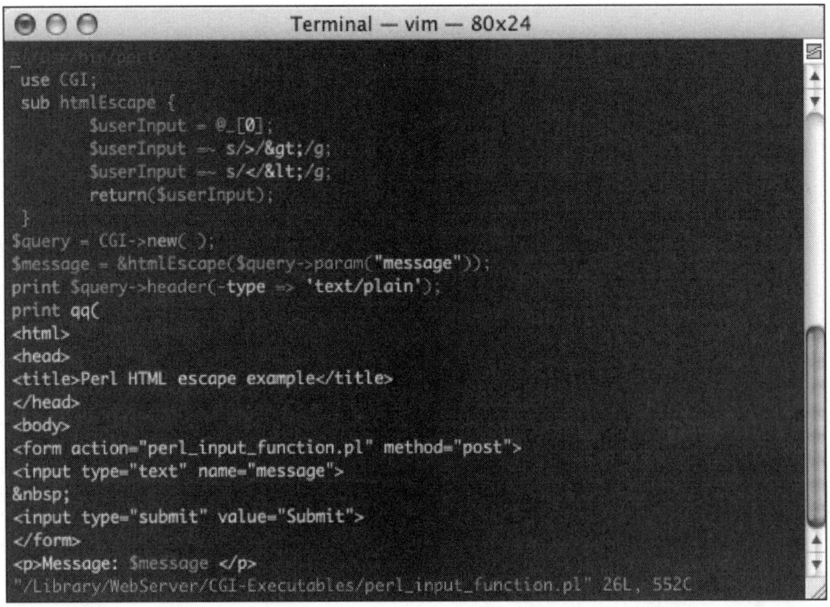

Figure 9-34. Syntax coloring in Vim

User input with PHP

If PHP is more to your liking, here's the same example, in PHP flavor.

1. Open a new document in BBEdit and save it as

/Library/WebServer/Documents/book/09/
➡php_input_function.php.

2. Your first line starts the PHP execution, so open the tags by typing the following:

`<?php`

3. Next, you define your `htmlEscape` function with a variable called `text` as a parameter by typing

`function htmlEscape($text) {`

4. The next line replaces the greater than symbol with the HTML entity equivalent using the `str_replace` PHP function. The `str_replace` function accepts three parameters: The first is the string to find, the second is the string to replace with, and the third is the variable to perform the operation on.

`$text = str_replace(">", "&gt;", $text);`

5. The line immediately after does the same thing but with the less than symbol.

`$text = str_replace("<", "&lt;", $text);`

6. Next, you use the `return` statement to return your replaced text.

`return($text);`

7. That's the function done with, so you can close it now with a right curly bracket:

`}`

8. Okay, now that the `htmlEscape` function is set up, you can use it to assign your message to a form variable called `message`.

`$message = htmlEscape`
➡`($HTTP_POST_VARS['message']);`

9. That's the end of the PHP code, so you can close those tags by typing

`?>`

10. As with the Perl version, you just need a very basic HTML form, where `<?=$message?>` outputs the message field you send with your HTML code (see Figure 9-36).

```
1    <?php
2    function htmlEscape($text) {
3        $text = str_replace(">", "&gt;", $text);
4        $text = str_replace("<", "&lt;", $text);
5        return($text);
6    }
7    $message = htmlEscape($HTTP_POST_VARS['message']);
8    ?>
9    <html>
10   <head>
11   <title>PHP HTML escape example</title>
12   </head>
13   <body>
14   <form action="php_input_function.php" method="post">
15   <input type="text" name="message">
16    
17   <input type="submit" value="Submit">
18   </form>
19   <p>Message: <?=$message?></p>
20   </body>
21   </html>
22
```

Figure 9-36. The finished PHP input code in BBEdit

```
<html>
<head>
<title>PHP HTML escape example</title>
</head>
<body>
<form action="php_input_function.php"
➡ method="post">
<input type="text" name="message">
 
<input type="submit" value="Submit">
</form>
<p>Message: <?=$message?></p>
</body>
</html>
```

By calling up `http://localhost/book/09/php_input_function.php` in your browser, you can test the script with another command that you probably wouldn't want to have run on your server, again for security purposes. That command is `<!--#exec cmd="ls -F" ->`, which lists the contents (as you should know by now), where -F lists an asterisk (*) after each file that is executable (see Figure 9-37).

Figure 9-38 shows the results of testing this function.

PHP contains many in-built functions that can perform useful tasks like this one. One such function is `htmlentities`, which replaces all HTML characters with their HTML entities. To find out more, visit the PHP website found at `www.php.net/`.

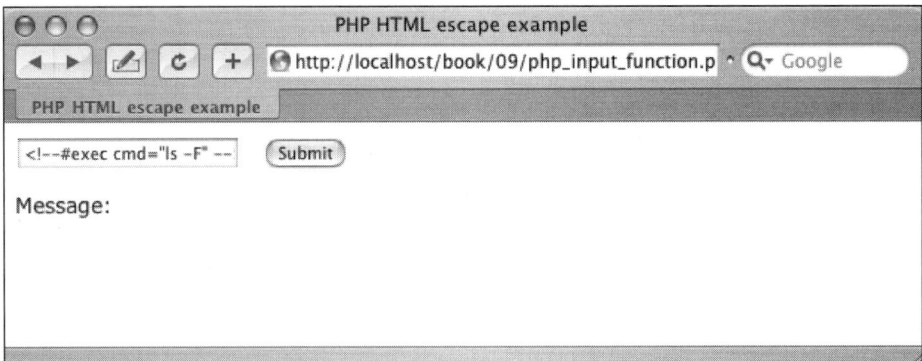

Figure 9-37. The finished PHP input function in Safari

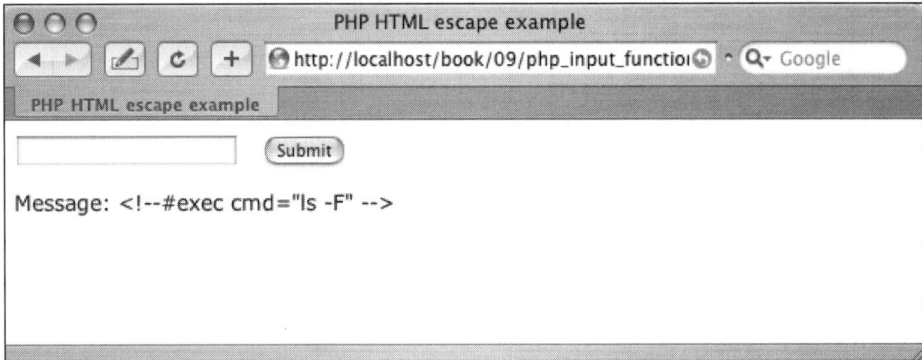

Figure 9-38. No malicious listing of files, thanks to the script

User input with JSP

Okay, it's time for the JSP version now. As this example does exactly the same job as the Perl and PHP versions in the preceding sections, let's get straight down to business.

1. Your first step is to change the working directory to your JSP web server root (the directory where all your JSP files are served). Type cd /usr/local/jakarta-tomcat-5.0.19/webapps/ROOT (remember, the Jakarta version may differ, depending on which version you installed).

2. Create a new text file by typing

```
pico jsp_input_function.jsp.
```

3. Your first line starts a JSP function or class block of code, so type

```
<%!
```

4. Next, you need to declare your htmlEscape function as follows:

```
public String htmlEscape(String text) {
```

5. As with the previous versions of this replacement example, you need some code to do the replacing. In this instance, you're going to use the replace function to remove the greater than symbol and replace it with the corresponding HTML character.

```
text = text.replaceAll(">", "&gt;");
```

6. The next line performs the same action as the previous line but using the less than symbol.

```
text = text.replaceAll("<", "&lt;");
```

7. The next line returns your replaced text.

```
return text;
```

8. That's the end of the function, so close with a right curly bracket:

```
}
```

9. Then close your function code block as follows:

```
%>
```

10. Next, you're starting a new block of JSP execution, so add an opening JSP code tag by typing

```
<%
```

11. You're going to assign a variable called message to your form field. To do this, use the request.getParameter() function as follows:

```
String message =
➡ request.getParameter("message");
```

12. The next line calls your function to remove < and > then assigns the result back to your variable.

```
message = htmlEscape(message);
```

13. The next block of code checks to see if the message variable has been set or not. If it has, it executes the function; otherwise, it assigns the message variable an empty value. If you don't add the following block of code, you'll get a nice Java exception error when you first visit the page.

```
if(message != null) {
message = htmlEscape(message);
} else {
message = "";
}
```

14. This is the end of your JSP execution, so close the tag:

```
%>
```

15. Again, as previously, the last block is just a basic HTML page that prints the message variable and shows the result.

```
<html>
<head>
<title>JSP HTML escape example</title>
</head>
<body>
<form action="jsp_input_function.jsp"
➡ method="post">
<input type="text" name="message">
 
<input type="submit" value="Submit">
</form>
<p>Message: <%=message%></p>
</body>
</html>
```

249

16. Save the code and exit Pico by pressing *CTRL+O*, and then *CTRL+X*. Once you've done this, you can preview the example in your browser by going to http://localhost:8080/jsp_input_function.jsp and using `<!--#exec cmd="ls -F" ->` as the test text, as shown in Figure 9-39. Figure 9-40 shows the results of the test.

You can find out more information on JSP's functions from Sun's website (Sun is the creator of Java and JSP) at http://java.sun.com/j2se/1.3/docs/api/index-files/index-1.html.

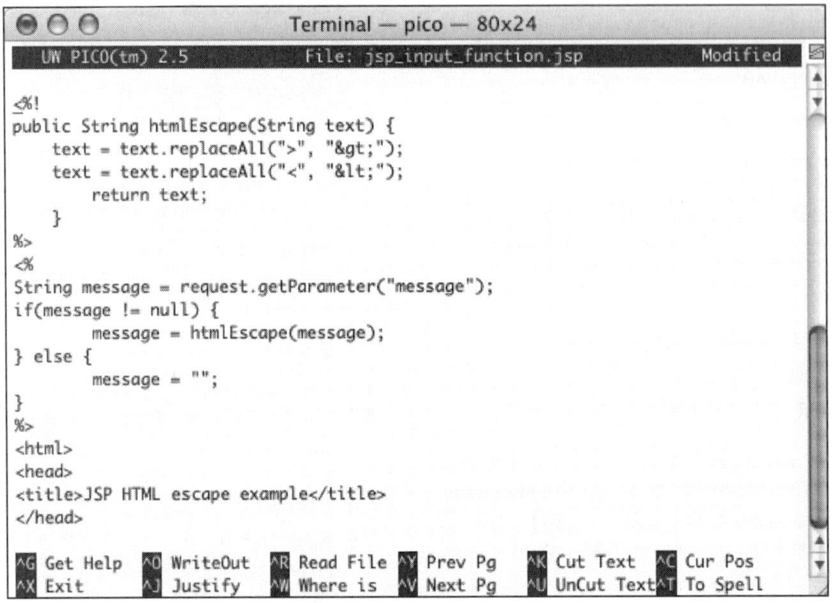

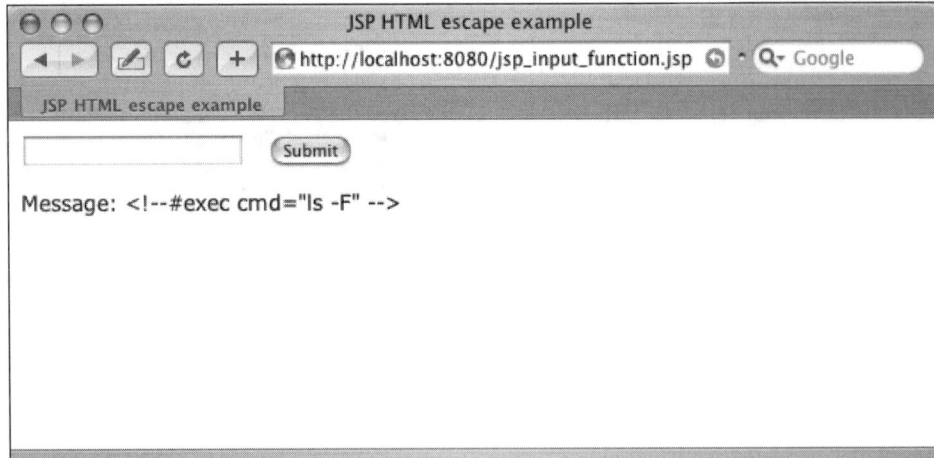

Figure 9-39. The finished JSP input function code in Pico

Figure 9-40. The finished JSP input function in Safari

Chapter review

I hope you've found this chapter interesting. The techniques discussed aren't necessarily the best way to perform the task in question, but I feel that they offer an easier way to learn some further basics about server-side language environments. Perl includes many options such as warnings and strict syntax that allow you to program better code. PHP supports object-oriented concepts. JSP allows you to program Java Beans and reuse them throughout different projects.

Once you have more experience in your chosen language, you can start to use these features and reduce programming time and increase your knowledge. Now that you've had a taste of these languages, you might have a clearer idea of which book to buy next time you're eyeing all those huge, thick, scary-looking code books at the book store.

If this chapter was a bit too code heavy for you, relax. The next chapter has sounds and moving things! Next stop, multimedia!

Chapter 10

MULTIMEDIA

What we'll cover in this chapter:

- Using Mac OS X's free resources
- QuickTime Pro
- Darwin (QuickTime) Streaming Server
- Flash

To the average person on the street, this is probably the only other chapter this Mac book should have, after the graphics chapter (Chapter 2). Even today, someone heard I was a Mac user and immediately launched in with the usual tirade of "Yeah, well, as multimedia stations, they're wicked, everyone knows that. They're rubbish for everything else though. They can't play games, and they haven't even got a proper operating system, ha ha!"

Sigh.

In this chapter, you'll take your proper operating system and put it to some serious use. We're going to be looking at what makes the web come alive: **multimedia**.

- Editing and exporting sound, video, and images for the web using the free iLife applications
- Streaming video files from your Mac using Darwin Streaming Server
- Embedding QuickTime content in your sites
- Incorporating Flash components and the **Flash Video** format (FLV)

Mac OS X comes complete with some great tools for the multimedia web developer. You might not think of them immediately, but the free iLife applications that come inside OS X—iMovie, iPhoto, and iTunes—are all useful for getting your sound and vision streamlined for web content. You made an iMovie? Use GarageBand to whip up a quick-and-easy royalty-free soundtrack to accompany it (though you have to buy GarageBand in the boxed version of iLife, depending on what software was bundled with your Mac).

To get those video files into shape for delivery to your end user, we'll be looking at QuickTime Pro. You'll also learn how to get Darwin Streaming Server—the open source, free cousin of Mac OS X's QuickTime Streaming Server (which is no longer free, since it comes bundled with Mac OS X Server)—installed and streaming media from your Mac.

This wouldn't be a proper multimedia chapter without a bit of Flash. Hold on; don't be put off by all the terrible examples of Flash you've seen. Flash can be an amazing tool when put to proper use and, with its drag 'n' drop components, can be quick to use.

Lest we forget: bandwidth! All of this is going to be friendly to that 56K modem user . . . wherever she is. Only joking. Always serving to the lowest common denominator, you are going to make multimedia available to the masses. Let's rattle those pots and pans, and make some (streamable) noise!

Using Mac OS X's free resources

Being a Mac user is great. You've read this far through the book, so you probably know this already. Why am I reminding you? Because of the stuff you get. The **free** stuff you get. When you turn that new machine on and Mac OS X boots up, there's a whole host of totally usable web development tools sat in the default dock. Take a look at Figure 10-1, if you don't believe me.

If you're staring and wondering which web development tools I'm referring to, I'm talking about iTunes, iPhoto, iMovie, and QuickTime. If you're thinking I've lost the plot, then you've not fully grasped what this chapter is all about yet.

Multimedia: *Human-computer interaction involving text, graphics, voice, and video.*

—*The Free On-line Dictionary of Computing* (http://wombat.doc.ic.ac.uk/foldoc/)

With these applications, you can take over the world! Yeah, okay, maybe not, but you can learn how to harness them in a way that will help you set the Internet ablaze with lightning download speeds and minimal bandwidth. Let's have a brief look at each one, before going head to head.

Figure 10-1. The default Mac OS X dock

- **iTunes:** Currently one of the most downloaded applications for managing digital audio, this thing is just on fire. "Rip, Mix, Burn," said the ad. They neglected to mention "convert big fat WAV and AIFF files to a far slimmer format suitable for use on the Web."

- **iPhoto:** Everyone has a digital camera these days. You just plug it into your Mac and iPhoto grabs your pictures. iPhoto also does a great job of simple photo retouching, removing red eye glare, and so on.

- **iMovie:** iMovie is so simple, even my mother could use it. It makes *anyone* a movie director in minutes. It will also convert those annoyingly huge DV files into a format that you can stream from your Mac.

- **GarageBand:** Depending on when you bought your Mac, you might find GarageBand preinstalled (or maybe you bought iLife '04). This application is really easy to use, and you'll be cranking out tunes in no time at all.

- **QuickTime:** QuickTime is the old family friend whom you remember from childhood. It used to play pretty much any video format you threw at it. Apple has lapsed a bit lately, and it seems like you need a new codec every other week. QuickTime Pro, however, is the Swiss Army knife of video editing and costs a meager $29.95. You'll be finding out what you can do with it in this chapter.

Now that your eyes are positively glinting with the shine of glory, let's get back down to earth and on with the show. First stop on this quick tour through the free applications is iTunes.

iTunes

Originally billed as just an MP3 player, iTunes has come a long way. Not only does it have network sharing (which is just awesome in an office with a central Mac serving as a jukebox!), and the iTunes Music Store, but also it now plays AAC files (also known as MP4 audio files). These things are even smaller in size than MP3 files, but with the same amazing quality. These are perfect for use over the Internet, as bandwidth is slashed.

Scenario: You have a movie file of a rock band called *Intentions Of An Asteroid* (as shown in Figure 10-2), which is almost 1GB, but you only need to get the

audio online as a downloadable file. Using iTunes, you can strip the audio track and have yourself a nice, small audio file in a couple of minutes. Here's how.

Figure 10-2. 1GB movie clip

1. Create a new iTunes playlist and drag the movie file into it.

2. Open Preferences ➤ Importing (or ⌘+,), and select the method of encoding you want to use. For now, select the default AAC Encoder at High Quality, as shown in Figure 10-3, and then click OK.

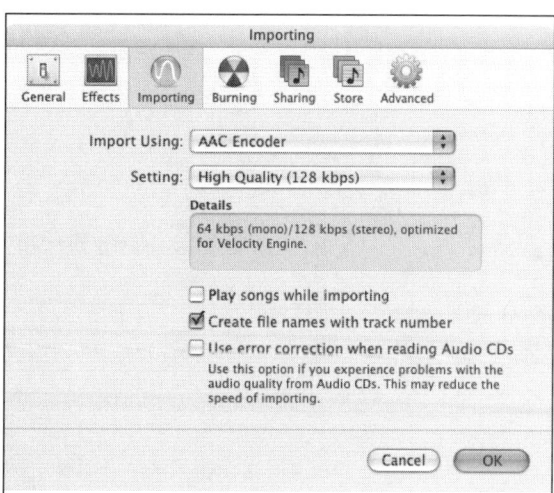

Figure 10-3. Choosing AAC encoding

3. With the video selected in the playlist, choose Advanced ➤ Convert Selection to AAC from the file menu, as shown in Figure 10-4.

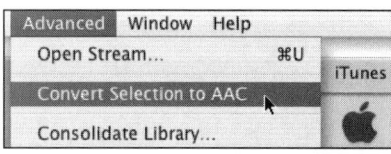

Figure 10-4. Converting the file

4. As you click that, a new playlist will appear called Converting Songs, as you can see in Figure 10-5. This will output the file to the directory you've specified in iTunes' preferences.

As AAC files are a relatively new format, and not all machines can handle iTunes, it makes sense to offer your site users an MP3 option too.

5. To do this, just change the Import setting in Preferences, as shown here in Figure 10-6, and repeat the convert process from step 3 earlier.

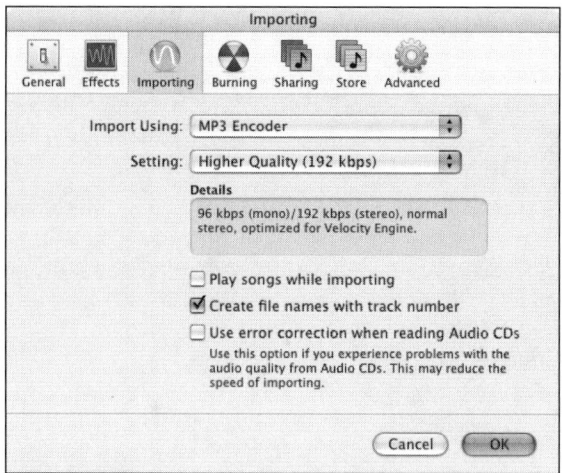

Figure 10-6. Be nice and offer an MP3 format too.

As you can see from Figure 10-7, iTunes has done a great job of shrinking that audio file down. When exported as an AIFF, the original movie file's audio track was a massive 46MB. The MP3 version is a slightly more respectable 6.2MB, but the AAC file comes in at just 3.5MB. All three formats have pretty much the same quality, but I know which one I would prefer to download over a 56K modem!

IOAA–Achieve.aif	46 MB
IOAA–Achieve.m4a	3.5 MB
IOAA–Achieve.mov	986.3 MB
IOAA–Achieve.mp3	6.2 MB

Figure 10-7. Finder reveals the wildly different file sizes.

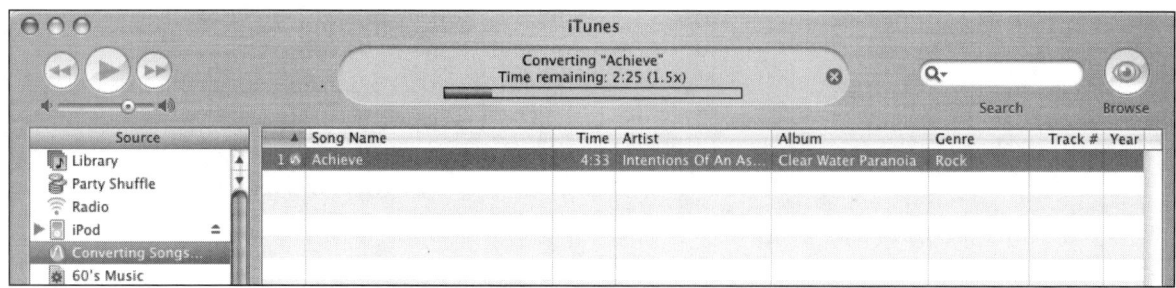

Figure 10-5. iTunes converting the file to AAC

iPhoto

iPhoto is great for organizing your digital photos. That's its job. It also has some useful little features built in, which are often the only effects some people use Photoshop for. Why spend all that money on Photoshop if you only crop, retouch, tint, and so on, when you can just edit with iPhoto's toolbar (see Figure 10-8)?

Scenario: You have a whole group of pictures to get online, but everyone looks like an alien in them, due to red eye. They could do with touching up in some areas too.

1. Open iPhoto (/Applications/iPhoto) and import the images by choosing File ➤ Import, and then selecting your images.

2. Select an image for editing by double-clicking it in the thumbnail view, or clicking the Edit button to open it in Edit view, as you can see in Figure 10-9.

3. Once open in Edit mode, use the cursor to highlight the eyes as shown in Figure 10-10, and then click the Red-Eye button. Done. Red eyes gone.

Figure 10-8. iPhoto's toolbar

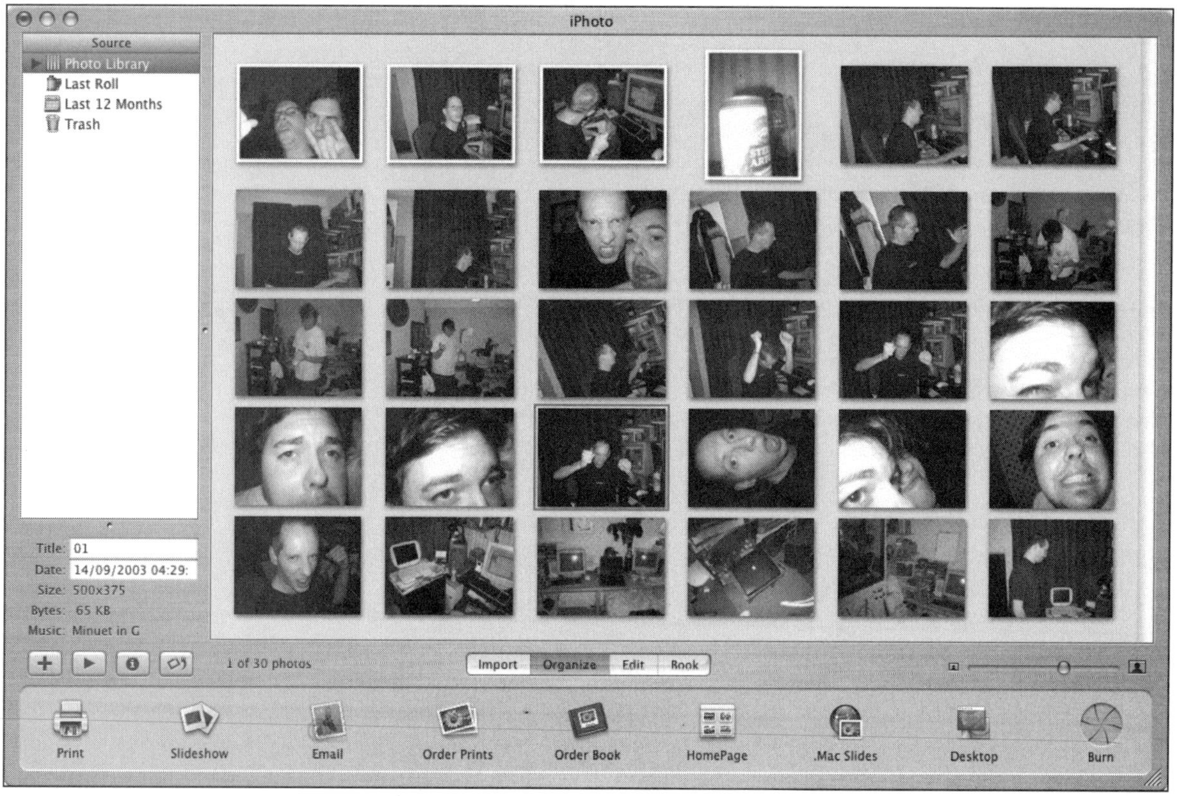

Figure 10-9. An image selected in iPhoto's Organize view

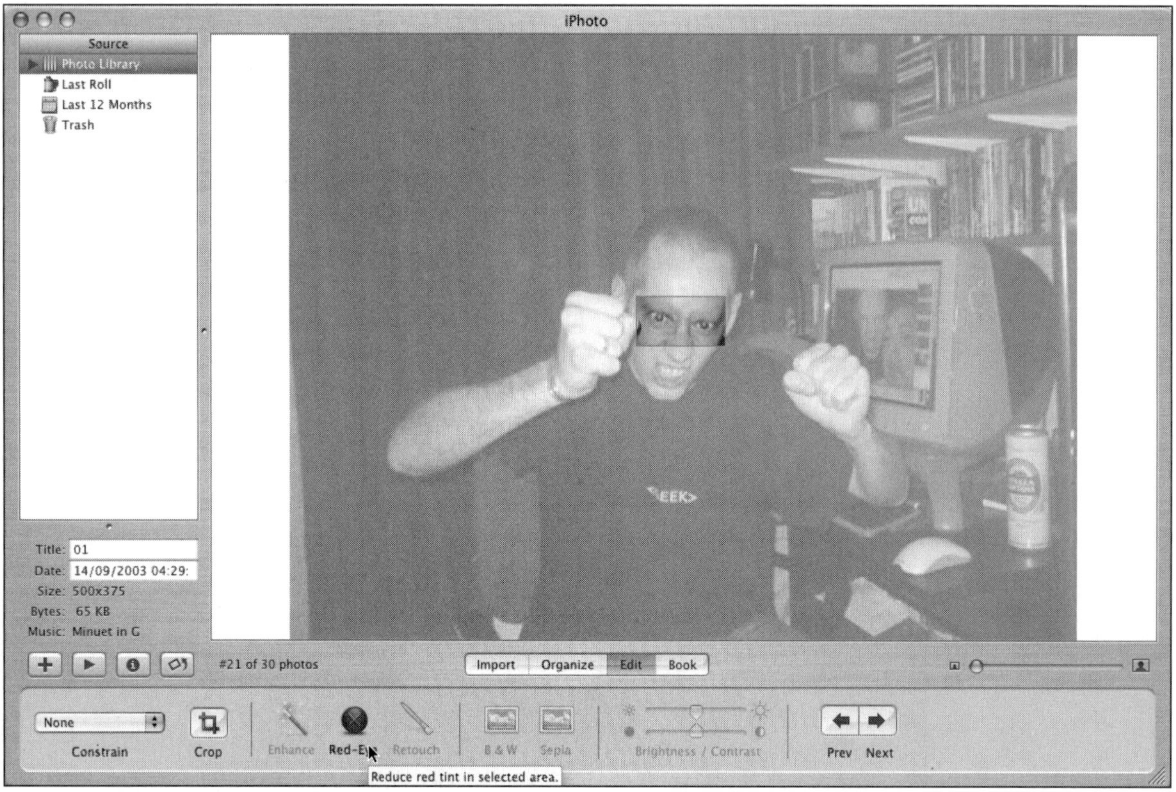

Figure 10-10. Selecting the red eyes on the image

Experiment with the other tools in here too. Enhance and Touchup can really make a difference to your images. The Brightness/Contrast sliders could come in handy too—remember though (from the "Color" section of Chapter 2) that Windows machines have a darker gamma setting than Macs.

Export a slideshow as HTML

iPhoto is great for exporting your images to get them on the Web. For a plain and simple page format, you're only a few clicks away.

1. Choose File ➤ Export from the File menu in iPhoto.

2. Click the Web Page tab, shown in Figure 10-11, and give the page a title and some colors.

3. Once you've done that, set the sizes for the images, and whether you want titles and comments, then click Export.

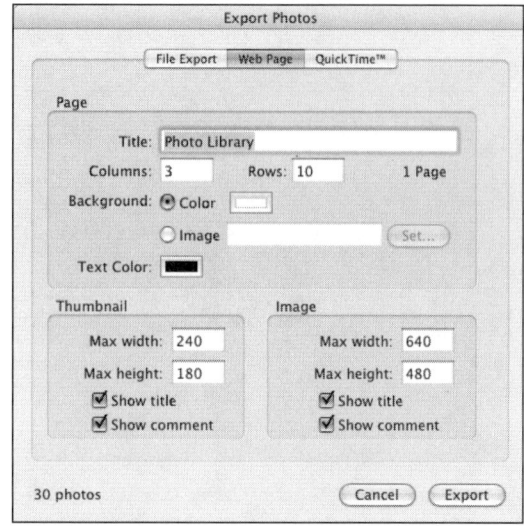

Figure 10-11. Configuring iPhoto's Web Page export

The files are exported to your `~/Sites` folder by default, as you can see in Figure 10-12.

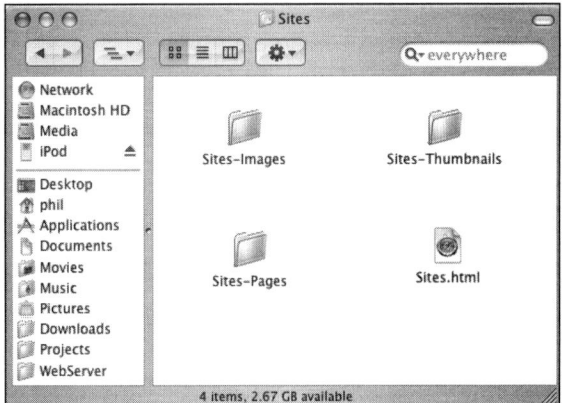

Figure 10-12. The exported photo gallery in Finder

Export a slideshow as a QuickTime movie

An even cooler feature is the ability to export your slideshow as a QuickTime movie, complete with audio. This is just as easy:

1. Click the Slideshow button on the iPhoto toolbar.

2. Choose the Transition effect, Direction, and Speed options on the Settings tab, and then configure the other options (if you want captions, for example), as I've done in Figure 10-13.

3. Next, click the Music tab and select which music you want as shown in Figure 10-14. This automatically reads your iTunes playlists, so make sure what you want is already set up in a playlist in iTunes. If you're going to display this movie on your website, this should be royalty-free music, such as your own GarageBand composition or that of a friend's band, for example.

4. Click Play to preview the slideshow.

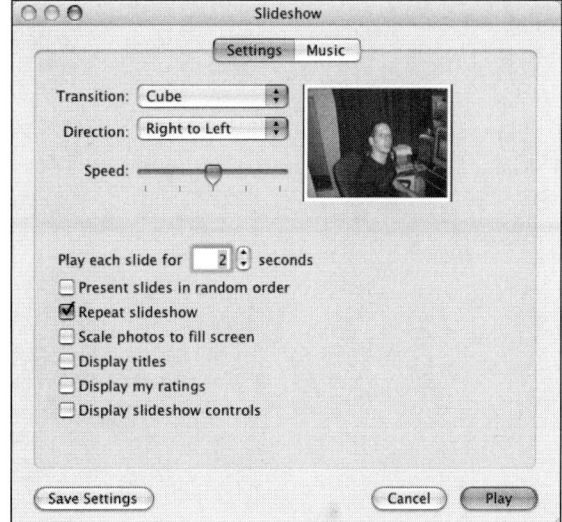

Figure 10-13. Configuring the export options for the QuickTime movie

Figure 10-14. Selecting a song to be the soundtrack

5. If all is well, choose File ➤ Export from the menu where you just have a couple more things to configure, as you can see in Figure 10-15.

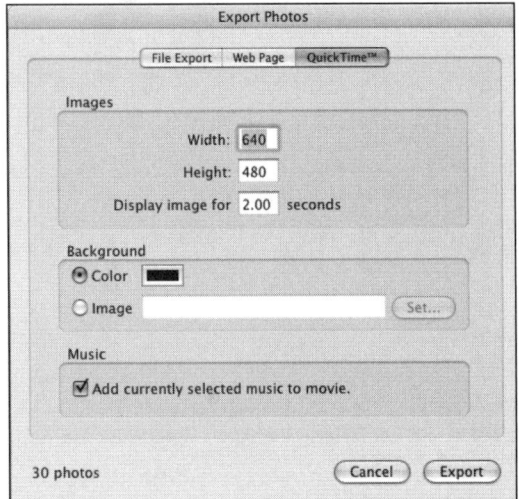

Figure 10-15. Setting the size and background color

6. Click the Export button, give the file a name, and you're in business. You have a nice little slideshow that you can put on your website.

As you can see then, iPhoto can perform some nifty tricks that you might not have known were available to you. You've got a few filters to play with, and you can crop and retouch. Being able to export gallery pages *with* thumbnails is a real timesaver too.

iMovie

Back in the old days, if you wanted to edit video on a Mac, you needed to get your head around Apple's Final Cut Pro or Adobe Premiere. These have quite steep learning curves and are certainly not the cheapest applications on the shelf. Apple changed that forever when they introduced iMovie.

iMovie is mind-bogglingly simple to use. Anyone can produce a great home movie with titles, effects, and music, and export it as a web-friendly QuickTime file. With clips imported directly from a DV cam or even just raw .dv files handed to you on some form of removable media, iMovie produces results within minutes of first using it.

For this quick example, I'm importing some footage from my DV camera, which my brother and I took in India a few years ago. If you haven't got a DV camera, but you have a load of raw .dv files, or even .mov files, the process is exactly the same once you've imported the clips.

1. When you open iMovie (/Applications/iMovie), you'll be asked what you want to do. Click Create Project as shown in Figure 10-16 and give the project a name.

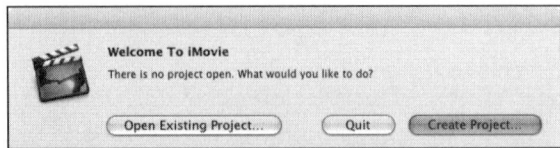

Figure 10-16. Creating a new iMovie project

2. Next up, open the Preferences dialog box and configure the options for your needs. As you can see in Figure 10-17, I chose PAL because I'm in the UK, whereas some of you are going to need NTSC. You may need to close the project and open a new one if you alter the PAL/NTSC setting here.

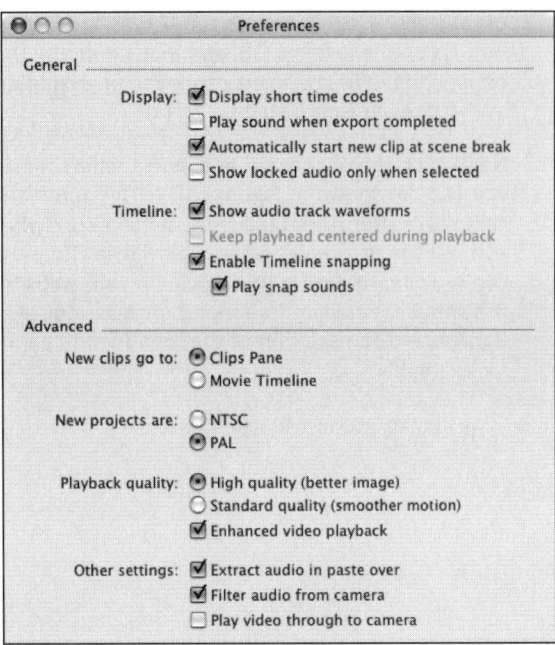

Figure 10-17. Setting your iMovie preferences

3. Now import your files. If you are using some external files, you can import them via File ➤ Import or by simply dragging them onto the Clips window. If you're importing from a DV camera, plug the camera into your Mac, switch it on, and click the Import button directly underneath the main window (see Figure 10-18). This will start the camera playing and import the video as **clips**. Each clip is determined by the points at which you originally started/stopped filming.

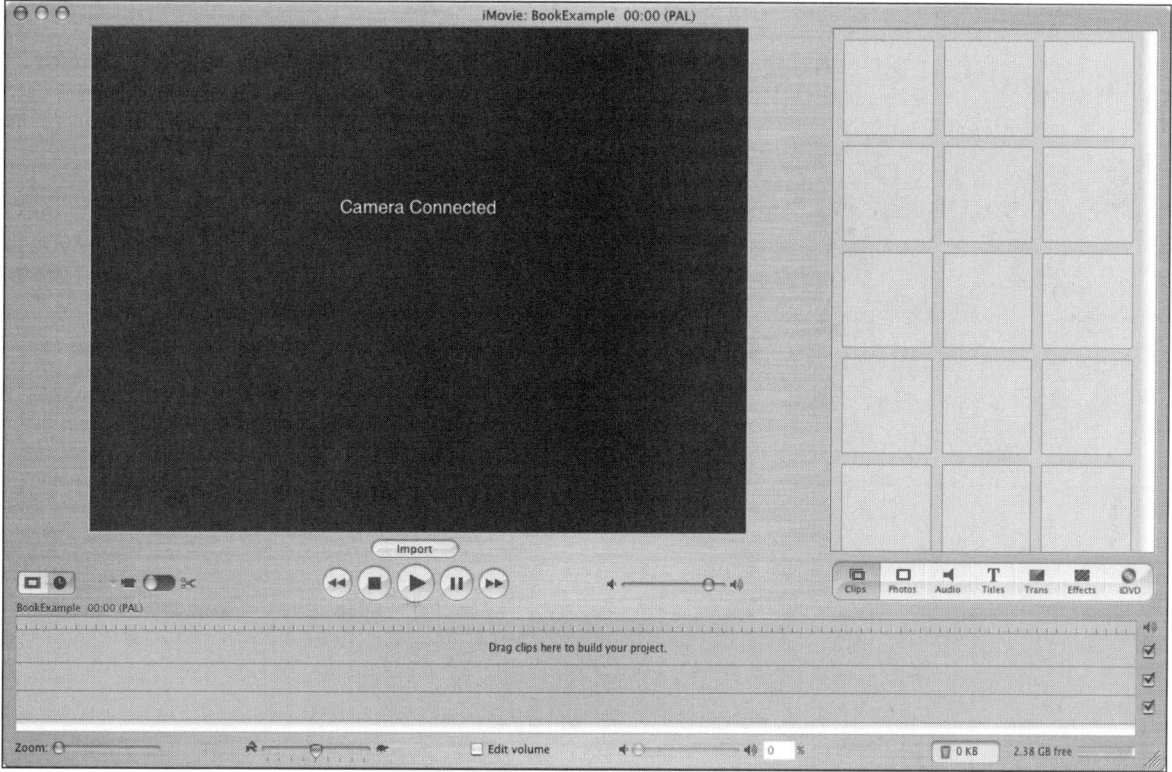

Figure 10-18. The blank iMovie window

4. As you can see in Figure 10-19, I've imported a few clips to work with, and they're all sat in the Clips window at the right of the interface. There might be a few second-long clips that you really don't need at all, so just drag those into the trash at the bottom right of the iMovie window, or select them and press *BACKSPACE*. Press ⌘+*S* to save the movie project with all the new data files.

5. Drag a few of your clips onto the timeline at the bottom of the iMovie window, arranging them in the order you think you might want them, as you can see in Figure 10-20.

You could just export it the movie like this, and the clips will just play one after the other, but that's a bit boring. Let's add some transition effects.

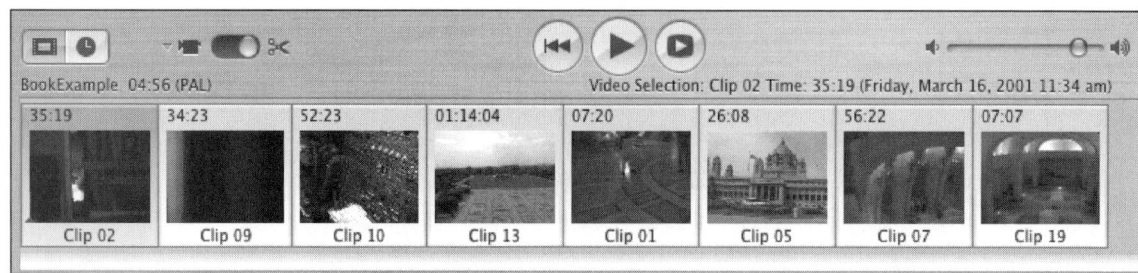

Figure 10-19. iMovie loaded with video clips and ready to go

Figure 10-20. The iMovie timeline with clips in place

6. Click the Trans button (short for transitions) under the Clips window to reveal the effects on offer, shown in Figure 10-21. Clicking each effect will give you a quick preview to give you have an idea of what effect you'll get.

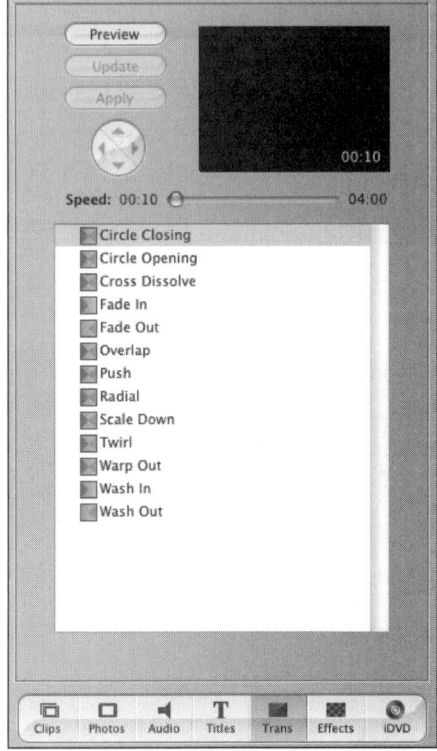

Figure 10-21. The transition effects window

7. Click the Cross Dissolve effect as shown in Figure 10-22 and adjust the speed to one that you like the look of.

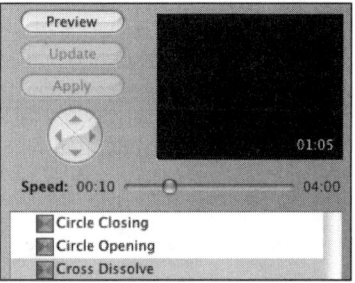

Figure 10-22. Choosing an effect to add to the movie clip

8. Click and drag the effect in between two clips on the timeline, and they'll nudge over, as you can see in Figure 10-23.

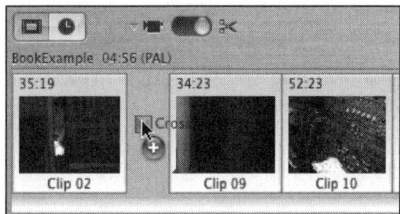

Figure 10-23. Dragging the transition

9. Drop the effect in there and you can see it join the two clips together (see Figure 10-24).

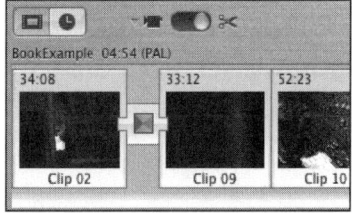

Figure 10-24. Dropping the transition

Using the same procedure, I've added another few transitions in between clips, just to make the viewing a bit smoother.

10. To view the clips with the transitions in place, ⌘-click a highlighted clip to deselect it. This will let you view the movie as a whole, rather than just playing the individually selected clip. Figure 10-25 shows my final timeline.

11. Once you've got your clips and transitions in place, you might decide you want to alter some of the transition speeds. To do this, toggle the timeline by clicking the clock icon just above the left corner of the timeline—the tooltip says "adjust audio and video timing in the timeline viewer." As you can see from Figure 10-26, the timeline has changed and has some controls underneath it.

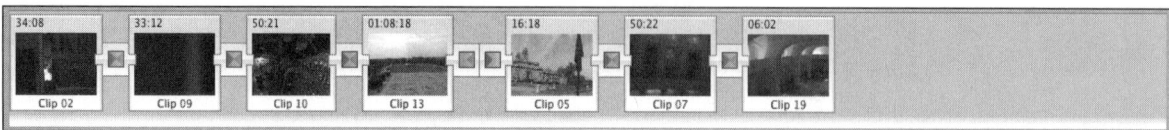

Figure 10-25. The timeline showing all the transitions in place

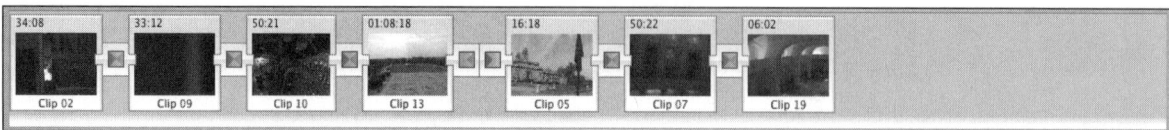

Figure 10-26. Toggling the timeline view to change the timing properties

12. To make a transition shorter, click to select it and then drag the slider shown in Figure 10-27. As you can guess from the hare and tortoise icons, dragging to the left makes the transition faster, and right slower.

Figure 10-27. Altering the transition speed with this slider

13. If you do change any of the transitions, you'll have to rerender it, as you can see from the pop-up message shown in Figure 10-28.

Figure 10-28. Rerendering the transition

Now you have a movie that plays well with some nice effects, but it would be good to have some information on there. Adding captions is easy enough, so let's add a title to the beginning of the movie.

14. Click the Titles button to reveal the Titles window (see Figure 10-29).

15. Next, choose the type of captioning you want. At the end of my movie, I've added some scrolling credits with Scrolling ➤ Scrolling Block. This just gives a nicer end to the movie and makes things look a bit more polished.

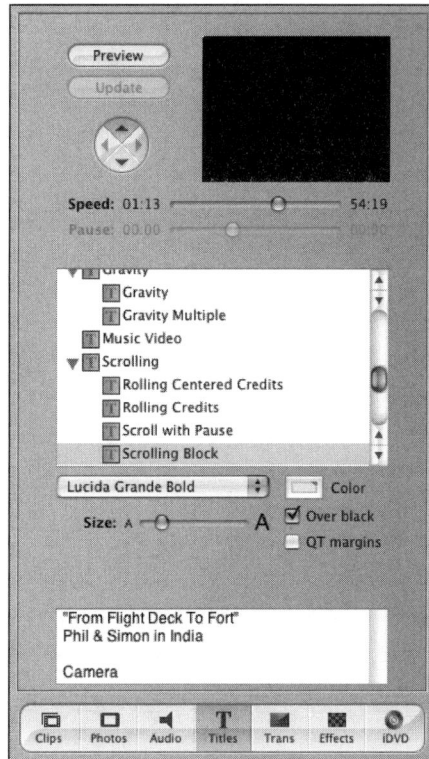

Figure 10-29. The Titles window

16. Moving along the buttons under the window at the right, you get to Effects. Click this button to check out the effects.

17. I'm going to add some ghost trails to my brother. To do this, I selected his clip on the timeline, selected the effect I want (Ghost Trails, shown in Figure 10-30), configured it, and then clicked the Apply button.

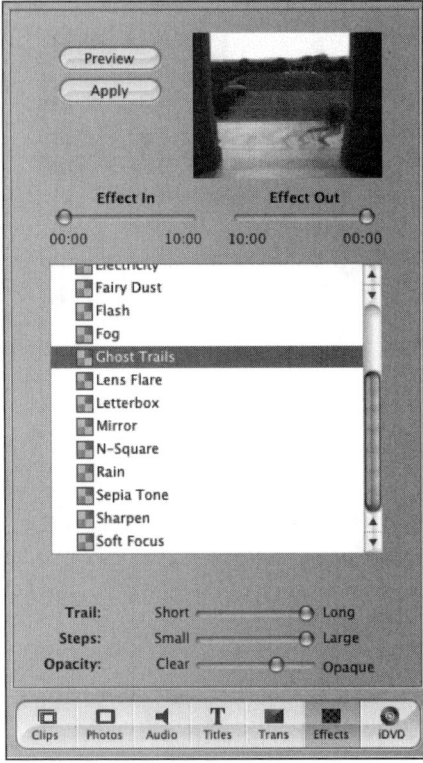

Figure 10-30. Configuring your chosen effect

So far, the movie is looking good, but what about the audio? All those video clips might look good together, but the accompanying soundtrack might be jumping all over the place with the commentary cutting off in mid-sentence. It's time to import an audio clip to lay across the whole thing. Ideally, this is a composition you made yourself in GarageBand (detailed in the next section), but any supported audio file can be used. Leaving this part of the movie until the end means that you can choose a piece of music that is the right length for the movie clip, as you can see in Figure 10-31.

18. Click the Audio tab, and choose your piece of music. Once selected, click the Place at Playhead button to import the audio file to the timeline.

Figure 10-31. Choosing a piece of music the same length as your movie

19. Check your movie all the way through and, once you're satisfied with it, select File ➤ Share to export it.

20. Click the QuickTime tab and compress the movie for web use by selecting Web in the drop-down menu. If you are going to be streaming this movie from Darwin Streaming Server (see later in this chapter), then you can select web streaming here. Click Share to export the movie as shown in Figure 10-32.

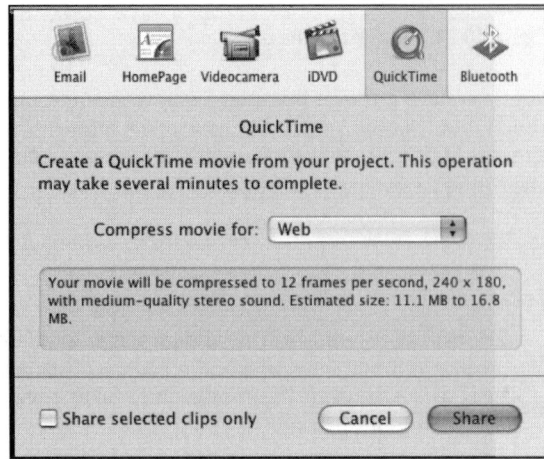

Figure 10-32. Compressing the movie for the Web

Obviously, there is a lot more to iMovie than what has been shown here, but hopefully this should give you a basic idea of how you can use it for getting your movies onto your website. Depending on how much bandwidth you have to play with, you might want to export bigger movies, because the web-optimized movies aren't very big, as you can see from Figure 10-33. As with everything I've shown you in this book, experiment; don't just take my word for it.

Figure 10-33. The finished movie, exported for web use

GarageBand

A lot of my friends and relatives have spent years making music, both professionally and as a hobby. If I have a question about Reason, ProTools, Cubase, or Logic Audio, I ask them. Thankfully, I don't need to use any of those applications now. GarageBand can make pretty much anyone into a professional-sounding musician in a matter of minutes. When you add this to iMovie as a soundtrack, watching the result is very satisfying, knowing that you've done the lot yourself.

You can plug instruments into GarageBand and go nuts with the arrangements, but for this simple exercise, you're going to create a short track simply by placing the loops available to you onto the timeline. Okay, the neighbors might start complaining a bit now because you're going to quickly make some noise (but probably nothing for Paul McCartney to get worried over). I've aimed for something loud and nasty, purely to test GarageBand's noise-making abilities, and everyone should rock out from time to time.

1. Open GarageBand (/Applications/GarageBand) and create a new track called "BookExample."

2. The default instrument is a piano, but we all know that a drum kit makes far more noise than a piano, so select Control ➤ Show Loop Browser (⌘+L), and click the Drums button, as shown in Figure 10-34.

Loops							Name ▲	Tempo	Key	Beats	Fav	
Reset ⊗	Drums	Piano	Rock/Blues	Single	Ensemble		70s Ballad Dr	80	C	8	☐	
Favorites	Drum Kit	Elec Piano	Urban	Clean	Distorted		80s Pop Beat	110	–	8	☐	
Bass	Beats	Organ	World	Acoustic	Electric		80s Pop Beat	110	–	16	☐	
Guitars	Percussion	Synths	Electronic	Relaxed	Intense		80s Pop Beat	110	–	16	☐	
Strings	Shaker	Horn	Country	Cheerful	Dark		80s Pop Beat	110	–	16	☐	
⊞	Scale: Any ▾	Q		796 items			80s Pop Beat	110	–	16	☐	
							80s Pop Beat	110	–	16	☐	

Figure 10-34. Lots of noisy drum loops

3. Check a few loops out by clicking them in the right side of the window. When you find one you like, drag it onto the timeline, like I'm doing in Figure 10-35. I've chosen Effected Drum Kit 03, because it sounds filthy.

4. When you drop the beats on the timeline, drag it hard left, so that it starts on bar 1, as shown in Figure 10-36.

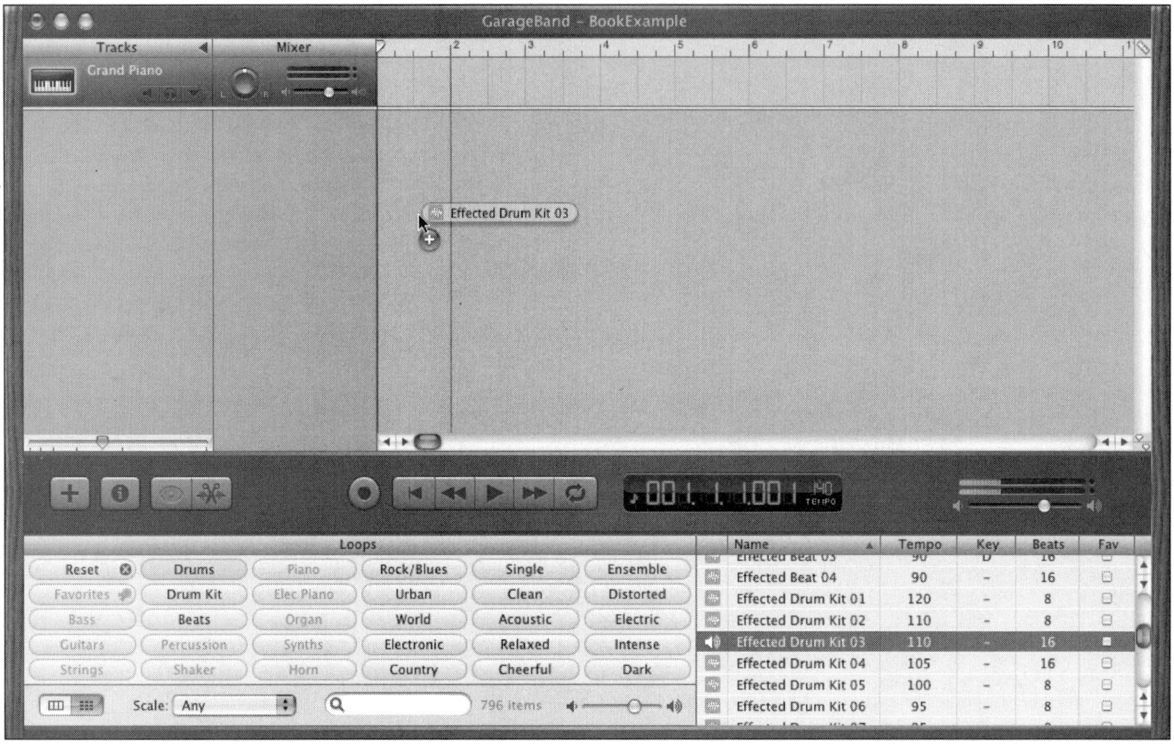

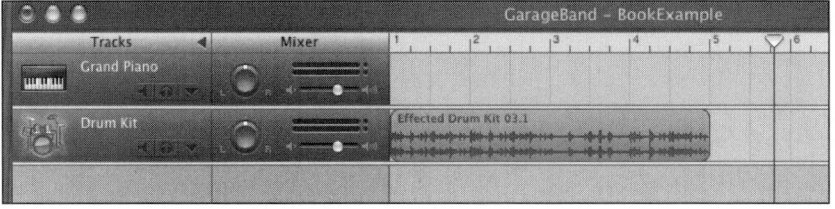

Figure 10-35. Dragging a loop to the timeline

Figure 10-36. Starting the loop at bar 1

5. When you hit the Play button, you should hear some noise for a few bars. To keep the beat going, grab the top-right corner of the drum beat in the timeline and then drag it along, like I've done in Figure 10-37. This will loop the beat. If you wanted the same one beat throughout the song, you would just drag this for as long as your tune needs to be.

6. Okay, time for some bass to go with those drums. Click the Reset button in the loop browser window, and then click Bass and select some bass. I've picked out Slow Sub Bass 01, which I've dragged to the timeline and started from bar 3 (I never did play bass according to any rules), as shown in Figure 10-38.

Figure 10-37. Stretching the beats over 12 bars

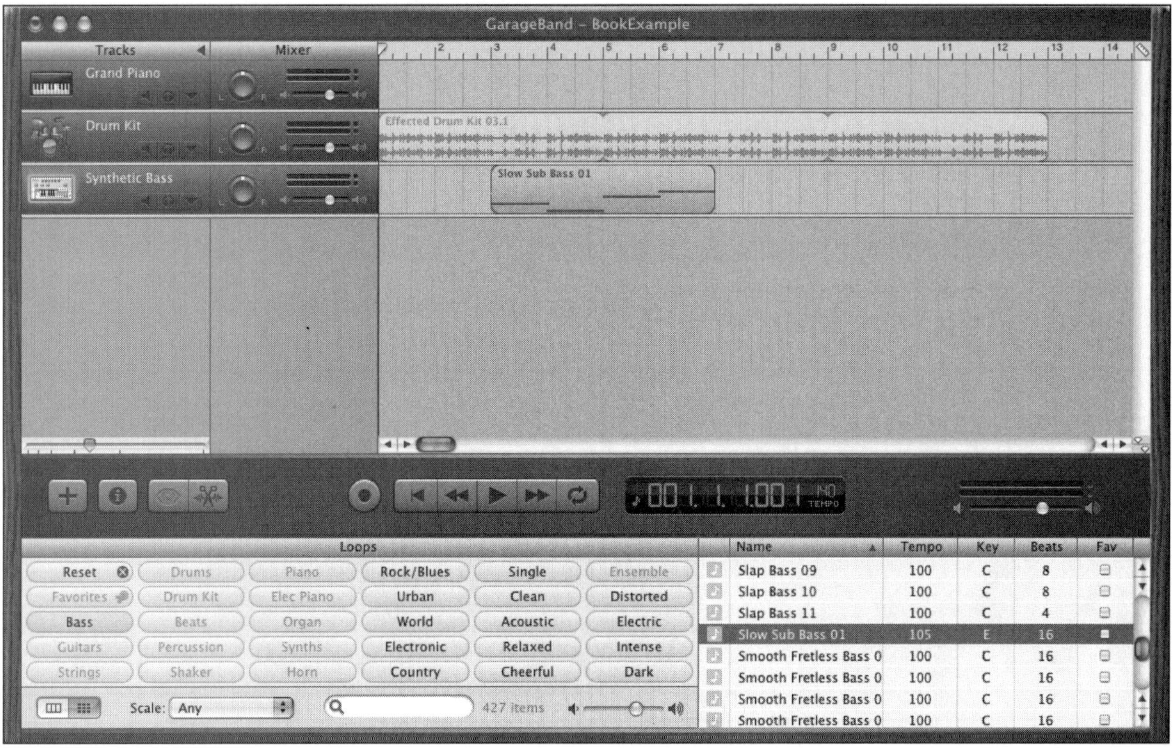

Figure 10-38. Adding some bass

7. Reset the loop browser, choose Percussion, and drag Djembe 03 out onto bar 7 of the timeline, as I have in Figure 10-39.

Figure 10-39. Adding some percussion

8. Upon playing that back, that new djembe sounds a bit loud when it comes in, so turn its volume down a touch with the slider in the mixer for that channel, which you can see in Figure 10-40.

Figure 10-40. Turning the percussion down a bit

9. Okay, still riding the Percussion train, I've gone for looping Exotic Beat 17 all the way through, so drag that to the timeline starting at bar 1 through to 12, as in Figure 10-41.

10. Save the document, click the Reset button, and select Synths.

Now you're going to add an effect to a couple of bars. This involves a few steps.

11. First, drag Techno Synth 04 onto bar 1 of the timeline and drag it out over 8 bars.

12. Drag it onto the timeline again, this time to bars 9 and 10.

13. Drag it out again, this time on to bars 11 and 12 but on the channel above, as shown in Figure 10-42.

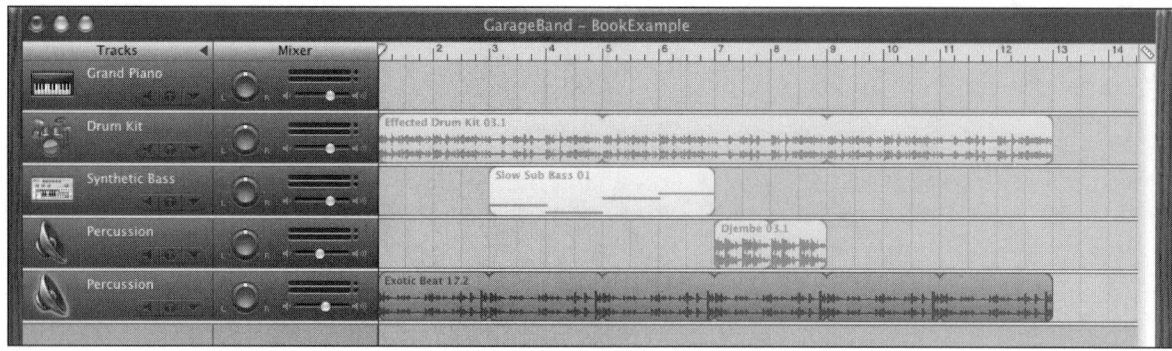

Figure 10-41. Adding another percussion track all the way through

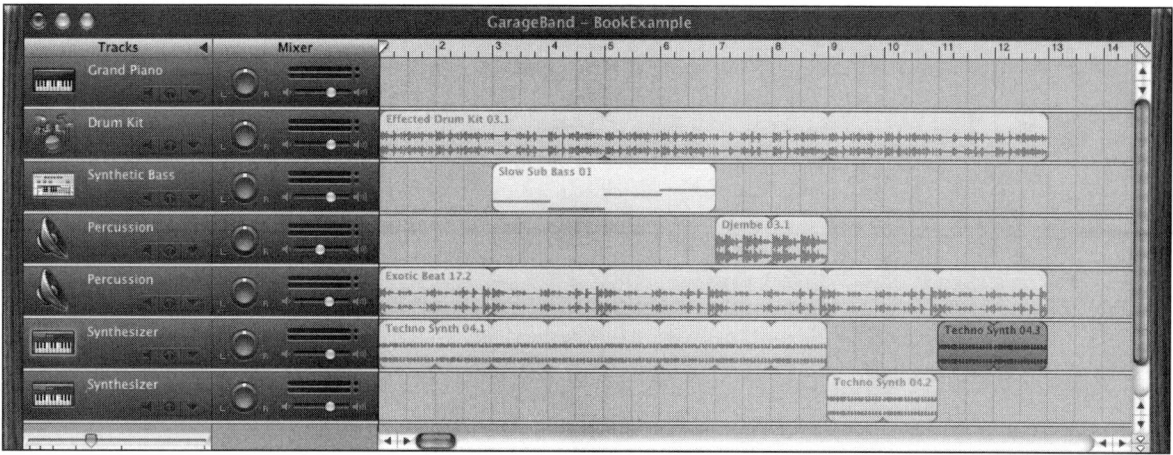

Figure 10-42. Splitting the synth onto two channels

14. As I mentioned just before step 11, you're going to add an effect to a couple of bars—not the whole channel. Select the bottom synth channel (bars 8–10), and click the Info button (or double-click the channel) to open the Track Info panel, which you can see in Figure 10-43, and then click the Details arrow to expand the panel.

15. As you can see in Figure 10-43, I've chosen to add a flanger effect to this channel, so check the box, and then select Flanger ➤ Full Range. This will sweep one full flange cycle over those two bars of synth, which will really make a difference to it.

16. Finally, fatten up that flanged section by adding another two bars of slow subbass on the bass channel, as you can see in Figure 10-44.

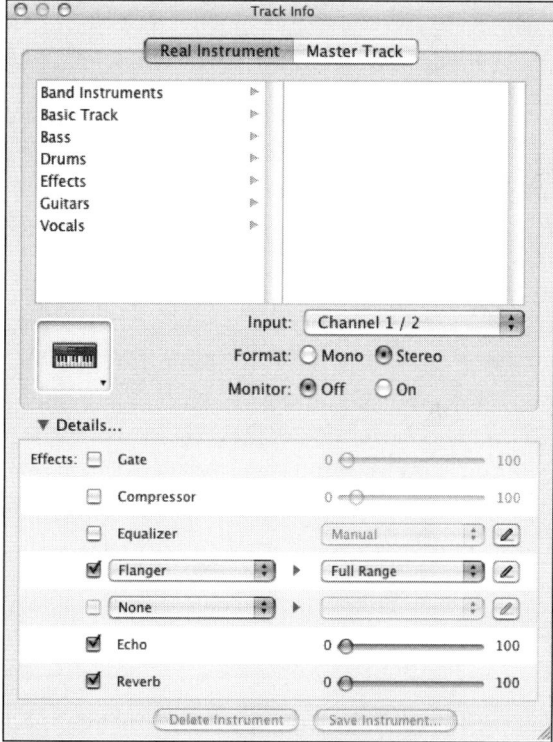

Figure 10-43. Adding a flanger effect

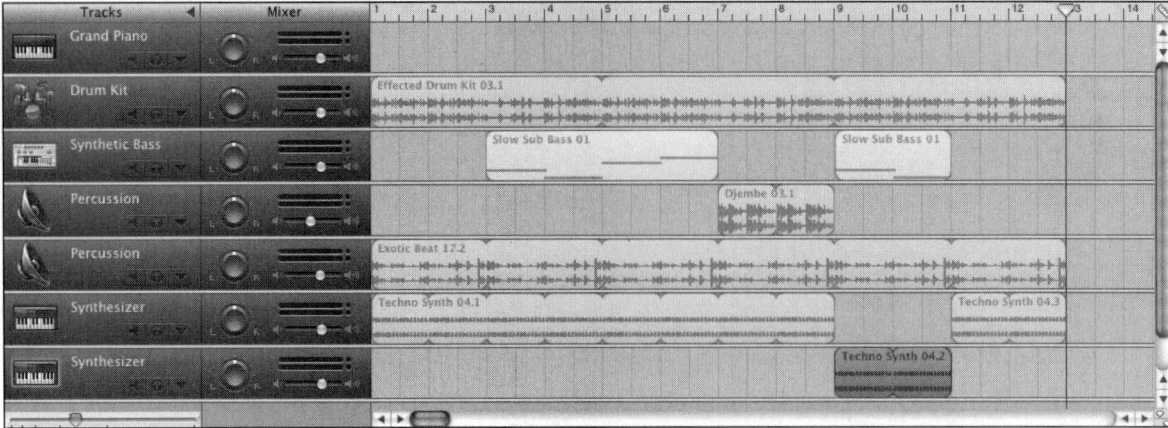

Figure 10-44. The finished loop

17. Exporting this loop couldn't be much easier. Save the file, and then select File ➤ Export to iTunes. Lo and behold, iTunes has a new playlist with your name on it and the exported tune sat in there (see Figure 10-45). At present, this is an .aiff file, so you'll probably want to convert it to AAC or MP3 format.

And there you have it. A triumph of Wagnerian volume and intensity! Okay, so it's not the best tune in the world, but it shows you just how easy it is to create some music for looping in Flash files or to use as background music in your iMovies. If you have a midi keyboard or a guitar, plug them in and get creative.

Now that I've made you play with the nasty loops, you can spend a nice quiet Sunday afternoon going through the more mellow loops. You have to admit, though, that flanger really pulled the tune together. Now, back to the movies.

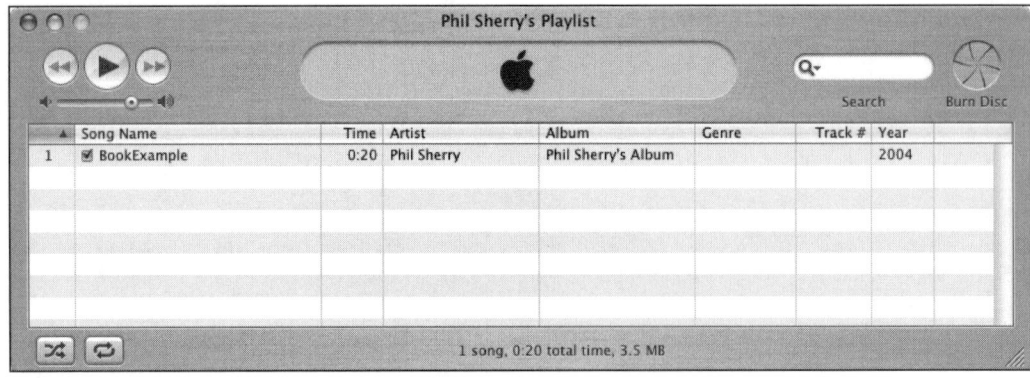

Figure 10-45. iTunes is ready to play your new tune.

QuickTime Pro

QuickTime has been preinstalled on new Macs since System 7. It does a pretty good job of playing video files, but for the extremely reasonable price of $29.99, you can get an absolute bargain in the form of Quick-Time Pro (www.apple.com/quicktime/upgrade).

At the start of this chapter, I referred to QuickTime Pro as "the Swiss Army knife of video editing." It can copy, paste, cut, extract, convert, import, export, or add effects. It can also play full screen, which is handy for presentations; save movies from web pages; create slide shows; and much more.

Export

Let's have a quick look at some different examples. Firstly, I'm going to tackle the same *Intentions Of An Asteroid* video clip as I used in the iTunes section of this chapter, purely because 1GB is a bit of a silly size to expect someone to go about downloading from your website. It's also 720×576px in size, which is unnecessarily large for a web download. If you want to see them that big, go to see the band live; that's my outlook. Finally, you'll prepare the video for streaming, which you'll learn more about in the section following this one.

As there's no DVD free with this book, and it would be a bit much to expect people to download 1GB files from the friends of ED web server, I'd suggest you use a big movie file from an enhanced music CD, or something similar, for this exercise.

1. Open your large movie file in QuickTime Pro.

2. As you can see in Figure 10-46, there are a lot of export options. For now, you're only exporting as QuickTime, so give the resulting file a name, and then choose File ➤ Export ➤ Movie to QuickTime Movie and then click the Options button. I added "_web" to the filename, so that I can tell which file is which in Finder later.

Figure 10-46. QuickTime Pro has a few export options.

3. Once you've clicked the Options button, you get the Movie Settings window. If you were to click that Settings button, you'd see more than enough options to confuse yourself with (as shown in Figure 10-47), but you want to make sure Sorenson Video 3 is selected for this example. Click the OK button and move on to the next step.

4. You'll get to that Filter button in the next example, so ignore that for now and click the Size button. As I said during the start of this exercise, I'm working with a huge video size. A good size for web video is 320×240 pixels, so alter the size settings for your video to match these.

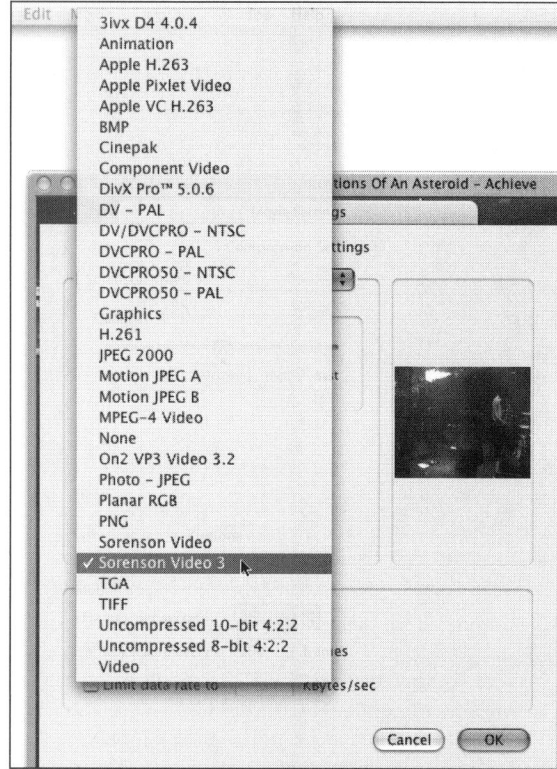

Figure 10-47. Selecting Sorenson Video 3

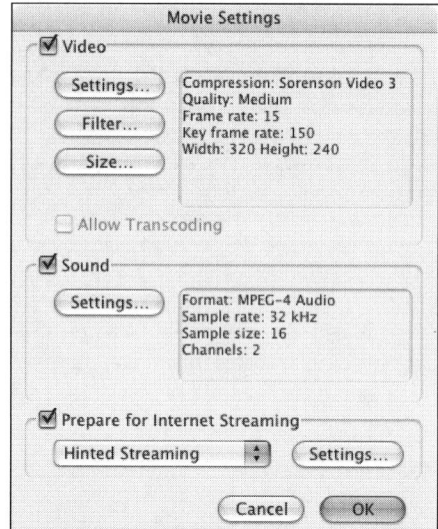

Figure 10-48. Preparing the video for Hinted streaming

Figure 10-49. Exporting may take a while, depending on the speed of your Mac and the size of the file.

5. Finally, check the Prepare for Internet Streaming option, which you can see at the bottom of Figure 10-48.

6. Click OK twice to export the video. This might take a while depending on the size of the clip, speed of your machine, and so on, but you'll have a nice progress bar like the one in Figure 10-49 to look at while this takes place.

The final output for my file was near identical in both audio and video quality, but obviously smaller in physical screen size. It was certainly smaller in file size too: 18.8MB. Result! And, it's hinted for streaming, which you'll learn more about soon. Okay, let's have another example.

Effects

In the last example, I mentioned an option called **Filters**. Using the output from the previous example, you're now going to add an effect to your movie clip.

1. Open your movie clip and choose File ➤ Export (⌘+E) and click the Options button, just as you did in step 2 of the last example. This time, I added "_filter" to the file name, for easy reference in Finder.

2. In the Movie Settings window, click the Filter button.

3. For this example, you're going to make the video clip look old by using the Film Noise filter. Click the triangle next to Special Effects and select Film Noise, as I've done in Figure 10-50.

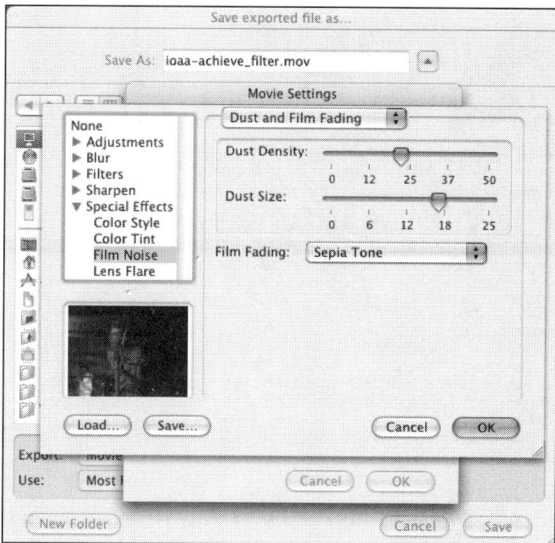

Figure 10-50. Selecting Film Noise and configuring the dusty bits

4. To make it look old, select Sepia Tone from the Film Fading menu.

5. You get a little preview of the effect, so play around with the settings and add different amounts of dust, hairs, etc., until you like the look of it (see Figure 10-51).

6. Okay the settings, check you added "_filter" to the filename, and click OK to export.

Figure 10-51. The effect movie clip with Sepia Tone and Film Noise

That's a pretty easy way to add a professional effect, and the file size is smaller (as there are less colors). Starting again with the unaffected movie clip, have a look at the other effects too, as they are all worth knowing. In fact, you'll need to experiment with the Blur filter, so that you have another effects-enhanced movie clip for the next section, so follow the same steps and save the output with "_blur" in the filename.

Cut/paste

Just like a word processor, you can cut and paste in QuickTime Pro. You are now going to splice a few movies together from the last exercise, in order to be dazzled by this feature. For this exercise, you will require three clips:

- The output from the export section
- The output from the effects section
- The blurred output from the effects section, which you made yourself

My movie clip just happens to be 4:33m long, so I'm going to chop it up into three sections of 1:31m and paste the different sections back together. Obviously, this kind of thing works best when you change the effect with the music back and forth between different effects all the time. This isn't Movie Making 101 though, so I'll just kick out a rough 'n' ready version in order to teach you the basics. Just remember my name if you ever make it big in movies.

1. Open your three movie clips, like I have done in Figure 10-52. In order to get them to play simultaneously, hold down OPTION+⌘+SPACEBAR. Use the same shortcut to stop them all too.

275

Figure 10-52. Opening all three movie clips

2. You need a new movie in which to save this slab of rock video, so choose File ➤ New Player (⌘+N), and a new player will open. Save this to the same directory as your other movie clips. I've added "effected_edit" to my filename, as you can see in Figure 10-53.

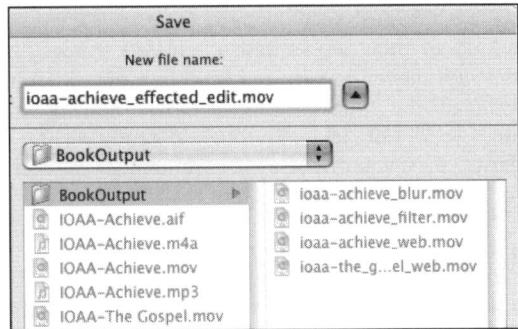

Figure 10-53. Save the new file before you start adding content.

3. Okay, turn your attention to the unaffected movie clip's timeline now and the two little triangular sliders underneath it as you see in Figure 10-54.

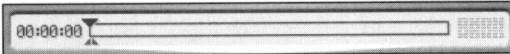

Figure 10-54. QuickTime's timeline

4. Click the right one, and drag it a third of the way along your timeline as shown in Figure 10-55.

As you might have guessed, this is selecting that section of the movie clip.

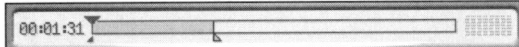

Figure 10-55. Selecting the first 1/3 of the movie clip

5. Now you want to copy that and paste it into the new movie clip you have waiting. So, choose Edit ➤ Copy (⌘+C), click the new movie clip to select it, and then choose Edit ➤ Paste (⌘+V), which then gives your new movie some content, as you can see from Figure 10-56.

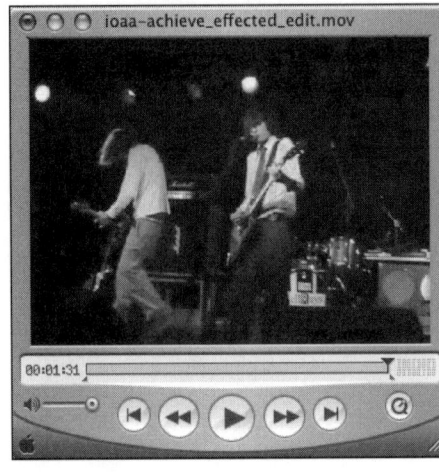

Figure 10-56. 1:31 of video successfully pasted into a new movie

6. Next, select the sepia (_filter) movie clip. Slide the right triangle to 2/3 of the way across (3:02 on mine), and the left triangle up to 1/3 (1:31 on mine), as shown in Figure 10-57. If you can't get the exact place you require by dragging with your cursor, get as close as you can, and then use the left and right cursor keys to move through the frames. Once you've got it sectioned off, copy it (⌘+C).

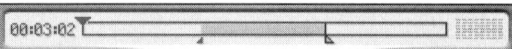

Figure 10-57. Selecting the middle 1/3 of the movie

7. Select the new movie clip again and paste the sepia section in (⌘+V), as I've done in Figure 10-58. If you play it through from just before the splice line, you'll see and hear how accurate you were when you chopped that last movie clip up. If you were wildly off, then just use Undo (⌘+Z) to take it out, recalibrate the sliders on the sepia clip, and try again.

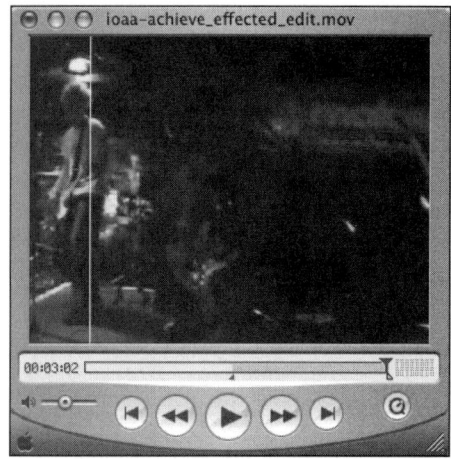

Figure 10-58. Selecting the middle 1/3 of the movie

8. Now click the blurred clip and use the sliders to select the final 1/3 of the movie. Again, if you're a few frames out here, you can just undo and try again. So, move that right-hand slider all the way to the right of the timeline, and the left to 2/3 (3:02 on mine), as I've shown in Figure 10-59, and then copy it (⌘+C).

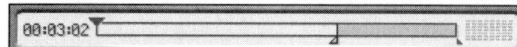

Figure 10-59. Selecting the final 1/3 of the movie

9. Paste it into the new movie clip, and then check how smooth an edit it was, in case you need to go back and adjust the slider to get it better. Save your final movie and that's it.

I think that's a cool way of getting some effects onto your video without spending big bucks on Final Cut Pro or another professional application, and obviously you'd do better to chop the clip up into relevant sections. Yes, Final Cut Pro is a much more professional tool, but with some time, effort, and imagination, you can get some great results for your $29.99. After that, I think you'd have to agree QuickTime Pro totally earns its "Swiss Army knife" reputation. For more QuickTime Pro facts, take a look at www.apple.com/quicktime/download/qtpro_faq.html.

Darwin (QuickTime) Streaming Server

Up until now, you've offered people the choice to see and hear files from clicking a link on a web page. From that link, their browser loads a video or audio file, both of which can then be saved to their local machine. There may be a time when you'd rather the user couldn't download that file. For instance, you would prefer them to have to return to your site in order to see that video clip, or listen to that audio file. For a band, this is a good way of keeping fans interested in the site, and traffic towards the site grows.

Enter **D**arwin **S**treaming **S**erver (**DSS**). DSS is the twin brother of QuickTime Streaming Server, which comes preinstalled on Mac OS X Server now. Using **R**eal **T**ime **S**treaming **P**rotocol (RTSP), Darwin Streaming Server effectively plays the file from your server, as opposed to the file being downloaded onto the user's computer first, and then playing back. This can be used for prerecorded files or even live broadcasts. Live broadcasts are a bit more involved though and require a camera and two machines (which I'm sure not everyone has), so I'm going to talk you through streaming some prerecorded files.

1. First of all, you need to download the installer file. In order to do this, you need to be a member of the **A**pple **D**eveloper **C**onnection (ADC) site, so go to `http://developer.apple.com/` to log in if you're a member or `http://connect.apple.com/` to sign up, if you haven't done so already. If you are a .Mac member, you can use your AppleID to log in (see Figure 10-60).

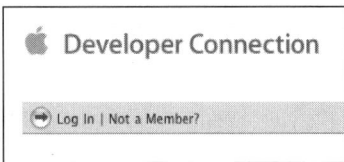

Figure 10-60. To use the ADC site, you must log in as a member.

2. Once you're logged in, navigate to the Darwin Streaming Server page at

`http://developer.apple.com/darwin/projects/` ➡`streaming/`

and download the Streaming Server package (`DarwinStreamingSrvr5.0.1.1.OSX.dmg`) from the link shown in Figure 10-61.

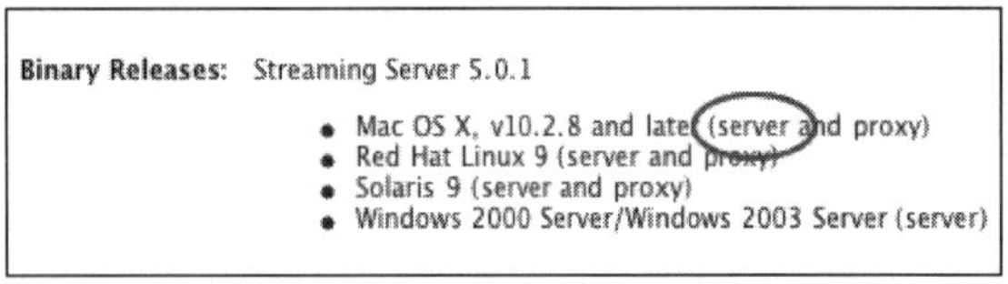

Figure 10-61. Selecting the server package link

3. Once downloaded, the disk image should automatically mount and open, as shown in Figure 10-62, so double-click the package installer.

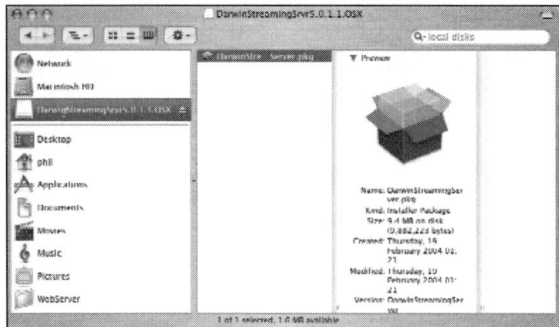

Figure 10-62. Double-click the installer to get things going.

4. Installation is a standard procedure, so select your installation volume (I chose my iMac's only volume in Figure 10-63), click the necessary buttons to continue, entering your password when asked to do so.

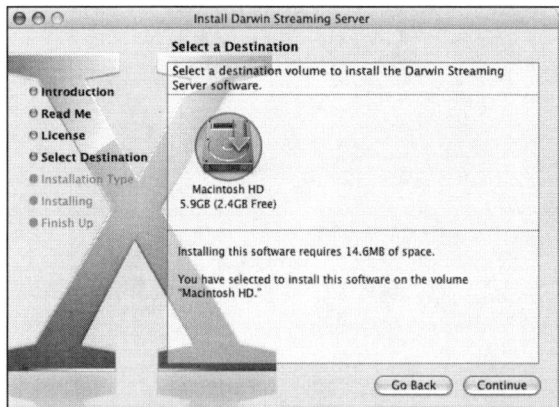

Figure 10-63. Selecting the installation volume

5. The last step of installation should open your browser to the Admin page. If this doesn't happen for some reason, you can access it by going to http://127.0.0.1:1220/. When you get there, you'll see a login panel like the one in Figure 10-64, asking you to enter a user name and password, so that you can administer the server. Keep things nice and simple, and use the same user name and password as your OS X login.

Figure 10-64. Entering an admin user name and password

6. Next step is showing you SSL. As SSL isn't set up out of the box, you can click Next and bypass this step (see Figure 10-65).

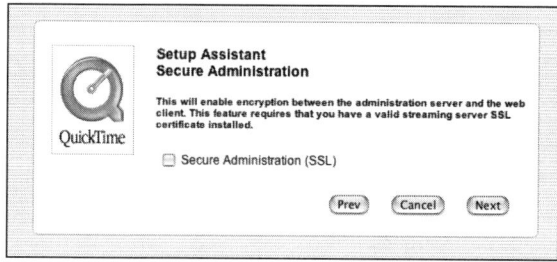

Figure 10-65. Skipping past SSL

7. Now you need to tell it where to find the media you want it to stream, so for the purposes of this exercise, you're going to use the default path of /Library/QuickTimeStreaming/Movies/ as shown in Figure 10-66.

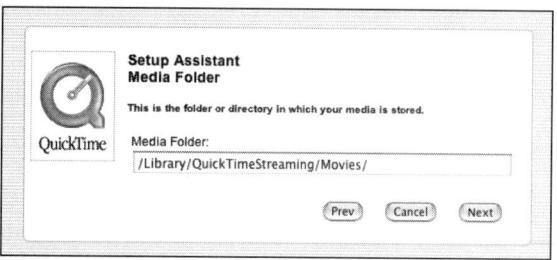

Figure 10-66. Selecting the media folder

8. Depending on your target audience, you may need to stream your media through firewalls. For this exercise, you're going to skip this for now (so it doesn't interfere with your web server), although I will show you where to enable it once you're through the setup stage. So, click the Finish button as shown in Figure 10-67.

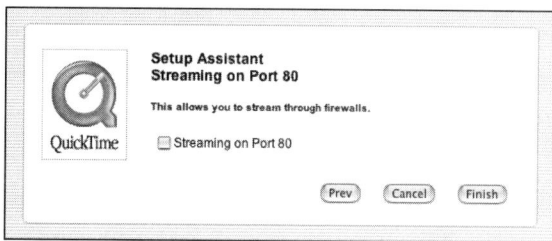

Figure 10-67. Are you going to be streaming via port 80?

9. Once you've completed these steps, you arrive at the main admin window, shown in Figure 10-68. From here, you set up your playlists. You can also specify how many connections can be made to your streaming server.

If you're serving this from home, your ISP isn't going to be very happy if you allow the default maximum number of connections, which, as you can see when you click the General Settings link in the menu at the left, is 1000. It's also very unlikely that you'd be able to manage such a thing, yet keep a decent quality of service.

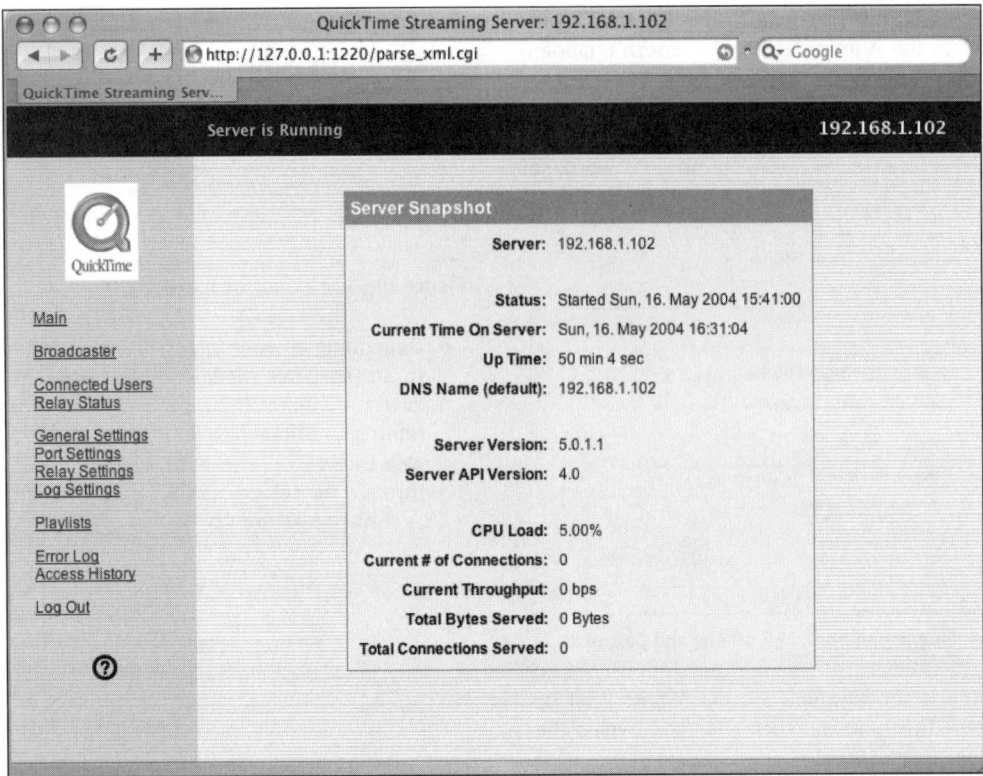

Figure 10-68. The main Darwin Streaming Server admin window

10. So, highlight those last two zeros and delete them (see Figure 10-69).

Figure 10-69. Altering the maximum number of connections

11. As mentioned in step 8, you can configure your streaming server to use port 80 if you need to stream through firewalls. To do this, click the Port Settings link. As hinted at in Figure 10-70 though, this is going to interfere with Apache unless you've configured Apache to run on a different port than its default of 80.

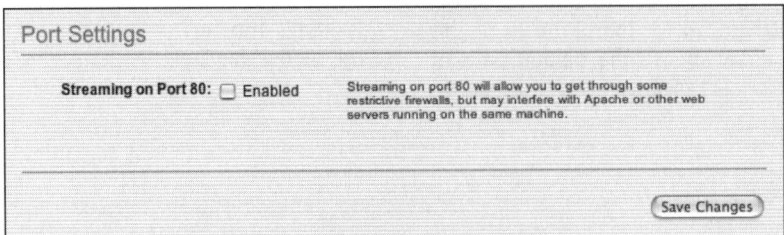

Figure 10-70. You can stream via port 80 by checking this box.

12. Next in the menu is Relay Settings (see Figure 10-71). Relays are used to accept a stream from one streaming server and send the stream on, or "relay" it, to another streaming server. This exercise won't be dealing with relays, so you can skip on to the next menu item.

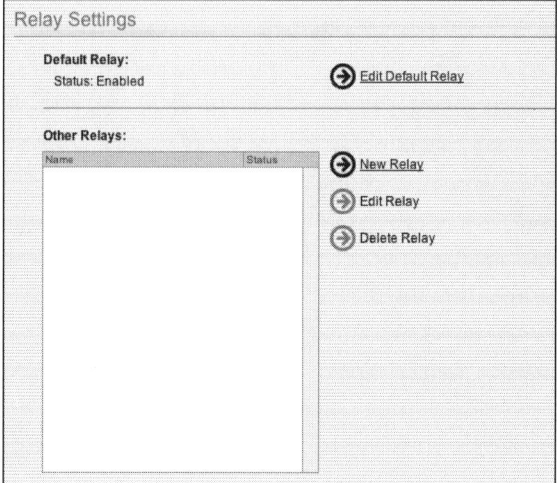

Figure 10-71. Use relays to relay your stream to another server.

13. Clicking the Log Settings link will let you configure the logging feature, which you can see in Figure 10-72. Depending on how much output your streaming server has, you may want to configure

these by size, rather than days. In any case, the outputted file will be something like `/Library/Quick-TimeStreaming/Logs/mp3_access.040507000.log`, which lets you see which date it was generated.

If, like me, you use a router to feed your cable connection around your network, you might have a local IP, similar to Figure 10-73. This is all very well if you only want to stream your media internally on your own **L**ocal **A**rea **N**etwork (LAN). If you want to stream outside of that LAN, you're going to have to bypass that router, so that you get an IP that the rest of the world can see.

14. If you have a domain name pointed towards your machine, meaning you're already able to stream from behind your LAN, then you will need to set up port forwarding to that machine. DSS uses ports 554 for video and 8000/1 for audio.

15. Once you do that, you need to reboot the machine, and you're greeted with a **W**ide **A**rea **N**etwork (WAN) IP when you run DSS Admin in your browser, as shown in Figure 10-74.

Figure 10-73. LAN IP address

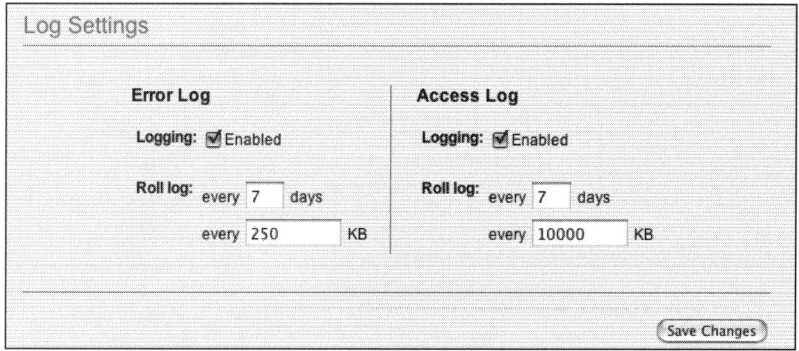

Figure 10-72. Enabling logs

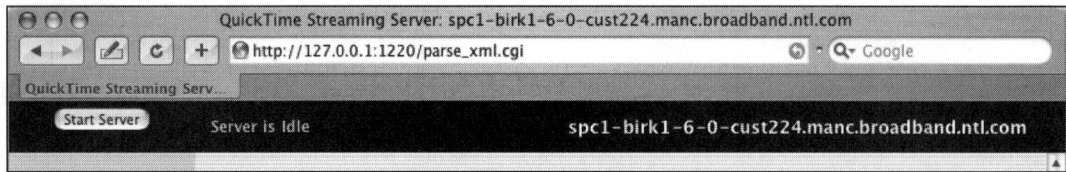

Figure 10-74. WAN IP address

16. Okay, before you can stream anything, you need a playlist. As you can see from Figure 10-75, there are no available playlists, so you'll have to create one. Click New MP3 Playlist.

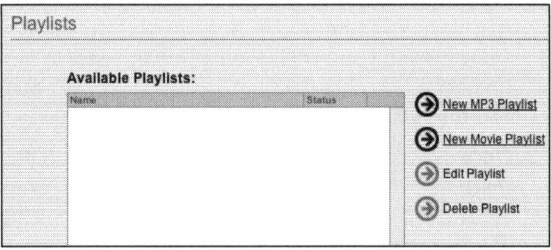

Figure 10-75. Creating a new MP3 playlist

17. Once you've clicked the link, give the playlist some details.

Name is the name you give your playlist and the name that appears in the iTunes window of the user. Mount Point is the path section of the URL you give to your users. In Figure 10-76, I've called this /ioaa, and this name must be unique; no two broadcasts can share the same name. Genre is pretty self-explanatory. With Play Mode set to Sequential Looped, your playlist plays the tracks in the order they appear and repeats the playlist in the same order when the last track has finished. Repetition lets you set the number of items that must play before an item can repeat. The default is 1, which you are going to use.

18. Underneath those settings, you'll see the available media from the specified media directory. By default, you should have a file called sample.mp3 in there. For this example, you'll be using six tracks by a fine English band called *Intentions Of An Asteroid*, which are included in the download files for this chapter. Add them to the media directory (that would then be /Library/QuickTimeStreaming/Movies/IOAA), as you can see in Figure 10-77.

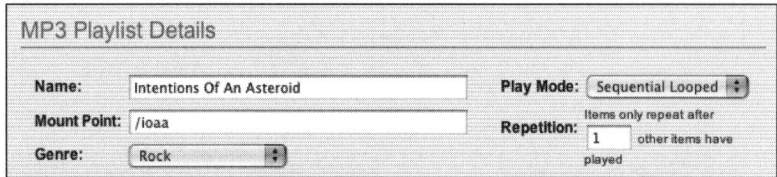

Figure 10-76. The playlist settings

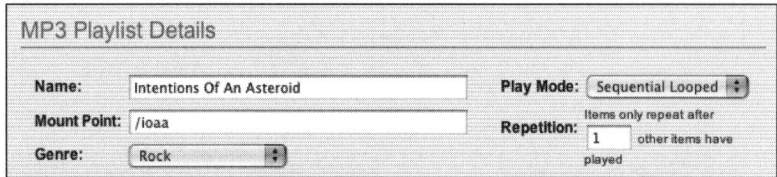

Figure 10-77. Available media shows up on the left.

19. Double-click the IOAA folder to open it and you'll see two additional folders: MP3 and Video. You'll read more about that Video folder later, so double-click the MP3 folder to open it. Inside there, you will find six tracks. Highlight all of them and drag them over to the right-hand playlist, as shown in Figure 10-78.

20. So you can see who's been accessing your streaming media, check the Log option shown in Figure 10-79, and then hit the Save Changes button. You're not sending this to a broadcast server, so you can leave that alone for this example.

21. Once you've saved those changes, your playlist is ready to rock. As you can see in Figure 10-80, there's one more thing to do: Start playing. Click the Play icon and the Status field will change to Playing, as shown in Figure 10-81.

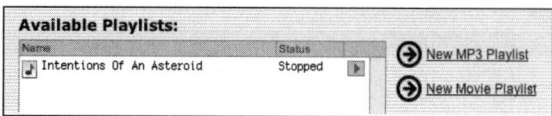

Figure 10-80. Clicking the Play button

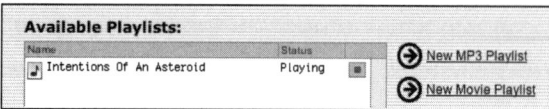

Figure 10-81. The playlist is playing!

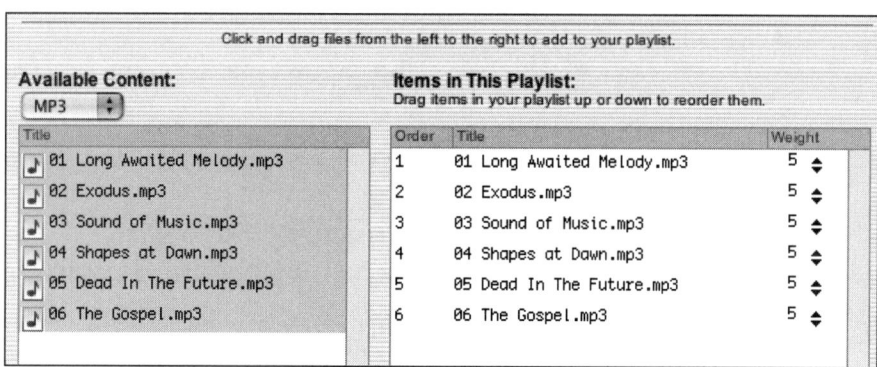

Figure 10-78. Dragging the tracks from the left to the right

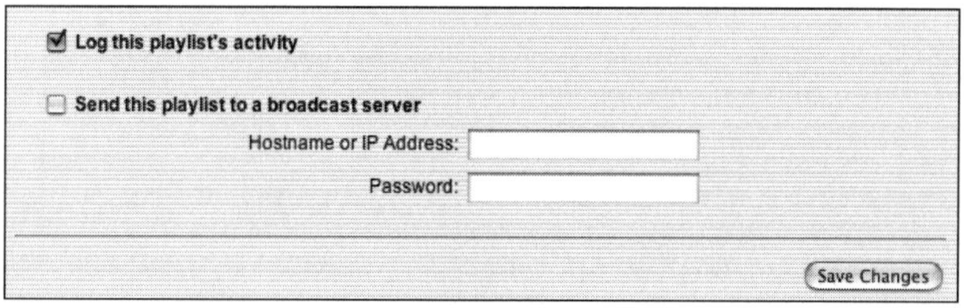

Figure 10-79. Logging the playlist's activity

22. Now would be a good time to test this out, so open iTunes and choose Advanced ➤ Open Stream (⌘+U), and enter `http://127.0.0.1:8000/ioaa` (see Figure 10-82).

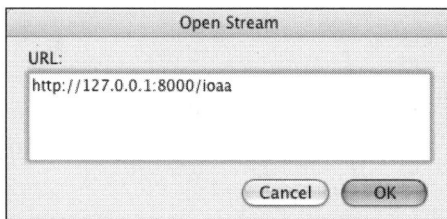

Figure 10-82. Entering the URL you wish to stream

If all went according to plan, iTunes should be serving up a large portion of ROCK, as in Figure 10-83. As I mentioned before, you'll have to do some tinkering to get this to work if you're behind a **N**etwork **A**ddress **T**ranslation (NAT) router. To test the stream in the outside world, replace `127.0.0.1` with your real IP. If you don't know this, you can find out easily enough by going to a site such as `www.whatismyip.com/`, which will tell you. If you have a domain name, you can use that instead.

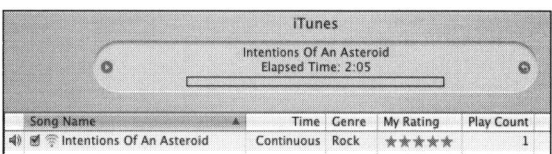

Figure 10-83. iTunes rocking out to the streaming media

Tip: If you plan on hosting from your Mac at home, buy yourself a domain name and use a dynamic IP forwarding service, such as DynDNS (`www.dyndns.org`) to point the domain towards your server. Then just add the domain name to the `ServerName` *section of your Apache configuration and you're hosting from behind your router!*

23. To add this link to a web page, you would code the following, obviously replacing *domain.com* for your IP or personal domain:

```
<a href="http://www.domain.com/ioaa.m3u"
➥ title="streaming Intentions Of An
➥ Asteroid songs">listen to some
➥ streaming ROCK</a>
```

You may be thinking "Hold on, what's an .m3u file, and where do I get one?" The .m3u file holds the playlist information for your media player, so it knows where to find the audio stream. As this isn't generated for you, you have to make one. This is dead easy.

24. Open a new text file in BBEdit and save it as `/Library/WebServer/Documents/ioaa.m3u`.

25. The file consists of one line of text: the streaming URL which you entered into iTunes in step 22, so type `http://www.yourdomain.com:8000/ioaa` and save the document.

That's all there is to it. You now have a fully functioning streaming media server, which you can link to from your web page. As the files aren't being served from the web server, nobody can download them. Result!

Streaming video with Darwin Streaming Server

Streaming video files is pretty much the same as streaming audio files, up to a point.

1. From the Playlist menu, click the New Movie Playlist link (see Figure 10-84).

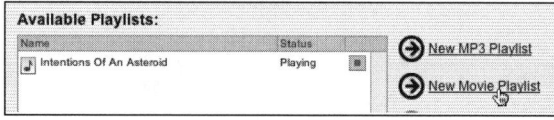

Figure 10-84. Adding a new movie playlist

2. Give the playlist some information to work with, but note that the playlist title must be different from the audio playlist title. As you can see in Figure 10-85, I've added the name of the song to the title. You'll notice the Mount Point already had a default extension of .sdp, so name it ioaa.sdp. If you leave Play Mode as Sequential, the video will play fine but then deliver a 415 error (unsupported media type) for everyone who turns up late for the show. You can avoid this by choosing Sequential Looped.

3. Navigate to the video directory in the left pane (/Library/QuickTimeStreaming/Movies/IOAA/Video), and drag the video file called ioaa-the_gospel.mov into the right-hand pane (see Figure 10-86).

4. Select whether you want activity logged or not, and then click the Save Changes button.

5. Start the playlist by clicking the Play button, as shown in Figures 10-87 and 10-88.

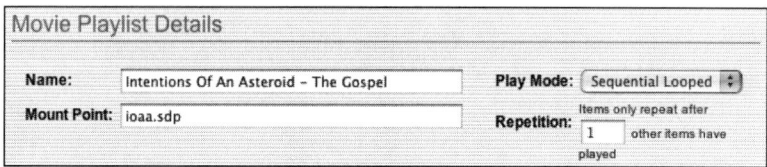

Figure 10-85. Filling in the movie playlist settings

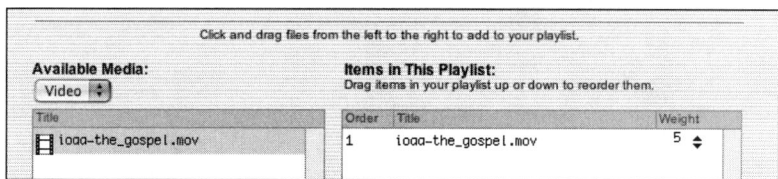

Figure 10-86. Dragging the file from the left into the playlist on the right

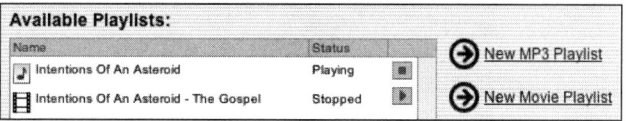

Figure 10-87. Click the play button . . .

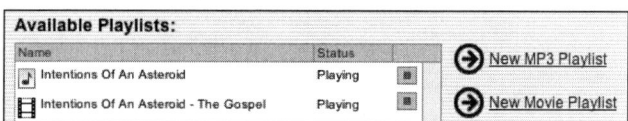

Figure 10-88. . . . to start the playlist.

6. Now that the playlist has started, you can test the file in QuickTime by choosing File ➤ Open URL in New Player (⌘+U) and entering the following URL: rtsp://127.0.0.1:8000/ioaa (see Figure 10-89).

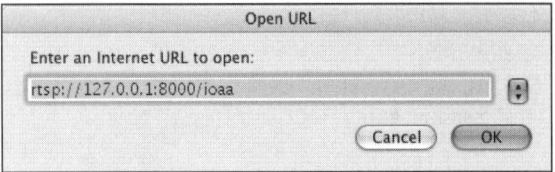

Figure 10-89. Entering the local URL to test the movie

7. When you click the OK button, you should now be able to see a Live Broadcast window playing The Gospel, as shown in Figure 10-90.

Figure 10-90. Live broadcast of ROCK!

Creating a reference movie

When you want to stream a file from a web page, you need a **reference movie**. The reference movie tells the browser where the QuickTime file is and is basically just a movie file that contains the address of your streaming movie. It then directs the QuickTime player to stream from that address. The reference movie is created using the **MakeRefMovieX** program, which can be downloaded from the Apple Developer Connection website (http://developer.apple.com/quicktime/quicktimeintro/tools/), and is located under "Webmaster Tools" (ftp://ftp.apple.com/developer/Quicktime/MakeRefMovieX.dmg.bin) as you can see in Figure 10-91.

1. Once MakeRefMovieX has downloaded, mount the disk image, drag the application into your Applications directory, and then open it.

2. Call the reference movie /Library/WebServer/Documents/ioaa_ref.mov, as shown in Figure 10-92. This reference movie will call upon the movie stream you created in the previous section.

3. Select Movie ➤ Add URL from the menu bar and then type in the path to your streaming movie. Use your real IP for this, as opposed to the local IP, which you used for testing. An example would look like rtsp://65.19.150.100:8000/ioaa as shown in Figure 10-93.

Webmaster Tools		
Plug-In Helper	tell me more	Mac OS	Win32
Associates URLs as well as stores QuickTime Plug-In settings inside a QuickTime movie.		
MakeRefMovie	tell me more	Mac OS	Win32
Creates alternate movies for various internet connection speeds, CPU's, languages, and more. This version allows you to create a reference movie that supports QuickTime 6.		
MakeRefMovie X	tell me more	Mac OS X	x
Creates alternate movies for various internet connection speeds, CPU's, languages, and more. This version runs on Mac OS X and allows you to create a reference movie that supports QuickTime 6.		

Figure 10-91. Clicking the Mac OS X link to download MakeRefMovieX

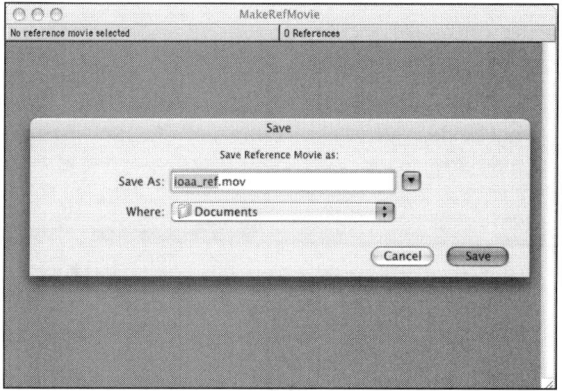

Figure 10-92. Saving the reference movie as `ioaa_ref.mov`

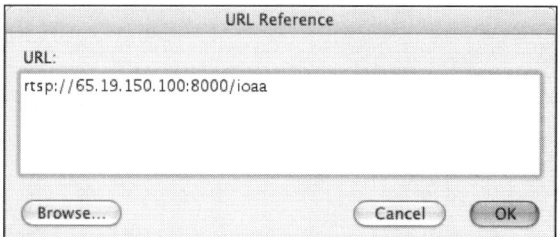

Figure 10-93. Adding the streaming URL to the reference movie

4. Set the minimum connection speed for the movie in the Speed: pop-up menu. As not everyone has broadband yet, don't set the speed too high. 256 Kbps is pretty much middle ground, so select that, as shown in Figure 10-94, along with the other settings I've shown there. Not all your users will have the current version of QuickTime installed, so give the v5.0.2 users a chance too. You can see which versions of QuickTime are currently available here: www.apple.com/quicktime/download/version.html.

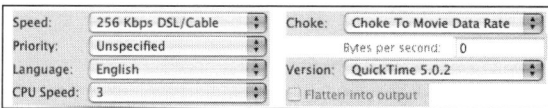

Figure 10-94. Configuring the reference movie

> *Tip: If you want to have different quality movies for different connection speeds, you can set the load order of the movies in the* Priority *menu. For example, you may want the reference movie to call the highest quality movie first, then the medium quality movie, etc. If there is more than one movie designed for the same connection speed, set a priority for which movie will load first.*

5. Save the reference movie with the new details.

That's all there is to it, but you need to get that movie into a web page now. Let's look at how to do that in the next section.

Embedding QuickTime vs. web standards

QuickTime is great. It's top quality and produces small files, and has always been the professional's format of choice. Back in the day, you could get away with just a few brief lines of code to embed your QuickTime movie into a web page.

Embedding QuickTime: Old style

```
<embed src="ioaa_ref.mov"
➥ width="320" height="256"
➥ autoplay="true"
➥ controller="true"
➥ loop="false"
➥ pluginspage=
➥ "http://www.apple.com/quicktime/">
</embed>
```

Those few lines of code would do the trick nicely, and were fairly easy to type from memory. Great stuff. However, with the release of Internet Explorer 5.5 SP2 and later, you must use an <object> tag in addition to the <embed> tag for your web pages to be compatible with both Netscape and Internet Explorer on Mac and Windows systems. Here's how you would code it these days.

Embedding QuickTime: New style

```
<object classid="clsid:
➥02BF25D5-8C17-4B23-BC80-D3488ABDDC6B"
➥ width="320" height="256"
➥ codebase="http://www.apple.com/
➥qtactivex/qtplugin.cab">
<param name="autoplay" value="true" />
<param name="controller" value="true" />
<param name="pluginspage" value=
➥"http://www.apple.com/quicktime/
➥download/indext.html" />
<param name="target" value="myself" />
<param name="type"
➥ value="video/quicktime" />
<param name="src"
➥ value="/ioaa_ref.mov" />
<embed src="/ioaa_ref.mov"
➥ width="320" height="256"
➥ autoplay="true" controller="true"
➥ border="0" pluginspage=
➥"http://www.apple.com/quicktime/
➥download/indext.html" target="myself">
</embed>
</object>
```

Blimey, there's a *little bit* more to the new code! If you want an in-depth explanation of all that, you can find one here: www.apple.com/quicktime/tools_tips/ tutorials/activex.html. Also of note is the fact that neither block of code is valid XHTML, because they rely on the <embed> tag, which has never been part of any *W3C* standard, despite being while widely supported by browsers. Herein lies a validation problem.

Do you employ a hack to work around this, or do you say, "What the hell, XHTML 2.0 will probably mock a lot of XHTML 1.1 hacks anyway, so it isn't worth it!" For those who insist on every page validating, even with QuickTime embedded, there is a way around this. Firstly, a quick explanation of how this came about.

Michael Zajac (http://zajac.ca/) originally suggested nesting <object> tags in order to display Flash movies successfully. He first posted this method on the *A List Apart* (ALA) Flash Satay article's discussion board (www.alistapart.com/discuss/flashsatay). Flash Satay was Drew McLellan's standards-compliant method of embedding Flash movies (www.alistapart.com/ articles/flashsatay), which eventually proved to be slightly less than hitch-free.

You might not be surprised to learn that good old MS/IE was the thorn in the side of this method. MS/IE displayed both sets of <object> tags, and stuck a rather ugly <textarea> on the screen. So, using Michael's idea, Ross Angus came up with a CSS method to hide the second set of <object> tags, which is detailed at this web page: realdev1.realise.com/ rossa/rendertest/quicktime.html.

> *"Ross Angus deserves all the credit for creating and developing the technique of hiding nested objects from MSIE using CSS. I merely coded a standards-based object tag, and mentioned that it would work virtually everywhere except MSIE/Win. Ross did the real creative work."* —Michael Zajac
>
> *"I've slapped together a page demonstrating an XHTML compliant method of embedding Quick-Time without client or server side scripting. It's a pretty ugly hack in places, and the only creative work I did was bringing together the work of others, but it seems to work OK."* —Ross Angus

Here's a quick look at the code you'd use to achieve such an effect. I'll leave the full explanation to Ross on his web page, where you can see it in action, complete with how it all works.

Michael chopped that big ugly block of code down to a more manageable chunk, as you can see:

```
<object classid="clsid:02BF25D5-
➥8C17-4B23-BC80-D3488ABDDC6B"
➥codebase="http://www.apple.com/
➥qtactivex/qtplugin.cab"
➥ width="320" height="260">
<param name="src" value="/ioaa_ref.mov" />
<param name="controller" value="true" />
<object type="video/quicktime"
➥ data="/ioaa_ref.mov" width="320"
➥ height="256" class="mov">
<param name="controller" value="true" />
<p>Error text goes here</p>
</object>
</object>
```

Then, Ross whipped up some nifty CSS to hide those extra <object> tags, like so:

```
<style type="text/css" media="screen">
/* hides the second object from all
➥ versions of IE */
* html object.mov {
 display: none;
}
/* displays the second object in all
➥ versions of IE apart from 5 on PC */
* html object.mov/**/ {
 display: inline;
}
/* hides the second object from all
➥ versions of IE >= 5.5 */
* html object.mov {
 display/**/: none;
}
</style>
```

Embedding with your chosen editor

So, if you feel you just can't let your validation slip for one second, you know which two guys to thank. If you aren't so concerned with your page being valid markup, then you have a few options, depending on which editor you favor.

Hand coders can just embed files using the *Embedding QuickTime—new style* code, which I showed earlier. So, whether you use BBEdit, Vim, Pico, or even TextEdit to create your pages, all you need to do is copy/paste your code in and change some values.

GoLive users have it easy, because GoLive has the *embed QuickTime* option right on the tool palette, which you just drag onto the HTML document (see Figures 10-95 and 10-96).

Figure 10-95. Drag the QuickTime icon from the toolbar . . .

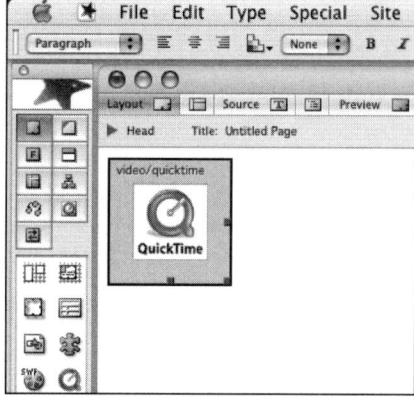

Figure 10-96. . . . then drop it in place on the page.

Once you've dragged and dropped, you can switch to code view and see all the code that it just created for you, as you can see in Figure 10-97. You don't even have to manually adjust the code, because Figure 10-98 shows you a nice little palette where you can adjust the properties.

Dreamweaver is a bit of a letdown when it comes to embedding QuickTime. There's no built-in option. Period. If you want to embed QuickTime with Dreamweaver, you have to add the code yourself. Luckily, one of the great things about Macromedia's applications is the Macromedia Exchange. They also have tons of extensions for Dreamweaver, Fireworks, ColdFusion, etc., including an extension to embed QuickTime. In fact, Brendan Dawes, who wrote the foreword in this very book, wrote the Official Macromedia QuickTime Extension. That was for the old-school code though, so if you were downloading the extension today, you'd look for the newest version, similar to the one shown in Figure 10-99, above Bren's extension.

If you don't already have a Macromedia ID, it's easy enough to get one. Head off to the Macromedia

Exchange (http://exchange.macromedia.com/) and sign up for an account. Take a good look around and you'll find a lot there to enhance your Dreamweaver experience. You can also find hundreds of prebuilt Flash components, smart clips, buttons, and much more really useful, timesaving stuff. Which leads us nicely into the Flash section of the chapter.

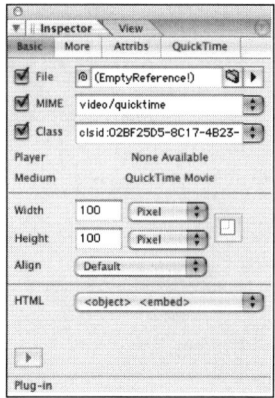

Figure 10-98. Configuring the movie properties from the palette

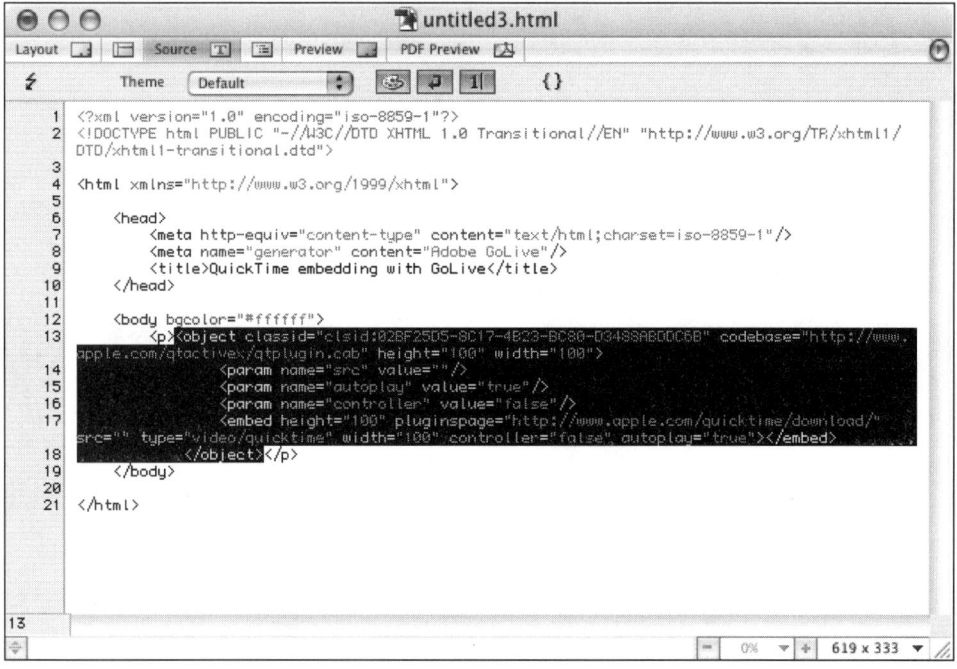

Figure 10-97. GoLive inserts all the necessary code for you.

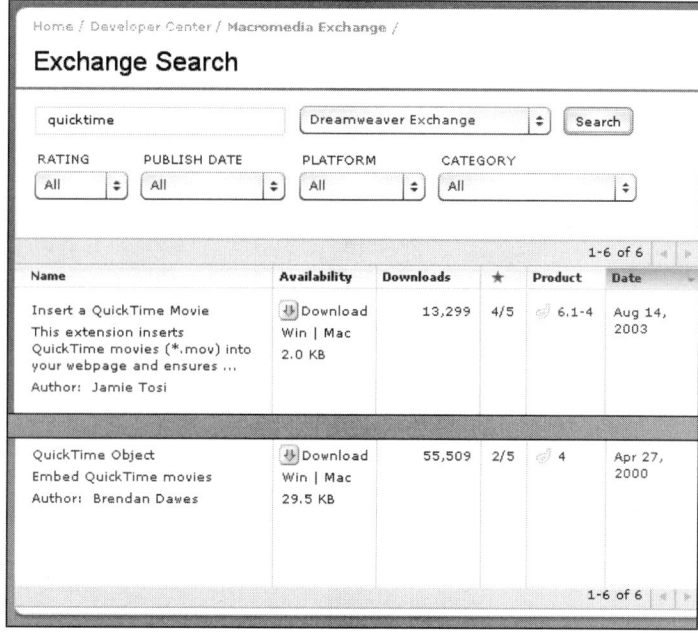

Figure 10-99. Downloading an extension to embed QuickTime with Dreamweaver

Flash

There can't be many people reading this book who haven't heard of Flash. In fact, if you're reading this chapter and you haven't heard of it, then you obviously weren't paying attention during Chapter 2's *"Vector animation: Adobe LiveMotion vs. Macromedia Flash"* section. This is akin to chewing gum in line, so go to the back of the class, and take Chapter 2 with you.

Flash gets a seriously mixed reaction from both web designers and web surfers. It's not so much a love/hate thing; it's more like worship/despise. This is not the fault of Flash, by any means. Flash is a wonderful tool, when used correctly. The witch-hunt tends to happen when people misuse Flash. And when Flash goes bad, it's not a pretty sight.

The most common mistake is usually too many bells and whistles. Example: You load a site and there's a huge intro with a bad techno loop (like the one you made earlier in this chapter!), with no way to turn the volume off, things are flashing all over the place, stuff is spinning around, and all for what? Apart from eventually forwarding you to an HTML page with some content, these intros rarely have any purpose, other than the designer saying, "Oooh, look what I learned in class this week." One function these intros definitely *do* serve is putting users off the site. Apart from changing the user's browser window size to open a site full screen, useless Flash intros are one of the most annoying things a designer can enforce on a user. So, if you're reading this and thinking of employing either of those techniques, do yourself a favor: Offer a text link to go full screen, and have a link to show the intro, or at least to skip it and go straight to the content. Your users will thank you for it; trust me.

If you have questions about Flash that need answering, a good place to start is the Flash support site at www.macromedia.com/support/flash/, which has a large FAQ database. Other good sites include www.actionscripts.org and www.flashkit.com, both of which have a large user base, tons of examples to download, tutorials, and message boards for interaction with other users who may have previously had and solved the problem you've got.

Components

There are already a ton of books about Flash and ActionScript by friends of ED, so it would be pretty pointless for me to cover the same ground in this book. For starters, that might be more advanced than some of you care to go. Instead, you're going to make use of one of the available prebuilt components within Flash.

What are components? A component is a movie clip with parameters that are set while authoring in Macromedia Flash that allow you to customize the component at runtime. Components are designed to allow developers to reuse and share code, and to encapsulate complex functionality that designers can use and customize without using ActionScript. In English, that means someone else has done most of the hard work, and you can just configure a few variables to get the thing working. Easy life! Fantastic.

So, what do they do? When you install Flash MX Professional 2004, you get a standard set of components preinstalled. To view these, you need the Components palette open, which you can do by choosing Window ➤ Development Panels ➤ Components (⌘+7). To configure a component, you need the Component Inspector open, which you can do with *Opt+7*.

There are three main sets of components: data components, media components, and user interface (UI) components. Figure 10-100 shows you the data components, which are used to hook Flash up to a database and interact with the data contained in it.

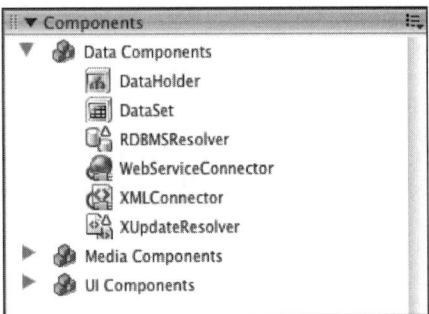

Figure 10-100. The Flash MX Professional 2004 Data Components panel

Next up are the media components, which are really easy to configure and have working. These are prebuilt media players that you will be meeting a bit closer in a minute. You can see those in Figure 10-101.

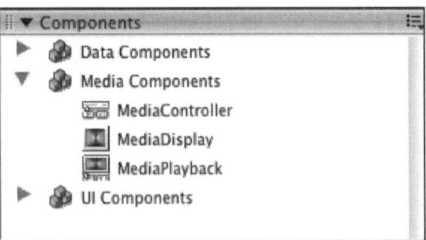

Figure 10-101. The Flash MX Professional 2004 Media Components panel

Lastly, Figure 10-102 shows you the user interface components. Believe me, in days of old, these would have saved a lot of nightmares, and maybe I wouldn't have deleted Flash off my machine as often! All these things had to be hand coded, previously. Now you can just drag them in and get on with fretting over whether the new boy in the office is going to make your tea the way you like it (and other such seriously important stuff).

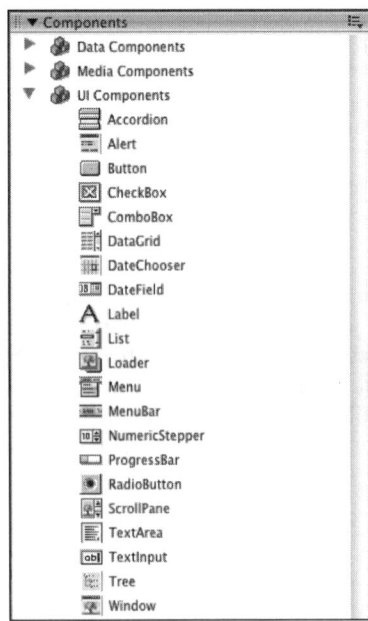

Figure 10-102. The Flash MX Professional 2004 User Interface (UI) Components panel

You know how to embed video into your HTML web page, but maybe you want to add an all-Flash version of the site too. Getting your video clip into Flash is a piece of cake now: Just hook it up with a component. To use a component, drag it onto the stage, and then configure it in the component inspector. If that sounds just a bit *too* easy, I'll expand on it.

Using the MediaPlayback component

For this example, you're going to use Flash and a splash of QuickTime Pro to create a nice Flash presentation of the *Intentions Of An Asteroid* video which you exported earlier in the chapter. These days, QuickTime Pro can export FLV files for use in Flash applications, as you saw back in Figure 10-46, so that is where you're going to start.

1. Open the video file, choose File ➤ Export ➤ Movie to Macromedia Flash Video (FLV), and click the Options button.

2. Most of the default properties are good to go, but there are two you're going to fiddle with. Change Quality to Medium, and Bitrate to 128 kbits/sec, as you can see in Figure 10-103, and click OK.

3. Export the video as ~/Sites/book/10/ioaa-the_gospel.flv.

4. While you're waiting for QuickTime Pro to export the movie, open a new document in Flash and save it as ~/Sites/book/10/ioaa-the_gospel.fla.

5. Open the Media Components section of the Components palette and drag the MediaPlayback component onto the stage. You can drop it anywhere because you're going to align it to the stage in a minute.

6. The component isn't quite the size you need it, so resize it to the same size as the stage. Click the component to select it, and then use the Property inspector (shown in Figure 10-104) to alter the size to 550 pixels wide × 400 pixels high.

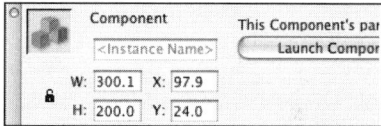

Figure 10-104. Configuring the video for FLV export

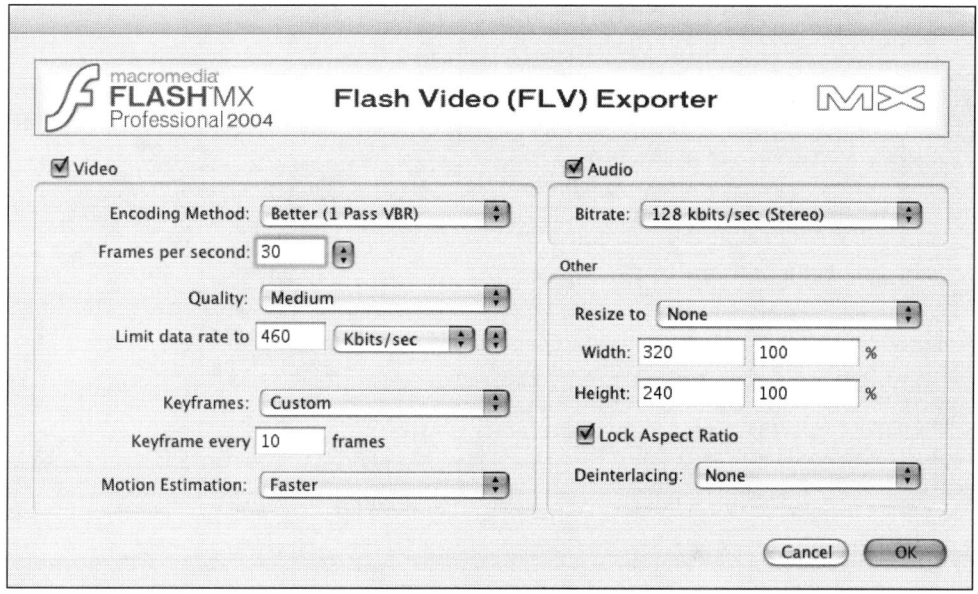

Figure 10-103. Configuring the video for FLV export

7. Next, align it so that it is central to the stage. As it's the same size as the stage now, you can just enter 0 as the x and y coordinates, which aligns it nicely. For future use, you can also use the Align palette for this (shown in Figure 10-105), which you can find by choosing Window ➤ Align (⌘+K).

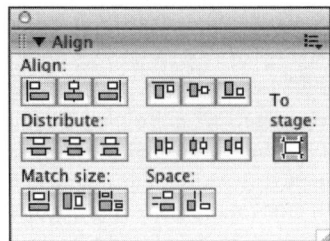

Figure 10-105. The Align palette

8. Now give the component an instance name of the_gospel in the Property inspector and you should have a view like that in Figure 10-106.

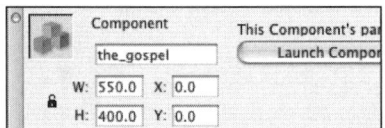

Figure 10-106. Configured properties

9. While the component is selected on the stage, you will notice that the component inspector has a few things going on, as you can see in Figure 10-107. This is where you configure the component to tell it where to find your video. With the FLV option selected in the Parameters tab, type ioaa-the_gospel.flv in the URL box, as I've done in Figure 10-107.

10. The media player controls are, by default, a bit like the Mac OS X dock, in that they show/hide according to mouse action. This might be a bit confusing on a web interface, so scroll down the Parameters panel and select Control Visibility ➤ On.

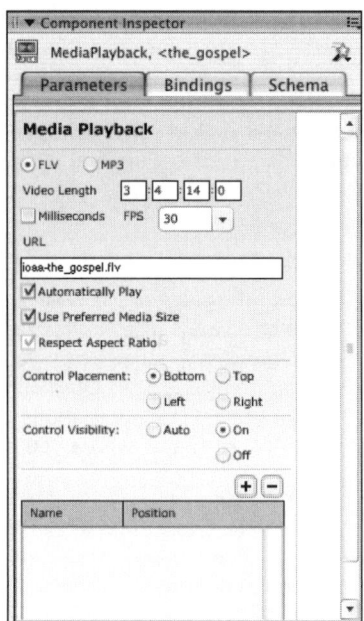

Figure 10-107. Configuring the component parameters

11. Save the document and choose Control ➤ Test Movie (⌘+*ENTER*) to preview it (see Figure 10-108).

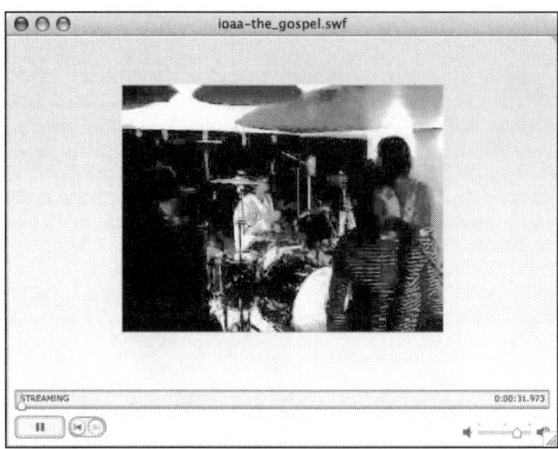

Figure 10-108. Streaming Flash video!

"Good grief, that was jolly easy," you'll be thinking by now, and rightly so. That really is all there is to it. The only things you might want to do now are personal preference things, like play around with the size of the window, or see if you prefer the controls on the top, hiding, etc.

If you don't like the default look of the player, you can alter the media components source document and change its assets so that it fits in with the look of your site. It is best to make a copy of this file and work from the copy, so that you will always have the installed source to go back to. You can find the media component source document here:

```
/Users/Username/Library/
➥Application Support/Macromedia/
➥Flash MX 2004/en/Configuration/
➥ComponentFLA.fla/MediaComponents.fla.
```

Publishing FLV

All you need now is an HTML page to load that file in to. You don't even need Dreamweaver for this (although you may prefer to use it).

1. With your Flash document still open, select File ➤ Publish Settings (*OPT+⌘+F12*), which brings up the settings window that you can see in Figure 10-109.

2. The default settings are just fine for testing, so click the Publish button, and then click the OK button when the files are published to return to the document.

3. That's it. You can test the page at

```
http://127.0.0.1/~username/book/10/
➥ioaa-the_gospel.html
```

as shown in Figure 10-110.

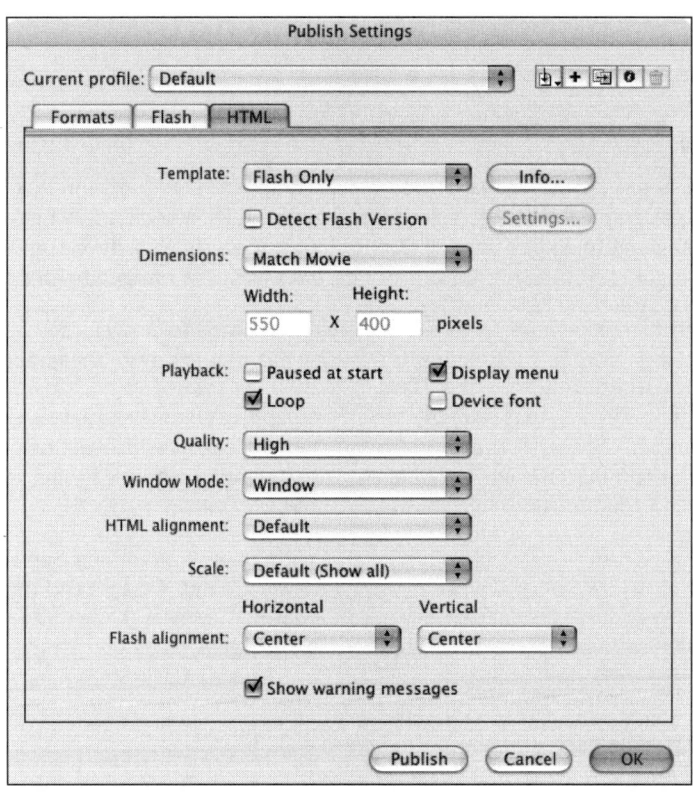

Figure 10-109. Flash publishing settings

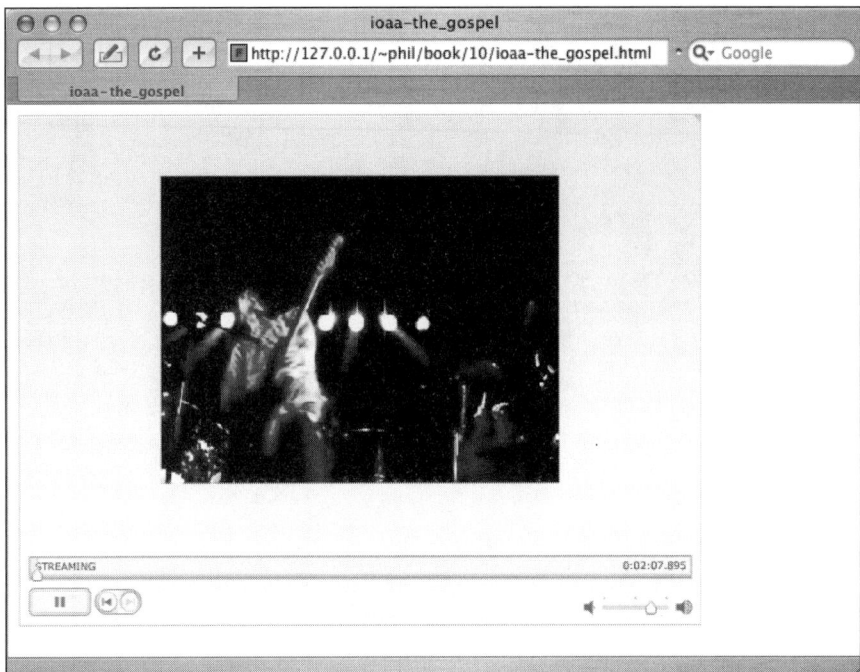

Figure 10-110. Flash's HTML output in Safari

At the risk of sounding like my dad, you kids today have got it easy! You'd get gray hairs and a migraine even *thinking* about attempting to embed some video and get streaming back in the days of Flash 4. You can use these components for streaming MP3 files too, in the same way.

So, there were no bells or whistles there, just a Flash application doing its job. Ideally, that would be accessed by a link, so the user knew what they were in for, meaning you're not imposing anything on their bandwidth. That makes for a good relationship with the user, so we're all happy now.

Chapter review

That lot should've given you a nice break from coding, which is what you need sometimes. If you're working on something difficult/annoying, have a break and make some noise! I'm sure you'll agree that there is plenty of fun to be had with iTunes, iPhoto, iMovie, and

GarageBand. All that, and they're free too, which is just absolutely marvelous. They're obviously extremely functional as web development tools too, which you may not have realized before now.

QuickTime Pro proves itself, once again, as the undisputed champion of "cheap applications that are worth their weight in gold." (If anyone can tell me how much an application weighs, I'd love to know.) It's a great little application, which will help you out of more than a few scrapes, without having to resort to more expensive programs.

With Darwin Streaming Server, you can stream your newly created GarageBand music from your Mac, and your new iMovies. Mine's all set to stream movies from my travels around the world, purely so I can show off my machine's new streaming capabilities!

And finally, you saw how easy Flash MX 2004 makes it to stream Flash video from your Mac. Those components totally rock.

INDEX

Z

friendsofed.com/forums

Join the friends of ED forums to find out more about our books, discover useful technology tips and tricks, or get a helping hand on a challenging project. *Designer to Designer*™ is what it's all about—our community sharing ideas and inspiring each other. In the friends of ED forums, you'll find a wide range of topics to discuss, so look around, find a forum, and dive right in!

■ **Books and Information**

Chat about friends of ED books, gossip about the community, or even tell us some bad jokes!

■ **Flash**

Discuss design issues, ActionScript, dynamic content, and video and sound.

■ **Web Design**

From front-end frustrations to back-end blight, share your problems and your knowledge here.

■ **Site Check**

Show off your work or get new ideas.

■ **Digital Imagery**

Create eye candy with Photoshop, Fireworks, Illustrator, and FreeHand.

■ **ArchivED**

Browse through an archive of old questions and answers.

HOW TO PARTICIPATE

Go to the friends of ED forums at **www.friendsofed.com/forums**.

Visit **www.friendsofed.com** to get the latest on our books, find out what's going on in the community, and discover some of the slickest sites online today!

friendsof

DESIGNER TO DESIGNER™

an Apress® company

1-59059-303-0 $29.99 [US]

1-59059-305-7 $34.99 [US]

1-59059-308-1 $34.99 [US]

1-59059-336-7 $34.99 [US]

1-59059-210-7 $34.99 [US]

EXPERIENCE THE DESIGNER TO DESIGNER™ DIFFERENCE

1-59059-306-5 $34.99 [US]

1-59059-238-7 $24.99 [US]

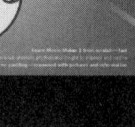

1-59059-149-6 $24.99 [US]

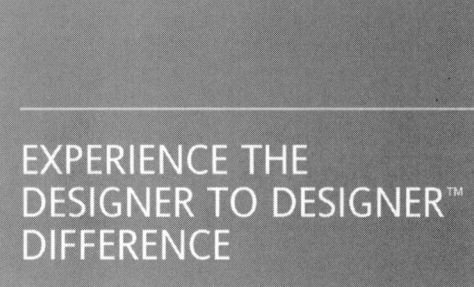

1-59059-224-7 $39.99 [US]

1-59059-221-2 $39.99 [US]

1-59059-236-0 $39.99 [US]

1-59059-372-3 $39.99 [US]

1-59059-262-X $49.99 [US]

1-59059-304-9 $49.99 [US]

1-59059-309-X $49.99 [US]

1-59059-399-5 $44.99 [US]

1-59059-110-0 $49.99 [US]

1-59059-231-X $39.99 [US]

1-59059-408-8 $34.99 [US]

1-59059-355-3 $39.99 [US]

1-59059-381-2 $29.99 [US]

1-59059-409-6 $39.99 [US]